Issues in American Political Life

FOURTH EDITION

Issues in American Political Life

Money, Violence, and Biology

Robert G. Thobaben
Donna M. Schlagheck
Charles Funderburk

Wright State University

Prentice
Hall

Upper Saddle River, New Jersey 07458

Library of Congress Cataloging-in-Publication Data

Thobaben, Robert G.
  Issues in American political life: money, violence, and biology/Robert G. Thobaben,
Donna M. Schlagheck, Charles Funderburk.—4th ed.
     p. cm.
  Includes bibliographical references and index.
    1. United States—Politics and government. 2. Political planning—United States. 3.
Policy sciences. I. Schlagheck, Donna M. II. Funderburk, Charles, III. Title.
  ISBN 0-13-033672-6 (alk. paper)

JK 271 .T46 2001
973.929–dc21
                                                                    00-053765

VP, Editorial director: Laura Pearson
Senior acquisitions editor: Heather Shelstad
Assistant editor: Brian Prybella
Editorial/production supervision and
   interior design: Barbara Reilly
Copy editor: Virginia Rubens
Editorial assistant: Jessica Drew
Director of marketing: Beth Gillett Mejia
Prepress and manufacturing buyer: Ben Smith
Cover art director: Jayne Conte
Cover design: Bruce Kenselaar
Cover photos: Richard Hutchins/Pearson Education;
   Steve Cole/Photo Disc, Inc.; Zigy Kaluzny/Stone

This book was set in 10/12 Palatino by Interactive Composition Corporation
and was printed and bound by Hamilton Printing Company.
The cover was printed by Phoenix Color Corp.

© 2002, 1998, 1995, 1991 by Pearson Education, Inc.
Upper Saddle River, New Jersey 07458

Printed in the United States of America
10 9 8 7 6 5 4 3 2 1

ISBN: 0-13-033672-6

Prentice-Hall International (UK) Limited, *London*
Prentice-Hall of Australia Pty. Limited, *Sydney*
Prentice-Hall Canada Inc., *Toronto*
Prentice-Hall Hispanoamericana, S.A., *Mexico*
Prentice-Hall of India Private Limited, *New Delhi*
Prentice-Hall of Japan, Inc., *Tokyo*
Pearson Education Asia Pte. Ltd., *Singapore*
Editora Prentice-Hall do Brasil, Ltda., *Rio de Janeiro*

Contents

4 The Politics of Crime in America   81

5 The Politics of Terrorism   109

Preface

In 1989, Texas Congressman Martin Leath offered an assessment of the problems confronting American society and concluded that "our resolve to deal with them is practically nonexistent." By the year 2000, he stated, "We'll go down on the list of world powers: Hopelessly in debt, hopelessly behind in technology and hopelessly in over our heads with a society dominated by the drug culture, and a population undereducated, unmotivated and woefully inadequate to compete in the world economic system."[1]

It is not necessary to agree with Congressman Leath's pessimistic scenario in order to conclude that the United States faces a number of serious issues as we begin the year 2001. *Issues in American Political Life, Fourth Edition,* is an introduction to the nature of major policy issues confronting American society and government. These issues are grouped under three broad headings: Money, Violence, and Biology. Each issue is discussed in terms of historical background, current status, and proposals and prospects for managing the problem. Our objective is to provide introductory-level students with information and analysis that will permit them to understand the issues and reach their own conclusions about future directions.

ACKNOWLEDGMENTS

We wish to recognize the contributions of a number of individuals and groups who gave us valuable assistance. Dean Mary Ellen Mazey and the faculty committee that administers the College of Liberal Arts Research Fund at Wright State University provided funds for typing. Joanne Ballmann and Renée Harber deserve special thanks for doing such a fine job in typing the manuscript and tables. Thanks to Eileen Kerr for providing invaluable research assistance, Tom Kerr for bibliographic assistance, and Bob and Terri Thobaben for their careful review and helpful suggestions associated with the chapters on biology. We are grateful for the helpful critique offered by Robin Ramey of Ohio University, reviewer for this edition. Finally, we are grateful to Beth Gillett Mejia of Prentice Hall for her commitment to this project.

NOTE

1. Representative Martin Leath is cited by Martin Gottlieb, "The Real Division in U.S. Politics Now," *Dayton Daily News,* December 6, 1989, p. 14A.

Introduction

Changes in American political life foretell many transformations in the issues and policy processes that will comprise American politics in the twenty-first century. Three basic values, however, will persist as the primary goals in American political life. The search for *prosperity, progress,* and *security* have been and will continue to be the fundamental social and political values on which the nation operates. Money, technology, and violence represent the primary means to those ends and dominate the American quest for abundance, improvement in the human condition, and guarantees of safety so that individuals and the nation as a whole may enjoy those values. In order to realize and allocate these important social goals best, human beings do two things—they establish security forces (police and armed forces) and political relations. The political leaders decide who gets what, when, and how, and the security system backs up these decisions with force. What is clear is that some individuals and groups have the power to make decisions (laws) that bind the entire community and that they are backed up by force.

Therefore, power is the central category of analysis in the study of politics. Political power may be based on a wide variety of attributes, but three of these factors seem to be particularly significant: control of money (wealth), violence (force), and biology (health and physical well-being). Four aspects of American society further define the relationships among money, violence, biology, and politics:

1. The transcendence of the industrial state
2. The shift from manufacturing to services
3. America as a consumer society
4. America as a superpower

1

THE TRANSCENDENCE OF THE INDUSTRIAL STATE

The first and foremost factor is the evolution of America from an industrial society to one based on technology and information. The fundamental change in contemporary America is that it is no longer primarily an industrial society. Various commentators have used different terms to describe the evolution of America from an industrial into a technological society. Harvard sociology professor Daniel Bell has analyzed the evolution of societies in terms of preindustrial, industrial, and postindustrial phases. Postindustrial societies are characterized by a shift from a manufacturing economy to one based on services, information, and technology. Both Bell and political scientist Everett C. Ladd contend that the United States is best understood as being qualitatively different from an industrial society. In his book *Megatrends* social forecaster John Naisbitt has described the transformation of America into an "information society" based on high technology.[1]

Social, economic, and political changes in contemporary America are best understood within the context of the evolution of the United States into a high-technology, information-processing society. The two major dimensions of postindustrial society, according to Bell, are the central importance of theoretical knowledge and the expansion of the service information sector as opposed to manufacturing. American society has entered a new era in which theoretical knowledge becomes the basis of new technologies.[2] In contemporary American society, economics and politics rest primarily not on manufacturing but on information and applied technology. Growth and development of new products in the economy are principally in the area of human services (health, education, and social services) and in the professional and technical areas (especially research and the processing and distribution of information).

A prime example of this trend is biotechnology. Scientists strive to produce new agricultural products that are resistant to certain diseases, able to survive longer periods without water, and reduce farmers' dependence on pesticides. Biotechnology is a powerful scientific tool used in struggling to save the environment from disasters such as oil spills and toxic waste and in helping to control diseases such as cancer and heart disease. Many benefits, both individual and social, are derived from biotechnology, but this new field also generates legitimate safety concerns requiring new regulation of products and of the complex relationships among government, business, and academe.

In summary, contemporary America may be described as an advanced technological society characterized by theoretical knowledge applied in new science-based industries such as computers, electronics, materials science, biotechnology, genetic engineering, and telecommunications. In addition, the American economy has experienced a decrease in manufacturing and industrial production and a shift to human and information services involving an expansion of the professional and technical sectors. This transformation of America into a society based on technology and information is fundamental to any discussion of government and public policy. Government policy and spending choices are constrained by the requirements of the postindustrial society and by problems created by the transition from industrial society.

THE SHIFT FROM MANUFACTURING TO SERVICES

The next aspect of American society that defines the relations among money, violence, biology, and politics is the shift from a social system based on manufacturing to a society focused on services. Manufacturing employment in the United States peaked at 21 million in 1979, dropped sharply during the subsequent recession of the early 1980s, and is now about 19 million. Many of the lost jobs were in well-paying unionized industries. The United Steelworkers, for example, has lost nearly half its members since 1974. These economic dislocations have been described as "the twilight of the big-paycheck blue-collar era."[3] This decline in the number of well-paying blue-collar manufacturing jobs is part of a larger trend as America shifts away from an industrial economy to one based on technology and information. A recent study by the Congressional Budget Office found that, in terms of real wages adjusted for inflation, the average income of a family headed by a person under the age of twenty-five fell 43 percent from 1973 to 1986. Opportunities are especially limited for workers with less education.[4] Much of the slack in income has been taken up by the increasing numbers of women in the work force.

These developments pose several issues for government economic policy. As is shown in subsequent chapters, the decline of American manufacturing capability is related to the balance-of-trade deficit and to the persistence of hard-core poverty and crime in inner cities. The transition the United States is undergoing raises issues of economic development, including protection of American industries from foreign competition, provision of expanded job training for displaced workers, provision of child care to assist working parents, and decisions on assisting failing industries.

The growth of the service sector is astounding. Of the 19 million new jobs created in the United States during the 1970s, 17 million did not involve the production of goods or commodities. Many of these involved either human services or the collection, analysis, and distribution of information or technical knowledge.[5] The educational requirements of jobs in the growth areas of the American economy constitute a major demand on government resources. More than 12 million Americans under the age of twenty-five attend a university or college. Expenditures by the federal and state governments for higher education exceed $100 billion per year.[6]

Two large and expanding areas of service associated with health include the new reproductive and life-maintenance technologies. For example, developments in the biological sciences have produced very complex moral and legal questions in the area of the new reproductive technologies. In the next few years, Americans will be faced with vital questions on eugenics and the ethics of manipulation of the basic material of life via genetic engineering. Technology is running ahead of our religious, moral, and ethical codes. In many ways, it stands in opposition to many values and beliefs Americans embrace today. The problem exists, and it must be resolved. For example, prolonging life through artificial means—experimentation, the status of frozen embryos, abortion, and many other issues—requires that Americans today face up to difficult philosophical questions.

The fastest growing economic group in American society is the professional and technical class. This is because emerging industries in America are, in the words of Robert Noyce, a founder of the Intel Corporation, "brain-intensive" as well as capital-intensive.[7] The growing reliance of American society on knowledge, information, and technology has altered the class structure and the nature of job requirements and, consequently, the demand for education and training. Advances in computer science and biotechnology have changed the nature of crime and law enforcement and have created new opportunities and ethical dilemmas in medicine and science. The restructuring of the United States into a society built on advanced technology, information processing, and services may ultimately prove to be as profound as the Industrial Revolution.

AMERICA AS A CONSUMER SOCIETY

The position of the United States as the world's leading consumer society has broad political and economic implications. Consequences of the cultural emphasis on consumption of material goods include pollution and waste disposal problems, a reliance on consumer debt, a low rate of savings, and lately, a large foreign debt. The rate of consumption has been high since the end of World War II, but with the recent decline of American manufacturing, the United States has become primarily a consumption-based, rather than a production-based, society. In the long run, consuming more than one produces tends to be expensive and requires abundant credit. Because of this emphasis on consumption, the rate of savings in the United States is among the lowest of the developed nations. This situation did not improve in response to the Reagan administration's experiment with supply-side economics.

The combination of lower levels of American manufacturing and higher levels of consumption means that much of what is now consumed is produced abroad. The United States now imports more than it exports, creating a trade deficit. The low rate of savings by Americans means that much of the credit needed to pay for consumer spending is now obtained from external (i.e., foreign) sources. To this must be added the hundreds of billions of dollars the U.S. government borrows to pay for deficit spending. Since 1981, the Treasury has borrowed well in excess of $1 trillion to make up for the fact that government spending substantially exceeded tax revenues. Borrowing heavily to pay for consumer and government debt has created a large foreign debt. Since 1983, the United States has become a debtor nation for the first time in the twentieth century. Strategies for managing environmental problems, budget, trade, and foreign debt will loom prominently on the government's agenda for the remainder of this century.

AMERICA AS A SUPERPOWER

In the years following World War II, the United States emerged, along with the Soviet Union, as one of the world's military superpowers. The United States assumed a national security policy of global containment of communism. This required a large military establishment, extensive worldwide treaty obligations, and involvement in an arms race with the Soviet Union for military superiority. During the Reagan-era military buildup, the U.S. government spent nearly $300 billion per year on national defense. Superpower status had additional costs, including the channeling of significant portions of society's educational, corporate, and technological resources into military purposes, undermining America's economic competitiveness. It was apparent that the economies of both superpowers strained under this burden as the United States spent 7 percent of its gross national product (GNP) on national security, and the Soviet Union spent 15 percent of its smaller GNP in order to compete. In 1991, the U.S.S.R. collapsed altogether.

Now that the Cold War has ended, the issues of priorities within the defense establishment and competition between defense and domestic programs must be addressed anew by government decision makers. The question "What makes the United States secure?" has become much more complex. The policy of containment of the U.S.S.R. was successful in forcing the Soviets to change their domestic and foreign policies. Initiatives in arms control are now developed and reach agreement more quickly than ever before in the history of superpower relations. Yet the American economy is more vulnerable than ever in the international marketplace, and American citizens are more vulnerable to crime at home and terrorism abroad. Military solutions to stop the flow of drugs into the United States or to liberate American hostages have failed to emerge, and "technical fixes" to crime (mandatory sentences) or the arms race (the Strategic Defense Initiative, or SDI) have created new costly problems such as overcrowded prisons and huge pressures on the federal budget. With security issues at home and abroad growing more complex, many Americans have begun to question whether their government can meet its most fundamental charge: to secure them in their life, liberty, and pursuit of happiness.

In the chapters that follow, the three types of challenges that confront Americans and their government in the twenty-first century are examined. In Part One, Money and Politics, the issues of poverty, healthcare, and corruption are discussed in the context of postindustrial society. In Part Two, Violence and Politics, the issues of physical security for Americans at home and abroad are examined in chapters on crime, terrorism, and arms racing. In Part Three, Biology and Politics, issues in the newest dimension of policymaking, that is, the realm of science and technology are raised. The chapters on biomedical, biotechnological, and environmental issues, which are new to the tradition of issues books, raise questions that can only increase in relevance as the twenty-first century begins. These chapters represent dominant issues in American political life as one age ends and another takes shape. The continuous threads of money, violence, biology, and technology in American politics, though, will continue to weave together the many diverse challenges that comprise the fabric of American political life.

NOTES

1. Daniel Bell, *The Coming of Post-Industrial Society: A Venture in Social Forecasting* (New York: Basic Books, 1973), pp. 1–265; Everett Carll Ladd, *The American Polity: The People and Their Government*, 2nd ed. (New York: W.W. Norton, 1987), pp. 17–51; John Naisbitt, *Megatrends: Ten New Directions Transforming Our Lives* (New York: Warner Books, 1984), pp. 1–33.
2. Bell, *The Coming of Post-Industrial Society*, pp. 1–164.
3. Spencer Rich, "The Twilight of the Big-Paycheck Blue-Collar Era," *The Washington Post National Weekly Edition*, June 13–19, 1988, p. 6.
4. Ibid.
5. Naisbitt, *Megatrends*, p. 8.
6. Ladd, *The American Polity*, pp. 23–24.
7. Noyce is cited in Naisbitt, *Megatrends*, p. 6.

PART I

Money and Politics

INTRODUCTION

Politics and economics are inevitably intertwined. Government decisions about taxing, spending, and borrowing have economic as well as political consequences. Since the beginning of the American republic, government has been involved in the nation's economic affairs through its activities in promoting commerce, regulating economic activity, and adjusting levels of taxation and spending in response to business cycles. The budgets of modern American government are sufficiently large that routine decisions about taxes and spending have significant economic impact.

How Much Government Costs

Table I.1 displays federal government spending for selected years from 1978 through estimates for 2008. Budgetary priorities refer to what government spends taxpayers' money for—that is, what goods and services government buys and what services it delivers. A glance at Table I.1 shows that there has been a gradual reordering of spending priorities in American government. Spending for defense, which was 27 percent of federal spending in 1988, equaled 17 percent in 1998 and is projected to be 15 percent of the total by 2008. Rather than reductions in the size of the defense budget, this percentage drop reflects a major reordering, with emphasis on *increases* in spending for human services and resources.

Entitlements and Indexed Programs.   Underlying this development are two concepts relatively new in American political economy. The first is the notion that citizens are entitled to certain economic benefits. Various government programs (called *entitlements*) have been enacted since the Great Depression. Entitlements are social programs providing services and benefits to which citizens have a legal right if they meet the qualifications for that program. Examples include Social Security, Medicare, and veterans' benefits. A second important development, which occurred during the 1960s and 1970s, is the concept of *indexed* programs, in which benefits increase automatically with the cost of living. The indexing of programs such as Social Security to increases in the Consumer Price Index ensures that benefits (and government spending) will increase with inflation. In addition to the proliferation of social programs and the expansion of benefits, the costs of medical care, technology, and human services have increased steadily as the American population has aged. The impact of entitlements on government spending is shown by the data in Table I.1. Social Security payments to retired persons, which totaled 19 percent of federal spending in 1978, are projected to increase to nearly one fourth of the total by the year 2008. Medicare is the program of health-care benefits for Social Security retirees. Medicare spending has increased from 5 percent of federal spending in 1978 to a projected 17 percent in 2008. This reflects both the increasing numbers of retirees in the United States and increases in the costs of health care and medical technology. During the thirty-year period shown in Table I.1, government spending for Social Security and Medicare combined is expected to increase from 24 percent to 40 percent of total spending.

Controlling the costs of entitlements is complicated by the fact that 60 percent of entitlement spending goes to pay for benefits for the elderly, mainly in the form of Social Security and Medicare. Although the elderly constitute only about 12 percent of the population, the number of elderly Americans is increasing rapidly, as is their political influence. There are more than 30 million recipients of Social Security and Medicare benefits, and the American Association of Retired Persons (AARP) has the largest membership of any organized interest group in the United States. Many elderly and retired Americans regard attempts to control the cost of entitlements as a direct assault on their interests. The political influence of Social Security beneficiaries has been demonstrated repeatedly. When the Reagan administration proposed reductions in Social Security benefits (for early retirees) and in cost of living increases, Congress was swamped with complaints from senior

TABLE I.1   Federal Government Expenditures 1978–2008

Category	Billions of Dollars (% of Total)			
	1978	1988	1998	2008 *(projection)*
Defense	118 (25%)	298 (27%)	302 (17%)	389 (15%)
Social Security	91 (19%)	214 (19%)	370 (21%)	587 (23%)
Medicare	25 (05%)	87 (08%)	217 (12%)	437 (17%)
Medicaid	11 (02%)	32 (03%)	102 (06%)	189 (07%)
Net Interest Paid	35 (07%)	148 (13%)	226 (13%)	150 (06%)
Surplus/Deficit	−32 (07%)	−121 (11%)	73 (04%)	113 (04%)
Total Spending	478	1119	1771	2538

Source: Bureau of Labor Statistics, Table 6, http://www.bls.gov/govs/cffr/99cffus.txt.

citizens. Democrats were quick to exploit this political advantage, denouncing the administration as unconcerned about the elderly. The result of the Reagan administration's painful lesson was that "social security became virtually untouchable."[1]

To summarize, sometimes decision makers *must* spend money because their options are limited by decisions that were made years, or even decades, earlier. Programs are created, benefits are conferred, expectations are established, and policies become entrenched. The beneficiaries of programs who become accustomed, or even entitled, to benefits constitute a political constituency in support of the programs. Governing consists partly of finding monetary sources to finance public services and partly of deciding who will pay these costs and who will receive the benefits. Politics is the process of deciding not only who gets what, when, and how, but also who pays and how much.

The U.S. government spends more than one fifth of the nation's gross national product (GNP) to deliver services, enforce regulations, and provide for national defense. To do this, the government must obtain upward of $2 trillion every year in the form of tax revenues and credit. Nearly half this sum is returned to individual citizens in the form of payments and benefits. The remainder goes to fund government programs in domestic politics and national defense; to pay the costs of government, including salaries and pensions of civilian and military employees; and to pay interest on money the government has borrowed. This last item is sizable because during the 1980s the U.S. government borrowed a significant amount of money to pay for spending not covered by available tax revenues. For example, in 1998 the government paid $226 billion to cover the interest due on the national debt.

Technological change plays a prominent role in American economics and politics. The pace of social change in America accelerated in the latter half of the twentieth century because of the impact of advanced technology. The questions of how society will pay for government programs (taxing and borrowing) and what government will spend the money for (policy priorities) have become increasingly important because advanced technology is expensive. Medical technology, computers, airplanes, and missiles are costly, as is the research and development needed to produce them.

The three chapters in Part I discuss questions of money and politics. These issues are analyzed in the context of the United States as a society based increasingly on advanced technology and information rather than manufacturing and on consumption rather than production. The implications of these transitions and the questions of persisting poverty and the costs of superpower status are considered.

Chapter 1, The Politics of Poverty and the Welfare State, discusses the scope and persistence of poverty in America and some of its causes and consequences. A substantial reduction in the level of poverty in the United States occurred from the end of World War II until the mid-1970s. But during the 1980s, poverty in America began to increase. This chapter addresses the causes and consequences of these changes in the economy and considers various proposals to mitigate the problem of poverty in America.

Chapter 2, The Politics of Health Care, examines the state of health care in the United States, including the cost, availability, and delivery of health services. These topics are analyzed within a comparative framework by discussing health care in several nations.

Chapter 3, Money in Public Office, addresses two issues, the first of which is the use of money to influence those in public office through bribery, corruption, and practices involving conflict of interest. The second issue this chapter considers is the relationship between money and campaigns for public office. Significant changes have occurred in campaign financing, fund raising, and expenditures; Chapter 3 discusses these developments and some of their consequences.

NOTE

1. Donald F. Kettl, *Deficit Politics: Public Budgeting in Its Institutional and Historical Context* (New York: Macmillan, 1992), p. 53.

SUGGESTED READINGS

HEILBRONER, ROBERT L. Chapter IX, "The Heresies of John Maynard Keynes." In *The Worldly Philosophers: The Lives, Times and Ideas of the Great Economic Thinkers,* 6th ed. New York: Simon & Schuster, 1986.

JONES, CHARLES O., ed. *The Reagan Legacy: Promise and Performance.* Chatham, NJ: Chatham House, 1988.

KETTL, DONALD F. *Deficit Politics: Public Budgeting in Its Institutional and Historical Context.* New York: Macmillan, 1992.

THE PUBLIC AGENDA FOUNDATION. *The Four Trillion Dollar Debt.* New York: McGraw-Hill, 1994.

SHUMAN, HOWARD E. *Politics and the Budget: The Struggle Between the President and the Congress,* 2nd ed. Upper Saddle River, NJ: Prentice Hall, 1988.

STOCKMAN, DAVID A. *The Triumph of Politics: The Inside Story of the Reagan Revolution.* New York: Avon Books, 1987.

Chapter 1

The Politics of Poverty
and the Welfare State

"The poor ye have with ye always." The belief in the inevitability of poverty is embedded in American culture and history. The question of which government policies and programs will best address the problem of poverty in America is part of a more fundamental debate over whether the government should help the poor at all. The notion that the national government should be involved in large-scale attempts to combat poverty is a relatively recent idea. The intense opposition to the expenditure of public money for poverty programs and welfare reflects an underlying contempt for the poor that is ingrained in American history, culture, and public policy.

SOURCES: THE WELFARE STATE IN AMERICA

Historically, poverty in America has been regarded not as a social problem but as a manifestation of individual weakness, moral deficiency, and shiftlessness. This is a reflection of American religious, cultural, and political traditions. The prevailing American ideology of liberal capitalism, in combination with the Protestant ethic of self-reliance, produced a highly individualistic political culture. Individuals were perceived as free to make choices, to pursue material self-interest, and to be held accountable for the choices they made. The primary role of government was to protect life, liberty, and property. The economic well-being of society was presumed to result from the interplay of competition and self-interest within the market economy. Impersonal economic forces interacted with talent and labor to produce a class structure. A few became rich, some merely comfortable, and many remained poor. One's place in the class structure was presumed to reflect individual motivation, industry, and achievement. Hard work was rewarded by success; idleness and indolence were punished by poverty.

The most extreme manifestation of this individualistic free market ideology was known as **Social Darwinism.** After the Civil War, this doctrine pervaded American culture as the Industrial Revolution reshaped the economy. Popularized by journalists, educators, and religious leaders, Social Darwinism profoundly affected politics and economics in the United States. Assumptions about wealth, poverty, and government were shaped by the widely held belief that social progress resulted from competitive economic struggle. The principle of survival of the fittest assured that there were winners and losers. The extremes of wealth and poverty that resulted were regarded as natural and morally appropriate. Social Darwinists contended that individuals received their due in accord with their talents and efforts and that the public interest was best served by permitting the competitive economic struggle to occur unimpeded. Consequently, the role of government ought to be limited to preserving order and guaranteeing the basic rights of life, liberty, and property.

Given this cultural heritage, it is not surprising that government assistance to the poor was deemed unnatural and undesirable. Historically, aid to the poor was a local task divided between charities and local government programs. State governments began to take a more active role in the latter half of the nineteenth century after industrialization, urbanization, and immigration created widespread conditions of congestion and squalor. Even so, prior to the Great Depression, state policies "consisted of a patchwork of very limited assistance in a few states and no aid at all in others."[1]

The Great Depression changed all that, of course. The Social Darwinist argument that the poor deserved their fate proved less than convincing to the 25 percent of the work force left unemployed by the Depression. Glorification of wealth became less acceptable as a public philosophy. The national government became permanently involved with the issues of unemployment, poverty, and welfare. Massive unemployment has proven to be a temporary, or at least cyclical, problem that can be addressed by government economic policy. Poverty programs and welfare, assumed initially to be temporary, have evolved into durable and expensive public responsibilities.

The various poverty and welfare programs that have evolved since the 1930s generally have at least one thing in common: They reflect the American heritage of liberal capitalism and competitive individualism. Government policies draw a distinction between those who deserve or have earned their benefits and those who receive unearned benefits. The former category of benefits are described as entitlements and social insurance. These programs have a large middle-class constituency, widespread political support, and generous benefits that have kept pace with the cost of living. The latter category of benefits is described as **public assistance** or, more commonly, as **welfare.** The recipients of welfare benefits, frequently stigmatized by other segments of society, are neither well organized nor politically powerful.

Welfare, or public assistance, benefits are distributed to recipients who are sufficiently impoverished to qualify. Because public assistance benefits are regarded as unearned welfare, recipients are frequently viewed with suspicion by authorities and much of the public. Not surprisingly, the level of public assistance benefits has not kept pace with increases in the cost of living since the mid-1970s.

Social Insurance

The Social Security Act of 1935 was the pivotal piece of social legislation in the development of the American welfare state. This law created the basic national programs in both social insurance and public assistance and established the fundamental distinction between them. "The Social Security Act segregated welfare recipients into two categories: those who would receive social insurance based on the philosophy that they had earned benefits and those who receive public assistance based on a demonstration of need."[2]

The basis for this distinction is that social insurance is a contributory program. Participants in the Social Security retirement system make contributions as employees by paying taxes into the system. Taxes paid by employers also help finance the system. Social Security retirees feel entitled to their benefits, perhaps believing that they are simply being repaid for contributions they made as wage earners. The reality is different. Social Security retirees are supported by taxes paid by the current generation of workers and their employers. Although not regarded as welfare, this social insurance program involves a transfer of wealth from one generation to another. Each year workers pay hundreds of billions of dollars in taxes to support retirees whose benefits may considerably exceed their contributions to the Social Security system. As the number of retirees and the amount of their benefits have increased, the tax burden has grown larger for the working generation. In 1956, disability benefits were added to the Social Security system. The Medicare program was established in 1965 to help pay the costs of doctor and hospital bills for retirees. Like the pension system, Medicare is a contributory program. In 1972, retirement benefits were increased by 20 percent and indexed to the cost of living, with cost of living increases distributed twice a year. There are more than 43 million Social Security beneficiaries, for whom expenditures for retirement and disability payments in 1998 totaled $403 billion and whose public health insurance (Medicare) cost $217 billion.[3] The unemployment compensation fund established in 1935 is also a contributory program, financed by taxes on employers and administered by the states.

Public Assistance

The public assistance components of the Social Security Act are not contributory. They are funded from the general revenues of the United States and participating state governments. These programs require a means test; that is, to be eligible, recipients must have very limited financial means. Included among these programs were old-age assistance for the impoverished elderly, aid to the blind, grants to states for public health and vocational rehabilitation, and most controversial, Aid to Dependent Children. Later known as **Aid to Families with Dependent Children (AFDC),** this aspect of federal policy incited considerable debate about deadbeats, chiselers, welfare Cadillacs, and widespread welfare dependence. Begun initially as a program of assistance to widows with young children, AFDC evolved into a major public assistance program with 14 million recipients, mostly women with young children. Many AFDC recipients were divorced or never married, were unemployed or underemployed, and had little education.

AFDC provided cash payments to households with dependent children if one parent was absent or, in some states, if the head of household was unemployed. This program was administered by the states, which determined eligibility and benefits. AFDC was financed by federal and state money, and benefit levels varied widely depending on the share contributed by each state. Expenditures for AFDC in 1996 totaled $32 billion, with the federal government providing $18 billion and the states furnishing the remainder.

Over time, AFDC became increasingly controversial, being criticized for encouraging welfare dependence, causing the disintegration of the family by contributing to the growth of female-headed families, and providing incentives for welfare mothers to have more children. Originally, the intent of AFDC was to enable widows to remain at home and raise their children. The welfare reform legislation enacted in 1996 (discussed later) to replace AFDC has the very different objective of forcing mothers of young children back into the labor market.

In-Kind Assistance

Additional federal programs have been established that do not provide cash payments to recipients, focusing instead on delivering goods and services. The provision of necessities in lieu of cash is described as in-kind benefits and includes the following.

Food Stamps.   The 1964 Food Stamp Act permits the federal government to sell food stamps to low-income households for the purchase of various types of foods. The cost of the stamps depends on the income of recipients but is always less than the face value of the stamps. To qualify for this program, a household must have an income below the poverty level. In 1996, more than 20 million American households received food stamps at a cost of $26 billion. In addition, the federal government and the states spent $5 billion on child nutrition and school lunch subsidies for low-income children. The welfare reform legislation of 1996 requires cuts in the food stamp program.

Medicaid.   The Medicaid program was established in 1965 to compensate doctors and hospitals for the cost of medical treatment for the impoverished. Like AFDC, it is a means-tested program in which the federal and state governments share the costs. In 1997, these costs totaled $111 billion. To qualify, a head of household must be eligible for public assistance. Medicaid excludes the working poor (those below the poverty level who do not qualify for welfare) from coverage. Consequently, a criticism of this program is that it discourages those on relief from accepting employment because they may lose medical benefits.

Housing and Education.   Additional services for the poor include low-income housing and vocational training. The federal government has provided for low-income housing in two ways: by helping the poor pay their rent (a rent subsidy) and by building low-income housing units. The latter practice was curtailed by the Reagan administration.

In 1964, President Lyndon Johnson moved the issue of poverty to the forefront of the American political agenda by declaring an "unconditional war on poverty." With congressional approval, the Office of Economic Opportunity was established to administer a number of programs to provide services and training aimed at improving the life prospects of the poor. Included were programs for preschool education (Head Start), compensatory education for public school children, and job training for disadvantaged youth (the Job Corps). These programs proved to be reasonably effective, and they survive in one form or another more than thirty years after they were created. In 1996, the federal government provided $16 billion in aid to education for low-income groups, including $8 billion in loans, grants, and work-study assistance targeted for lower-income college students, and nearly $1 billion for low-income preschool children (Head Start). The federal budget also included nearly $4 billion for job training and placement for low-income individuals.

In summary, in designing and administering the welfare state since the 1930s, government policymakers distinguish between two types of programs. Social insurance requires recipients to contribute to the programs by paying taxes as wage earners. Public assistance relies on general revenues of federal and state governments to provide aid and services to low-income families. Since the 1960s, policymakers have explored alternatives to direct cash payments to the poor (AFDC) and have relied increasingly on in-kind benefits, including medical care, food stamps, housing, and education programs. Welfare reform legislation enacted in 1996 replaced AFDC family support payments with block grants to the states.

For the remainder of this chapter, we analyze how social welfare programs have interacted with economic growth to reduce poverty in America since the 1950s. We consider the implications of the economic dislocations and stagnation that occurred in the 1970s and the prospects for continued progress in the reduction of poverty in America.

STATUS: POVERTY IN AMERICA

Before considering the causes of poverty and the impact of economic change and government policy, we must address more basic questions: What is the scope of poverty in America? How many people are poor? Who are they?

The Poverty Level

The United States began the process of identifying the poor in 1959. The Census Bureau provides a statistical estimate of the size and characteristics of the population that lives in poverty. This figure, revised annually, is used to determine the amount of federal funds provided to states to operate public assistance programs. The Department of Health and Human Services uses the poverty level as an income guideline to determine eligibility for some federal programs.

TABLE 1.1   Defining Poverty: The Poverty Level
for Different Family Sizes, 1999

Number of Persons	Poverty Level
1	$8,677
2	$11,156
3	$13,032
4	$17,184
5	$20,723
6	$23,835
7	$27,425

Source: U.S. Bureau of the Census, *Current Population Survey,*
http://www.census.gov/poverty99.

The poverty level is derived by estimating the amount of money required to purchase a minimally adequate market basket of food that will provide families with a diet meeting basic nutritional standards. Until 1986, the poverty level was calculated by multiplying the cost of the food basket by three. This was based on a 1955 Department of Agriculture survey that found that, on the average, low-income families spent one third of their incomes on food. In 1986, the multiplier was changed to 3.4, reflecting increases in the cost of living.[4]

Table 1.1 displays the poverty levels established by the government for different sized families in 1999. For example, the table estimates that in 1999 a family of four needed a before-tax income of $17,184 to purchase necessities in the United States. A family of six needed $23,835.

Like any statistic, the poverty level can be, and has been, criticized as inaccurate. Advocates for the poor contend that the poverty level underestimates the number of people living in poverty because it relies on census data, which fail to count millions of the destitute and transients. Others insist that the poverty level overestimates the number of poor people because low-income individuals are eligible for non-cash benefits such as food stamps and Medicaid, which improve their standard of living. In addition, it is argued that many low-income individuals earn money by participating in an underground economy and neither report nor pay taxes on this income.

Despite possible shortcomings of the government-established poverty level, data collected systematically for more than forty years permit comparison between social groups over time. Table 1.2 summarizes the results of the government's research from 1959 to 1998.

Progress Against Poverty in the United States

The pattern in the data shows that during the 1960s and 1970s poverty in America decreased rapidly, but in the 1980s progress against poverty stopped and some of the gains of the previous decade were reversed. In 1959, nearly 40 million Americans lived below the poverty level. The poor constituted more than one fifth

TABLE 1.2   Persons below Poverty Level, 1959–1998

Year	Number below Poverty Level (in millions)				Percent below Poverty Level			
	Total	White	Black	Hispanic	Total	White	Black	Hispanic
1959	39.5	28.5	9.9	NA	22.4%	18.1%	55.1%	NA
1970	25.4	17.5	7.5	NA	12.6	9.9	33.5	NA
1978	24.5	16.3	7.6	2.6	11.4	8.7	30.6	21.6%
1983	35.3	24.0	9.9	4.6	15.2	12.1	35.7	28.0
1990	33.6	22.3	9.8	6.0	13.5	10.7	31.9	28.2
1994	38.1	25.3	10.2	8.4	14.5	11.7	30.6	30.7
1998	34.5	23.4	9.1	8.1	12.7	8.2	26.1	25.6

Source: U.S. Bureau of the Census, *Statistical Abstract of the United States: 1996* (114th ed.). Washington, DC: 1996, Table No. 7307, p. 472, and U.S. Census Bureau 1998 Web site.

of the population, and more than half of all African Americans were below the poverty level. By 1970, the number of poor had declined to 26 million, less than 13 percent of the population. The poverty rate among African Americans decreased to one third. Although poverty among African Americans and Hispanics remains high (around 25 percent), this should not obscure the fact that a majority of poor people (69 percent) are white.[5]

The decline in poverty is even greater if the figures are projected back to an earlier time. The estimate for the poverty rate in 1949 is 32 percent.[6] This means that the poverty rate decreased almost 20 percentage points between 1949 and 1970. Poverty continued to decline at a slower rate until 1979, when the rate again began to rise. After peaking at 15 percent in 1983, poverty declined somewhat but has remained higher than at any time since the late 1960s.

Who Are the Poor?

In the midst of an overall reduction in poverty, some social groups have fared better than others. Poverty is increasing among some groups, including, unfortunately, the nation's children. Table 1.3 shows this trend from 1970 to 1998. The most dramatic decline in poverty has occurred among those aged sixty-five and older. The decrease in poverty among the elderly (from 25 to 10 percent) is directly attributable to the increase in government and private sector expenditures for social insurance. Social Security retirement payments with automatic cost of living increases (COLAs) constitute one of the American welfare state's most effective antipoverty programs.

The reduction of poverty among the elderly is not mirrored for the youngest age groups. During this period the rate of poverty among American children increased from 15 to 21 percent. By 1994, two of every five African American and Hispanic children in the United States lived in households with incomes below the poverty level. Comparison with other industrial democracies shows that the poverty rate is higher in the United States. In a comprehensive study, the United Nations

TABLE **1.3**   Poverty and Age, 1970 to 1998

Year	Children below the Poverty Level		Elderly below the Poverty Level	
	Number (in millions)	Percent	Number (in millions)	Percent
1970	10.2	15%	4.8	25%
1994	14.6	21	3.7	12
1998	13.5	19	3.4	10

Source: U.S. Bureau of the Census, *Statistical Abstract of the United States: 1996* (116th ed.). Washington, DC: 1996, Table No. 733, p. 473.

Children's Fund (UNICEF) reported in 1993 that the United States ranks behind other industrialized countries in providing a safety net for children. The poverty rate of 21 percent for American children is double the rate of any other industrialized country. The UNICEF study showed that the United States ranks nineteenth in child mortality, behind Western Europe, Japan, Hong Kong, and South Korea.[7] Government estimates in Table 1.3 show that in 1998 nearly 13.5 million American children lived in poverty, a number equal to nearly one fifth of the nation's children. This trend is most evident in the largest cities. In New York, 700,000 children (about 40 percent of the city's children) live in families with incomes below the poverty line.[8]

Single Mothers and Poverty.   The issue of children in poverty is closely related to changes in American family structure, especially the rise in the number of households headed by single women. Since 1959, the divorce rate has doubled and the number of babies born to unwed mothers has tripled. These factors have doubled the number of children living in families headed by a single parent. The poverty rate for this type of family exceeds 50 percent, and the number of families in this category has increased from 4 million in 1959 to almost 7 million. One fifth of all children in the United States lived in a family headed by a single woman in 1991, double the rate in 1959. A majority (56 percent) of children in female-headed households lived below the poverty level. Of that number, more than half were African American. Families headed by men, and two-parent families, experience less poverty (about 14 percent).[9]

The Concentration of Poverty

In the 1980s, poverty became more concentrated within the poor areas of American cities. The National League of Cities reported that between 1979 and 1985 the number of poor people in metropolitan areas increased by 7.6 million. The number of poor residents living in poverty areas (meaning neighborhoods in which at least 40 percent of the residents are below the poverty line) increased from 16 percent in 1970 to 24 percent ten years later.[10] Sociologist William Julius Wilson reports that between 1970 and 1980 in America's five largest cities (New York, Los Angeles, Chicago, Philadelphia, and Detroit), the poverty population increased by 22 percent, and that nearly half of the total poor population in the nation's fifty largest cities live in these five locations.[11]

The Working Poor

Some poor people cannot find jobs, but millions also are poor despite the fact that they work. The working poor and their dependents total about 5 million, many of whom do not receive either medical insurance coverage on the job or Medicaid benefits available to welfare recipients. The working poor and their dependents make up about 13 percent of the poor, while another 17 percent of the poor live in families where the wage earner is underemployed. This means that nearly one third of the poor live in families in which the head of household is employed, either full or part time. Another one third are elderly or disabled, and one fourth are single parents with young children.[12] Most of the poor do not live in families with an able-bodied head of household who simply refuses to work. Hundreds of thousands of poor Americans have low-paying jobs in hospitals, nursing homes, convenience stores, and other retail outlets. The number of working poor has increased 52 percent since 1975.

The Underclass: The Permanently Poor?

William Echikson, a Paris-based staff writer for *The Christian Science Monitor,* in 1989 made this comparison between French and American cities: "Nowadays France does not suffer from such sharp divisions of wealth as one finds in the United States. . . . None of the inner cities except perhaps Marseilles has turned into an angry, empty shell like American urban ghettos."[13] In 1984, a panel of the Conference of Catholic Bishops stated in a pastoral letter: "In our judgment, the distribution of income and wealth in the United States is so inequitable that it violates [a] minimum standard of distributive justice."[14]

These assessments of American urban poverty describe different aspects of the same paradox: Despite the great wealth in the United States, and despite a gradual reduction in poverty since 1949, there is an emerging urban underclass that is perhaps permanently impoverished. Millions of citizens are trapped in urban poverty, geographically and socially isolated, poorly trained for the emerging information-based labor market, and residentially segregated into crime-ridden slums.

The urban underclass is composed of groups that have been left behind by economic change. They constitute a distinctive subgroup, not simply an economic category. The poverty areas of American cities are heavily populated by the most disadvantaged segments of the urban population, those who lack training and skills and who experience long-term unemployment, poverty, and welfare dependence. Poverty neighborhoods are characterized by the breakdown of social organization, very high unemployment, a high percentage of female-headed households and out-of-wedlock births, and a high rate of violent crime. As a group, the urban underclass is isolated from mainstream norms and behavior patterns and is economically and geographically segregated.[15]

Changing income patterns have contributed directly to the rise in urban poverty. Increasingly, there is a division of American families into two-paycheck families on the one hand and female-headed families on the other. Likewise, the income gap between the less educated and the college educated is growing. Jobs for those with less than a high school education are evaporating as the labor market reflects trends toward an information- and technology-based economy. The income gap between two-income families and female-headed families, and between better educated and less educated individuals, is increasing. Urban poverty areas are characterized by large numbers of female-headed families and individuals with less than a high school education. The groups most heavily disadvantaged in relation to economic trends are, as a result of historical migration patterns, concentrated in America's large cities.

Economic Change and Social Disorganization

Changes in the structure of the American economy in the 1970s, which created dislocations and unemployment in the economic mainstream, were devastating for low-income residents of inner cities. According to Wilson, "inner-city communities prior to 1960 exhibited the features of social organization including a sense of community, positive neighborhood identification, and explicit norms and sanctions against aberrant behavior."[16] These communities were class integrated, meaning that different segments of the urban African American population (the lower, working, and middle classes) lived in the same communities, sent their children to the same schools, and shopped in the same areas. Today, this is no longer true. Black middle-class professionals often live and work outside the inner city, and the working class is moving out of the ghetto into better neighborhoods. These are the groups whose "very presence provided stability to inner-city neighborhoods and reinforced and perpetuated mainstream patterns and norms of behavior."[17]

The mobility of the African American middle class is only the tip of the iceberg. In parts of the United States, the inner-city manufacturing economy has nearly collapsed. The process of **deindustrialization** has taken a toll. Many smokestack industries have closed plants or relocated to more profitable settings. Jobs for workers with little education and weak skills have vanished, to be replaced by information- and technology-based jobs for which less educated inner-city residents are unable to compete. This irreversible transformation of urban economies has resulted in a mismatch between the needs of the labor market and the skills and training of many inner-city residents. For example, in New York City the number of jobs in industries with lower education requirements decreased by nearly 500,000 between 1970 and 1984, while jobs with higher education requirements increased by 239,000.[18]

These urban economic dislocations are compounded by a housing situation that produces increased concentrations of poverty. The shortage of affordable urban housing for those with low incomes forces the poor to gravitate to deteriorating areas or to rely on public housing. Much of the housing built and operated by the government in large cities is in the form of huge projects and high-rise structures. The concentration of public housing further segregates and isolates the poor from the mainstream and, in addition, sometimes creates dreadful living conditions. In his book *The Truly Disadvantaged,* Wilson describes conditions in the Robert Taylor

Homes, the largest public housing project in Chicago. This complex of twenty-eight high-rise buildings covers ninety-two acres and is home to more than 25,000 people, two thirds of whom are minors. Ninety-three percent of the families with children are headed by a single parent, nearly all of whom received AFDC funding. Unemployment approaches 50 percent. In 1980, about 10 percent of Chicago's murders, rapes, and aggravated assaults were committed in the Robert Taylor Homes.[19]

The plight of the urban underclass has resulted from patterns of migration as well as changes in social and economic organization. Until about 1970, there was a significant migration of African Americans to northern industrial cities. Historic patterns of racial discrimination in housing and employment laid the foundation for an urban underclass. The recent migration of the black middle and working classes from the inner cities has left behind a hard core of urban poor who are economically, socially, and racially isolated. Changes in the urban economy and the job market limit their prospects. African Americans and other inner-city blue-collar workers have been hurt because of their concentration in automobile, steel, and other heavy industries.

The urban manufacturing sector did not bounce back from deindustrialization. Heavy industry has been displaced by a technological economy with higher education requirements for employment. The urban underclass has been left behind in the process, unable to benefit from economic recovery. This is illustrated by the fact that unemployment in the United States reached a fifteen-year low of 5.1 percent in March 1989.[20] At the same time, the poverty rate was 13 percent, higher than at any time during the 1970s. There are underlying economic and social problems, especially in American cities, that economic recovery is not able to solve. Contrary to the cliché, a rising tide has not lifted all boats.

Because analysts use differing definitions, there is a wide range of estimates regarding the size of America's underclass. Conservative estimates, based on the number of poor living in poverty areas, place the figure at approximately 2 million. When defined more broadly as the long-term poor, the estimate reaches 8 to 11 million.[21] In keeping with the definition of the underclass as a distinctive subgroup that is isolated from the mainstream, we regard a more conservative estimate of 2 to 4 million as appropriate because research has shown that most people who are poor do not remain that way. Long-term studies tracking welfare recipients show that most people who become poor at some point in their lives experience poverty for an average of fewer than two years. There are a substantial number of long-term poor, and among this group, female-headed families remain in poverty the longest—an average of twelve years.[22] The underclass is a minority of the poor, but because of the growth of chronic poverty and social deviance, it experiences a disproportionate share of social problems.

The Homeless

In 1985, more than 1,000 people died in the United States from exposure to cold weather. This was a 137 percent increase from the 427 freezing deaths reported in 1976. Dr. Edwin Kilbourne, a researcher for the national Centers for Disease Control, attributed a large part of this increase to the growing numbers of people who have no shelter.[23] In November 1993, Yetta M. Adams, a homeless woman, died in near-freezing weather in Washington, D.C. Her death drew attention from media and government because Ms. Adams died while sleeping on a bus bench across the street from the headquarters of federal housing officials in the offices of the Department of Housing and Urban Development (HUD). Within one week of Ms. Adams's death, HUD officials pledged an additional $25 million for care of the homeless during the winter.[24]

Images of the homeless are now a routine part of American media coverage of social problems. Stories of people living in the subway systems of cities, in shelters, in cars, in cardboard boxes, or spending the night on heating grates or park benches are commonplace. More systematic assessments of the homeless suggest that they are best described as being composed of several distinct groups.

The Congressional Research Service reported in 1989 that the actual incidence of homelessness is unknown. Estimates range from 300,000 to 3 million homeless. Research indicates that there are at least five factors contributing to homelessness: substance abuse, mental illness, desperate economic circumstances, family disintegration, and a shortage of low-income housing.

Substance Abuse.   Some of the homeless are so dependent on or addicted to alcohol or other drugs that they have ceased to function in the mainstream and have gravitated to the margins of society. They are the down and out, "bums, winos, and druggies" who have dropped out of society. Given their circumstances, and the shortage of shelters and low-income housing, some of these people inevitably end up out in the cold. Estimates are that upward of one third of the homeless are chronic substance abusers.[25]

Mental Illness.   Recent studies suggest that from 20 to 40 percent of the homeless population are chronically mentally ill, that there is substantial overlap between mental illness and substance abuse, and that it is difficult to determine whether the substance abuse began before or after the homelessness. It is clear, however, that a systematic policy of deinstitutionalization of the mentally ill has produced significant numbers of homeless citizens. This policy, more popularly known as "dumping," resulted in the discharge of more than 400,000 patients from mental hospitals between 1950 and 1980. Supporters of this practice claimed that advances in drug therapy and treatment made it feasible to integrate mental patients back into the community. But the community-based treatment facilities required to follow up this policy were never provided in adequate numbers. Expected to fend for themselves, former mental patients often ended up in shelters or on the streets.[26]

Those who are homeless for more than two years may be described as long-term homeless. This group fits the traditional conception of the homeless, being comprised primarily of substance abusers, the mentally ill, and those with prison records. Recently, the ranks of the homeless have been increased by the addition of other groups, frequently on a temporary basis, due to personal and economic circumstances.

Economic Circumstances.   Some people have become homeless as a result of unemployment or economic difficulties. A study of homelessness in Ohio found that unemployment and economic problems were major reasons for about half of the state's homelessness. Research in Minneapolis indicated that a portion of that city's working poor was homeless; that more than one third of the city's homeless were working, although most were not working full time; that another third were on public assistance or Social Security; and that approximately one fifth had no income at all.

Family Conflict.   Stress within the family, domestic violence, and family dissolution contribute to homelessness. Women (frequently with young children) and runaway youths leave home to escape domestic violence. This has created the relatively new phenomenon of the homeless family. One fifth of the sample in the Ohio study reported that family conflict was the major reason for their homelessness.

Housing.   Those in dire economic straits have difficulty finding affordable housing. Urban redevelopment and gentrification (the refurbishing of older neighborhoods) displace low-income housing with more profitable middle-class units. This not only inflates housing costs in the area but eliminates low-income units as well. In Los Angeles, 40 percent of the women surveyed reported that they were homeless as a result of eviction.[27]

Given the transient lifestyle of many of the homeless, it is difficult to estimate their numbers. The Department of Housing and Urban Development estimated the number of homeless in the United States at between 250,000 and 350,000. Advocacy groups for the homeless insist that there are between 2 and 3 million,[28] but such claims appear to be exaggerated. The nonpartisan Urban Institute estimates that there are about 600,000 homeless individuals in the United States.[29] To put this issue into historical perspective, a congressional investigation reported that in 1937, during the Great Depression, there were 5 million homeless Americans.[30]

Welfare and Poverty

Defenders of the welfare state contend that social spending has reduced poverty and could decrease it even more if government restructured its priorities. Critics of social welfare are equally certain that government programs, especially public assistance, are a big part of the problem, not the solution, of poverty.

In their analysis of the development of American public policy, David Robertson and Dennis Judd conclude that the United States is an exception to the generalization that as societies become wealthier they become more willing and able to provide extensive welfare state benefits. "American government, especially in light of the nation's wealth, has been slower to offer social benefits, more

TABLE 1.4   Federal Social Welfare Spending, 1970–1995 (in billions of dollars, rounded off)

Year	Social Insurance (Social Security and Medicare)	Welfare (Public Aid and Food Stamps)	Other (Veterans, Education, Housing)	Total
1970	45 (58%)	10 (13%)	23 (30%)	77
1980	191 (63%)	49 (16%)	62 (21%)	302
1992	496 (66%)	139 (18%)	115 (15%)	749
1995	580 (65%)	170 (19%)	137 (16%)	888

Source: U.S. Bureau of the Census, *Statistical Abstract of the United States: 1996* (116th ed.). Washington, DC: 1996, Table No. 733 p. 473, and U.S. Census Bureau Web site, http://www.census.gov/hhes/poverty98.

austere in the benefits it offers, less willing to guarantee benefits to its poorest citizens, and extremely resistant to reducing income disparities."[31] We believe that an analysis of social welfare spending and priorities in America confirms Robertson and Judd's appraisal.

Spending on Social Welfare.   Table 1.4 shows that in 1995 the U.S. government spent $888 billion for programs classified as social welfare expenditures. This table also shows that most of this spending was for entitlements and contributory programs, not for welfare and aid to the poor. More than two thirds of U.S. government social welfare expenditures pays the costs of social insurance, including Social Security (retirement, survivors', and disability), Medicare for retirees, and public employee retirement programs. Spending for social insurance has grown from 58 percent of the total in 1970 to 65 percent in 1995, due to increasing numbers of retirees, longer life spans, and soaring medical costs.

Public aid programs, or "welfare," include cash payments to the nonelderly poor, food stamps, medical care for the destitute (Medicaid), and aid to the impoverished elderly and blind. Spending for these programs totaled $170 billion in 1995, an amount equal to 19 percent of federal social welfare expenditures. Cash payments to welfare mothers (AFDC) totaled $14 billion (2 percent of the total), with the states contributing an equivalent amount, and spending for food stamps was $23 billion. An analysis comparing the level of welfare benefits in different states showed that only in Alaska and Hawaii did the combined benefits for AFDC and food stamps exceed the poverty level. In two states, benefits were less than half the poverty level, and in half of the states, benefits were less than three fourths of the poverty level.[32] The policy in many states is that unearned benefits should be low enough to reduce their attractiveness as an alternative to working.

An examination of government spending and priorities shows that most social welfare spending in America is allocated to social insurance and public education. Social insurance primarily aids the retired or their survivors and has contributed to poverty reduction among the elderly. Social insurance costs equal two thirds of all federal social welfare spending. About one fifth of social spending is intended to assist poor and low-income Americans by providing cash payments or in-kind benefits. Welfare benefits, as measured by combined AFDC payments and food stamps, have been below the poverty level in forty-eight of the fifty states for those on public assistance.

PROSPECTS: SOCIAL PROGRAMS AND WELFARE REFORM

For social programs, assessment of the impact and prospects for success is difficult, and the outcome of an appraisal is likely to reflect economic, social, and political assumptions made by the analyst. Presumptions about the causes of poverty influence perceptions about solutions. For purposes of comparison, we have grouped policies and proposals regarding poverty and welfare into three broad categories. Some analysts regard economic growth as the key to understanding and reducing poverty. Others contend that government social programs have reduced poverty and that an expansion of the welfare state will decrease poverty in America. Welfare reform is the primary objective of those who believe that welfare and social programs are out of date and need to be revised or that welfare actually contributes to poverty by discouraging work and promoting dependence.

Economic Growth

Analysts who place primary emphasis on economics assume that people are poor because they are unemployed or underemployed. Poverty is seen as a consequence of poor economic performance and long-term changes in the economy. Frank Levy explains the decline in poverty during the 1960s as a response to economic conditions. A booming economy based on industrial manufacturing expanded at a rate sufficient to generate growth in real income. As incomes went up, poverty went down. A period of economic stagnation beginning in 1973 and lasting through the early 1980s accounts for the upsurge in poverty beginning in the late 1970s. Levy describes this period of stagnation as a hidden depression consisting of a series of recessions and inflations triggered by economic restructuring and deindustrialization. Five million workers, half of whom were in manufacturing, were displaced during the hidden depression. Real family income stagnated for most of this period and actually declined during the late 1970s. When incomes fall, more people become poor. In Levy's analysis, this decline in the growth of economic productivity is at the root of the increase in poverty during the 1980s.[33]

William Julius Wilson employs a similar mode of analysis to explain the growth of urban poverty. Wilson contends that irreversible economic changes have transformed large American cities. Thousands of blue-collar workers have been displaced, and an impoverished and poorly educated underclass has become stranded in the central cities, unable to participate in the technologically complex economy.

The supposition that poverty is attributable primarily to low incomes and slow economic growth has implications for the direction of government policy. The hidden depression of the 1970s left behind permanent changes in the American economy. Successful policies must address the requirements of a postindustrial economy, especially the need for a technically trained and educated labor force suited to the changing labor market. This will require a greater commitment to retraining displaced workers and providing training and skills to those left behind by economic change. Advocates of this point of view must also address the fact, as shown in Table 1.2, that during the lengthy period of economic expansion in the 1990s, poverty in the United States declined only marginally.

Expanding Social Welfare Programs

While acknowledging the importance of a sound economy, some analysts believe that strong, sustained growth will not be sufficient to produce a further substantial reduction in poverty. An expansion of government social programs is necessary, they believe, because the private sector has demonstrated indifference or inability to handle the challenge of poverty and because hard-core poverty is barely affected by a return to economic prosperity. There are several areas in which expanded social programs might have an impact on poverty in America.

Education. Isabel Sawhill of the Urban Institute has argued persuasively that raising the levels of education and literacy among the children of poor families is a key to breaking the cycle of poverty. About half of poor adults have less than a high school education. Lack of education and deficiencies in skills contribute to unemployment, crime, welfare dependence, and out-of-wedlock births. Compensatory education programs increase the likelihood of high school completion and successful employment. Preschool programs have been shown to be especially effective. However, less than one fifth of the children eligible for Head Start are enrolled.[34] This program could be a candidate for expansion if greater support is made available for early childhood education.

Employment. Programs targeted at reducing unemployment among the poor have had a measure of success, especially when job training is combined with placement services. The Job Corps is a program for disadvantaged youths who have dropped out of school. By combining remedial education, job training, and health and placement services, the Job Corps increases employment prospects and earnings.[35] Although a relatively expensive program (about $15,000 per trainee), it has been reasonably effective.

The role of the private sector in providing job training could be expanded. A Massachusetts Institute of Technology study reported that Japanese and West German corporations invest far more than most American companies in training and retraining workers.[36] Government incentives could be used to encourage greater participation by American companies in training disadvantaged youths and retraining displaced workers. The case for expanding these and similar programs rests not only on enhanced earnings for the program graduates but on social benefits such as the reduction in crime and welfare dependence.

Health Care. The absence of government- or employer-provided health-care coverage for many low-income workers may be a reason some people choose to remain on welfare. Providing health-care benefits would make working in low-paying jobs a more attractive alternative; for example, the Medicaid system could be expanded to cover the working poor. Alternatively, Congress could require employers to provide minimum coverage to all full-time employees, as President Clinton proposed. The question is whether the government or the private sector will absorb this expense at a time of rapidly rising health-care costs.

Housing.   As urban real estate values have continued to rise, many low-income families have found themselves priced out of the housing market. The amount of low-income housing built with the aid of federal Community Development Block Grants has not kept up with demand. Further, as rents have increased, the poor have been forced to accept substandard dwellings. The federal government also provides rent subsidies, but at the present level of funding, fewer than one in four welfare families receives a subsidy.[37] This means that 3 million renters on welfare did not receive government assistance to pay their rent. Federal housing assistance "is allocated on a first-come, first-served basis. It is a lottery, not an entitlement."[38]

The cutbacks in federal housing support have come at a time of growing awareness that low-income, high-rise public housing projects must be replaced. The concentration of poverty and crime associated with high-density public housing projects, as well as high maintenance costs, limits their utility. A report submitted to the mayor's office in Chicago recommended that the city demolish most of its 168 high-rise public housing buildings and find new homes for 70,000 tenants, preferably by relocating them throughout the metropolitan area.[39] The dispersal, rather than the concentration, of poverty would likely be an improvement. However, construction of low-income housing units in middle-class neighborhoods is inevitably controversial.

Racism and Discrimination.   In his book *Poverty in America,* historian Milton Meltzer cites past and present racism as a cause for high rates of poverty among minorities.[40] Past patterns of discrimination in housing and employment led to the segregation of the poor by reducing their geographic and economic mobility. This assessment of the impact of past discrimination is widely accepted. There is less agreement about the scope and impact of present discrimination against women and minorities and about appropriate remedies. For example, Wilson agrees that historic racism explains the concentration of minorities in urban ghettos but regards overt racism and discrimination as a less compelling explanation for the development of the contemporary urban underclass. Because a significant increase in the size of the underclass has occurred since 1970, after the civil rights and antipoverty programs were enacted, Wilson attributes the increase in urban poverty primarily to economic factors.[41]

Contemporary discrimination, while perhaps less blatant, cannot be dismissed as a factor contributing to minority poverty. Research on hiring practices suggests that some employers are reluctant to hire disadvantaged minority youths, perhaps believing them to make poor employees. A comparison of urban youths of similar age and education showed that African Americans received far fewer job offers than did whites when they applied for similar jobs.[42]

Government policy has approached the issue of bias in hiring by providing means for investigation and adjudication of complaints and by affirmative action policies that encourage the employment and promotion of women and minorities. The net effect of preferential employment policies has been to benefit the better educated and trained minority applicants.[43]

Welfare Reform

Those who believe that poverty is a manifestation of individual and cultural traits rather than economic and social causes are likely to advocate different solutions. Critics of the welfare state often regard the poor, rather than poverty, as the problem and believe that the root causes of poverty are found in the personal attributes of the poor. Consequently, they advocate policies aimed at changing the poor by reshaping their attitudes and work habits. This will be accomplished, welfare critics believe, by policies providing incentives for working and removing incentives for not working. From this perspective, the welfare state contributes to poverty by rewarding the poor for not working and by encouraging welfare dependence. George Gilder, author of *Wealth and Poverty*, and Charles Murray, in *Losing Ground*, contend that welfare programs, especially AFDC, have discouraged the poor from working, thereby perpetuating poverty.[44] Rather than regarding poverty as a result of unemployment, the welfare state critics believe that unemployment is partly a result of poverty. The poor, due to lack of motivation and poor work habits, choose welfare dependence, which perpetuates their lack of motivation and poor work habits. The result is a self-perpetuating cycle, or culture of poverty, fostered and maintained by welfare programs. Welfare reforms, especially work requirements, are seen as crucial to breaking this cycle and forcing the able-bodied back into the labor market.

Workfare.   Perspectives on the appropriate relationship between work and welfare have changed over time. The premise of the original Aid to Dependent Children program was that the interests of society and its fatherless children were best served if mothers of young children were not obligated to work outside the home. This point of view has changed as the economy, the family structure, and the roles of women have changed. The change is symbolized by the growing popularity of the notion of workfare. The essence of the workfare argument is that welfare recipients ought to be required to work for their benefits by performing unpaid clerical and maintenance services. While working off their public assistance payments, the poor will learn proper work habits and values that will enable them to become self-sufficient. The simplicity of this "no work, no benefits" approach has popular and political appeal, but successful workfare programs involve expensive training, placement, and child-care services. After evaluating experimental programs in several states, a Congressional Budget Office report concluded that carefully designed work-related programs for AFDC recipients can be moderately successful. Specifically, programs that include training and placement assistance usually increase the average earnings of participants. Savings generated by reduced welfare expenses helped pay some, but not all, of the costs of the programs.[45]

Ending Welfare As We Know It: The Welfare Reform Act of 1996

The Clinton administration proposed to "end welfare as we know it" by overhauling the welfare system. The plan relied on a carrot-and-stick approach, the stick being a two-year limit on eligibility for welfare benefits. The carrots included proposals to expand job training and child-care programs so that welfare mothers could acquire job skills and enter the work force. In the 1994 congressional elections, the Republicans won control of both houses of Congress. The president, faced with a conservative Congress more than willing to overhaul the welfare system in a dramatic fashion, signed the welfare reform bill in August 1996. During his televised announcement, President Clinton said, "Today, we have a historic opportunity to make welfare what it was meant to be: a second chance, not a way of life."[46] A significant departure from welfare policies of the last sixty years, this law eliminated AFDC, reduced food stamp expenditures, and placed new limits on eligibility for welfare benefits. Specifically, the welfare reform law of 1996 provides for the following.[47]

Ending AFDC.　The welfare reform law replaces AFDC, the nation's largest cash welfare program, with a grant program called Temporary Assistance for Needy Families (TANF.) This consists of federal payments to state governments totaling $16 billion yearly. Since the states will determine who is eligible for welfare benefits, poor people will no longer automatically be entitled to cash benefits, and eligibility and benefits will likely vary from state to state. There is no longer a federal guarantee of welfare assistance to all eligible low-income families.

Cuts in Benefits.　The welfare reform law requires $54 billion in reductions in social welfare programs over a five-year period. Most of these reductions are to come from cuts in the food stamp program and limits on benefits for legal immigrants. Illegal immigrants are denied benefits. States have the option of denying benefits to children born to welfare recipients and to unwed parents under the age of eighteen. Half of the forty governors who submitted state welfare plans to the federal government stated that they will not increase payments to women on public assistance who have additional children.[48]

Work Requirements.　Welfare recipients will be required to begin working within two years. Parents with children under one year of age may be exempt, if a state chooses, but not for more than one year. Federal grants of approximately

$2 billion per year are provided to the states to pay for child-care programs to enable former welfare recipients to work. The welfare reform law grants states wide discretion in developing specific regulations and in awarding benefits, and many states are adopting stricter work requirements and shorter time limits. Some states, such as Indiana, decided to enforce work requirements by reducing welfare payments to those who refuse to cooperate. Pennsylvania, on the other hand, attempts to reward those who do work by increasing the amount they are permitted to earn before they are forced off the welfare roles.[49]

Republican Governor Tommy Thompson of Wisconsin signed a bill known as "Work Not Welfare," which imposed a two-year limit on welfare benefits. Governor Thompson vetoed a proposal to provide health care for the poor once welfare is abolished.[50] Whether the state will provide job training and child care to assist the poor remains to be seen. The state of Michigan abolished much of its welfare program for those who are not disabled and who do not have children, resulting in the elimination of General Assistance benefits for 81,000 people. Republican Governor John Engler said that those whose benefits were cut off should find jobs or move in with relatives. Some welfare counselors in Michigan advised their clients without food or shelter to "commit a simple larceny" because being jailed for commission of a nonviolent crime would provide the clients with basic necessities.[51]

Drugs.   States may deny welfare benefits and food stamps to individuals convicted of felony drug offenses. As of 1997, more than twenty states reported that they planned to do this, and only Oregon indicated that it will not deny welfare benefits to convicted drug offenders.[52]

Evaluating Welfare Reform

Preliminary assessments of the impact of welfare reform indicate that significant numbers of welfare recipients have moved off of the welfare roles since 1997. In his remarks before the House Committee on Education and the Workforce, Alvin Collins, Director of the Office of Family Assistance, attributed this to numerous factors, including

- welfare reform
- strong economic growth
- increasing the minimum wage
- the Welfare-to-Work grant program
- tax credits to encourage hiring of welfare recipients (12,000 businesses have hired 410,000 welfare recipients)
- funding welfare-to-work transportation assistance ($75 million in 1999)
- support for welfare-to-work housing vouchers (50,000 enacted so far)

Specifically, government data show that in 1997 nearly 4 million families (11 million recipients) were receiving Temporary Assistance for Needy Families. By

1999, TANF recipients had declined to 2.7 million families and 7.3 million individuals. Collins's report shows that by 1999, nearly one fourth of welfare recipients were employed compared with 7 percent in 1992. While stating that many of these working families are better off financially than they were on welfare, Collins stressed the need for systematic follow-up and additional welfare-to-work efforts.[53]

Conclusion.   As previously discussed, most spending in the social welfare expenditures category provides insurance and medical benefits for retirees and veterans, not aid to the poor. These entitlement programs are very popular and are protected by powerful political interests. The welfare, or public assistance, portion of the budget, consisting of public aid for the poor and food stamps for low-income Americans, is much smaller but not as well protected by political interest groups. Consequently, welfare provides a convenient target for politicians. In both political and economic terms, it is easier to attack welfare than to attack poverty. Since most of the budget is spent on entitlements, it will be difficult for welfare reform programs to compete for money. For welfare reform to succeed over the long run, it is important that job training and child-care programs be funded at levels sufficient to provide these services for most welfare recipients.

Traditionally, poverty in America has been regarded as a manifestation of individual weakness and failure rather than as a social problem. A national welfare system was not established until 1935, and systematic antipoverty programs were enacted only in the 1960s. A significant reduction in the level of poverty in the United States occurred because of a period of sustained economic growth from the end of World War II until the mid-1970s and because of government spending on welfare and poverty programs. During the 1980s, poverty in America began to increase, due primarily to fundamental changes in the economy. Addressing the consequences of these economic changes requires American political leaders once again to acknowledge that poverty is a social and economic problem. How well these latest welfare reforms will work remains to be seen. Success will depend on continued economic growth and on how much money is actually forthcoming from federal and state governments to pay for job training, placement, and child care.

STUDY QUESTIONS

1. How does the U.S. government define poverty? Do you agree with this definition?
2. Approximately what percentage of the U.S. population lives in poverty?
3. Is the poverty rate in the United States higher or lower than in other industrial democracies?
4. For which social groups has poverty increased? For which groups has poverty decreased?
5. What is welfare? Are Social Security retirement payments welfare? Why or why not?
6. What was AFDC? How does the welfare reform law of 1996 change the welfare system?

7. Who are the working poor?

8. Define the urban underclass.

9. How many homeless people are there in the United States? What are some of the causes of homelessness in America?

10. What are some of the causes of poverty? Which ones are the most important?

NOTES

1. David B. Robertson and Dennis R. Judd, *The Development of American Public Policy: The Structure of Policy Restraint* (Glenview, IL: Scott, Foresman, 1989), p. 203.

2. Ibid., p. 214.

3. Congressional Budget Office statistics, reported in *U.S. News and World Report*, February 20, 1995, p. 38.

4. Thomas P. Gabe, *Progress Against Poverty in the United States (1959–1986)* (Washington, DC: Congressional Research Service, The Library of Congress, 1987), pp. 3–5.

5. Ibid., p. 20.

6. Frank Levy, *Dollars and Dreams: The Changing American Income Distribution* (New York: W.W. Norton, 1988), p. 170.

7. Eugene Robinson, "The Poor Children of the World's Greatest Superpower," *The Washington Post National Weekly Edition*, October 4–10, 1993, p. 37.

8. Levy, *Dollars and Dreams*, p. 1.

9. Gabe, *Progress Against Poverty*, pp. 18–20. See also The Public Agenda Foundation, *The Poverty Puzzle* (New York: McGraw-Hill, 1994), pp. 4–10.

10. "New Study Finds the Poor Getting Poorer, Younger and More Urban," *The New York Times*, December 27, 1987, p. 5E.

11. William Julius Wilson, *The Truly Disadvantaged: The Inner City, the Underclass, and Public Policy* (Chicago: University of Chicago Press, 1987), p. 46.

12. Isabel V. Sawhill, "Poverty and the Underclass," in Isabel V. Sawhill, ed., *Challenge to Leadership: Economic and Social Issues for the Next Decade* (Washington, DC: Urban Institute Press, 1988), p. 228.

13. William Echikson, "The French Revolution," *World Monitor*, vol. 2, no. 4 (April 1989), p. 31.

14. Cited in Levy, *Dollars and Dreams*, p. 13.

15. Wilson, *The Truly Disadvantaged*, pp. 1–12.

16. Ibid., p. 3.

17. Ibid., p. 7.

18. Ibid., pp. 39–41.

19. Ibid., p. 25.

20. "Jobless Rate Drops to 15-Year Low," *Dayton Daily News*, March 11, 1989, p. 7B.

21. Isabel Wilkerson, "Growth of the Very Poor Is Focus of New Studies," *The New York Times*, December 20, 1987, p. 15.

22. Wilson, *The Truly Disadvantaged*, p. 10.

23. "Deaths by Freezing Increase," *Dayton Daily News*, December 23, 1988, p. 2A.

24. "Woman's Death Prompts Release of $25 Million to Help Homeless," *The New York Times*, December 5, 1993, p. 21.

25. The description of the homeless population is based on a report by Ruth Ellen Wasem, "Homelessness: Issues and Legislation in the 101st Congress," in *CRS Issue Brief* (Washington, DC: Congressional Research Service, The Library of Congress, January 19, 1989), pp. 1–14.

26. Michael Fabricant and Michael Kelly, "The Problem of Homelessness Is Serious," in David Bender, ed., *How Should Society Deal with the Homeless?* (St. Paul, MN: Greenhaven Press, Opposing Viewpoints Pamphlets, 1988), pp. 989–1004.

27. The Ohio, Minneapolis, and Los Angeles studies are reported in Wasem, "Homelessness: Issues and Legislation in the 101st Congress," pp. 4–7.

28. Susan Schillmoeller and Karen Spar, *The Homeless: An Overview of the Problem and the Federal Response* (Washington, DC: Congressional Research Service, The Library of Congress, 1987), p. 18.

29. David Whitman, "Shattering Myths About the Homeless," *U.S. News and World Report,* March 20, 1989, p. 27.

30. Ibid., p. 2.

31. Robertson and Judd, *The Development of American Public Policy,* p. 85.

32. "Welfare and Poverty Among Children," *Congressional Research Service Review,* vol. 8, no. 7 (July 1987), p. 6.

33. Levy, *Dollars and Dreams,* pp. 1–7, 74–100.

34. Sawhill, "Poverty and the Underclass," pp. 245–246.

35. Ibid., p. 246.

36. "Work Best for Training, Report Says U.S. Depends Too Much on Schools," *Dayton Daily News,* May 3, 1989, p. 7B.

37. Vee Burke, "Welfare," in *CRS Issue Brief* (Washington, DC: Congressional Research Service, The Library of Congress, December 29, 1988), p. 11.

38. Sandra J. Newman and Ann B. Schnare, "Housing and Welfare: A Logical Link," *The New York Times,* January 5, 1988, p. 25.

39. "Raze Housing, Chicago Urged," *The New York Times,* July 17, 1988, p. 12.

40. Milton Meltzer, *Poverty in America* (New York: William Morrow, 1986).

41. Wilson, *The Truly Disadvantaged,* pp. 10–12.

42. Sawhill, "Poverty and the Underclass," p. 240.

43. Wilson, *The Truly Disadvantaged,* pp. 114–116.

44. George Gilder, *Wealth and Poverty* (New York: Basic Books, 1981); Charles Murray, *Losing Ground: American Social Policy, 1950–1980* (New York: Basic Books, 1984).

45. *Work-Related Programs for Welfare Recipients* (Washington, DC: Congressional Budget Office, April 1987), pp. 1–78.

46. Jeffery Katz, "After 60 Years, Most Control Is Passing to States," *Congressional Quarterly Weekly Report,* August 3, 1996, p. 2190.

47. Ibid., pp. 2190–2194.

48. Robert Pear, "Rewards and Penalties Vary in States' Welfare Programs," *The New York Times,* February 23, 1997, p. 16.

49. Ibid.

50. Ruth Conniff, "Wisconsin's Work Not-Welfare Program Is Warfare on the Poor," *Dayton Daily News,* December 17, 1993, p. 19A.

51. "Sick, Homeless Told to Commit Crime," *Dayton Daily News,* October 7, 1991, p. 8B.

52. Pear, "Rewards and Penalties Vary in States' Welfare Programs," p. 16.

53. Statement on Welfare Reform by Alvin C. Collins, Director, Office of Family Assistance, U.S. Department of Health and Human Services, Before the House Committee on Education and the Workforce, Subcommittee on Postsecondary Education, Training, and Life-Long Learning, September 9, 1999. Available on HHS Web site http://waisgate.hhs.gov/cgi-bin/waisgate.

SUGGESTED READINGS

GILDER, GEORGE. *Wealth and Poverty.* New York: Basic Books, 1981.

HARRINGTON, MICHAEL. *The Other America: Poverty in the United States.* New York: Penguin Books, 1981.

LEVY, FRANK. *Dollars and Dreams: The Changing American Income Distribution.* New York: W.W. Norton, 1988.

MARMOR, THEODORE R., JERRY MASHAW II, and PHILIP HARVEY II. *America's Misunderstood Welfare State.* New York: Basic Books, 1990.

PHILLIPS, COVEN. *The Politics of Rich and Poor.* New York: Harper, 1991.

ROBERTSON, DAVID B., and DENNIS R. JUDD. *The Development of American Public Policy: The Structure of Policy Restraint.* Glenview, IL: Scott, Foresman, 1989.

ROSSI, PETER H. *Down and Out in America: The Origins of Homelessness.* Chicago: University of Chicago Press, 1989.

SCHWARZ, JOHN E. *America's Hidden Success: A Reassessment of Twenty Years of Public Policy.* New York: W.W. Norton, 1984.

WILSON, WILLIAM JULIUS. *The Truly Disadvantaged: The Inner City, the Underclass, and Public Policy.* Chicago: University of Chicago Press, 1987.

Chapter 2

The Politics of Health Care

cost

The politics of health care has at least three different interrelated aspects. The aspect of the health-care issue that is most visible is the *cost* of medical care in the United States. The cost of health care in America is the highest in the world when measured either as a percentage of gross national product (GNP) or as cost per person. From 1970 to 1992, health-care costs in the United States increased about 10 percent per year. The rate of increase slowed somewhat during the 1990s, due presumably to tighter controls imposed by health maintenance organizations (HMOs). More than any other aspect of the health-care issue, it is the cost of health care that is driving the debate about the need for reform. In addition to the questions of how the costs of medical care should be paid and who should pay them, the problem of controlling the costs of medical care must be addressed by any serious attempt at reform.

coverage

The second aspect of the health-care reform issue is *coverage.* Most Americans have reasonably good health-care insurance, provided most often by their employer. A significant minority of Americans, estimated at around 40 million, do not have health-care insurance. Most are working people (and their dependents) whose jobs do not provide health insurance as a fringe benefit. Other uninsured individuals are unemployed or work part time. During the 1990s the percentage of Americans without health insurance increased from 14 percent in 1990 to 16 percent in 1999.

allocation

Finally, in addition to costs and coverage, there is the question of *allocation,* or "rationing," meaning restrictions on the types of medical services patients may receive. Many Americans object to the idea of rationing health care, but clearly, the present system rations health care by excluding 40 million Americans from coverage. Health maintenance organizations and insurance companies ration health care by determining which types of services most Americans can receive.

SOURCES: HEALTH CARE IN THE UNITED STATES

For most Americans, health insurance is a fringe benefit of employment. People employed in well-paying jobs with good fringe benefits usually have adequate health-care insurance. Those who are self-employed, who work part time, or who work in low-paying, low-benefit jobs may have very limited coverage or none at all. Many of these citizens would have great difficulty paying for private health insurance, even if it were available. Most elderly and retired citizens are insured through **Medicare,** a government program. Extremely poor people may be covered through the **Medicaid** program, but many poor citizens are unable to qualify for Medicaid, even though their family income is well below the poverty level.

The current system of health care in the United States links insurance to employment or to government programs that cover specific groups of people, including the elderly and the very poor. This patchwork of health insurance coverage results from historical circumstances. As the present system evolved, it proved generally satisfactory for workers, employers, insurance companies, and health-care providers. Until the 1980s, health insurance was a benefit that employers could provide to workers at relatively reasonable cost while passing the cost on to consumers. Health insurance was part of a benefits package, along with wages and working conditions, that could be negotiated periodically. Employers received tax advantages and group discounts, and workers enjoyed generous benefits.[1]

After years of steadily rising health-care costs, this situation has changed. Health insurance, at one time encouraged by employers as an alternative to larger wage increases, has become the Frankenstein monster that threatens to devour corporate profits. General Motors, for example, spent more than $3 billion for health benefits in 1990.[2]

The system of health care prevalent in the United States has several consequences. Since the system is not universal, there are millions of Americans with no health insurance. Despite the exclusion of many Americans from coverage, health care in America is the most costly in the world. As is shown in the discussion that follows, the way in which health care is distributed is related to the costs of medical services. Because care is provided mostly by means of private insurance, with few controls on medical fees or on patients' access to costly medical services and technology, spending on health care has risen rapidly.

The Costs of Health Care

Americans spend more money on health care than do citizens of other countries partly because Americans have more money and can afford quality health care. The estimate for health-care costs in the United States for 1998 was $1.15 trillion. This is more than $3 billion per day, or $3,600 per person. In 1960, the United States spent 5 percent of GNP on health care. In 1990, health-care spending had climbed to 12 percent of GNP; it rose to 16 percent in 1995; and it was projected to reach 18 percent of GNP by the year 2000.[3] Health policy and budget experts are questioning whether the American economy can continue to absorb increases at this rate.

Health-Care Coverage

The current system of employer-based health insurance, in combination with government programs, provides coverage for most Americans. Although employers are not legally required (or "mandated") to provide health insurance for employees and their dependents, about 57 percent of the population is insured through employer-sponsored programs. About 8 percent are covered by health insurance policies purchased privately. This means that private insurance companies provide health-care coverage for 65 percent of the population. About 20 percent of Americans are covered under government programs, including Medicare for the elderly (12 percent) and Medicaid for the very poor (7 percent). This leaves 16 percent of the population (about 40 million Americans) with no health-care coverage. The number of uninsured increased from 34 million in 1988 to nearly 36 million in 1990, and approached 40 million by 1997.[4] Businesses and governments have reacted to rapidly rising health costs by reducing insurance coverage and benefits and by increasing employees' share of health costs.

In 1998, federal and state governments spent more than $500 billion for health-care services and supplies. This included federal expenditures of $217 billion for Medicare to pay medical expenses of retirees, $102 billion for Medicaid for the poor, medical care for veterans, and state Medicaid expenditures. The costs of Medicaid coverage for the poor are rising rapidly, and state governments are scrambling to find the money to pay them. Under financial pressure, states have changed eligibility requirements to make it more difficult for the poor to qualify for Medicaid. The result is that fewer than 40 percent of poor people are eligible for Medicaid. The federal government estimates that Medicare and Medicaid expenditures will total $620 billion yearly by 2008.[5] A variety of reforms have been proposed to extend health insurance coverage to the uninsured. Extension of health benefits to millions of uninsured Americans will have significant implications for the allocation and costs of health care in the United States.

STATUS: ALTERNATIVES IN HEALTH CARE

Cost Factors in Health Care

The cost of health care and the allocation of medical services are closely related. The current system of health care in the United States encourages demand for care while doing little to control the cost or availability of expensive medical services and technology. This is true for several reasons.

1. Insurance encourages demand for medical services.
2. Medical fees are higher in the United States than in other countries.

3. Political leaders have been reluctant to impose controls on the costs, fees, and availability of medical services.
4. Expensive medical technology is readily available and is widely used in the United States.
5. Administrative overhead costs are high in the American health-care system.
6. Malpractice insurance and litigation contribute to rising costs.
7. The population in the United States is aging.

Insurance.　Patients who are insured bear only a small part of the total cost of their health care. This is especially important to those who are seriously or chronically ill because this minority of the population accounts for most spending on health care.[6] Insurance also increases demand for other types of care, including preventive services, mental health, dental services, and expensive diagnostic and technical procedures.[7]

Given these facts, health-reform proposals for expanding insurance coverage to the uninsured are likely to have the effect of increasing demand for health services. Many countries with comprehensive health-care coverage have dealt with this problem by controlling costs through health-budget limits, fee schedules, and limits on availability of expensive medical technologies, resulting in waiting lists for patients for nonemergency procedures.[8] Whether American political leaders are willing and able to enact effective cost controls, and whether the public will accept them, remain to be seen.

Medical Fees.　Doctors' fees, hospital bills, and costs for medical services are higher in the United States than in other countries. Research comparing physicians' fees in different countries found that doctors' fees in the United States averaged 139 percent higher than in Canada and that charges for routine surgeries were about eight times as high as in Europe.[9] In 1992, the average income of a cardiovascular surgeon in the United States was $547,769. For orthopedic surgeons the average was $339,829, and for radiologists the figure was $309,556. Average income for family practitioners was $168,476.[10] One result of this fee structure is a preponderance of medical specialists in relation to general practitioners in the United States.

Government Controls.　The government has been reluctant to regulate fees and health-care costs in the United States. When the Medicare program was enacted, the government agreed to reimburse physicians for "customary and reasonable" charges. During the Carter administration, Congress rejected the president's proposal for implementing cost containment for hospitals in the Medicare program. Starting in the 1980s, Congress began to take some measures to control the costs of this program. Under Medicare's Prospective Payment System (PPS), the government pays hospitals a set price for each diagnosis, based on the average cost of such diagnoses. This decision reflects a move away from a system in which government allows health-care providers to determine how much they will be paid. There was a modest slowdown in hospital cost increases when PPS went into effect.[11]

The Cost of Medical Technology. The widespread availability of new and expensive medical technologies and procedures has contributed significantly to the rapid rise in health-care costs in the United States. This is a difficult issue to address because cost containment will involve decisions about allocation of medical resources. This may require not only some limits on fees or reimbursements for procedures, but also limits on patients' access to expensive technology and costly procedures.

Medical technology is developing at a rapid rate. Complicated and expensive procedures, such as coronary bypass operations and organ transplants, are now commonplace. As sophisticated equipment is developed, it rapidly becomes widely available in the United States. The increasing availability of new procedures and of the latest equipment is a characteristic of the American health-care system. This is a major reason why American health care is both effective and costly. Americans expect good health care, feel entitled to it, and want it to be readily available at their local hospital.

Hospital treatment in the United States is expensive partly because it is more intense and technologically sophisticated than in other countries. There are significantly more coronary units, radiation therapy units, and magnetic resonance imaging (MRI) units per million population in the United States than in England, Germany, or Canada.[12] More than 2,000 MRI scanning machines, which can cost upwards of $2 million each, have been installed in American hospitals. The widespread availability and use of these sophisticated machines adds more than $5 billion per year to the cost of health care.[13] The availability of treatments for serious and chronic diseases also contributes to rising health costs. The estimated costs of treating all Americans infected with the HIV virus in 1995 exceeded $10 billion. The cost of treating an individual with drug-resistant tuberculosis was $250,000.[14]

Dr. Willard Gaylin, in his critique of the Clinton administration's health-reform proposal, contends that health costs are rising because American medicine has been successful in healing the sick and prolonging life. "People will pay anything to defend against the possibility of death, all the more so when the money involved doesn't come directly out of their own pockets."[15] The American appetite for costly health services is, Dr. Gaylin contends, practically unlimited. The reality, however, is that we cannot do everything for everybody. Dr. Gaylin's conclusion is that controlling health costs will require allocation. "The first step is to admit the cruel necessity of rationing health care. The second is to set limits on health care according to principles of equity and justice."[16]

The high costs and extensive availability of new technologies and new treatments are fundamental factors pushing up health-care expenses in the United States. Health-policy expert Henry Aaron has concluded that controlling the allocation of health services will be required to contain costs. According to Aaron, a "sustained reduction would require the curtailment of care that is beneficial but is deemed to be excessively costly, in other words, the rationing of health care."[17] The prospect of allocation of health services is in stark contrast with popular beliefs. One survey of public opinion found that 70 percent of Americans believe that medical costs can be substantially reduced without affecting the quality of care.[18]

Administrative Costs.   In the United States, many medical bills are paid by **third-party payers,** meaning insurance companies or government agencies. There are about 1,500 insurance companies using a bewildering array of forms and procedures in processing claims. One estimate is that this administrative system costs more than $100 billion per year. This means that between 10 and 15 percent of health-care expenses result from the costs of processing claims for reimbursement.[19] Proposals to make the system more efficient include the adoption of a single-payer system, as in Canada, or a requirement for a single, simplified insurance form, as proposed by President Clinton.

Malpractice Insurance.   The number of malpractice suits in the United States increases yearly. To protect themselves against lawsuits, doctors and hospitals pay $7 billion per year in premiums for malpractice insurance.[20] These insurance costs are passed on to health-care consumers. Although the cost of malpractice insurance is less than 1 percent of the cost of health care, the constant threat of lawsuits may cause doctors and hospitals to practice "defensive medicine." Various tests and procedures may be ordered simply to minimize the risks of litigation and large jury awards. Studies have estimated that as many as 39 percent of medical procedures may be unnecessary.[21] Whether the motives for these procedures were to earn extra profits or to reduce the threat of malpractice litigation is difficult to determine. In either case, the practice drives up medical costs. One survey found that 78 percent of physicians ordered tests they considered unnecessary out of fear of the threat of malpractice suits.[22]

An Aging Population.   As more Americans live longer, the number of elderly citizens has increased, producing a greater demand for health care. Elderly people have more illnesses, need more health care, and require more costly health services. The impending aging of America's large middle-aged generation (the "baby boomers" born shortly after World War II) will produce another surge in demand for health care early in the twenty-first century. These demographic trends suggest that it would be preferable to deal with the questions of health-care reform and cost containment sooner rather than later.

Alternative Approaches to Health Care

Americans spend more on health care than citizens of any other country. There are a wide variety of alternative approaches to health care throughout the world that have one thing in common: They are less costly than the American system. A comparative approach permits an assessment of the advantages and weaknesses of various systems of health care. The comparison that follows is limited to countries that have a level of economic development similar to that of the United States.

Socialized Medicine.   Britain's National Health Service (NHS) is a nationalized system of health care. Following World War II, the Labour Party enacted a socialist program nationalizing numerous industries and the health-care system. Although most of the industries have subsequently been denationalized (sold back to the private sector), the system of nationalized health care has proven to be popular and has been retained. This system permits the government to control fees, costs, and allocation of health services.

The British system is universal and comprehensive, meaning that all citizens have health coverage and that most illnesses and treatments are covered. Each citizen enrolls with a general practitioner, usually one close to his or her residence. Health services are provided regardless of the patient's ability to pay, and most services are provided without charge to the patient. About 12 percent of British citizens purchase private insurance as a supplement to NHS. Most doctors in Britain contract with the NHS to provide health services for a salary, the amount of pay depending on the number of patients they see. Including physicians, specialists, and hospital staff, the NHS is one of the largest employers in Europe.[23] A centralized system of nationalized health care has obvious advantages in the areas of finance and cost controls. The NHS is financed from general tax revenues, spreading the cost of health services among all taxpayers. Some services and tests involve a modest fee directly to the patient. The British government controls health costs by limiting health-care expenditures. This is done by means of an annual health budget allocated to the regional health authorities.[24]

The shortcomings of the British NHS also result from the centralized system of budgeting and government control. Tight health budgets have resulted in low levels of investment in technology and facilities, shortages of the latest equipment, and waiting lists for nonemergency procedures. But more than fifty years after its creation, the British NHS still functions as a system that delivers basic health care to all citizens at a modest cost.

National Health Insurance.   The method of providing health care in Canada is often cited as an alternative that retains most features important to Americans, including the patient's freedom to choose doctors and hospitals, while reducing costs by means of a single-payer system of reimbursement. In effect, the government functions as the insurance company, reducing administrative costs by providing centralized and simplified reimbursement procedures. The government also regulates the health-care system extensively and imposes cost controls.

The national health insurance plan is financed by a variety of taxes and administered by the provincial governments. The Canadian central government and the provinces share costs. All legal residents are insured, regardless of their income or employment status. Doctors retain their private practices and are reimbursed by the provincial governments on a fee system. Dental care, eye care, and prescriptions are not covered, although most Canadian employers provide supplemental insurance coverage for these services. Doctors' fees are regulated, as are hospital charges by means of a health budget that is negotiated with the provincial authorities. Allocation of health services is controlled by means of government regulation of hospital budgets. For nonemergency procedures, a waiting list is created. Fewer units of expensive equipment are purchased per hospital than in the United States, so costly technology is less readily available locally.[25]

The health plans of the provinces are not identical, but all provide universal and comprehensive coverage, a single-payer method of reimbursement, and control of physicians' fees and hospital budgets. Spending for health care per person in Canada is two thirds of the cost in the United States.

Universal Health Insurance.   Germany, the Netherlands, Japan, and, in the United States, Hawaii, all use a system of health care that is universal, comprehensive, and private. In each case, the health-care system rests on an **employer mandate** whereby the government requires employers to provide comprehensive health insurance for their employees. In all cases, physicians are in private practice, and there are multiple payers and providers. Private insurance is used as a supplement by a minority of patients.

In the German, Dutch, and Japanese systems, there is regulation of private medicine to control costs, including physicians' fees and hospital budgets. In these systems, universal health care is financed by a variety of taxes, including employer contributions, payroll deductions for employees, and general taxes. One additional cost control of the German and Dutch systems is that insurance funds administering the system are nonprofit insurance organizations and must cover everyone. Taxes and government programs pay for coverage for the unemployed and the retired. The Dutch system also provides for coverage of nursing-home and long-term care. In Germany, the Netherlands, and Japan, the government plays a much greater role than in the United States in controlling health-care costs by regulating fees and hospital budgets and ensuring that all employers and workers pay for insurance premiums.[26] This reduces the number of people without coverage, who must rely on hospital emergency rooms for care. President Clinton stated in an address to Congress, "When people don't have any health insurance, they still get health care, but they get it when it's too late, when it's too expensive, often from the most expensive place of all, the emergency room."[27]

In the United States, Hawaii provides the closest approximation to the European and Japanese systems just discussed. The State of Hawaii Health Insurance Plan (SHIP) is universal, comprehensive, and emphasizes preventive care. The Prepaid Health Care Act established the universal health-care system in 1974. SHIP expanded the system in 1989 to emphasize preventive, as well as comprehensive, health services. Workers and employers share financing for this system. There is a supplemental fund to assist small employers in paying the premiums. The law mandates employer-sponsored health insurance for anyone not already covered and specifies that coverage must provide benefits equal to the average plan in the state. The law relies on the private insurance system to administer the program. SHIP provides a fund for the purchase of insurance for those who are not otherwise covered but who are not eligible for Medicaid. Insurance coverage is provided for a fee based on a sliding scale according to the citizen's income. In recent years, coverage has been extended to include some mental health benefits, alcohol and drug treatment, and mammography.[28]

Hawaii's universal coverage has not led to soaring health-care costs. Insurance premiums in Hawaii are below average and only about half the cost in the most expensive states. According to Dr. John Lewin, Hawaii's director of health, the key to Hawaii's lower health-care costs is the decision by the state to emphasize prevention. "We have twice as many outpatient visits—that is, people see their doctors several times a year—and half as many hospital stays, as the national average."[29]

Rationing Health Care.   In 1989, Oregon enacted a sweeping proposal to guarantee health care to individuals living below the poverty level. The Oregon Basic Health Services Act (OBHSA) creates a process to establish a basic level of services that will provide the most health care to the largest number of poor people. The controversy surrounding the *allocation* and *cost control* mechanisms in the Oregon plan provides a preview of the kinds of political and ethical issues that the United States must eventually address.

To provide health coverage for its citizens living below the poverty level and to control the costs of these health services, Oregon rations the amount of money and services available through the Medicaid system. The law created a Health Services Commission to conduct public hearings and then to establish a *priority list* of health services. Organ transplants, for example, are not paid for by the state. The amount of money available for Medicaid is decided by the state legislature. Health care for the poor is allocated based on the ranking of various services on the priority list and on the amount of money available. The available funds are used to purchase a package of health services for each recipient. The range of services offered is determined by how far down the priority list the total amount of money will permit the state to select. The state ranked 688 medical conditions and procedures and drew the line at number 568. Conditions and treatments above that line are covered; those below the line are not. To contain costs, services will be purchased from health maintenance organizations (HMOs) and other managed care providers.[30]

After the Oregon plan became law, a number of critics, including then-Senator Albert Gore (D-Tenn.), attacked it as unfair to the poor. The criticisms continued despite the fact that the priority allocation system would allow Oregon to extend coverage to 78,000 new recipients during the first year of implementation.[31] The process of obtaining a Medicaid variance from the U.S. government delayed implementation of this plan during the Bush administration. The Clinton administration gave Oregon approval to proceed with the plan.

PROSPECTS: MANAGED CARE

The health-care reform plan proposed by the Clinton administration addressed the issues of insurance coverage and health-cost containment. The Health Security Act proposed to make health insurance coverage universal. A variety of cost containment provisions, based on managed care, were included to slow down the rate of growth in health-care costs. The Health Security Act proposed by the Clinton administration would have expanded health insurance coverage to all Americans by means of an employer mandate. In a plan similar to the German system, employers would have been required by law to provide health insurance to their employees. Self-employed and unemployed people were also to be covered by paying a share of the cost of insurance premiums based on a sliding scale, depending on their incomes. Employers would have been required to offer their employees a choice of a number of alternative insurance plans. All plans, even the least expensive, would have been required to offer a comprehensive package of health benefits, including preventive care and prescription drugs.[32]

Managed care

A key concept of the Health Security Act was the idea of managed care. The proposed expansion of health coverage, and the provisions for cost control of health services, depended on the effectiveness of managed care concepts in organizing health-care delivery and controlling health costs. **Health maintenance organizations (HMOs)** were of particular importance for the management of health care in the Health Security Act. HMOs are organized to use market forces to inject competition into health-care delivery and provide health services at reduced cost. HMOs help to reduce health costs by offering a variety of services, providing care for a predetermined fee, and emphasizing preventive medicine. Network-based managed care plans limit consumers' choice of health-care providers to a specified network, regulate payment method and rates, and establish controls over hospitals and specialist physician services. Medical costs for consumers served by HMOs are lower than for those receiving traditional care.[33] Following the example of Hawaii, the Clinton plan emphasized preventive care, including immunizations, mammograms, well-baby care, and periodic medical exams and screening tests.

Critics of the Clinton health-reform proposal, including insurance companies, the medical establishment, and opponents in Congress, mobilized quickly to defeat the plan.[34] Attacking the president's proposal as a government takeover of the health-care system, congressional opponents warned against increased bureaucracy, higher taxes, and reduced choice for health-care consumers. Ironically, despite the defeat of the Clinton health-care proposal by Congress in 1994, the growth of managed care in the health industry has produced greater bureaucracy, more cost controls, and, in some instances, reduced health-care options. Insurance companies and health maintenance organizations are imposing many controls on health costs and benefits to consumers through the private sector.

Although the Health Security Act did not pass in Congress, some of the HMO cost control features have been imposed, not by the government, but by private health plans and insurance companies. More than 50 million Americans are enrolled in HMOs, and the number is increasing rapidly. In 1994, half of those insured through their employers were covered by some type of managed care plan. By 1997, this percentage had increased to three quarters.[35] A 1996 survey found that companies of all sizes have reduced the number of alternative health plans offered to their workers and that many employers now offer only one plan. Only one fourth of workers are enrolled in traditional fee-for-service plans that allow free choice of provider, down from three fourths in 1988.[36] Rather than enacting a comprehensive plan, Congress has adopted a piecemeal approach to try to address specific consumer complaints. For example, some of the managed care plans were so restrictive that they limited hospital stays for new mothers to twenty-four hours. In response to complaints about "drive-through deliveries," Congress passed a law in 1996 requiring health insurance companies to guarantee maternity patients a hospital stay of at least forty-eight hours.

The Kennedy-Kassebaum Bill.   After the failure of the Health Security Act, President Clinton joined with Senators Edward Kennedy and Nancy Kassebaum to enact a much more modest health-reform bill. The centerpiece of this bill is health insurance "portability," meaning that individuals who lose their jobs can maintain their health insurance coverage. The law also includes provisions for tax deductions for the cost of health insurance for the self-employed and for long-term care, but does not regulate the cost of health insurance.[37]

The Kennedy-Kassebaum bill represents a very modest response to the issue of health-care costs and availability in the United States. This legislation attempts to protect those who already have health insurance coverage from the prospect of losing their coverage. It does not address the cost of insurance and does little for the 40 million Americans without health insurance. Preliminary results indicate that insurance companies have found ways to skirt the Kennedy-Kassebaum law by refusing coverage for people with medical problems or by charging very high premiums.[38]

The SCHIP Program.   The State Children's Health Insurance Program (SCHIP) is the largest expansion of health insurance coverage for children in more than thirty years. This legislation was proposed by President Clinton and enacted in 1997 to expand health-care coverage for some of the 11 million American children who are uninsured. The program was designed to reach uninsured children of working families with incomes too high to qualify for Medicaid. As of September 1999, 2 million children had been covered by SCHIP. The costs of the program are shared by the federal and state governments, so eligibility and coverage varies depending on the state. President Clinton's proposals for the 2001 budget included provisions giving states the option of extending SCHIP to children up to age twenty, increasing outreach efforts to enroll children in SCHIP and Medicaid, and expanding SCHIP to parents of eligible children.[39]

The failure of President Clinton's health-reform bill was followed by a piecemeal approach that has produced some modest reforms. Despite the passage of several laws intended to expand coverage, the number of uninsured Americans has increased each year since 1987 and now exceeds 41 million, approximately one sixth of the population.[40] America's political leaders have decided that the difficult decisions about health-care cost and availability are best made by insurance companies, HMOs, and employers. By doing so, politicians have avoided much of the fallout that will accompany decisions to control costs and availability of health care in the United States.

STUDY QUESTIONS

1. Distinguish between socialized medicine, national health insurance, and universal health insurance.
2. Identify some of the factors that are causing the cost of health care in America to increase rapidly.
3. What policies might help control health-care costs? What are some of the difficulties political leaders face in attempting to enact these policies?
4. What does it mean to "ration" health care? Is this a good idea? Why or why not?
5. What are some of the problems with the American health-care system? What are the positive aspects of the American system?
6. What are some advantages and problems of health-care systems in other countries, such as Canada, England, and Germany?
7. What is the Kennedy-Kassebaum bill?
8. Discuss the SCHIP Program.

NOTES

1. Henry J. Aaron, *Serious and Unstable: Financing America's Health Care* (Washington, DC: The Brookings Institution, 1991), p. 3.
2. The Public Agenda Foundation, *The Health Care Crisis: Containing Costs, Expanding Coverage* (New York: McGraw-Hill, 1992), p. 7.
3. The source for these estimates is the Health Care Financing Administration, reported in Steven Pearlstein, "A Hard Pill to Swallow," *The Washington Post National Weekly Edition,* May 17–23, 1993, p. 7.
4. Public Agenda Foundation, *The Health Care Crisis,* pp. 5–6; and Table 6, Federal Government Receipts and Expenditures, at the Bureau of Labor Statistics Web site: www.bls.gov.empmaco6.htm.
5. Ibid., p. 7.
6. Henry J. Aaron, "Health Care Financing," in Henry J. Aaron and Charles L. Schultz, eds., *Setting Domestic Priorities: What Can Government Do?* (Washington, DC: Brookings Institution, 1992), p. 33.
7. Aaron, *Serious and Unstable,* p. 12.
8. Ibid., p. 13.
9. Ibid., p. 81.
10. Erik Eckholm, "Health Plan Is Toughest on Doctors Making Most," *The New York Times,* November 11, 1993, sec. 1, p. 13.
11. Judith Feder, "Health Care of the Disadvantaged: The Elderly," in Lawrence D. Brown, ed., *Health Policy and the Disadvantaged* (Durham, NC: Duke University Press, 1991), p. 10.
12. Aaron, *Serious and Unstable,* pp. 85–86.
13. Public Agenda Foundation, *The Health Care Crisis,* p. 13.
14. Joseph A. Califano, Jr., "A Three-headed Biomedical Monster Threatens America's Health Landscape," *Dayton Daily News,* January 2, 1993, p. 11A.

15. Willard Gaylin, M.D., "Faulty Diagnosis: Why Clinton's Health-Care Plan Won't Cure What Ails Us," *Harper's,* October 1993, p. 61.

16. Ibid., p. 63.

17. Aaron, *Serious and Unstable,* p. 53.

18. Public Agenda Foundation, *The Health Care Crisis,* p. 8.

19. Public Agenda Foundation, *The Health Care Cost Explosion* (New York: McGraw-Hill, 1993), p. 10.

20. Ibid., p. 9.

21. Public Agenda Foundation, *The Health Care Crisis,* p. 8.

22. Public Agenda Foundation, *The Health Care Cost Explosion,* p. 9.

23. Laurene A. Graig, *Health of Nations: An International Perspective on U.S. Health Care Reform,* 2nd ed. (Washington, DC: Congressional Quarterly, 1993), pp. 148–153.

24. Ibid., p. 154.

25. Ibid., pp. 50–59.

26. Ibid., pp. 81–84, 95–96, 117–119, 130.

27. "Address of the President to the Joint Session of Congress," September 22, 1993, in *Health Security: The President's Report to the American People,* p. 114. This document is part of a larger publication: *The White House Domestic Policy Council, The President's Health Security Plan* (New York: *Times Books,* 1993), pp. 1–165.

28. Dean Neubauer, "Hawaii: The Health State," in Howard M. Leichter, ed., *Health Policy Reform in America: Innovations from the States* (Armonk, NY: M.E. Sharpe, 1992), pp. 155–168.

29. Timothy Egan, "Hawaii: Setting an Example for the Rest of the Nation," *The New York Times,* November 14, 1993, sec. 4, p. 8.

30. Howard M. Leichter, "Rationing of Health Care: Oregon Comes Out of the Closet," in Leichter, *Health Policy Reform in America,* pp. 117–120. See also the Associated Press report, "Oregon to Provide Rationed Health Care," *Dayton Daily News,* March 20, 1993, p. 7A.

31. Leichter, "Rationing of Health Care," p. 133.

32. The discussion of the specifics of the Health Security Act is based on *Health Security: The President's Report to the American People.*

33. *Managed Health Care,* Report to the Chairman, Subcommittee on Health, Committee on Ways and Means, House of Representatives, United States General Accounting Office, Washington, DC, October 1993, pp. 8–9. See also National Issues Forum, *The Health Care Crisis,* p. 38.

34. Robin Toner, "Foes Take to the Grass Roots on Clinton Health Proposal," *The New York Times,* December 5, 1993, sec. 1, p. 18.

35. "Consumers and Managed Care," *The New York Times,* February 9, 1997, sec. 4, p. 14.

36. Robin Toner, "Health Cares: Harry and Louise Were Right, Sort Of," *The New York Times,* November 24, 1996, sec. 4, p. 1.

37. Steve Langdon, "Kennedy, Kassebaum Steer Insurance Bill to Safety," *Congressional Quarterly Weekly Report,* August 3, 1996, pp. 2197–2200.

38. Robert Pear, "Policy Changes Fail to Fill Gaps in Health Coverage," *The New York Times,* August 9, 1998, p. 1.

39. U.S. Department of Health and Human Services, *HHS Fact Sheet,* February 24, 2000. www.hhs.gov/news/press/2000.

40. Pear, "Policy Changes Fail to Fill Gaps in Health Coverage," p. 1.

SUGGESTED READINGS

AARON, HENRY J. *Serious and Unstable: Financing America's Health Care.* Washington, DC: Brookings Institution, 1991.

AARON, HENRY J., and CHARLES L. SCHULTZ, eds. *Setting Domestic Priorities: What Can Government Do?* Washington, DC: Brookings Institution, 1992.

BROWN, LAWRENCE D., ed. *Health Care and the Disadvantaged.* Durham, NC: Duke University Press, 1991.

GAYLIN, WILLARD. "Faulty Diagnosis: Why Clinton's Health-care Plan Won't Cure What Ails Us." *Harper's,* October 1993, pp. 57–64.

GRAIG, LAURENE A. *Health of Nations: An International Perspective on U.S. Health Care Reform.* 2nd ed. Washington, DC: Congressional Quarterly, 1993.

LEICHTER, HOWARD M., ed. *Health Policy Reform in America: Innovations from the States.* Armonk, NY: M.E. Sharpe, 1992.

THE PUBLIC AGENDA FOUNDATION. *The Health Care Cost Explosion.* New York: McGraw-Hill, 1993.

THE WHITE HOUSE DOMESTIC POLICY COUNCIL. *Health Security: The President's Report to the American People.* Washington, DC: U.S. Government Printing Office, 1993.

Chapter 3

Money in Public Office: Campaign Finance, Graft, and Corruption

Where there is a quid, there is a quo.

—Retired Air Force Major General Richard V. Secord,
director of the "Enterprise"[1]

I can't be bought, but I can be rented.

—Congressman John Breaux[2]

On May 31, 1989, Speaker of the House Jim Wright announced that he intended to resign, effective June 6. Wright's resignation as Speaker came in response to a year-long investigation by the House Committee on Standards of Official Conduct, better known as the ethics committee. On April 17, 1989, the ethics committee had announced that it had found reason to believe that Wright had violated House rules in sixty-nine instances. The most damaging allegations were that the Speaker had violated rules prohibiting acceptance of gifts and limitations on outside income. Five days before Wright made public his unprecedented decision to resign as Speaker, House Majority Whip Tony Coelho of California announced that he was resigning from Congress rather than endure an ethics investigation of his personal finances. Two weeks earlier, Congressman Coelho acknowledged that he had failed to report a $50,000 loan he obtained to finance the purchase of junk bonds issued through the investment firm of Drexel Burnham Lambert. Coelho also admitted that, with the help of a savings and loan executive, he had purchased the bonds at a lower price than they were selling for at the time.[3] Two months earlier, the Senate had rejected the nomination of former senator John Tower to be secretary of defense, partly because of allegations of improper financial dealings and partly because of the widespread perception that he had a drinking problem.

In autumn of 1989, the role played by five U.S. senators in assisting a financially shaky savings and loan business became the focus of public debate.

Charles H. Keating, a wealthy Phoenix businessman and chairman of Lincoln Savings and Loan, was accused by federal regulators of fraud and other illegal activities that caused Lincoln to lose more than $1 billion in federally insured deposits. During the investigation of Lincoln in 1987, the senators personally intervened with federal bank regulators to press for more sympathetic treatment of Lincoln. The senators became known in the media as "the Keating Five" after it was disclosed that Keating and his associates had contributed more than $1 million to campaign organizations controlled by the five senators.

Similar ethical issues arose again during the 1996 election campaigns. President Clinton, whose finances and business dealings were already under investigation by special prosecutor Kenneth Starr, became enmeshed in a controversy involving questionable campaign contributions. Speaker of the House Newt Gingrich, who had earlier led the Republican assault on Jim Wright, found his own ethics under attack by House Democrats. The ethical issues involved in the cases of Congressmen Wright, Coelho, and Gingrich; Senator Tower; the Keating Five; and President Bill Clinton illustrate a much larger issue—the relationship between private money and public officials.

SOURCES: MONEY, ETHICS, AND CORRUPTION

The word *corruption* has a variety of meanings, the most common of which includes immorality or dishonesty. In a broader sense, corruption refers to a process that destroys or subverts honesty or integrity. Analyses of political corruption use the term in both its narrow and broader meanings. Defined narrowly, political corruption refers to acts by public officials that are dishonest and illegal. Taking a bribe is an obvious example. Viewed more broadly, corruption may encompass actions by public officials that are not illegal but are questionable in terms of the integrity of a system of democratic government. For example, consider the decision by an elected official to accept a large campaign contribution from a wealthy individual or to accept a $10,000 lecture fee for giving a campaign speech to an interest group. Even though campaign contributions and lecture honoraria are legal, the ability of a public official to make an independent decision in the public interest may be compromised by their acceptance. It is, in fact, sometimes difficult to distinguish clearly among bribes, gifts, favors, honoraria, and campaign contributions.

These issues are addressed in the following discussions of politics as a *business* and politics as an *investment*. Most of the activities described in "politics as a business" are illegal. Many of the activities discussed in "politics as an investment" are legal. Whether these activities are corrupt is left to the reader to decide.

POLITICS AS A BUSINESS

Public office provides many opportunities for private gain. To prevent greed, conflict of interest, and outside financial interest from influencing public decision making, various activities have been prohibited, although not eliminated, from government.

Bribery and Extortion

For much of American history, bribery and extortion have been the most common types of political corruption. A bribe consists of an offer of money or other inducements by an outside party to secure desired action from government officials. A demand by a public official for money or gifts constitutes **extortion.** The recipients of bribes are more likely to be convicted than are those who offer bribes.[4] One of the more notorious bribery cases in American history was the **Teapot Dome** scandal during the administration of President Warren G. Harding (1921–1923). This scandal involved the use of bribes by oil companies to secure leases for drilling rights on public lands (the Teapot Dome and Elk Hills reserves). Secretary of the Interior Albert Fall was convicted and sent to prison for accepting a bribe. Oilman Harry Sinclair was acquitted of offering the bribe, leading to the popular journalistic outcry, "You can't convict ten million dollars!"[5] During the Truman administration (1945–1953), Internal Revenue Service officials were jailed for soliciting and accepting bribes.

Bribery scandals erupt with some regularity in state legislatures. A sting operation dubbed Desert Shame resulted in the indictment of seven Arizona legislators and several lobbyists in 1991. The Arizona lawmakers (some of whom were videotaped taking bribes) were indicted for accepting more than $100,000 in cash from an informant posing as a political consultant for casino gambling interests.[6] Although bribery of public officials has probably decreased since the decline of urban political party machines, the **Koreagate** and **Abscam** scandals (to be discussed later) show that the practice is still alive, even in the U.S. Congress.

The Disguised Bribe

A somewhat more subtle transaction, the disguised bribe involves the sale of influence in exchange for a commodity, usually securities or real estate. The commodity is purchased by the public official at a cost well below the market value and resold later at a handsome profit. An example is the case of Governor Otto Kerner of Illinois (1961–1968), who paid $18,000 for racetrack securities that he later resold for $116,000. The donor of these securities was the racetrack owner who benefited from Governor Kerner's influence in securing favorable legislation and regulations.[7] On the witness stand, Kerner "scoffed at the suggestion that his ownership of stock in horse-racing enterprises regulated by the state might constitute a conflict of interest."[8] Kerner eventually was convicted and served seven months in prison.

Kickbacks

Government officials may use their bargaining power with contractors and their discretion in awarding contracts to obtain a fee or service charge for arranging the contract. A percentage—usually 5 percent—of the contract is returned, or kicked back, to the public official by the contractor. The attractiveness of a **kickback** arrangement for contractors is that they are using the government's money to pay off corrupt officials. Spiro Agnew, while a Baltimore County official, governor of Maryland, and vice president, received payments from engineering firms that had contracts with Baltimore County and the state of Maryland. Agnew's kickback rate was 5 percent.[9] A variation of this theme occurs when officials use their power over government employees to extort kickbacks. Employees are assessed a percentage of their salaries (usually 2 to 5 percent) to be kicked back to the party as a contribution. This practice has been outlawed for many years by federal civil service regulations. The seventeen-count federal indictment against Congressman Dan Rostenkowski of Illinois in 1994 included allegations of kickbacks from office employees.

Insider Trading

The legendary George Washington Plunkitt of Tammany Hall described insider trading as **honest graft.** By using inside information, politicians and officials make a profit doing business with the government.[10] An example is Thomas Keane of the Daley organization in Chicago who, while floor leader in the Chicago city council, regularly advised his friends in real estate, who bought property that they then resold to the Chicago Housing Authority. Keane eventually went to jail.[11]

Misuse of Public Property and Funds

Control of public property provides opportunities for mismanagement and corruption. During the heyday of the urban political machines, the Tweed Ring of New York actually sold City Hall and had the city buy it back.[12] A more contemporary example is the **Iran-Contra affair,** in which profits from the sale of U.S. government property (antitank and antiaircraft missiles) were diverted to private arms dealers and to counterrevolutionaries in Latin America. Misappropriation of public funds may range from small-scale to enormous amounts. Former Philippines president Ferdinand Marcos was accused of stealing millions of dollars, much of it in American foreign aid. The Robin HUD scandal in the Department of Housing and Urban Development is discussed later in this chapter.

Influence Peddling

Individuals with access to people in high places are sometimes tempted to trade on the influence of high-ranking government officials. There is money to be made through sale of access, the arrangement of contacts and meetings, and timely intervention to secure favorable disposition of regulatory decisions and government contracts. The use of these kinds of connections for personal gain is usually described as influence peddling. Two examples, one petty and one brazen, illustrate this technique. During the Eisenhower administration (1953–1961), the president's chief of staff, Sherman Adams, became very influential in Washington. On numerous occasions, Adams intervened with government agencies to assist various private interests. Adams's activities included personal intervention with the Federal

Trade Commission (FTC) on behalf of textile manufacturer Bernard Goldfine. At Adams's behest, the FTC rejected a staff recommendation for criminal charges against Goldfine's company. For this favor Adams received various gifts, including an Oriental rug and a vicuña coat. After these activities were disclosed, Adams maintained that the gratuities were simply an expression of friendship and not a payoff. Amid mounting political pressure, President Eisenhower reluctantly asked for Adams's resignation.[13]

A more blatant example of large-scale influence peddling in Washington is the case of Robert Gene "Bobby" Baker. A protégé of Senate Majority Leader Lyndon B. Johnson, Baker became a high-ranking member of the Senate staff. Between 1955 and 1963, he used his influence with members of the Senate to secure government contracts for various private interests, including his own business. Baker was indicted and convicted for theft, defrauding the government, and tax evasion. He served a year and a half in prison.[14]

Patronage

The assignment of government positions to political supporters has long been a practice in politics. While civil service regulations at the national and state level have effectively curtailed the number of patronage jobs, political appointments still occur at the top levels of government, and they provide a legitimate way for elected politicians to influence bureaucracy through the appointment of loyal executive officials. The process becomes corrupt when appointees are expected to pay for their jobs. The custom of rewarding wealthy campaign contributors with appointments as ambassadors has been traditional in presidential politics. For example, Herbert Kalmbach, President Richard Nixon's personal attorney and fund-raiser, pled guilty to a charge of promising a European ambassadorship in exchange for a $100,000 campaign contribution. The Senate Watergate Committee's investigation disclosed that eight ambassadors appointed after the 1972 election contributed a total of $706,000 and that all ambassadorial appointments combined produced nearly $2 million in presidential campaign funds.[15]

The sale of government jobs and widespread illegal campaign contributions disclosed during the **Watergate** scandal were part of a pattern of illegal activities committed not for business reasons (personal gain) but as a means to political power. Campaign contributions are the way elected officials pay the costs of communicating with voters in order to win elections. From the standpoint of the donors of campaign funds, contributions are an investment in politics. Most campaign contributions are a legal method by which private interests ensure access to politicians and to the resources politicians control.

POLITICS AS AN INVESTMENT

Democracy is expensive. Lengthy election campaigns involve substantial media and advertising expenses. In 1986, for example, the total costs of campaigns for Congress were estimated at slightly more than $450 million.[16] The costs for state and local elections and presidential campaigns add millions more to the total. The Federal Election Commission reported that during the 1996 election cycle (from January 1, 1995, to November 25, 1996) the Democratic and Republican parties raised $881 million to spend in election campaigns. This was a 73 percent increase over the 1991–1992 election cycle. During the 1996 cycle, Republican Party committees raised $549 million, and Democratic committees collected $316 million. To put these figures in perspective, consider that in 1996, the U.S. automobile industry spent more than $11 billion advertising its products. Total advertising expenditures in the United States for 1996 are estimated at nearly $67 billion. For the month of January 2000, the auto industry spent more than $1 billion on advertising. American political parties were expected to spend about one-tenth that amount to elect the president and Congress in 2000. At a cost of less than $6 per voter, this is a relatively efficient use of advertising money.[17]

In the American political system, the vast majority of money for the election campaigns of public officials consists of private contributions. Donors to campaigns may be individuals, political parties, interest groups, and **political action committees (PACs).** Contributions may be large or small, legal or illegal, but they consist mostly of private money. Since 1976, presidential nominations and elections have been partially funded by tax money, and several states have provisions for limited public funding of some campaigns. With these exceptions, campaign finance in America requires the procurement of significant amounts of private money.

The role of private money in elections, and the relationship between public officials and their campaign contributors, have been troublesome issues for American democracy. Historically, the source of campaign finance has moved from dependence on large contributors to greater involvement of small contributors and political action committees, with a limited role for public funding. This progression is illustrated by trends in the financing of presidential campaigns. Prior to 1964, both major parties relied primarily on large contributions to finance campaigns. Approximately three fourths of all contributions to presidential campaigns were in amounts exceeding $500, and contributions of $10,000 or more were not unusual. A handful of wealthy individuals made huge contributions. In 1968, Nelson Rockefeller received a contribution of nearly $1.5 million from his stepmother, Mrs. John D. Rockefeller. The Nixon campaign in 1972 received at least two contributions of $1 million or more, one from insurance millionaire W. Clement Stone, who gave $2 million, and another from oil and banking heir Richard Mellon Scaife, who contributed $1 million. The campaign of Democratic candidate George McGovern received $400,000 from General Motors heir Stewart Mott and nearly that much from Xerox stockholder Max Palevsky.[18]

Beginning in 1964, presidential candidates rediscovered the small contributor. Senator Barry Goldwater, the Republican candidate for president, was successful in using televised and direct-mail appeals to raise $6 million in contributions of $100 or less. Prior to that time, it was assumed that appeals to small contributors would generate barely enough money to cover the costs of the mail-out or television time. Subsequently, solicitation of small contributions has become a routine part of campaign fund-raising. The application of telemarketing and computerized direct-mail techniques to political fund-raising has made it cost-effective to reach millions of small contributors. In addition, campaign finance regulations have been changed to provide citizens with incentives to make political contributions.

STATUS: MONEY AND CORRUPTION IN AMERICAN POLITICS

Laws regulating campaign finance in the United States have traditionally had two distinguishing features. First and foremost is the legitimization and protection of the *private financing* of nomination and election campaigns. Limitations have been placed on the sources and size of contributions, but private financing has survived every reform in campaign finance law. Federal public funding, when implemented in 1976, applied only to presidential campaigns. Second, campaign finance laws and court cases interpreting them have been generous in the creation of numerous loopholes—provisions permitting candidates and campaign committees to circumvent limitations and to disclaim responsibility for "unintended" violations and actions by independent committees.

According to Herbert Alexander, the regulation of campaign finance has, with varying degrees of success, approached the issue of private money in politics from four different perspectives.[19]

- *Public disclosure* provides the public with knowledge of the sources of monetary influence on elected officials, the assumption being that public exposure reduces abuses.
- *Limits on campaign spending* address the rising costs of campaigns and the disparity of resources between candidates. The 1976 Supreme Court decision in **Buckley v. Valeo** (discussed later in this chapter) has diminished the utility of limitations on campaign spending.
- *Restrictions on contributions* limit the influence of large donors and have, on occasion, been effective. A change in the law (the 1979 **soft money** amendment) has created a giant loophole in the regulations.
- *Public funding* provides an alternative source of money to replace contributions that have been prohibited. At the federal level, public funding is limited to presidential campaigns. In 1974, the Senate passed a bill extending public funding to congressional campaigns, but this proposal failed in the House of Representatives. Sixteen states have some variation of limited public support for election campaigns.

Consideration of the status of current campaign finance regulations shows that the United States relies mainly on public disclosure and limitations on the size of political contributions to regulate the relationship between money and election campaigns. Spending limits have not proven feasible, and public financing plays a significant but limited role in presidential politics and in several states. As always, there are loopholes, one created by the Supreme Court in 1976 and another established by legislation in 1979.

The Federal Election Campaign Act

Current federal campaign finance regulations began to take shape in 1971, when Congress passed the **Federal Election Campaign Act (FECA).** This legislation was amended in 1974 in response to the Watergate scandal, and again in 1976 and 1979. In 1976, the Supreme Court significantly modified the FECA by declaring unconstitutional the provisions placing limitations on campaign spending.

As enacted in 1971, the FECA placed limits on media expenditures for federal nomination and election campaigns and limited the amount candidates and their families may contribute to their own campaigns. The act established detailed provisions for public disclosure of contributions, requiring candidates to report the names and occupations of anyone whose contributions exceeded $100. The lists of donors proved to be enlightening and led, after the Watergate scandal, to the imposition of limits on the size of contributions.

Watergate. In 1972, the Watergate hotel, apartment, and office building complex in Washington, D.C., was the location of the offices of national Democratic Party headquarters. Democratic Party offices were burglarized twice by operatives working for the Finance Committee to Reelect the President (CREEP, as it came to be ridiculed). During the second break-in, while attempting to replace a malfunctioning electronic listening device, the burglars were apprehended. One of the burglars had on his person the telephone number of E. Howard Hunt, an employee of the committee to reelect President Richard Nixon. Following up this lead, the *Washington Post* reporters Carl Bernstein and Bob Woodward uncovered a series of sensational revelations about politics in Washington, resulting in a Senate investigation that led to impeachment hearings in the House Judiciary Committee. After the Judiciary Committee voted three articles of impeachment against President Nixon, the president resigned in August, 1974 to avoid impeachment by the House and a trial in the Senate. The articles of impeachment accused the president of obstruction of justice and abuse of executive power.

It was the involvement of President Nixon and his aides in a coverup that nearly caused the president to be impeached. Of more relevance to the issue of money and politics are the things they attempted to conceal. Investigations by journalists, special prosecutors, and congressional committees uncovered a network of illegal activities by White House operatives. These activities included the extortion of illegal campaign contributions from corporations, the laundering of money in foreign banks to make it difficult to trace its sources, secret cash slush funds, illegal contributions from foreigners, and use of this money to finance other illegal activities, including payoffs to the burglars to keep them quiet.

Between 1972 and 1974, twenty-one companies, including Gulf Oil, American Airlines, and Goodyear Tire and Rubber, were charged with making illegal contributions totaling nearly $1 million. Although most of this money ($842,500) went to the Nixon campaign, several prominent Democrats received illegal contributions, including presidential candidate George McGovern, former vice-president Hubert Humphrey, and former vice-presidential candidate Edmund Muskie. Testimony by corporate executives indicated that public officials were using high-pressure fund-raising tactics bordering on extortion.[20]

Although some corporate contributions were given out of fear of government retaliation, others were donated with specific benefits and favors in mind. *Quid pro quo* is a Latin term meaning "something for something," or an equal exchange. In these cases, the exchange was one of money for influence. The *quid* was money, the *quo* was favorable treatment by the government. Two of the most publicized and best-documented cases of using campaign contributions to purchase political influence involved the nation's large dairy cooperatives and the International Telephone and Telegraph Company (ITT).

The objective of the dairy cooperatives was an increase in milk price supports paid by the government. Unable to persuade the secretary of agriculture, representatives of the dairy cooperatives met privately with President Nixon. This meeting was followed by a conference between Treasury Secretary John Connally and the attorney for Associated Milk Producers, who urged the administration to reconsider the price support matter. Two days later, the government announced a higher level of milk price supports. Shortly thereafter, large sums of dairy money began to flow into the Nixon campaign coffers, eventually reaching a total of $427,500. In terms of actual dollars, the decision cost the U.S. Treasury in excess of $125 million and resulted in a profit of $700 million to the milk industry.[21]

The dairy industry is not the only one that has successfully milked the government and the taxpayers. International Telephone and Telegraph also received a good return on its political investment. At a time when an antitrust suit against ITT was pending before the Justice Department, ITT pledged $400,000 to underwrite the cost of the 1972 Republican presidential convention. Eight days later, settlement of this suit on terms favorable to ITT was announced.[22]

Needless to say, in the wake of these disclosures, a clamor arose for further reform of campaign practices. In response, the FECA was amended, leading to public funding of presidential campaigns, limits on campaign spending and contributions, and a proliferation of political action committees.

Public Funding of Presidential Campaigns. The foundation of public financing of presidential campaigns was the Revenue Act of 1971, which established an income tax checkoff system to subsidize presidential campaigns. The 1974 amendments to the FECA provide public money for presidential primaries, conventions, and the general election. American taxpayers may contribute to the presidential campaign fund by consenting to have $3 of their income taxes placed into the fund administered by the Federal Election Commission (FEC). The number of tax returns making contributions to the FEC fund declined from 28 percent in 1980 to 18 percent in 1992. Because campaign and election costs have continued to increase during this period, in 1993 the FEC recommended, and the Congress approved, an increase in the taxpayer checkoff from $1 to $3 to avert a shortage in the FEC fund for the 1996 campaign.[23]

Tax money for the conventions and the general election consists of grants to each major party (and under certain circumstances, to third parties). Federal

TABLE 3.1   Funding Sources of Presidential Nominees, 1992–2000 (in millions of dollars, rounded off)

	1992			1996			2000* (through May 31, 2000)	
	G.H. Bush	Clinton	Perot	Clinton	Dole	Perot	Gore	G.W. Bush
Primary Elections								
Contributions from individuals and PACS	27	25		27	30		34	85
FEC Matching Funds	11	13		13	14		14	—
Presidential Election								
FEC Grant	55	55		62	62	29	70*	70*
Candidate's personal funds			68			8		

*Estimate.

Sources: The Federal Election Commission, *The Presidential Public Funding Program* (Washington, DC: U.S. Government Printing Office, 1993), p. 31, Chart 4-1; FEC Web site, www.fec.gov (August 31, 1996 and May 31, 2000).

matching funds are available to presidential candidates in the primaries in an attempt to make presidential candidates less dependent on large contributors by providing public funds to match small private contributions of $250 or less. Donations from committees and interest groups are not eligible to be matched, and only the first $250 of individual contributions are matched with tax money. To qualify for matching funds, a candidate must raise $5,000 in small contributions in twenty different states. The matching funds provision, plus limits on campaign contributions, ensures that presidential candidates must raise some of their money in small amounts. A presidential candidate who accepts matching funds cannot legally receive contributions greater than $1,000 from individuals and $5,000 from PACs. Table 3.1 shows the funding sources of the major-party presidential nominees from 1992 through May 31, 2000. The table shows that Republican nominee George W. Bush declined matching funds in 2000 so as not to be subject to contribution limits.

Political Action Committees.   The FECA, as amended, permits business, corporate, labor, professional, ideological, and issue groups to establish PACs to raise and spend political funds and to make campaign contributions. The growth of PACs is also encouraged by the contribution limits in the FECA. Although individuals may contribute only $1,000 per candidate in each election, PACs are permitted to contribute $5,000 to a candidate in each election. The number of PACs registered with the FEC increased from 608 in 1974 to 4,211 in 1987. Of these, 42 percent (1,779) were business and corporate PACs.[24]

Independent Spending.   Most of the campaign spending limitations contained in the FECA were declared unconstitutional by the Supreme Court as a violation of the First Amendment. The Supreme Court, in the case of *Buckley v. Valeo* (1976), concluded that spending by individuals and groups in support of a candidate is a form of political expression and is protected by the First Amendment. A candidate's supporters may legally spend an unlimited amount to help elect the candidate, provided that this spending is done independently, meaning without any contact with or coordination by the candidate's campaign committee. In summary, the *Buckley* decision ruled that expenditures for speech are substantially the same as speech itself and, therefore, are protected by the First Amendment. This decision struck down limits on campaign expenditures as unacceptable restrictions on freedom of expression. At the same time, the Court upheld the limits on contributions to candidates by individuals and by PACs and the system of public financing of presidential campaigns.

Evaluating Campaign Reform.   The FECA reforms have broadened the base of contributors in American politics. About 15 million Americans now contribute to candidates, parties, and PACs, much of it being contributed in relatively modest amounts. Public funding now plays an important role in presidential selection. Political action committees are significant in collecting and dispensing contributions, as well as independent spending. The advent of PACs permits corporate, labor, professional, and ideological interest groups to function in a more open and legal manner and enables the public to be better informed about their activities. Supporters of the present system of campaign finance feel that it is a significant improvement over the pre-Watergate era.

Others are less sanguine about the state of campaign finance in America. Criticisms of current practices are numerous, focusing in particular on the issues of spending and influence. Advocates of new spending limits propose them as a means of bringing skyrocketing campaign costs under control. Since spending limits are legal when candidates accept public funds, public subsidy of congressional campaigns has been proposed as an enticement for candidates to comply with spending limits. The most straightforward proposal for spending limitations is a constitutional amendment sponsored by Senator Ernest Hollings of South Carolina that would overrule *Buckley v. Valeo* and permit enactment of spending limitations on political advertising. Neither of these proposals has been able to muster a majority in Congress. Concerns about money and influence have to do not only with the amounts of money spent in politics but also with the process of soliciting and collecting money.

The commitments politicians make to raise money and the degree to which private contributions create obligations for public officials are of central concern to those who advocate complete public financing of congressional campaigns. Only public financing of campaigns can ensure the independence necessary to permit the public interest to prevail over private interests. A leading advocate of this position is political commentator Elizabeth Drew, author of *Politics and Money: The New Road to Corruption*. As the title indicates, she argues that campaign contributions and the pressure to raise them have distorted both the process and the policies of American government. The "threshold of principle" of American politicians has been lowered by the need to hustle ever greater amounts of money from private interests. Drew asserts that the "role that money is currently playing in American politics is different both in scope and in nature from anything that has gone before."[25]

Soft Money.   Of special concern to Drew are the changes made in the FECA in 1979, especially the so-called soft money amendment. This permits state parties to raise and spend unlimited amounts for party-building activities, including get-out-the-vote drives and campaign materials for voluntary activities. Soft money is exempt from federal reporting and disclosure requirements despite the fact that national parties have become involved in raising and distributing soft money. This provision is essentially a major loophole that circumvents contribution limits and disclosure requirements. In the future, it may be necessary to apply the same limitations and disclosure requirements for soft money as for other contributions. Federal Election Commission data show that soft money contributions are increasing rapidly. Republican Party committees raised $141 million in soft money in 1996, an increase of 183 percent over 1992. Democratic Party committees collected $122 million in soft money during 1996, a 257 percent increase over 1992. The FEC reported that 43 percent of the $72 million in soft money raised by the national party committees in 1992 came in donations of $50,000 or more, frequently from corporations or labor unions.[26]

A Question of Access.   Those who believe that campaign finance should remain a private matter contend that accepting contributions from supporters is different from the sale of influence. The money buys only the right to be heard—the assurance that decision makers will listen to one's point of view. In political parlance, this is known as *access*. Until his resignation, Congressman Tony Coelho was a successful Democratic congressional fund-raiser. He described the situation this way: "Access. Access. That's the name of the game. They [contributors] meet with the leadership and with chairmen of committees. We don't sell legislation; we sell the opportunity to be heard."[27]

According to this interpretation, contributions are simply an investment in politics that ensures the right to a hearing—perhaps a sympathetic hearing. Interest group activity is inevitable in democratic politics. Citizens have a right to be heard, as well as a right to spend money in order to express their opinions. Public officials need to be informed about the preferences of their constituents to better represent them.

Finally, there is the question of the corrupting influence of private money—the *quid pro quo*. It is sometimes difficult to discern the difference between the acceptance of a campaign contribution and the sale of influence. According to the late congresswoman Millicent Fenwick of New Jersey, "When [a member of Congress] will tell you quite frankly, 'Yes, I'm going to vote that way, because I took fifty-eight thousand from such-and-such a group and they want it,' I call that corruption."[28] Advocates of private campaign financing would view this not as an argument for public funding but rather for public disclosure and limits on the size of contributions. A system of regulated private campaign financing is, they insist, most compatible with democratic government and the right of free expression.

Corruption in the Congress

Various types of graft and corruption were discussed earlier in this chapter. Direct bribery of public officials has probably declined, although kickbacks, padding of government contracts, and conflicts of interest remain serious concerns as the complexity of government programs and the size of budgets and contracts increase. A series of scandals in Congress during the 1970s showed that old-fashioned bribery has not disappeared.

The Constitution gives each house of Congress the power to punish its members for misconduct. But historically, Congress has been very tolerant of questionable conduct by its members, based on the belief that the voters should be the final judges of a politician's behavior.[29]

Investigations and disclosures during the 1970s created political pressures for ethics reform. In 1972, Martin Sweig, a top aide to Speaker of the House John McCormack, was convicted of influence peddling. In the same year, Representative Cornelius E. Gallagher of New Jersey was indicted for tax evasion, perjury, and conspiracy in a kickback scheme. After a guilty plea, he was sentenced to two years in prison. The pivotal year in congressional ethics reform was 1976. Criminal proceedings were brought against five members of Congress for a variety of offenses, including bribery, kickbacks, illegal campaign contributions, and soliciting prostitution. In addition, ethics investigations were initiated against two members—Robert Sikes of Florida for financial misconduct and Wayne Hays of Ohio for trading government jobs for sexual favors. Sikes was reprimanded and Hays resigned.[30]

Concern about ethics in government increased as a result of the Watergate scandal. It was several years, and several scandals, after Watergate when members of Congress confronted the issue of ethics in Congress. A new code of ethics in 1977 and the Ethics in Government Act in 1978 were the result. The ethics committees in Congress have gradually become more diligent in enforcing the code. As a result of stricter enforcement, one member of Congress (Representative Michael "Ozzie" Myers of Pennsylvania) was expelled and several others resigned to avoid expulsion. Included among these was one senator, Harrison A. Williams of New Jersey. Two former members of Congress were convicted for crimes committed while they were members of Congress. Several members, including Speaker of the House Jim Wright, resigned amid ethics committee investigations.

Koreagate. In October 1976, the *Washington Post* reported that the Justice Department was investigating allegations of congressional corruption involving an influence-buying scheme in which agents of the South Korean government dispensed as much as $1 million a year in cash and gifts to members of Congress. This scandal, which became known as Koreagate, involved payoffs by Tongsun Park to several congressmen. Park was a rice dealer as well as an agent of the South Korean Central Intelligence Agency. Park's testimony indicated that many of the payoffs exceeded $200,000 and that several former members of Congress were implicated.[31] The House Ethics Committee recommended censure of one representative and reprimands for two others. The House chose to reprimand all three. This milder punishment was justified by the belief that most of the large payoffs went to former members, not to sitting representatives.

The Code of Ethics.   In 1977, the House and Senate adopted new codes of ethics for their members and employees. Although differing slightly in each body, both codes contained some limits on outside income (law practices and lecture honoraria), abolished office accounts where unreported contributions could be hidden, and required public disclosure of members' and spouses' income, debts, gifts received, and financial transactions. The codes prohibit members and employees from accepting gifts worth more than $100 from lobbyists and foreign nationals. In 1978, Congress passed the Ethics in Government Act, which made these provisions legally binding on members of Congress and required financial disclosure for other high-ranking government officials. The act contains conflict of interest provisions, including "revolving-door" restrictions, which prohibit retired executive officials from lobbying their former agencies for one year after leaving government service.

Abscam.   In 1980, another scandal in Congress demonstrated the need for the new codes of ethics and the willingness of the ethics committees to enforce them. The Abscam investigation was an undercover operation in which FBI agents posed as wealthy Arabs offering money in return for help in obtaining U.S. residency for other Arabs and help in securing government grants and gambling licenses. Making use of surveillance technology, the FBI videotaped meetings between congressmen and "the Arabs." Videotape recordings shown at the trials, and subsequently on television, included, among other things:

- Congressman "Ozzie" Myers of Pennsylvania accepting a $50,000 cash payoff and agreeing to take an additional $85,000 while boasting about his connections with the Mafia.
- Congressman John W. Jenrette, Jr. of South Carolina admitting, "I've got larceny in my blood." He took a $50,000 payoff and agreed to accept another $100,000.
- Congressman Richard Kelly of Florida stuffing $25,000 into his pockets and asking if the money made conspicuous bulges in his clothing.[32]

In 1981, seven members of Congress (six representatives and one senator) were convicted in the Abscam scandal. Representative Myers was expelled from Congress; three others, including Senator Harrison Williams, resigned to avoid likely expulsion; and the remaining three were defeated by the voters.

Between 1968 and 1997, there were more than thirty-five investigations by congressional ethics committees. Twenty-six of these investigations have occurred since 1980, reflecting increasingly strict enforcement of standards by the committees. Commenting on the case of former Speaker of the House Jim Wright, R. W. Apple stated in the *New York Times*:

> Once upon a time, no one would have paid any attention. Mr. Wright is a product of that time, and of a place—Lyndon B. Johnson's Texas—where rich friends routinely did

favors for politicians, and where the politicians often grew rich themselves. But standards are unquestionably higher now, and what Mr. Wright and his wife are accused of doing . . . is definitely not Congressional "business as usual" today.[33]

Newtgate. After succeeding in forcing the resignation of Democratic Speaker of the House Jim Wright in 1989, Congressman Newt Gingrich was elected Speaker by the Republicans following the 1994 congressional elections. A controversial and combative Speaker, Gingrich soon became the subject of an ethics investigation resulting from a wide-ranging complaint brought by House Democrats. Among other charges, the allegations included:

- Gingrich misused funds collected by a Republican PAC that he chaired. Specifically, that as chair of GOPAC, Gingrich made personal use of its resources, including a $250,000 per year slush fund.
- Gingrich violated the tax code by using tax-exempt funds collected by a foundation for political purposes.[34]

In January 1997, the House of Representatives voted by a wide margin to accept the recommendation of the ethics committee to reprimand Mr. Gingrich and to impose a $300,000 fine for actions of his that brought discredit on the House. Despite the ethical controversy, the House Republicans reelected Gingrich as Speaker. Gingrich eventually retired from the House.

Corruption in the Executive Branch

While corruption was pervasive and routine in the administrations of Presidents Grant and Harding, the Watergate scandal involving illegal contributions, burglary, extortion, payoffs, abuse of executive authority, and obstruction of justice is perhaps the high-water mark for executive corruption in American national government. The flurry of post-Watergate reform was short-lived, as a major scandal developed in the Reagan administration.

The Iran-Contra Affair. On November 3, 1986, *Al-Shira,* a Lebanese weekly newspaper, reported that the United States had secretly sold weapons to Iran. At first, the reports seemed dubious, and President Reagan repeatedly denied that they were true. The administration had forcefully stated on numerous occasions that American policy was to refuse to deal with terrorists or to sell arms to the terrorist government of Ayatollah Khomeni. Within a few days, however, it was evident that the reports were true. The Reagan administration had sold weapons—primarily TOW antitank missiles and HAWK antiaircraft missiles—in an attempt to obtain the release of American hostages held by pro-Iranian groups in Lebanon. The next startling revelation came three weeks later, when Attorney General Edwin Meese announced that some of the profits from the Iran arms sales had been diverted to anticommunist rebels in Nicaragua (the Contras) at a time when federal law prohibited American military aid to the Contras.

A formal congressional inquiry began on January 6, 1987. The Senate and House Select Committees took the unusual steps of merging their investigations and hearings and issuing a joint report. The committees investigated four areas: sale of weapons to Iran, diversion of money to the Contras, violations of law, and the role of the National Security Council (NSC) staff in the affair. After forty days of public hearings reviewing 300,000 documents and examining 500 witnesses, the committees issued their report.[35]

The findings of this report described the interplay of money and politics in the Iran-Contra affair. On two occasions, Congress passed measures containing amendments sponsored by Representative Edward Boland of Massachusetts prohibiting the U.S. government from attempting to overthrow the government of Nicaragua. The second Boland amendment prohibited agencies involved in intelligence activities from spending money to aid the Contras. The president felt strongly about the Contras, however, and ordered his staff to find a way to keep the Contras' "body and soul together."[36] Denied funding by the Congress, the president and his staff turned to foreign governments and private sources. In a year and a half, they secretly raised $34 million for the Contras from foreign sources and $2.7 million in private contributions. In July 1985, Lieutenant Colonel Oliver L. North, a member of the NSC staff, was assigned control of these funds.

The Enterprise.   Following the suggestion of CIA Director William J. Casey, North recruited retired Air Force Major General Richard V. Secord to assist in directing money to the Contras. Using Swiss bank accounts and a network of field operatives, Secord and his associate Albert Hakim created what they called **the Enterprise.** The Iran-Contra report describes the Enterprise as a private organization designed to engage in covert operations on behalf of the U.S. government.

> The Enterprise, functioning largely at North's direction, had its own airplanes, pilots, airfield, operatives, ship, secure communication devices, and secret Swiss bank accounts. For 16 months, it served as the secret arm of the NSC staff, carrying out with private and non-appropriated money, and without the accountability or restrictions imposed by law on the CIA, a covert contra aid program that Congress thought it had prohibited.[37]

Iran entered the picture in the summer of 1985, when the government of Israel proposed that missiles be sold to Iran in return for Iran's assistance in securing the release of seven American hostages held in Lebanon. The secretaries of state and defense opposed the plan on the grounds that the United States should not pay ransom to terrorists and that the sales would violate the Arms Export Control Act as well as the American arms embargo against Iran. Despite these objections, the president authorized Israel to ship TOW and HAWK missiles to Iran, with the promise that the United States would promptly replenish Israel's supply of missiles. The Enterprise received a $1 million advance from Israel, part of which North diverted to the Contras. Beginning in January 1986, the president authorized direct shipments of missiles to Iran by the United States. The Enterprise was used to carry out these sales.

Despite the fact that Iran repeatedly failed to deliver the hostages, the arms sales continued. One reason for this was the profits that the arms sales generated for the Enterprise. The committees' report shows that of the $16.1 million in profits from the sale of arms to Iran, only about $3.8 million actually went to support the Contras. Ultimately, three hostages were released but three more were taken, yielding a net gain of zero. Among the conclusions of the committees' report on the Iran-Contra affair were the following:

- The failure of the Reagan administration to inform Congress of the arms sales to Iran violated the reporting requirements of the National Security Act and the Arms Export Control Act.
- A substantial portion of the profits from the arms sales ended up in the personal bank accounts of the individuals executing the sales.
- The NSC staff turned to private parties and foreign governments to fund and implement foreign policy goals rejected by Congress.
- The diversion of money from the arms sales to benefit the Contras violated the law and constituted a misappropriation of government funds derived from the transfer of U.S. property.
- Finally, the report emphasized that under the Constitution, only Congress may provide funds for the executive branch.[38]

The investigation into the Iran-Contra affair by independent counsel Lawrence Walsh took six years and resulted in fourteen indictments and eleven convictions. On December 24, 1992, President George Bush issued executive pardons to Caspar Weinberger, Elliott Abrams, Robert McFarland, and three CIA officials for their involvement in the Iran-Contra affair. The president justified the pardons by stating that none of these executive officials had profited from their involvement. The convictions of Oliver North and John Poindexter were overturned on legal technicalities. Of the more than $47 million that North helped raise for covert operations (which Secord and Hakim put into Swiss bank accounts), $10 million is still unaccounted for.[39] In June 1994, Oliver North was nominated as the Republican candidate for the U.S. Senate from Virginia, but he was defeated by Democratic Senator Charles Robb.

Consultants and Beltway Bandits. A network of interstate highways connects the center of American government in Washington, D.C., with the outlying areas. The beltways are home to a variety of companies, including many consulting firms that sell information, political analysis, and legal advice to government agencies and to other companies doing business with the government. The beltway consulting firms surround Washington in the same manner that an amoeba envelops its food. The specialized information, expertise, and political connections of the consultants make them players in the money and politics game. Some consultants are former government employees who are able to use their political connections to build a consulting business. Because government contracts and large—sometimes exorbitant—consulting fees are at stake, the temptation to purchase political influence is ever present, as is the temptation to commit fraud and theft.

Michael Deaver and Lyn Nofziger are former aides to President Reagan who were found guilty of lobbying illegally on behalf of private firms and foreign governments. They were convicted of violating the revolving-door restrictions requiring former executive officials to refrain from lobbying their former agencies for one year after leaving the government. Nofziger was convicted of lobbying illegally for the Wedtech Corporation, a multimillion-dollar defense contractor. Wedtech obtained some of its contracts by buying influence. Although Nofziger's conviction was overturned on appeal, seven other public officials were indicted and convicted, including two New York congressmen. All told, there were twenty-one indictments, including that of E. Robert Wallach, a longtime friend of former attorney general Edwin Meese.

In June 1989, following an investigation of corruption in the Pentagon, Federal District Judge Richard L. Williams had this to say as he passed sentence on two vice presidents of Teledyne Electronics:

> This trial was a window to Defense Department procurement procedures. Those procedures are so outrageous that a world of so-called consultants—and as far as I am concerned that is another word for rogue—are permitted to live a parasitic life off the government.[40]

The Teledyne vice-presidents were convicted of hiring a consultant to bribe a Navy official in order to obtain inside information that helped Teledyne get a $24 million government contract.

The HUD Scandal. A combination of lax management, unscrupulous consultants, influence peddling, bribery, and embezzlement occurred in the Department of Housing and Urban Development (HUD) during the Reagan administration. The embezzlement of government funds came to be known as Robin HUD. This scandal was so named by the media because one of the embezzlers claimed she stole $5 million to give to the poor. Private escrow agents under contract with HUD to oversee the sale of government property stole a total of at least $20 million.

A second aspect of the HUD scandal provides a textbook illustration of influence peddling and conflict of interest. In one instance, an adviser to the campaigns of Presidents Bush and Reagan and a past business partner of Republican National Committee Chairman Lee Atwater admitted that his lobbying firm was able to steer millions of dollars in federal housing funds to a housing project that he owned. His firm was paid $326,000 in consulting fees to provide public relations and lobbying services for the project. When asked by a House subcommittee to describe those services, he replied, "I would stipulate that for purposes of today, you could characterize this as influence peddling."[41] Lest the irony be lost: In essence, he was paid a six-figure consulting fee to arrange federal rehabilitation funding for a housing project of which he was part owner.

The HUD scandal involved bribery as well as influence peddling and favoritism. In 1993, three people, including a former top aide to HUD Secretary

Samuel Pierce, were convicted of offering gratuities to HUD officials. During their trial, a former deputy assistant secretary in charge of awarding urban grants testified that he accepted more than $400,000 in bribes while working at HUD.[42]

In summary, the government investigation of HUD uncovered millions of dollars in payments to politically connected consultants who were hired to help their employers win HUD contracts for housing the poor. In one instance, consulting fees of $5.7 million were paid for a single housing rehabilitation program. The consultants included politically influential Republicans and former agency officials.[43]

The Road to Impeachment

Whitewater.   During President Clinton's first year in office, his administration became enmeshed in an imbroglio involving a failed real estate deal and a bankrupt Arkansas savings and loan company. At issue were the president's past connections, while governor of Arkansas, to Madison Guaranty Savings and Loan and to Whitewater Development Company, a real estate venture jointly owned by the Clintons and James McDougal, the owner of the S&L. A federal investigation into the failed S&L disclosed that depositor funds from the S&L may have been diverted improperly to Clinton's 1984 campaign for governor. Questions of possible conflict of interest and political favoritism arose because President Clinton and his wife, Hillary, were business partners with the S&L owner. Specifically, Hillary Rodham Clinton represented the S&L before a state regulator appointed by her husband. This raises the possibility that lenient treatment for their business partner may have permitted an insolvent S&L to stay open long after it should have been closed by regulators. Under a subpoena from the Justice Department, the White House agreed to turn over documents about Whitewater that were found in the office of Deputy White House Counsel Vincent Foster after he committed suicide in July 1993.[44] In January 1994 President Clinton, against the advice of some of his staff, asked Attorney General Janet Reno to appoint an independent counsel to investigate the Whitewater affair.

In order to understand how a small-scale real estate deal escalated into an impeachment inquiry, bear in mind three important points:

1. The independent counsel was granted extremely broad investigative authority.
2. The individual selected as independent counsel was a political enemy of the president.
3. President Clinton is a ladies' man without a great deal of discretion. Ultimately the president would find himself on trial not for his real estate dealings but for his sexual activities.

The Independent Counsel.   In addition to questions of financial impropriety and possible misuse of S&L deposits, the independent counsel was also charged with investigating any other crimes discovered during the course of the primary investigation. The independent counsel was authorized to investigate the possibility that members of the Clinton administration had engaged in illegal actions in office to cover up or obstruct investigation of these matters and, more importantly, to investigate new allegations uncovered during the investigation. As some in the president's staff had feared, the independent counsel was granted an unrestricted hunting license and an unlimited budget to investigate the administration. The first independent ethics counsel was Robert Fisk. However, after a meeting between a federal judge and Senators Jesse Helms and Lauch Faircloth, both conservative Republicans from the judge's home state of North Carolina, Fisk was replaced by Kenneth Starr, a conservative with ties to the Christian right. The nightmare scenario feared by the president's staff was beginning to take shape: The Office of the Independent Counsel was in the hands of the president's enemies.

Monicagate.   In a strange juxtaposition of events, the president provided his foes with ammunition and nearly served up his own head on a platter. Allegations of sexual harassment and misconduct expanded the Whitewater affair from an inquiry about an Arkansas real estate venture into an investigation of the president's personal life. When the president gave misleading testimony under oath, he provided congressional Republicans with an excuse to impeach him. The sexual aspect of the scandal began to pick up steam when Paula Jones, an Arkansas state employee sponsored by the Conservative Political Action Conference, filed a sexual harassment lawsuit against President Clinton in 1994. Jones alleged that on May 8, 1991, Governor Clinton asked her to perform a sexual act in a room of the Excelsior Hotel in Little Rock. Two subsequent events elevated Jones's civil suit into a constitutional crisis. First, in an unprecedented decision, the Supreme Court permitted Jones's lawsuit to proceed while President Clinton was still in office. No one had ever before filed a civil suit against a sitting president involving the president's private behavior. Secondly, during Jones's suit her attorneys sought to strengthen their case by asking for the names of other women with whom the president had been sexually involved. One of the women subpoenaed was a White House intern named Monica Lewinsky. It was President Clinton's tortured denials under oath of his involvement with Lewinsky that precipitated his impeachment by the House of Representatives and subsequent trial and acquittal in the Senate. Ironically, Jones's case was dismissed, and prosecutor Kenneth Starr found no evidence of wrongdoing by the president regarding the Whitewater real estate venture. Assessing this sorry situation, a *New York Times* editorial concluded: "It has been clear from the opening days of the trial that the partisan passions that stirred the House to impeach Mr. Clinton never migrated across the Capitol to the Senate. . . . The problem is that the House Republicans misused the power of impeachment to deal with Presidential misconduct that deserves formal rebuke but not the ultimate constitutional sanction of overturning an election."[45]

PROSPECTS: ETHICS AND REFORM

Certain kinds of political corruption, such as kickbacks and misappropriation of funds, are partly a result of lax management practices. The HUD scandal is a good example. HUD Secretary Samuel R. Pierce was known in Washington as "silent Sam." His tenure at HUD was described by the *New York Times* as "eight years of hands-off management." Jack Kemp, Pierce's successor at HUD, characterized the department as "a swamp" of mismanagement.[46] Sound management requires having honest and qualified public officials working under effective supervision according to clearly established standards.

The codes of ethics, disclosure requirements, and conflict of interest rules enacted since the 1970s have undoubtedly tightened up standards of ethics in government. There are clearly limits, however, on the ability of Congress to impose management standards on the executive branch. The president, cabinet, and senior executive officials set the tone. Consider, for example, the fate of whistle-blowers in executive agencies. Whistle-blowers are government employees who risk reprisal by reporting wrongdoing within their agencies. Congress has enacted provisions to reward, or at least protect, whistle-blowers. Despite this, the agencies' control of rewards and sanctions frequently results in retaliation against public servants who disclose misconduct in the bureaucracy. In 1989, Internal Revenue Service (IRS) agents testifying before a congressional subcommittee stated that they were demoted, threatened, and intimidated by their superiors after reporting that IRS auditors had accepted gratuities from a businessman who owed $400,000 in back taxes. In response to their disclosure of agency misconduct, their superiors told them, "The organization will get you, you whores."[47] The objective of their superiors at IRS was to prevent the disclosure of misconduct to protect the service's public image.

A variety of campaign finance proposals have been introduced in Congress, including bills to change limits on contributions, tighten disclosure requirements, regulate soft money, eliminate PAC contributions, and permit public funding of congressional campaigns. Partisan bickering has stalled or blocked nearly all of these. In 1992, Congress passed legislation to provide public funding and other incentives, including vouchers to buy discounted television advertising, to congressional candidates who agreed to abide by campaign spending limits. President Bush vetoed this bill, and the Senate failed to override the veto.[48]

In the area of campaign finance, advocates of public funding of election campaigns face an uphill, and probably insurmountable, struggle. Private financing of campaigns is deeply rooted in American political tradition. The burden of proof rests with the reformers, and those they must persuade—the elected officials— clearly prefer the existing system of private contributions. This is hardly surprising, considering the reelection rates for incumbents. In Congress, more than 90 percent of members who seek reelection are returned to office. There are other advantages of incumbency in addition to superior fund-raising ability, including higher name recognition and greater visibility; but the ability of public officials to attract more campaign money than their opponents contributes significantly to their high rate of reelection. It seems unlikely, in the absence of another major scandal and public outcry, that elected officials will enact measures giving substantial assistance to potential opponents. The present system is heavily one-sided in favor of incumbents who, in all likelihood, will vote to keep it that way.

Finally, realism requires the acknowledgment that a certain amount of corruption is attributable to human nature. Opportunities for corruption exist in public office and in complex government organizations. Greed is a motivation for some public servants as it is for private citizens. Ethical standards in American government are undoubtedly higher as a result of reforms enacted during the 1970s and 1980s. Both major parties rely, to a greater extent, on money donated by small contributors and PACs. There are limits on the size of campaign contributions and requirements for public disclosure. Public funding permits less-known candidates to compete in presidential primaries. There are also very large loopholes in the regulation of campaign finance. Tighter ethical standards are required of members of Congress and executive officials. As desirable as these changes may be, the series of scandals since Watergate shows that ethics in government must remain a matter of concern for citizens.

STUDY QUESTIONS

1. Define bribery, extortion, kickback, and conflict of interest.
2. Distinguish between a bribe, an honorarium, and a campaign contribution.
3. What methods are used in the United States to regulate the impact of private money in campaigns for public office?
4. What is the FECA and what does it do?
5. What is soft money and why is it important?
6. What are the similarities and differences between the Watergate scandal, the Iran-Contra affair and the Whitewater scandal?
7. Should public financing of campaigns be extended to congressional elections? Why or why not?
8. What is the revolving door and why is it important?
9. What are whistle-blowers? What often happens to them in government bureaucracies?
10. What are some of the issues raised by the Whitewater affair?
11. Who was Paula Jones and why was she important?

NOTES

1. Secord is quoted in Joel Brinkley and Stephen Engelberg, eds., *Report of the Congressional Committees Investigating the Iran-Contra Affair*, abridged ed. (New York: Times Books 1988), p. 26.
2. Breaux is cited in Amitai Etzioni, *Capital Corruption: The New Attack on American Democracy* (San Diego: Harcourt Brace Jovanovich, 1984), p. vii.
3. Janet Hook, "Passion, Defiance, Tears: Jim Wright Bows Out," *Congressional Quarterly Weekly Report*, June 3, 1989, pp. 1289–1294.
4. George C.S. Benson, *Political Corruption in America* (Lexington, MA: Lexington Books, 1978), pp. 5–6.
5. Burl Noggel, *Teapot Dome: Oil and Politics in the 1920s* (Baton Rouge: Louisiana State University Press, 1962).
6. "Another Arizona Political Scandal Erupts," *Dayton Daily News*, February 11, 1991, p. 3C.
7. Benson, *Political Corruption in America*, p. 7.
8. George Amick, *The American Way of Graft* (Princeton, NJ: Center for Analysis of Public Issues, 1976), p. 107.
9. Benson, *Political Corruption in America*, p. 8.

10. William L. Riordon, *Plunkitt of Tammany Hall* (New York: Alfred A. Knopf, 1948).

11. Benson, *Political Corruption in America*, p. 8.

12. Ibid., p. 12.

13. John C. Bollens and Henry J. Schmandt, *Political Corruption: Power, Money, and Sex* (Pacific Palisades, CA: Palisades Publishers, 1979), pp. 42–43.

14. Ibid., p. 44.

15. Larry L. Berg, Harlan Hann, and John R. Schmidhauser, *Corruption in the American Political System* (Morriston, NJ: General Learning Press, 1976), p. 92.

16. Frank J. Sorauf, *Money in American Elections* (Glenview, IL: Scott, Foresman, 1988), p. 1.

17. "Political Parties' Fundraising Hits $881 Million," Federal Election Commission News Release, January 10, 1997, contact: Ron Harris@www.fec.gov. The advertising statistics are found in Keith Bradsher, "How to Pooh-Pooh $70 Million War Chests," *The New York Times*, April 30, 2000, sec. 4, p. 6.

18. Herbert E. Alexander, *Financing Politics: Money, Elections, and Political Reform*, 3rd ed. (Washington, DC: Congressional Quarterly, 1984), pp. 59–62.

19. Ibid., p. 19.

20. Ibid., p. 86.

21. Bollens and Schmandt, *Political Corruption*, p. 58.

22. Ibid.

23. The Federal Election Commission, *Record*, vol. 19, no. 9 (September 1993), pp. 1, 2.

24. Sorauf, *Money in American Elections*, p. 78. See Table 4-1.

25. Elizabeth Drew, *Politics and Money: The New Road to Corruption* (New York: Macmillan, 1983), p. 1.

26. The Federal Election Commission, *The Presidential Public Funding Program*, p. 32; "Political Parties' Fundraising Hits $881 Million."

27. Coelho is cited in Jay Hedlund, "Lobbying and Legislative Ethics," in Anne Marie Donahue, ed., *Ethics in Politics and Government* (New York: N.W. Wilson, 1989), p. 126.

28. Drew, *Politics and Money*, p. 96.

29. For a historical survey, see *How Congress Works* (Washington, DC: Congressional Quarterly, 1983), pp. 193–210.

30. Ibid., p. 195.

31. *CQ Almanac 1978* (Washington, DC: Congressional Quarterly, 1978), p. 804.

32. *How Congress Works*, pp. 196–198, 207.

33. R.W. Apple, Jr., "Washington's New Wave of Ethics Anxiety," *The New York Times*, April 23, 1989, sec. 4, p. 1.

34. Jackie Koszczuk, "Gingrich Troubles Not Over After Committee Report," *Congressional Quarterly Weekly Report*, October 5, 1996, p. 2840.

35. Brinkley and Engelberg, *Report of the Congressional Committees Investigating the Iran-Contra Affair*. The summary of the Iran-Contra affair is based on pp. 1–88 of this report.

36. Ibid., p. 12.

37. Ibid., p. 13.

38. Ibid., pp. 26–27.

39. Martha Sherrill, "Bullet Proof," *Esquire*, February 1994, p. 88.

40. "Judge Sentences Two in Pentagon Corruption Case," reported by the Associated Press in the *Dayton Daily News*, June 8, 1989, p. 10A.

41. "GOP Consultant Admits 'Influence Peddling,'" *Dayton Daily News*, June 21, 1989, p. 6A.

42. "3 Men Found Guilty in HUD Scandal," *Dayton Daily News*, January 6, 1993, p. 1.

43. "HUD Probe Uncovers More Payments," *Dayton Daily News*, August 3, 1989, p. 4A.

44. Susan Schmidt and Michael Isikoff, "Whitewater Rapids," *The Washington Post National Weekly Edition*, January 10–16, 1994, p. 13.

45. "Witness for the Defense," *The New York Times*, Feb. 7, 1999, sec. 1, p. 16.

46. E.J. Dionne, Jr., "Pierce at HUD: Eight Years of Hands-off Management," *The New York Times*, June 18, 1989, p. 1.

47. "Intimidation of Whistle-blowers Kept Lid on at IRS, Panel Hears," *Dayton Daily News*, July 27, 1989, p. 10A.
48. "Bush Rejects Campaign Finance Legislation," *CQ Almanac, 1992* (Washington, DC: Congressional Quarterly, 1992), p. 63.

SUGGESTED READINGS

ALEXANDER, HERBERT E. *Financing Politics: Money, Elections, and Political Reform.* 3rd ed. Washington, DC: Congressional Quarterly, 1984.

BENSON, GEORGE C.S. *Political Corruption in America.* Lexington, MA: Lexington Books, 1978.

BOLLENS, JOHN C., and HENRY J. SCHMANDT. *Political Corruption: Power, Money, and Sex.* Pacific Palisades, CA: Palisades Publishers, 1979.

BRINKLEY, JOEL, and STEPHEN ENGELBERG. *Report of the Congressional Committees Investigating the Iran-Contra Affair.* New York: Random House, 1988.

DELEON, PETER. *Thinking About Political Corruption.* Armonk, NY: M.E. Sharpe, 1993.

JACKSON, BROOKS. *Honest Graft: Big Money and the American Political Process.* New York: Alfred A. Knopf, 1988.

The Knapp Commission Report on Police Corruption. New York: George Braziller, 1973.

SORAUF, FRANK J. *Money in American Elections.* Glenview, IL: Scott, Foresman, 1988.

STEWART, JAMES B. *Blood Sport: The President and His Adversaries.* New York: Simon & Schuster, 1996.

Glossary

Abscam   An FBI undercover operation in 1980 that disclosed bribery and payoffs in Congress.

Aid to Families with Dependent Children (AFDC)   A federal social welfare program that supported poor, unmarried mothers of young children.

bribe   An offer of money or other inducements in order to secure favorable action from government officials.

Buckley v. Valeo   The 1976 Supreme Court decision that declared limits on independent campaign spending to be unconstitutional.

deindustrialization   The process by which the industrial sector of the economy decreases as the service sector increases.

employer mandate   A government policy requiring employers to pay for part of the costs of health insurance for their employees.

the Enterprise   A private, profit-making organization that conducted arms sales to Iran for the United States and transferred some of the profits to counterrevolutionaries in Latin America (the Contras).

extortion (political)   A demand by a public official for money or gifts.

Federal Election Campaign Act (FECA)   Legislation that, as amended, limits the size of campaign contributions, requires public disclosure of the names of contributors, and establishes the Federal Election Commission (FEC) to administer public funds in presidential primaries and elections.

health maintenance organization (HMO)   An organization set up to provide comprehensive health services in a cost-efficient manner, often using prepaid plans permitting a range of services.

"honest graft"   The use by politicians and public officials of inside information to make a profit doing business with the government.

Iran-Contra affair   A scandal during the Reagan administration involving sales of U.S. weapons to Iran and diversion of some of the profits to the Contras in Nicaragua.

kickback   A percentage of government contract payments returned to public officials by the contractor.

Koreagate   A bribery scandal during the 1970s involving payoffs by a Korean agent to current and former members of Congress.

Medicaid A noncontributory medical care program for the very poor.

Medicare A contributory health insurance program for the elderly.

national health insurance Health insurance provided by the government and paid for by taxes, as in Canada.

political action committee (PAC) A voluntary organization created to collect, dispense, and spend political contributions.

poverty level The U.S. government's measurement of poverty in America, computed based on the cost of food and other necessities.

public assistance Noncontributory social welfare programs funded from general revenues.

quid pro quo A Latin term meaning "something for something," or an equal exchange.

Social Darwinism The view that society progresses only through a competitive struggle among individuals. The poor are regarded as having failed in this competition and, consequently, as not being worthy of assistance or welfare.

social insurance Government retirement and medical care programs in which beneficiaries have made a contribution to the cost of the program.

socialized medicine A system of nationalized health care operated by the government, as in Great Britain.

soft money Contributions to state party committees that are exempt from federal contribution limits and disclosure requirements.

Teapot Dome A scandal during the administration of President Warren G. Harding involving bribery to secure oil leases on public land.

third-party payer The party who is billed for medical services provided to a patient (the first party) by a doctor or hospital (the second party) under various insurance plans. The third-party payer may be an insurance company or a government agency.

underclass The long-term poor living in urban, high-poverty areas.

universal health insurance A system of health insurance providing coverage for all residents within a state or country, as in Germany, Japan, and Hawaii.

Watergate The scandal during the administration of President Richard M. Nixon involving illegal campaign contributions, burglary, "dirty tricks," and obstruction of justice.

welfare Those government social programs (public assistance) in which recipients have not made a direct contribution to the cost of the program.

Whitewater The investigation, initially of Bill and Hillary Clinton's business dealings in the Whitewater real estate development in Arkansas, that expanded into a sex scandal and led to charges of perjury for which the president was impeached in 1999.

workfare The idea that welfare recipients should work for their public assistance benefits.

PART II

Violence and Politics

INTRODUCTION

> *We the people of the United States, in Order to form a more perfect Union,*
> *establish Justice, insure domestic Tranquility, provide for the common*
> *defence, promote the general Welfare, and secure the Blessings of Liberty to*
> *ourselves and our posterity, do ordain and establish this Constitution for the*
> *United States of America.*
>
> —*Preamble, Constitution of the United States of America (1789)*

Since the American Revolution, one of the central responsibilities of the U.S. government has been to secure individual Americans and their country from the threat of violence. Domestic tranquility and national security, concerns of the drafters of the Constitution, continue to play a key role in American political life today and figure prominently on the national agenda as the United States enters the twenty-first century. Violent crime threatens Americans in their homes and cities, undermining domestic tranquility in the world's most modern and powerful society. National security is still perceived to be at risk, with 3,500 Russian intercontinental ballistic warheads still able to reach the American nation,[1] and with growing numbers of countries able to build weapons of mass destruction, both chemical and biological, as well as nuclear. In addition to the inherited and persistent problems of crime and national security, the United States confronts new sources of violence because of two critical developments in the twentieth century. First, the accelerating rate of technological change has created new weapons (nuclear explosives, ballistic missiles, Stinger missiles, chemical and biological poisons) and new vulnerabilities (international commerce, travel, and communication). Second, the United States today must defend its role and status as a superpower and leader of the free world.

Since World War II and the onset of the Cold War, security and violence have become increasingly complex issues in American politics. In this part of the book, three areas in which violence and politics intersect—crime, terrorism, and the proliferation of weapons of mass destruction—are examined.

The Politics of Crime

In May 2000, the FBI reported that violent crime had declined nationally for the eighth straight year, although Americans still felt threatened by crime and at least 200 million guns were in private hands. Nationwide, prisons were full and exceeding their capacity. School and workplace shootings, carjacking, and stalking were widely covered by the media, leaving Americans feeling unsafe at home, at work, at school, and at play. The presidential campaign of 2000 saw the major candidates concur on their basic support for the death penalty and continuing tough anticrime legislation. The type of crime experienced by a nation provides many insights into the character of that society, and a nation's policies on crime also reveal how well that society and its government work together to solve this basic threat to individual security. Who commits crime? What types of crimes are perpetrated? How does the criminal justice system prosecute and punish criminals? How much are Americans willing to spend on law enforcement and criminal rehabilitation? These questions all bear on the political nature of crime in the United States, crime's sources, remedies, and nagging persistence.

Because experts have failed to agree on the causes of crime—whether the source is poverty, age, drugs, alcohol, heredity, or weak moral character—the assignment of blame becomes a social and political act with remedies following from the identified cause or causes of crime. In nineteenth-century America, when crime was viewed as the aberrant behavior of the morally inferior, prisons operated to punish and deter criminal activity. In twentieth-century America, crime was often viewed as the result of economic hardship, subsequently adding rehabilitation to the set of tasks prisons were asked to perform on incarcerated criminals. Simultaneously, politicians campaigned on getting-tough-with-crime platforms (a major platform position of the presidential campaigns of Richard Nixon in 1968, George H. Bush in 1988, Bill Clinton in 1992 and 1996, and Al Gore and George W. Bush in 2000), which included capital punishment, tougher drug laws, and gun control debates as the United States approached the twenty-first century.

The politics of crime also run parallel to social and technological changes occurring in the United States in the late twentieth and early twenty-first centuries. The transition to a postindustrial economy, which had raised concerns over worsened urban problems of poverty, homelessness, unemployment, and crime, instead witnessed the longest peacetime economic expansion ever enjoyed in the United States, as well as a steadily declining violent crime rate. At the same time, crime has become more technologically sophisticated, as the criminal justice system scrambles to cope with computer theft and nuclear espionage conspiracies. While some types of crime have been deemphasized through policy changes—for example, the legalization of gambling or the decriminalization of marijuana—other crimes have been spotlighted by social awareness and new legislation concerning issues such as child pornography and spouse battering. Crime in America also reflects political constants in our society: 95 percent of state prison inmates in 1999 were repeat offenders or were serving time for violent crime;[2] African Americans typically receive longer jail sentences than white Americans; and African Americans and Hispanics make up 60 percent[3] of the prison population, although they constitute less than 30 percent of the U.S. general population. The criminal justice system, statistics reveal, focuses on violent and repeat offenders and reflects prevailing racial attitudes as well as class- and race-related problems in the United States. In Chapter 4, The Politics of Crime in America, the types and causes of crime are examined, and the different solutions that have been tried or are being considered are discussed. The threat to the security of the individual American, how government responds to that threat, and what lessons may be drawn from both the problem and the response are discussed. Special attention is given to the changing debate on the death penalty.

The Politics of Terrorism

The politics of terrorism involves a different type of violence confronting Americans both at home and abroad. Motivated by political objectives rather than personal gain or psychological imbalance, terrorism is not a new problem on the American political agenda. At home, terrorism is as old as the American Revolution of 1776, in which political violence was directed at people (Tory sympathizers) and property (stamp houses) to trigger a revolutionary uprising. The targeting of a symbolic victim to obtain political concessions from a third party identifies the species of violence known as terrorism.

The Ku Klux Klan and abortion clinic bombers have been prominent employers of terrorist violence against Americans at home, but the greater threat of violence has, with just a few notable exceptions (World Trade Center 1993, Oklahoma City 1995), targeted Americans abroad. The occupation of the American embassy in Tehran (from 1979 to 1981); the bombing of the U.S. Marine barracks in Beirut (1983); the assassination of the president of Pakistan, Zia ul-Haq (1988), which also killed American Ambassador Arnold Raphel and chief U.S. military attaché Brigadier General Herbert Wassom; and the Pan Am 103 bombing over Lockerbie, Scotland (1988) have placed terrorism high on Americans' political agenda; but it took the deaths of 168 Americans in Oklahoma City in April 1995 to bring home the reality of terrorism—by way of graphic video footage and photographs—to the average American.

Terrorist attacks typically are designed to demonstrate a government's inability to protect its people, and publicity is a key element in the demonstration effect. The technology of instantaneous global communication has enabled terrorists to attack Americans abroad or at home and have an immediate effect on U.S. public opinion. This creates pressure on the government to respond to avoid the appearance of impotence that plagued Jimmy Carter in 1980 and that contributed to the Reagan administration's sale of TOW missiles to Iran in 1986. The technology that enables Americans to travel abroad and conduct business on a global scale has also been used to make them targets of international terrorism. Americans (tourists, business professionals, diplomats, and military personnel) represent attractive, vulnerable targets when terrorists seek to obtain concessions from the U.S. government.

The nature of domestic and international terrorism and the manner in which the U.S. government has responded are the subjects of Chapter 5, The Politics of Terrorism. As with crime in America, there are many possible remedies for a terrorism problem, and the U.S. government employs a wide range of options. Law enforcement, diplomacy, economic sanctions, technical fixes, military rescues, and reprisals all figure in American responses to terrorism. Like crime, the choice of a response to terrorism often follows from a particular understanding of its causes. In both crime and terrorism, however, the violent threat to Americans' security remains a persistent problem. Nonetheless, American citizens look to their government for protection, expecting to live and work without the fear of violent assault. The pressure on the United States to secure its people from the threat of violence will increase as the American presence abroad continues to grow and as groups like those led by Islamist radical Osama bin Laden increasingly focus on Americans as their preferred targets. Understanding the politics of terrorism becomes increasingly important as Americans enter the new millennium.

The Politics of Arms Racing and Weapons of Mass Destruction

All states are obliged to protect their people and their territory from violent assault, but the responsibility for national security took on new meaning for the United States when it emerged from World War II as a superpower. Having ended the war with Japan by exploding one uranium and one plutonium bomb over Hiroshima and Nagasaki, the United States found itself militarily supreme, with a nuclear monopoly and an undamaged homeland. However, only two years later, in 1947, the United States would confront a new and unprecedented challenge to its national security—the Cold War with the Soviet Union. The Cold War was the source of a new type of conflict in the international system: Incompatible ideologies, hostile rhetoric, conflicting interests, competition for global influence, arms racing, and the building of weapons of mass destruction all characterized a conflict that fell short of traditional outright war. In Chapter 6, The Politics of Arms Racing and Weapons of Mass Destruction, this source of international competition and conflict is examined. Many new concepts introduced by the Cold War era must be assimilated by students living in the age of superpower politics. Familiarity with the nuclear, biological, and chemical **arms race** and how it is managed through **arms control** and **deterrence** are essential to an understanding of the politics of international violence and national security that will dominate the American agenda in the twenty-first century.

The U.S.–U.S.S.R. arms race, which ended in 1991, was composed of four interdependent elements:

1. perception
2. money
3. technology
4. numbers

Perception.　Underlying and fueled by all arms races is the participants' shared perception of mutual hostility and threat. Arms control efforts include confidence-building measures designed to neutralize the sense of mutual threat. In August 1988, for example, American observers witnessed the Soviet destruction of three SS-20 missile launchers, and Soviet observers witnessed a U.S. underground nuclear test to evaluate a measurement device (CORRTEX—Continuous Reflectometry for Radius versus Time Experiment) for nuclear testing agreements. The United States and Soviet Union, however, had forty-five years of mutually hostile perceptions to overcome as they engaged in arms control talks. From 1981 to 1988, the Reagan administration's evolution in its perceptions of the Soviet Union illustrated the connection between perceptions and behavior and the different roles played by public opinion, bureaucratic interests, and individual leaders in arms racing and arms control. During the Clinton administration, with the progress in strategic arms reductions, we have seen how former adversaries can escape the arms race spiral and modify their relationship, which now includes joint construction of a space station with Canada, Russia, the European Union, and Japan. In 2000, the Russian parliament finally ratified the Strategic Arms Reduction Treaty II, but concerns about a renewed arms race were raised by the American interest in building a ballistic missile defense system to guard against a nuclear threat from Iran or North Korea.

Money.　National spending on deterrent and defensive weapons systems is a key measure of whether or not nations are engaged in an arms race. Soviet and U.S. military spending was more or less constant after World War II until the 1960s. "An arms race, of course, need not imply an upward spiral, but it does imply competition. If two long-distance runners maintain a steady pace, we consider them to be in a race just as much as if their speed were continually increasing; it is the element of competition, or interaction, that makes the race."[4] The United States still spends like a superpower on its national security concerns, using 5 to 8 percent of its gross national product (GNP) for military purposes, compared with 3 to 4 percent by the Germans and 1 percent by the Japanese.[5]

The Soviet Union made perhaps the greatest sacrifice for national security, reportedly spending upwards of 15 percent of its GNP on defense until the USSR collapsed.

Technology.　Spending is a reflection of both arms racing and the cost of developing the sophisticated technologies of the nuclear age. What one rival develops, the other must counter and/or match (see Table II.1). The United States still approaches its arms control talks in eight categories that reflect technological research and development (1–6) and, to a lesser extent, politics (7–8):

1. strategic weapons
2. intermediate-range weapons
3. conventional weapons
4. chemical weapons
5. space weapons

TABLE II.1   Weapons System Competition

	Year Deployed	
Technology	U.S.	U.S.S.R.
Atomic Bomb	1945	1949
Thermonuclear Bomb	1952	1953
Intercontinental Ballistic Missile (ICBM)	1960	1957
Multiple Independently Targetable Reentry Vehicle (MIRV)	1970	1975
Cruise Missile	1976	1980
Strategic Defense Initiative	?	

6. nuclear testing

7. nuclear nonproliferation

8. confidence-building measures

Numbers. Numbers, finally, represent the last and most traditional aspect of arms racing. The most difficult to verify and the most susceptible to political exploitation, the statistics of the arms race came under the spotlight again as the Reagan administration successfully concluded its negotiation of an Intermediate-Range Nuclear Force (INF) reduction agreement with the Soviet Union. That treaty subsequently focused attention on strategic weapons (U.S.–U.S.S.R. range) and the imbalance of conventional (Warsaw Pact and NATO) forces in Europe. Plans to reduce strategic weapons by up to two thirds are underway. Chapter 6 examines the basic concepts (national security, deterrence, Cold War, etc.) and characteristics (perceptions, money, technology, and numbers) of the competitive and conflictual relationship that the United States and Soviet Union waged until one of the adversaries collapsed in 1991, and outlines changes in the realm of weapons of mass destruction, arms racing, and proliferation since then.

NOTES

1. *Arms Control Update* (Washington, DC: Office of Public Affairs, U.S. Arms Control and Disarmament Agency, July 1988), no. 7.
2. *1986 Report on State Prison Inmates* (Washington, DC: Bureau of Justice Statistics, U.S. Department of Justice, 1986).
3. Ibid.
4. Bruce Russett, *The Prisoners of Insecurity* (New York: W.H. Freeman, 1983), p. 70.
5. John Kenneth Galbraith, "Guns or Butter," *Bulletin of the Atomic Scientists,* June/July 1981, p. 13.

CHAPTER 4

The Politics of Crime in America

Serious and violent crime (murder, rape, robbery and aggravated assault) declined by an average 7 percent in 1999, continuing a pattern begun in 1991, and representing the longest continuous decline on record.

—FBI (2000)

Now is not the time to become complacent. Let's try harder. We must redouble our efforts by providing alternatives to crime, as well as tough enforcement.

—Attorney General Janet Reno (May 2000)

The primary purpose of the U.S. government is to secure American citizens' lives and property. This purpose, stated explicitly in the Preamble to the Constitution, has remained a difficult challenge in postindustrial America. The economic security of U.S. citizens is threatened by technological changes in our society, such as the shift away from manufacturing and toward a more high-tech and service-oriented workplace. In addition to economic insecurity, crime continues to pose a threat to Americans, with 6 homicides per 100,000 adults 25 years or older reported in 1999. This is sharply down from the rate of 8.1 per 100,000 in 1981, according to the FBI, but oddly, Americans do not seem to feel much safer, and U.S. taxpayers now spend more on prisons than on schools. Crime in America has also grown more complex and more difficult to control. While authorities wrestle with the persistent traditional forms of violent crime against persons (assault, robbery, rape, murder) and property (burglary, motor vehicle theft, arson, larceny), social and technological changes in our society have produced new types of crime (cybercrime, hate crimes, carjacking). Physical and economic security, and the evolving threats to them, remain high on the political agenda as the United States enters the twenty-first century.

Crime, in both its traditional and its new dimensions, is the focus of this first chapter in Part II, Violence and Politics. The many dimensions of crime in America—the persistent types of crime as well as new types of criminal activity—are examined, beginning with the debate over the sources or causes of crime.

SOURCES: CRIME

Criminals target either people or property, committing crimes that traditionally have been categorized in one of two ways: violent crimes (those that result in personal injury, such as murder, rape, assault, child abuse) and crimes against property (robbery, arson, theft). In addition, suicide represents a crime against oneself (in 1999, suicide was the leading cause of death among American teenagers), and with the prevalence of computers in America's homes and workplaces, theft of intellectual property or damage caused by viruses and worms, as well as espionage, is now a leading concern for law enforcement.

Crimes, especially the most deviant and violent crimes, are usually explained by one of several competing theories on the causes of crime. These theories do not represent merely an intellectual debate. Theories on the causes of crime are reflected in policies regarding the appropriate punishment of crimes and methods for the prevention of criminal behavior.

Environmental Causes of Crime

The 1960s and 1970s were a period in which liberal theories identified environmental factors as causes of crime; that is, poverty and social deprivation were seen as root causes of crime, and broad social and economic reform programs were designed to alleviate or remedy these conditions. Studies had shown, for example, that low-income areas have higher crime rates[1] and that 8 percent of the sons of unemployed men have a record of violent crime, compared with 2 percent of those whose fathers are employed.[2] Likewise, assault is more often committed by the sons of unemployed fathers.[3] Programs that included CETA (Comprehensive Education Training Act) and Head Start were designed to alleviate problems (unemployment, child neglect) thought to underlie the obvious problem of crime.

The policymakers of the 1980s, placing more emphasis on individual responsibility and responding to a public perception that crime was increasing, emphasized tougher law enforcement, longer and mandatory jail sentences, and the priority of victims' rights above those of the accused. (The public's perception of a rising crime rate was accurate until 1991, when a steady decline in violent crime began. The Department of Justice's National Crime Survey found that violent crime rates dropped nearly 11 percent from 1973 to 1986, but the number of injuries—roughly 2.2 million each year—did not decline at all. Serious and violent crime rates began dropping in 1991 and now represent the longest decline since 1970.) The conservative approach focused on deterring undesirable individual behavior instead of placing the blame for crime on other sources.

Convinced that swift and severe punishment would deter potential criminals as well as repeat offenders, conservative policymakers of the 1980s put record numbers of Americans in jail, with nearly 3 percent[4] of American adults in prison, on parole, or on probation by the end of 1996. The 1980s approach to the crime problem, however, also failed to alleviate personal and property crimes. The percentage of victims of rape, robbery, and assault who were physically injured during the attacks increased from 1979 to 1986;[5] the increase in the overall number of offenses during 1987 and 1988 reversed a five-year decline in crimes reported by victims.[6]

Continuing through the late 1980s and into 1990, violent crime showed a disturbingly steady increase, rising 10 percent from 1989 to 1990. FBI figures on violent crime for 1991 and 1992 began to reflect a decline in this trend, but as a result of aggressive policing and prosecution, the United States now faces the problem of severely overcrowded prisons, with taxpayers reluctant to spend more money on new prison facilities. By 1990, forty-two states were under court orders to reduce overcrowding in prisons and jails, which were at 122 percent capacity.

The Bureau of Justice Statistics reported in 1999 that the large number of drug offenders was a major reason for the increase in the prisoner population. In 1977, 11.5 percent of commitments to prison were for drug-related offenses, but by 1990, nearly 33 percent of new prisoners were drug offenders. New prison beds, however, cost taxpayers $50,000 each to build and $15,000 to $40,000 per year to maintain. This creates a situation that Senator Phil Gramm (R-Tex.) described as follows: "In America today, we have crime without punishment. Forty thousand people were arrested on felony charges last year [1988] in the District of Columbia, but only 1,400 of them went on to prison."[7]

As law enforcement officers arrest more suspects than the criminal justice system can prosecute or incarcerate, the problem of recidivism also grows more obvious. In the United States, 69 percent of prisoners received another conviction within six years of their parole, in a system that tried 1.5 million cases in 1988, with more than 1 million convictions.[8]

Senator Gramm has called for the construction of 70,000 more prison beds. "We want a national crime emergency to allow us to go out on closed military bases, pitch tents, use temporary buildings, put the violent criminals in jail and keep them there. And do it now."[9] In reply, Representative Charles Rangel (D-N.Y.) said, "It's absolutely ridiculous to believe that our first line of defense should be spending the billions of dollars that we are building jails, without being willing to spend millions of dollars in finding out the reasons why people have this antisocial behavior."[10]

While state and federal authorities debated rising crime rates and prison overcrowding, the problem reached a crisis stage at the Southern Ohio Correctional Facility in Lucasville, Ohio. Inmates there took control of L Block on April 1, 1993, and held it for eleven days protesting prison conditions. The siege became the longest such uprising in U.S. history. Prisoner demands included a reduction in overcrowding, a revision of visitation and phone privileges, and an end to integrated cell assignments. Six guards were captured; one guard and nine inmates died in the savage prison riot. The Ohio legislature responded by approving the hiring of more guards, but by 1999, the Ohio prison system remained at 175 percent capacity. For the United States overall, the prison population in 1999 stood at 680 people incarcerated per 100,000. This figure is ten times higher than the rate in any Western European nation. The only comparable imprisonment rate is in Russia, which is experiencing a serious crisis following the collapse of the communist state in 1991.

Reflecting these statistics, law and order issues were consistent themes in the 1996 presidential campaign. Candidates Clinton and Dole both called for tougher anticrime measures, and both supported the death penalty. Dole supported the "three strikes and you're out" policy of life sentences for third-time felony offenders, while Clinton took credit for tough new gun control legislation (the Brady Law and the assault weapons ban) and for measures to assist local communities in hiring more police officers. The unresolved question of environmental causes of crime (e.g., unemployment and the rise in drug-trafficking arrests) has recently been joined by an alternative approach to crime called the genetic or biological approach. If borne out by research, this new approach may lead to an entirely new set of American policies on crime.

Genetic Causes of Crime

The most important genetic factor in crime is gender. Men in prison greatly outnumber women who are incarcerated (over 90 percent of the 2 million Americans in state and federal prisons in June 1999 were male).[11] In addition, men are responsible for five times more violent crime in the United States, and mounting research indicates that the causes of that violent behavior include both sociological and biological factors, such as gender, age, intelligence, and temperament. American social convention, which expects and tolerates more aggressive behavior from men, does not explain the significantly greater criminality in males. Research across cultures indicates that men are generally more aggressive than women, but more important, these gender differences are found much too early in children to be the product of socialization. Researchers have found that aggressiveness can be altered in experiments that modify levels of sex hormones.[12]

The biology versus environment (or nature versus nurture) debate has been investigated by C. Robert Cloninger, a psychiatrist at the Washington University–St. Louis School of Medicine, who found that adopted male children with criminal birth parents were four times more likely to become criminals themselves than were adopted boys whose birth parents had no record of criminal behavior. Dr. Cloninger observed, "I don't think there's a specific gene for criminality itself, only genetic factors that influence susceptibility."[13] Psychologist Sarnoff Mednick also found an environmental correlation in a study at the University of Southern California. Dr. Mednick's study included more than 14,000 Danish boys who had been adopted between 1924 and 1947. In that sample, 24.5 percent of the boys with both criminal birth parents and criminal adoptive parents had criminal records. Twenty percent of the adoptees whose birth parents had criminal records but whose adoptive parents did not were convicted of a crime. When only the adoptive parents had criminal records, 14.7 percent of the boys were convicted; and finally, when neither birth nor adoptive parents had a criminal record, only 13.5 percent of the children had criminal convictions.

Among other genetic factors, low intelligence has increasingly been linked to criminal behavior, especially violent, impulsive crimes such as robbery and rape. James Q. Wilson and Richard J. Herrnstein argue in *Crime and Human Nature* that low intelligence quotient (IQ) test scores relate to criminals' diminished ability to grasp the consequences of their behavior. Low IQ scores often cause children difficulty in the classroom, instilling anger and frustration that can later contribute to delinquency and criminal behavior.

A study currently underway at the University of Minnesota examining identical twins separated at birth and adopted by different parents has confirmed the heritability of temperament or behavior patterns such as shyness or boldness. Criminals, especially recidivists, often dispay temperamental traits of impulsiveness and an inclination to take risks—characteristics they may have inherited.[14]

A Danish study of identical and fraternal twins conducted by Dr. Karl O. Christiansen further confirms the genetic connection. Christiansen's study found that if one fraternal twin had a criminal conviction, the other twin likewise developed a criminal record 12 percent of the time. Among identical twins, the rate jumped to 35 percent, consistent with the greater genetic similarity in identical twins.[15] Identical twins, however, are also more likely to be treated alike, making it difficult to separate environmental from genetic factors in this study, in which the twins had not been separated since birth.

In 1993, Han Brunner, a geneticist at University Hospital in Nijmegen, the Netherlands, added another piece to the genetic puzzle. He studied a Dutch family known for its history of aggressive behavior from 1870 to 1978. The researcher found a pattern of uncles and male cousins who were prone to impulsive outbursts that ranged from exhibitionism to arson to attempted rape. Women in the family showed no signs of abnormal behavior. DNA studies of seventeen male family members aged twenty to fifty revealed that the five who were occasionally aggressive or impulsively violent were deficient in a gene that affects the chemical transmission of messages to the brain. The twelve who behaved normally did not exhibit this mutation. The defective gene was not producing normal levels of the enzyme monoamine oxidase (MAOA), which causes the decomposition of serotonin, another brain chemical. The altered metabolism of serotonin is known to affect aggression in animals, and researchers believe a similar pattern will prove to be the case in humans as well. The Dutch researchers expect to find this condition in other men, and they believe it can be treated with diet, drugs, and, in the future, with gene therapy (see Chapter 8, Biotechnology).

Gender, intelligence, and temperamental heredity are outranked, however, by youthfulness as the established leading predictor of criminal behavior. Crimes are committed by more than 80 percent of children under eighteen years of age. Only 3 percent of these offenders are actually arrested and prosecuted for their crimes,[16] because American society and its criminal justice system treat criminal minor children like offenders with diminished capacity to comprehend their actions and their consequences. First offenses usually are not prosecuted at all. Despite the public's horror and outrage at teenagers involved in school shootings such as the 1999 Columbine High School disaster, the Justice Department's Office of Juvenile

Justice and Delinquency Prevention reported in November 1999 that violent crime by juveniles had fallen to its lowest level in a decade, declining 30 percent since 1994. The decline was attributed to a decline in the demand for crack cocaine, truces between crack gangs, and stiffer sentences for repeat offenders.

Criminal justice experts identify several causes of juvenile crime, including an increase in leisure time, a 60 percent teen unemployment rate, peer pressure, lack of parental supervision, and child abuse. Despite uncertainty over the causes of juvenile crime, demographics account for the generational impact that teenage baby boomers had on the crime rate in the 1960s—a sharp increase over the previous decade—and the similar surge in crime among their children in the 1980s. As these individuals age, the crime rate attributed to them also decreases. Prevention programs and increased community support for first-time offenders have also been credited by Attorney General Janet Reno with lowering the incidence of juvenile offenses.

Public concern over violent juvenile crime remains so intense, however, that several states now are moving to impose capital punishment on sixteen- and seventeen-year-olds convicted of murder after having prosecuted them as adults in the criminal justice system. Because the juvenile murder rate tripled from 1950 to 1993, and gang activity grew at a similar rate, the public's attention to and concern with law enforcement will not abate until a steady downward trend in juvenile crime has been established. Nonetheless, the impact of age on crime should be clear: When the national crime rate was peaking in the 1980s, the baby-boom generation was about sixteen to thirty-four years old, the age group most likely to commit crime. In 1999, that generation ranged in age from thirty-four to fifty-three—past the prime age for criminal activity.

The newest theory about why crime has declined among youth was put forward in a report published by economists John J. Donohue (Stanford Law School) and Steven D. Levitt (University of Chicago). They contend that fewer crimes are being committed because many potential juvenile criminals were never born. Their study found that the decline in youthful crime coincided with the period when children born after the legalization of abortion (*Roe v. Wade*, 1973) would have attained the peak age for criminal activity. They found that states with the highest abortion rates saw greater reductions in crime than states with low abortion rates. Critics of the report note that many factors have contributed to the decline in juvenile crime, including low unemployment, the end of the crack epidemic, and the rise of the prison population.

Drug-Related Causes of Crime

In addition to the environmental and biological causes of crime, researchers, law enforcement officials, and policymakers agree that crack cocaine use is directly related to violent behavior. Scientists have long known that alcohol depresses inhibitions and impairs physical functions, contributing to a variety of crimes such as assault, drunk driving, and murder. Heroin addicts frequently are arrested for committing violent crimes when the drug is wearing off and they need money to obtain their next fix. However, in a national study conducted through a cocaine crisis hot line, crack users revealed a tendency to commit violent crimes while high on the drug.

Of the cocaine users who called the toll-free hot line during the autumn of 1988 (200 women, 450 men):

- 45.7 percent said they had violent arguments or fights while intoxicated on cocaine
- 13 percent admitted to robbery while on the drug
- 7 percent reported spouse- or child-battering while under the influence of crack
- 1 percent admitted committing murder while stoned[17]

A 1998 study by the Justice Department and the Census Bureau confirmed arguments made by law enforcement officials that the drug-related crime that plagued America's major cities most severely in the late 1980s and early 1990s was due to the spread of the cheap, smokable form of cocaine known as crack. Violent crime surged with the crack epidemic beginning in 1985, and both violent crime and the use of crack took an unpredicted nosedive in 1991.

Are certain individuals genetically predisposed to drug dependence, or are drugs an environmental cause of crime, a hazard that many children in poor, urban settings cannot avoid? (Scientific studies have established, for example, that male children of alcoholics are four to five times more likely to become dependent on alcohol.) The use of designer drugs and heroin is increasingly noted among middle-class teenagers and college students, while rape drugs and binge drinking continue to be associated with violent crime across the United States, disregarding boundaries of race and class.

Cocaine, of course, was not confined to America's slums; it found its way into middle-class junior and senior high schools, as well as into corporate offices. Like other facets of crime in postindustrial America, cocaine use and the criminal activity associated with it have become widespread and complex problems. Of concern to lawmakers today is the discrepancy in sentencing between crack and powder cocaine possession. The status of these problems—how American society and law enforcement are responding—reflects the many changes our society is undergoing and represents at least some new problems that will persist in the new century.

STATUS: AMERICA'S WAR ON CRIMINALS

In August 1993, President Clinton introduced a major crime bill that included $3.4 billion for 50,000 new police officers, a diversion program to send youthful first-time offenders to "boot camps," a gun control component (known as the Brady Bill, mandating a five-working-day waiting period on handgun purchases), and the death penalty for forty-seven crimes, including drive-by shootings. During the 1996 election, he proudly noted having assisted local communities in hiring over 20,000 law enforcement personnel and pointed to a decline in gun violence in 1994 and 1995 due to the Brady Law waiting period to buy a handgun and the ban on assault weapons. As the FBI reported a 7 percent drop in serious crimes (murder, rape, assault, robbery, burglary, auto theft, and larceny) in 1999, the eighth consecutive year of decline in crimes reported by 17,000 police agencies across the nation, President Clinton noted "this confirms our anti-crime strategy—more police officers on the beat, fewer illegal guns and violent criminals on the street—is having a powerful impact." These three policy emphases of the 1990s are being carried forward as the United States enters the twenty-first century—policies that continue to focus on

1. more resources devoted to prosecution and punishment of criminals, including the death penalty;
2. gun control;
3. a "war" on drugs.

A New Approach to the War on Crime

President Clinton campaigned in 1992 on a platform that called for reducing the federal budget deficit, but his 1993 crime bill called for new anticrime spending. Republicans generally supported the proposal for its "tough on crime" measures—putting more police officers on the streets and limiting prisoners convicted of capital crimes to filing no more than one "habeas corpus" appeal after their final state appeal. Republicans also widely supported the expansion of categories of crime subject to the death penalty. Democrats supported the more liberal and innovative proposals in the crime package that would provide an alternative criminal justice approach to juvenile offenders and drug offenders, and they were more supportive of the Brady Bill. The Clinton crime package offered something to both liberals and conservatives, and it sought both tougher and more innovative remedies for the nation's crime problems. Paying for the proposals at a time when balancing the budget was a priority, and with the public still opposed to new taxes, was nearly as difficult as finding viable solutions to crime. Both the White House and Congress recognized the existence of a crisis in law enforcement that state and local police describe as a war they cannot win with the resources now available to them. The crisis has two dimensions:

1. The introduction of aggressive law enforcement and mandatory sentencing that took place in the 1980s;
2. The failure to match these aggressive new steps with legislation for more spending on judges, prosecutors, public defenders, jails, and prisons (see Figure 4.1).

In 1978, there were 284,000 inmates in state and federal prisons; in 1988, more than 627,000 inmates were housed in overcrowded facilities. By 1993, the inmate population exceeded 925,000, and in 1996, the prison population exceeded 1,690,940. At the close of 1999, 1.8 million inmates were being held in prison. Court dockets are clogged, and inmates are spending less and less time in jail. The percentage of prisoners serving six months or less rose from 8 percent in 1982 to 44 percent in 1998. The forty-two states under court orders to reduce overcrowding often must release some inmates to make room for more violent criminals, such as rapists and murderers. Plea bargaining is increasingly used to keep some offenders out of prison or to impose shorter sentences on them. The result of the prison overcrowding problem is that the average prison term has dropped from eighteen months to one year,[18] and criminals are back on the streets more quickly than ever.

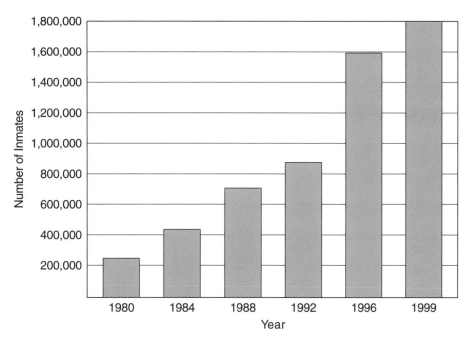

FIGURE 4.1 U.S. Inmate Population (state and federal prisoners)

Source: Bureau of Justice Statistics (Washington, DC: U.S. Government Printing Office, 2000).

The 1989 war-on-crime package included $1 billion to expand federal prison facilities for an additional 24,000 prisoners, as well as funds to hire 1,600 new federal prosecutors and 825 new agents for the FBI, the U.S. Marshal's Service, and the Bureau of Alcohol, Tobacco, and Firearms. Unfortunately, these facilities and personnel had no impact on the crimes that concern most Americans: murder, rape, assault, robbery, and violent drug-trafficking offenses. State and local police fighting these crimes did not enjoy any benefits from the anticrime package. Only 120 of the 47,700 prisoners in federal penitentiaries are serving sentences for murder. Of federal prison inmates, 83 percent currently serve time for federal offenses such as tax evasion, embezzlement, counterfeiting, and nonviolent drug offenses.

America's cities and states, having stepped up the war on crime, now confront serious problems not only in law enforcement but also with legislatures and executive officials who have underfunded and understaffed their courts, jails, and prisons. The state of Texas, for example, spent $288 million in 1983 expanding its prison system, another $500 million in 1988, and it was still unable in 1994 to house all the men and women convicted in Texas courts. The city of Washington, D.C., gave early releases to more than 3,000 inmates from 1987 to 1989 to relieve prison overcrowding. Los Angeles resorted to erecting tent jails in 1988 to house a flood of summer prisoners from drug crackdowns before prisoner advocates forced the city to dismantle the facility. Tougher law enforcement (demanded by the public),

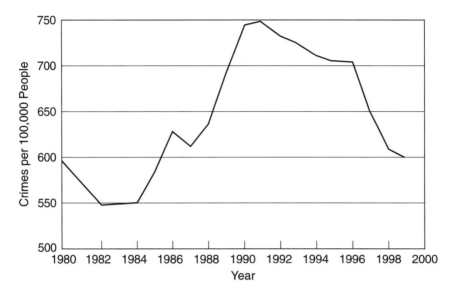

FIGURE 4.2 Annual Violent Crime Rate per 100,000 Population

Source: Federal Bureau of Investigation, *Uniform Crime Report* (Washington, DC: U.S. Government Printing Office, 2000).

underfunding (the result of tax-shy legislators), and a relatively high crime rate have combined to create a crisis in America's prison system. In Figure 4.2, the trend in the crime rate is depicted.

Despite the lack of substantial new resources to fight crime, or perhaps because old methods were not working and new resources were not forthcoming, an important change in the philosophy of policing has been underway since the late 1980s known as "community policing." New York, Chicago, and Detroit accounted for a 32 percent drop in the nation's homicide rate in 1995, and all three share a similar shift to aggressive tactics to put more uniformed officers on the streets and to get guns off the streets.

But the public sends its legislators mixed signals. Elections through 1996 rewarded candidates with platforms that were tough on crime and promised no new taxes, which contributed to the fiscal crisis in the criminal justice system. Recent public opinion polls, however, indicate Americans' willingness to spend more money fighting crime, indicating that Americans continue to fear violent crime, despite a steady five-year decline in its incidence.

Capital Punishment

In his anticrime package, President Clinton also raised the ultimate political issue in law enforcement: the death penalty. During President George H. Bush's administration (1989–1993), capital punishment was reinstated for murders committed by hired killers, hostage takers, terrorists, and racketeers. The president also proposed amending federal laws so that the death penalty for bank robberies resulting in death, train hijackings, murders committed by federal prisoners serving life sentences, espionage, treason, and assassination of federal officials all would come into compliance with Supreme Court procedural requirements and, thus, be enforceable. (The death penalty for murders committed in the course of drug conspiracies was revised and enacted in 1988.) By his actions, consistent with his campaign platform in 1992, President Clinton joined one of the most intense political debates in the arena of American criminal justice.

Most of the developed Western democracies, including Great Britain, Canada, France, Federal Republic of Germany, the Netherlands, Switzerland, Denmark, Norway, Sweden, Belgium, and Italy, have abolished or suspended the death penalty. Capital punishment has also been abolished in Australia, New Zealand, Brazil, Argentina, Colombia, Venezuela, Finland, Iceland, Portugal, and Costa Rica, among others. The United States (where only thirty-seven states currently impose death sentences) finds itself in the company of more than 100 nations, such as Russia, India, and most Arab states, that still practice capital punishment. The United States observed a court-ordered moratorium on capital punishment from 1967 to 1977 because the inequitable imposition of the death penalty was determined to violate the Eighth Amendment's prohibition of cruel and unusual punishment. Most of the individuals subjected to the death penalty prior to 1967 had murdered a white victim or had raped a white woman. (University of Iowa Professor David Baldus found in a 1983 study that the murderer of a white victim was 4.3 times more likely to be given the death sentence in Georgia than the killer of a black victim. In another study of executions of rapists between 1930 and 1964, 455 men were executed, 405 of them black. In the South, blacks who raped white women were eighteen times more likely to be sentenced to death than were blacks who raped blacks or whites who raped whites or blacks.)

Since 1977, however, thirty-seven states have revised their laws and sentencing guidelines to conform with the Supreme Court's standards, and capital punishment again is carried out in the United States. Seventeen states and Washington, D.C., use the electric chair; ten states employ the gas chamber to execute prisoners convicted of capital crimes and sentenced to death; four states hang convicts or employ lethal injections; one state offers a choice of hanging or the firing squad. With increased public concern over rising crime rates, support for capital punishment increased in the 1990s until doubts again were raised by studies showing that the penalty has not been fairly imposed, as well as by the freeing of seventy death row inmates due to DNA evidence that exonerated them. From 1976 to May 1998, 373 executions were carried out by thirteen states. Since 1983, there has been an average of nineteen executions per year. More than 3,500 inmates were on death row by mid-1999, having postponed their punishment through a complex appeals process, which both President Clinton and the Congress have worked to shorten. Those legal remedies are nearly exhausted, and capital punishments will continue to take place—although at least one state, Illinois, has suspended executions. Illinois Governor George Ryan issued a moratorium on executions when he learned in February 2000 that thirteen inmates from his state's prison system had been released since 1987 because of flaws in the criminal justice system that had placed them on death row. In June 2000, Columbia University released a study led by law professor James S. Liebman that examined state and federal court records of death penalty trials. Considered to be the most extensive study of its kind ever conducted, the report found that two of every three convictions were overturned on appeal due to serious errors by defense attorneys or prosecutors and withholding of evidence by police. While more states are expected to join Illinois' suspension of executions, public opinion remains strongly in support of the death penalty, with polls showing between 70 and 80 percent favoring capital punishment. During the 2000 presidential race, candidates George W. Bush and Al Gore both campaigned as supporters of capital punishment.

Like the debate over the root causes of crime, capital punishment is intensely debated as either a powerful deterrent or as an inhumane, immoral remedy and punishment. Although the Supreme Court has prohibited the inequitable imposition of the death penalty, it has not objected to the principle of capital punishment. The court's 1976 decision in *Gregg v. Georgia* upheld the death penalty imposed through "guided discretion," wherein juries and judges weigh aggravating and mitigating circumstances. (Proof of an unusually cruel murder would be considered an aggravating circumstance, whereas proof that showed the murderer was raised in a violent and abusive home might be considered a mitigating circumstance.) The debate over capital punishment appears to have left the courts and returned to the states' executive and legislative branches and to the public arena in general. The debate involves many arguments and claims, including the following in favor of capital punishment:

1. Frightening and irreversible punishment deters capital crime.[19]
2. Society owes the victims of heinous crimes swift and terrible punishment of the perpetrators of those crimes.
3. Capital punishment prevents recidivism.
4. Society should not have to pay to support dangerous criminals serving life sentences.
5. Capital punishment will prevent criminals from passing undesirable hereditary traits to their offspring.
6. The Bible's Old Testament, in Exodus 21:23–25, clearly establishes the morality of punishment proportional to the crime. "If there is serious injury, you are to take life for life, eye for eye, tooth for tooth, hand for hand, foot for foot, burn for burn, wound for wound, bruise for bruise."
7. Capital punishment will prevent an aroused public from taking justice into its own hands, as in the case of vigilantism.
8. Not all criminals can be rehabilitated.

Arguments against capital punishment include the following:

1. Society should not punish a violent crime with an equally violent act. Capital punishment diminishes the value society places on life.

2. Two wrongs do not make a right. Incarcerated criminals can perform acts of restitution and may be rehabilitated. Executed prisioners can do neither.

3. Any form of murder is morally wrong, even if it is authorized by the legal system.

4. Capital punishment does not deter crime.[20]

5. Capital punishment has not been meted out fairly in the American criminal justice system.

6. The innocent may be executed unfairly, as, for example in the case of Randall Dale Adams, who was saved from a wrongful execution in 1989 by the documentary film *The Thin Blue Line*. Since the return of capital punishment in 1976, 87 inmates have been freed from death row because of errors in the legal process. DNA testing may free even more.

7. The United States Constitution's Eighth Amendment states "excessive bail shall not be required, nor excessive fines imposed, nor cruel and unusual punishment inflicted."

8. The Bible states clearly in the Fifth Commandment, "Thou shalt not kill," and in the New Testament, "Do not take revenge, my friends, but leave room for God's wrath, for it is written: 'It is mine to avenge; I will repay.'"(Romans 12:19)

Guns and Gun Control

A well-regulated militia being necessary to the security of a free state, the right of the people to keep and bear arms shall not be infringed.

—Second Amendment, Constitution of the United States

Prisons, capital punishment, gun control, and drugs dominated the political agenda on crime control in the 1990s, and will dominate it in the twenty-first century. The issue of gun ownership and gun control reappeared on the political horizon in the 1980s. Several dramatic events focused public and law enforcement agencies' attention on the widespread ownership of guns in America:

- In 1981, President Reagan was nearly killed by John Hinckley Jr., who had also tried to smuggle a handgun on board an airliner in 1980.

- Police agencies throughout the 1980s found themselves outgunned by criminals using automatic and semiautomatic weapons.

- Tragic murders of children in grade schools in Winnetka, Illinois, in 1988, and in Stockton, California, in 1989, by mentally disturbed individuals using firearms drew intense media coverage and finally triggered bans on semiautomatic assault rifles in some cities and states. President Bush also requested that Congress ban the importation of foreign-made assault rifles but allow U.S. manufacturers to continue making and selling the weapons.

- In 1992, rioters in Los Angeles targeted gun stores and pawnshops, stealing at least 1,700 weapons. And in 1993, the murder of foreign tourists in Florida and the killing of James Jordan (father of NBA superstar Michael Jordan) preceded President Clinton's announcement of new gun control measures. He sought a five-day waiting period for the purchase of guns (the Brady Bill) and signed an executive order to ban the import of assault pistols while expanding controls on gun dealers to include fingerprinting and background checks. In 1999, two teenagers killed a dozen of their classmates at Columbine High School before killing themselves.

What is meant by gun control, and how might it ameliorate America's crime problem? Gun control is an umbrella term encompassing a wide range of measures regulating the behavior of gun manufacturers, wholesalers, retailers, and purchasers. Gun control may involve legislation to require the registration of guns or permits to carry them; recently, legislation has emphasized heavier sentences for crimes committed with the use of guns. President Bush's crime package proposed to double the five-year minimum sentence for using a semiautomatic firearm in a crime. Even the ammunition guns require is subject to gun control. Local, state, and federal governments have passed laws regulating ammunition, firearms, and explosives since the early 1900s. The shipping of concealable firearms by mail has been banned since 1927; the 1934 National Firearms Act established the first tax and registration requirements on gun owners.

Licensing of firearms and ammunition dealers and manufacturers began in 1938. Federal regulation of interstate transport of guns and ammunition began that year as well. The 1954 Exportation-Importation of Firearms Act expanded federal control of guns, and the 1958 Federal Aviation Act banned firearms from commercial aircraft. In 1968, the Gun Control Act sought to tighten further the transport and sale of firearms, empowering the Bureau of Alcohol, Tobacco, and Firearms (part of the U.S. Department of the Treasury) to enforce the federal regulations. Cities and states, however, supervise how citizens may acquire and own guns, and there is great variety in the purchase, waiting period, and registration requirements they impose on gun dealers and owners. Estimates vary, but from 20 to 25 percent of all American families may own handguns.[21] Widespread gun ownership, however, is matched by widespread support for gun control. In a 1993 Yankelovich poll, 92 percent of Americans favored a five-day waiting period before a gun could be purchased to enable law enforcement to conduct background checks. Sixty-five percent agreed that stricter gun control laws are a necessary part of any anticrime bill.[22] President Bush in 1991 and 1992 opposed the Brady Bill, which proposed a waiting period prior to handgun purchase to permit background checks and to provide a "cooling off" period for those buying a weapon in a fit of rage. The bill failed in 1992 when Senate opponents filibustered the legislation. President Clinton supported the Brady Bill and signed it into law in November 1993, after approval in the House and Senate.

Why do Americans simultaneously own guns and favor gun control? In 1992, 1.9 million violent offenses were reported in the United States, including 22,540 homicides. A firearm was used in seven of every ten murders.[23] Table 4.1 shows that, compared with other developed democracies, our society suffers an extraordinarily

TABLE 4.1   Cases of Violent Crime Involving a Firearm, 1996

United States	340,000 per 248,000,000
Great Britain	360 per 57,000,000
Federal Republic of Germany	300 per 60,000,000
Japan	171 per 123,000,000

Source: Bureau of Justice Statistics (Washington, DC: U.S. Government Printing Office, 1997).

high rate of violent crime using firearms. Gun violence rose steadily in the United States from 1985 to 1994, when a decline in armed violence began to appear. In October 1996, the FBI reported that murders committed with a gun dropped 11.6 percent from the previous year.

Repeated gun control efforts, including the May 1986 measure by which Congress effectively doubled the price of machine guns by banning future manufacture for private sale, and the signing of the assault weapons ban by President Clinton in September 1994 that outlawed the sale and possession of nineteen types of assault-style rifles for a decade, reflect the public's tolerance for gun control measures in the face of high levels of violent crime. (President Clinton also went on several well-publicized hunting trips during 1994 to show that he was a sportsman who enjoyed hunting, hoping to retain the support of fellow gun hunters.) Unlike the other nations described in Table 4.1, which forbid private ownership of guns or heavily regulate it, the United States remains unable to regulate illegal gun ownership by private citizens. Even under new guidelines and waiting periods for background checks, many states still lack the technology to check a criminal record in all fifty states, and any prospective gun buyer who is at least eighteen years old can check the "no" boxes on questions inquiring whether he or she is a convicted felon or whether he or she had ever been imprisoned or jailed for drunkenness, drug addiction, or mental illness, and likely can obtain a gun within five days of the original inquiry.[24]

Despite efforts by the powerful anti–gun control lobby, led by the National Rifle Association (NRA), to slow or block any further restrictions on gun ownership, however, cities and states have begun considering legislation to control or ban assault rifles and other semi- and fully automatic weapons. In May 1989, California Governor George Deukmejian signed two bills that banned the sale of fifty-five semiautomatic assault rifles, pistols, and shotguns beginning January 1, 1990. The laws permit people who currently and legally own such firearms to keep them if they obtain a permit from the state. This legislation was instigated by the January 1989 attack at an elementary school in Stockton by Patrick Purdy, who killed five children and wounded thirty others with an AK-47 assault rifle and then killed himself. Other states, including Colorado, Louisiana, Michigan, and Rhode Island, saw similar bills introduced, as did numerous cities, among them Los Angeles, Cincinnati, and Dayton, Ohio.

Gun control legislation passed in 1994 in the first term of the Clinton administration focused on gun dealers, requiring face-to-face interviews with federal inspectors, fingerprinting, and higher license fees. In 1997, three years after its passage, this new policy led to a 57 percent drop in the number of gun dealer licenses, according to the Treasury Department; in 1997 124,286 gun-dealer licenses were held in the United States, the lowest number in twenty-two years. In 1999, Congress rejected gun control legislation aimed at tightening oversight of gun shows where unlicensed private individuals buy and sell weapons without conducting background checks.

The violent crime problem facing the United States in the 1990s also has a drug connection, which law enforcement and publicly elected officials are finding as difficult to control as guns.

Drugs and Crime

As the 1980s drew to a close, the connection between illegal drugs and the most pressing crime problems in America became clearer. The nation's capital led the country's murder rate statistics (76 per 100,000 population), due primarily to the violence that accompanies drugs, especially crack.[25] The rise in homicides across the country marked a change in the murder rate, which experts thought had peaked in 1980 with 23,044 victims. The homicide rate dropped in the early eighties, to 18,692 in 1984, but it rose again until 1991. The year 1984 marked the arrival of crack in the United States. With a price tag of $5 for a "rock" or $15 for a vial, crack is a cheap and highly addictive drug that provides an intense but short high and often triggers violent mood swings in its targeted market—the young and poor—especially in the ghetto. After a decade of popularity, crack usage began to fall steadily in the late 1990s, and with it the homicide rate fell once again (see Table 4.2).

In October 1993, Mayor Sharon Pratt Kelly of Washington, D.C., wrote to President Clinton and requested personal authority to deploy National Guard troops to assist D.C. police. (The president said no.) District of Columbia police number approximately 4,500, or roughly twice as many officers per capita as other large cities. The combination of poverty, drugs, and crime in Washington has led to the presence of National Guard troops assisting local police since 1989. The Bureau of the National Guard reports that police in almost every state have been using guard troops since 1989 in support roles to battle drug traffic and the violent crime that accompanies it.

Illegal drug trafficking, especially of crack, produced a set of interrelated crime problems. Drug arrests swamped the criminal justice system. New York City police, for example, made more than 20,000 arrests for crack alone in 1988. By contrast, they had made no crack arrests at all prior to June 1985. Nationally, drug arrests in 1988 totaled 35,261,226, representing a 24 percent increase over 1987.[26] These arrests inundated the courts and filled America's jails and prisons. Not only was the U.S. criminal justice system underequipped to manage a criminal drug problem of these proportions, but the problems created by illegal drugs, and crack in particular, were affecting a growing segment of American society. Six percent of high school seniors admitted in a 1988 survey that they had tried crack. Fourteen percent admitted using some form of cocaine, and the survey did not include dropouts.[27]

By 1995, interest in crack had begun to diminish among teenagers, but newer intoxicants had entered the picture. Khat, the drug of choice in Somalia, is popular

TABLE 4.2   Change in Homicide Rate, 1999

Washington, DC	down 15%
Columbus, OH	down 9%
Chicago, IL	down 9%
Dallas, TX	down 29%

Source: Bureau of Justice Statistics (Washington, DC:
U.S. Government Printing Office, 2000).

in Detroit. Hallucinogens, especially LSD, have reappeared in high schools and on college campuses. Ecstasy, a potent amphetamine, is in vogue in colleges across the country. Marijuana has made a comeback, joined by new designer drugs such as GHB, or gamma hydroxy butyrate, which is often mixed with amphetamines. And the classic hard drug, heroin, is also back in vogue.

Crack has been implicated in the increase in gang activity in large cities. Drive-by shootings in the summer of 1992 terrorized residents of poor neighborhoods in Washington, D.C., while the FBI reported that California gangs like the Bloods and the Crips were franchising their operations into forty-six cities in the Midwest. Law enforcement now confronts at least three types of "organized" crime involvement in drug traffic: street gangs and motorcycle gangs that participate heavily in the crack and speed (amphetamines) traffic; foreign groups, including Jamaicans (known as posses) and Colombians, who deal in marijuana and cocaine; and the traditional branch of organized crime, sometimes called the Mafia, which dominates heroin trafficking. Drugs have overburdened police and the courts, created a problem of overcrowding in America's jails and prisons, led to a jump in the national homicide rate, and contributed to a resurgence in gang activity in our major cities. A research group known as The Sentencing Project reported in 1995 that the "war on drugs" had fallen disproportionately on young black men, who now represent 74 percent of prisoners serving sentences on drug-related charges. Citing U.S. Justice Department figures, 32 percent of black men aged twenty to twenty-nine are in prison or on parole, compared with 6.7 percent of young white men. By 1999, state and federal law enforcement were examining sentencing discrepancies and reporting that the crack market and related violent crimes, including murder and robbery, had all declined simultaneously.

Drugs, including alcohol, are implicated in other threats to public safety as well, including drunk driving, which killed more than 22,000 Americans in 1992, but less than 15,000 in 1999. The spread of the AIDS virus by intravenous (IV) drug users poses perhaps the quietest threat to the public's well-being, although public sympathy for (and media attention paid to) addicts who inject heroin, morphine, or cocaine is extremely low. Confronting such a diverse array of problems stemming from illegal drugs, what are American law enforcement and the nation's political leadership doing to confront this crisis? Figure 4.3 shows the agencies currently involved in the drug enforcement effort.

> *I will not say "we will prevail." It's essential that we win, but it's not inevitable. It may take ten, fifteen or twenty years. . . . I have no illusions that in the course of four years I'm going to solve the drug problem.*
>
> —William J. Bennett, drug czar

Like the war against terrorism, which we study in the next chapter, the war on drugs is an unconventional, low-intensity conflict that involves more than thirty congressional committees and more than thirty-five agencies and organizations, all members of a large bureaucracy with little tradition of interagency cooperation. To enhance their ability to cooperate and coordinate the war on drugs, in 1989 newly

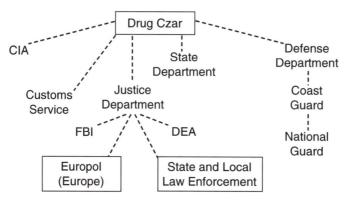

FIGURE 4.3   Agencies Coordinated by the Director for
National Drug Control Policy

elected President Bush appointed the first drug czar, William John Bennett, the former secretary of education. In addition to improved coordination of the bureaucratic effort, Presidents Bush and Clinton and Congress have directed increasingly large amounts of money toward the war on drugs. Between 1981 and 1988, for instance, the United States spent over $20 billion in the fight against drugs. The U.S. Customs Service has spent $700 million to construct and operate a sophisticated system to detect aircraft smuggling drugs across the border, although only 20 percent of the cocaine traffic enters the United States via private planes. Another $50 million has been spent by Customs on a new intelligence system, C3I (Command, Control, Communications, and Intelligence), although the Drug Enforcement Administration (DEA) refuses to permit an interface with its own computer system to share information. Of growing concern is the $250 million the United States spent in Colombia in 1999 to fight the cultivation and trafficking of drugs, making that country third only behind Israel and Egypt as a recipient of foreign aid. Building on a bureaucratic base that spans the Justice, State, and Defense Departments and the CIA, elected officials are providing funds and better coordination to accomplish three tasks in the war on drugs:

1. attack the source
2. target the dealers
3. reduce demand

The U.S. State Department spearheads diplomatic efforts to curtail the foreign supply of drugs (cocaine, marijuana, hashish, heroin) through crop eradication and local law enforcement programs. Colombia, Mexico, and Peru are primary targets, but these efforts are undermined by Latin America's addiction to drug revenues. The CIA has created a new antinarcotics unit to lend analytical and operational support by collecting intelligence and possibly employing covert operations against foreign drug cartels that have established their own well-equipped private armies. The CIA's Counter Narcotics Center includes personnel from the National Security

Agency (providing satellite and other electronic intelligence), the Drug Enforcement Administration, the Customs Service, the Coast Guard, and other agencies.

The Coast Guard and Customs Service attempt to interdict the flow of drugs entering the United States by air, land, and sea. Customs successfully confiscated over $1 billion in 1988, twice its operating budget, from drug traffickers in the form of airplanes, boats, and other property. It is building a new center in Oklahoma City to coordinate the air war. The FBI and DEA target traffickers in the United States and have 12,000 and 3,000 agents, respectively. State and local police also enter the picture at this stage, although they have not enjoyed the funding or coordination available to the federal agencies. In 1999, a joint sting operation in Miami led to the indictment of 58 baggage handlers for American Airlines, along with three law enforcement officials who had been corrupted by drug money from Colombia.

On the demand side, the FBI has established a Drug Demand Reduction Program designed to bolster efforts of local law enforcement. Social and educational leaders around the country have undertaken drug awareness programs, first spotlighted by former first lady Nancy Reagan's "Just Say No" campaign, which was echoed in Bob Dole's 1996 campaign theme "Just Don't Do It." Wider drug testing by employers, including the Zero Tolerance program to test federal employees for drugs begun by President Reagan shortly before leaving office, have also targeted consumers. During Reagan's administration, Secretary of Education Cavazos acknowledged that "as long as our citizens demand illegal drugs, criminals will do whatever is necessary to supply the demand." If the street or retail price of cocaine is an indicator, then the supply has not been reduced. In areas where supply has been at least temporarily staunched, local entrepreneurs have begun manufacturing synthesized drugs such as methamphetamine. William Bennett's prediction of a ten- to twenty-year-long war on drugs may prove to have been overly optimistic.

President Clinton's administration modified the approach taken by his predecessors Reagan and Bush. Clinton trimmed the staff of his first drug czar, Lee P. Brown, from 146 to 25, but he also sought a 7 percent increase in funds for law enforcement and an additional $800 million for drug control and demand-reduction programs targeted at youths. A review of military efforts to interdict drug trafficking got underway in 1993, and two years later, the president appointed retired army general Barry McCaffrey to lead antidrug efforts in his administration. Clinton and Attorney General Janet Reno believed that nonviolent drug offenders should be diverted to drug rehabilitation or reeducation programs, keeping jails and prisons for "unsalvageable thugs." Since 70 percent of the nation's prison inmates are estimated by the administration to have drug problems, they too are a target of treatment programs. Overall, the Reagan/Bush policy of focusing 70 percent of federal antidrug spending on law enforcement and 30 percent on treatment was under scrutiny in 1993 and 1994, with a view to shifting the emphasis to treatment and rehabilitation. The Clinton administration doubled spending on preventive education, but enforcement still consumes 50 percent of anti-drug spending.

President Clinton also received a report from Vice President Al Gore recommending the consolidation of the FBI and DEA to enhance performance and reduce duplication. Stopping short of that goal, the attorney general gave FBI Director

Louis Freeh authority to coordinate investigations with the DEA, Border Patrol, and U.S. Marshal's Service. The administration hoped this move would eliminate instances of FBI and DEA agents refusing to share information, even when investigating the same individual.

The large and complex threat drugs pose to American well-being and security ranges from foreign policy issues to the sociopsychological question Why are Americans so fond of drugs? Alcohol dominates the reasons people check into substance abuse centers, followed by cocaine and heroin use. This particular challenge to law enforcement will persist, and increase, as several states passed legislation legalizing marijuana for medicinal use in 1996 referenda, confirming many observations about Americans' deep-seated ambivalence toward drug use and abuse.

New Crimes on the Political Agenda

In the late 1980s and early 1990s, the issues of punishment (longer prison sentences, the death penalty), violent crime, gun control, and drugs dominated the discussion of crime in America. The debate over victimless crimes—those in which theoretically the only harm done is self-inflicted to the perpetrator (such as gambling and prostitution)—receded against a background of debate involving violent crime and drugs. The crime issue emerging in the 1980s, but still in the shadow of violent crime, was white-collar crime. Violent crimes based on gender (such as stalking and partner battering) or race emerged as dominant issues for the 1990s.

White-collar crime, an umbrella term coined in 1949 by Edwin Sutherland, implies a violation of the law by an individual who uses his or her position or influence for the purpose of illegal gain. In the 1950s and 1960s, criminologists specializing in this new field usually studied antitrust offenses. During the 1970s the emphasis shifted to illegal corporate activity, such as harming workers in nuclear facilities, causing injury to consumers, or damaging the environment. In the late 1980s the focus shifted to the deviant behavior of individuals in the white-collar workplace, with emphases on the stock market and computers. White-collar crime costs U.S. businesses between $40 and $200 billion annually,[28] and the FBI's white-collar crime section is devoting more resources to this problem than ever before, having declared it in 1988 to be one of the top national investigative priorities, along with organized crime, terrorism, and espionage.

In 1986, two well-known figures on Wall Street, Dennis Levine and Ivan Boesky, pleaded guilty to charges of insider trading. Levine paid an $11 million fine, and Boesky agreed to a plea-bargained arrangement in which he paid $100 million in penalties and was sentenced to three years in a minimum-security prison. The Securities and Exchange Commission (SEC) and the FBI continued the investigations, bringing charges against Drexel Burnham Lambert and Michael Milken, the junk bond czar. Because the RICO (Racketeering Influenced and Corrupt Organization) Act was invoked, and Drexel Burnham Lambert might have had its assets seized, the company agreed to a settlement that stripped Milken of millions of dollars in bonuses and benefits. (Milken made $550 million in 1987.) The firm pleaded guilty to six federal felony charges and paid $650 million—a fine four times larger than the SEC's annual budget—to close the largest securities fraud case in history. Federal investigations expanded in 1989 to examine possible trading practice violations on Chicago's two commodity exchanges and four New York futures exchanges. What exactly is insider trading, and why did it assume such a high profile for law enforcement in the 1990s?

The Securities Exchange Act of 1934 prohibits fraud in connection with the sale of any securities, and Rule 14e-3 specifically makes it illegal for anyone with inside information regarding a pending takeover to trade the targeted company's stock. The exotic world of speculating on stock became a major enterprise in the 1980s when American businesses conducted a record number of corporate takeovers and mergers. Firms like Drexel Burnham Lambert traded in high-risk "junk" bonds to bankroll some of the biggest corporate takeovers in history. Insider information regarding those takeovers enabled traders like Levine, Boesky, and some employees at Drexel Burnham Lambert to make huge illegal profits from other investors who did not have the advantage of insider information as to when and what to buy and sell. Risk arbitrage, as speculating in the stock of companies subject to possible takeover bids is known, has focused the attention of Congress and law enforcement on all the futures exchanges, where a broad range of speculative buying and selling is conducted. Congress has the option of strengthening the powers of the Commodity Futures Trading Commission (CFTC) to police the speculators, although the heads of each of the markets continue to lobby Congress for less regulation. As 1999 gave way to 2000, white-collar fraud had moved from junk bonds to illegal trading in stocks of high technology companies about to go public and offer Initial Public Offerings, or IPO's.

Computer Crime

In an economy increasingly dependent on technology, computer crime—the type of crime that businesses most fear—is the category that the public least understands. The prevalence of computers in the U.S. private sector is tremendous, with countless desktop computers engaged in commerce and management of sales and service, not to mention the reliance of major corporations on over 560,000 mainframe computers.[29]

Government and academia also have grown dependent on the computer, as was revealed by a November 1988 computer program that infected thousands of military and university computers. A Cornell University graduate student in computer science introduced a *worm*—that is, an independent program that endlessly duplicated itself, tying up more than 6,000 computer systems around the country in the Pentagon's communication system, Arpanet. Technically, the program was not a *virus*, which reproduces itself after entering a host computer's operating program. One month later, another intruder penetrated the computer system linking the unclassified Milnet system, which includes hundreds of government research centers and private defense contractors. In 1992, the Michelangelo virus temporarily disabled computers across the country, heightening awareness of the systems' vulnerability and the danger of sharing floppy disks. In 2000, the "I Love You" virus, sent from Manila in the Philippines, caused even greater damage to government and private computers via e-mail. The good news, however: The millennium bug did not crash computer systems nationally or overseas, as many doomsday scenarios had predicted would occur on January 1, 2000.

What exactly is computer crime? A computer crime involves the use of a computer to commit a broad range of offenses, including fraud, theft, vandalism, sabotage, embezzlement, tax evasion, treason, and espionage. Computer crimes fall into one of three categories. *Hacking* is unauthorized access to a computer system. Some hackers simply want to enter well-protected, high-security systems because they represent a challenge. In 1999, an Israeli teenager hacked his way into highly classified Department of Defense computers. Other hackers seek to steal or destroy data stored in the computer system. Where the average low-tech bank robber steals $5,000, the average hacker nets $500,000.[30] One quarter of American businesses report losses due to hacking totaling over $700 million annually.[31] Many more companies do not report such losses, fearing embarrassment and loss of customers. The FBI has authority to investigate such crimes under the Computer Fraud and Abuse Act of 1986. The National Security Agency is responsible for protecting government computers.

A second type of computer crime involves the duplication of copyrighted software without the permission of the copyright owner. This is the most commonly committed computer crime, depriving publishers of profits and authors of royalties. A third type of computer crime, called *phreaking* by those in the industry, involves the use of calling cards. Phreakers use computers to randomly dial eleven-digit phone numbers until they find an account's access code. The account is then used to charge long-distance phone calls anywhere in the country—or the world. These numbers may be posted on one or more of the 1,000 bulletin boards around the world.

Other games and crimes committed by hackers include *time bombs*—programs inserted in a system and left hidden until triggered to perform some task; the *Trojan horse,* a program that seems useful but that can destroy a database; and *superzapping*—bypassing all system controls. Computer crimes are very difficult to detect, and criminals know how to erase the evidence of their illegal activity, which may have lasted only milliseconds. Victims often refuse to report or prosecute, and they may take weeks even to discover that a crime has been committed against them.

The number of computers and computer crimes continues to grow. The computer security industry is beginning to benefit from the skills of retired or reformed hackers, and fortunes wait to be made writing vaccine programs to protect systems from viruses. Law enforcement is handicapped by a slow investigatory process and lack of technical expertise, although that too is changing. The prosecution of criminal hackers now receives high priority and media attention. The Cornell graduate student—who said he "intended no harm"—did an estimated $100 million in damage, partly due to interruptions in work from shutdowns; he was prosecuted by the U.S. attorney's office on criminal charges and was convicted in 1990. The Georgia World Congress Center spent over $25,000 to restore data destroyed by hackers in 1985; and in the case of a Fort Wayne, Indiana, insurance firm that had 168,000 files destroyed by a former employee's virus, the perpetrator was successfully prosecuted.

In 1989, a Canadian woman was arrested by the U.S. attorney on conspiracy charges involving theft of computer and phone service and trafficking in illegal credit cards and telephone calling card numbers. Federal agents reported that she had up to fifty co-conspirators, including teenagers in Ohio, Michigan, Boston, Georgia, and Los Angeles. The computer theft ring infiltrated corporate and government electronic mailboxes, bought Western Union money orders, and stole service from Home Box Office and RCA Telephone System Sales. Adult members of the ring faced up to ten years in prison for the illegal use of computer-access equipment, five years for wire fraud, and five more years for conspiracy.

Tough prosecution and intense publicity, prosecutors hope, will deter the spread of these types of crime. Computer systems cannot be made absolutely safe unless they are completely isolated from other computers, but then the power and efficiency of the interconnected system is lost.

Gender-Based Crime

In 1993, the U.S. Senate Judiciary Committee issued a report entitled *Violence Against Women: A Week in the Life of America.* The report indicated that more than 1 million incidents of domestic violence were reported in 1992, and that perhaps 3 million additional domestic assaults went unreported. Violence was determined to be the primary cause of injury suffered by females aged fifteen to forty-four—greater than the harm inflicted by cancer deaths, auto accidents, and muggings combined. Nearly 100 women are murdered every week, one third to one half of them by lovers or spouses. Women are six times more likely than men to be assaulted or murdered by an intimate. Domestic violence accounts for 20 to 35 percent of the visits women make to emergency rooms. The National League of Cities reports that an estimated 50 percent of women will experience some violence in their marriage. The March of Dimes reports that battering of pregnant women causes a significant number of birth defects.

Gus Kaufman, Jr., cofounder of Men Stopping Violence in Atlanta, Georgia, says, "Male violence against women is at least as old an institution as marriage." Police traditionally have preferred not to intervene in or prosecute domestic violence cases, and hot lines and shelters for battered women fleeing domestic violence typically receive less public funding than animal shelters.

The term *battered woman syndrome* entered our vocabulary in 1984, when psychologist Lenore Walker began publishing studies on abused women. This syndrome has figured prominently in the legal defense of women who, in small but growing numbers, have killed the partners who batter them. Twenty-seven states now have recorded clemencies granted to such women, a trend that attracted great media attention in 1990, when outgoing governor Richard E. Celeste of Ohio commuted the sentences of twenty-seven women who had murdered or attempted to murder a battering lover or spouse.

Why do men batter their partners? Why do women stay in violent relationships? Like all human relationships, these phenomena are complex and not readily explained. Control and low self-esteem are the concepts that experts use most often in trying to explain them. Why does the criminal justice system ignore violence against women? Again, the issue is complex, but concerns about power, family, and social hierarchy figure prominently in the arguments activists make when they try to alter the status quo. Violence can be a tool used to keep women in a subordinate role. The criminal and civil trials (1996 and 1997) involving the murder of Nicole Brown Simpson raised many of these questions, but resolved few of them. In December 1996, the Justice Department released a study entitled *Female Victims of Reported Crime,* which noted that one of every 270 American women was raped in 1994 and that 78 percent of women knew their attacker. In the same year, forty-one of every 1,000 women were victims of violent crimes, compared with sixty of every 1,000 men. Not all women choose to continue to be victims. Gun ownership among women, according to *The American Handgunner* (January 1997) comprises over 17 percent of American gun ownership, and the rate is rising.

In addition to the new focus on domestic violence against women, sexual harassment and stalking have been added to the criminal repertoire of violence usually based on gender. Sexual harassment in the workplace is prohibited by law. It became a *cause célèbre* during the confirmation hearings for Supreme Court nominee Clarence Thomas in October 1991, when law professor Anita Hill alleged that he had sexually harassed her while she worked for him at the Equal Employment Opportunity Office. Social and legal debate continues on this subject, as women now constitute more than 40 percent of the U.S. work force and social norms about female-male relations struggle to adapt. Surveys of women who claim to have been sexually harassed at work have revealed how widespread the problem is. Sixty-four percent of women in the military said they had endured sexual harassment (1990), and 77 percent of clergywomen in the United Methodist Church report having experienced sexual harassment. Legal recourse and attempted remedies have often proven to be futile, due to the absence of witnesses or of physical evidence. Increasingly, victims have begun to covertly tape their harassers to successfully document their complaints. The technology of miniaturized video cameras placed in briefcases or purses may prove to be the victims' best offense and defense against sexual harassment.

In 1990, the young star of the television program *My Sister Sam,* Rebecca Schaeffer, was murdered by a fan who had stalked her for several months. Stalking received a name, and legal remedies eventually followed, with thirty-one states having recorded antistalking ordinances by late 1993. "Stalking is going to be the issue of the '90s," said Cheryl Tyiska, who directs victim services at the National Organization for Victim Assistance. *Stalking* is defined as the intentional, repeated, and malicious following or harassment of another person with a credible threat of violence. Threats by letter or telephone calls and destruction of personal property or reputation typically occur during stalking. Most cases are believed to take place following a broken relationship, but in some stalking cases, the victim does not know the stalker. Law enforcement authorities can now have restraining orders issued to discourage stalkers, but little aggressive action can be taken against a stalker until he or she is caught.

The addition of this form of gender-based violence has expanded our concept of crime, now covering a spectrum from sexual harassment to stalking to assault, rape, and murder. How do we explain American society's seeming tolerance of continued high levels of violence against its most nonviolent citizens? Efforts by the women's movement and educators who raise broad questions about violence in our culture have focused attention on these issues. The crimes now have names, and remedies are taking shape. In the meantime, women constitute the fastest-growing group of handgun owners in the United States, and are a key market for the handgun industry, as exemplified by the new "ladies' line" sold by Smith and Wesson: the Lady Smith.

Race-Based Crime

In March 1991, Rodney King was beaten by Los Angeles police officers after he attempted to elude them in a high-speed automobile chase. The officers who were charged in the case were acquitted in April 1992, triggering three days of looting and rioting that left 53 people dead, 2,383 injured, and nearly $200 million in property damage. Sixteen hundred stores owned by Koreans were burned. (The following year, two of the officers were convicted in federal court of violating King's civil rights.) After the riot, 7,066 people were arrested (853 white, 3,517 Hispanic, 2,564 black, 132 other).[32]

The L.A. riots brought together the explosive ingredients of racial tension, police brutality, poverty, and the rage pent up in the American urban underclass. In November 1992, four Detroit police officers (three white, one black) were charged and later convicted of beating another black motorist, Malice Green, to death after they stopped him near a crack house. Over the course of one year, the issue of police brutality and race relations in the prosecution of our criminal justice seized the public's attention.

In 1997, New York City became the focus of concern about police brutality following a sexual assault by police officers on Abner Louima, a Haitian immigrant who was in their custody; and, in 1999, the Amadou Diallou case, in which police shot and killed an unarmed African immigrant who they thought was about to shoot them, raised further concerns about racism on the police force. The city's aggressive war on crime came under intense scrutiny, and public debate spilled over to a discussion of **racial profiling.** "Driving while black," or DWB—the practice by some law enforcement officers of pulling over and interrogating drivers based on their race or ethnicity—and more serious police mistreatment of minorities, reminds us that the problem of equal justice for all is a principle not yet completely available to all Americans.

American citizens who are poor and/or minorities are disproportionately likely to be victims of crime and to be convicted, imprisoned, and executed for the commission of crimes. (African Americans constitute one eighth of the U.S. population and one third of prison inmates.) Hate crimes that target African Americans, such as the 1993 New Year's Day abduction and setting on fire of Christopher Wilson in Florida or the police brutality exemplified in the attack by New York police on Abner Louima, exacerbate the fear of crime among African Americans. There was an epidemic of arson fires against black churches in 1996, and the FBI reported in 1996 that more than three out of five hate crimes in 1995 were motivated by race. The failure of the American criminal justice system to deliver security to Americans and to protect their lives, liberty, and property raises serious questions as to whether the system may collapse under the weight of drugs, poverty, and guns.

PROSPECTS: TRENDS IN CRIME AND ITS PREVENTION

Crime in America continues to make Americans feel insecure in their homes and cities, despite efforts by policymakers and law enforcement agencies to find remedies to secure the public's safety (see Table 4.3). The problems of drug-related crime and prison overcrowding have created a demand for spending more tax dollars at the same time the national debt of $5 trillion has created pressure for spending cuts. Working with existing resources, policymakers and law enforcement encounter the problem of bureaucratic reluctance to cooperate with other agencies and public resistance to measures that might possibly ease America's crime problems—for example, drug decriminalization, drug testing, and increased social welfare spending. There are no easy solutions to difficult problems on the horizon for the public, policymakers, or those in the criminal justice system. Limited resources, controversial remedies, and American impatience militate against dramatic improvement in the problem of crime in America.

Technology does offer some hope of progress, both in the prevention and the prosecution of crime. Biotechnological prosecution of criminals gained momentum in the late 1980s, as DNA (deoxyribonucleic acid) codes were used to implicate suspects in crimes. DNA samples are matched using skin, blood, or semen left at crime scenes and now are admissible in court as evidence, since all individuals except identical twins are genetically unique. Retinal patterns also are used to enhance security at facilities that seek to restrict admission to tightly screened individuals, and DNA, retinal patterns, and electronically scanned fingerprints all promise better tracking of suspects and convicted criminals through a high-tech law enforcement database. Police now use lasers to lift fingerprints once invisible to the eye, and computers in squad cars can almost instantaneously print out photographs, fingerprints, and the criminal records of individuals who are in the database. Surveillance of suspects now involves the use of satellites in orbits 300 miles high and infrared beams to listen through windows and walls. As we reach the year 2001, law enforcement has become better equipped to locate and prosecute criminals. The question remains whether the public and elected officials will provide the judges, jails, juries, defenders, and prisons to accommodate the convicted.

Illegal drugs will continue to play a major role in American's recreational and criminal lifestyles. As society becomes increasingly competitive, some experts predict

TABLE 4.3   Change in Violent Personal
                      Crime Rates, 1998 to 1999

Rape	down 7%
Robbery	down 8%
Burglary	down 7%
Murder	down 8%
Overall	down 7%

Source: Federal Bureau of Investigation,
Uniform Crime Report (Washington, DC: U.S.
Government Printing Office, 2000).

that consciousness-altering drugs will be joined increasingly by performance-enhancing drugs, like steroids and amphetamines, and memory-enhancing drugs. The deepening involvement of juvenile gangs in drug production and marketing will continue, especially if the dropout and unemployment rates in America's poorer neighborhoods remain constant or worsen, which many fear if and when the economic expansion of the 1990s ends. Crime in America has an insidious number of dimensions, with no generally acknowledged causes or remedies, and the threat to Americans' physical and mental sense of well-being continues. Of the many challenges confronting lawmakers in the years ahead, addressing the national problem of crime will be of paramount importance as the United States enters the twenty-first century.

STUDY QUESTIONS

1. Compare and contrast three different theories on the cause of crime. Discuss the solution each theory might offer for America's crime problem.
2. Why is it so difficult for Americans to address the problem of crime? Discuss the problem of (a) local versus federal problems and remedies, (b) the financial crisis in law enforcement, (c) the pervasiveness of drugs and guns, (d) the sophisticated technology of modern white-collar crime.
3. Should capital punishment be suspended? Should a DNA database for all crime be established?
4. Define gun control. How might gun control ease America's crime problem? Can criminals be prevented from obtaining guns? Why did the framers of the Constitution write the Second Amendment, which establishes the right to keep and bear arms?
5. How should white-collar criminals be punished? Given the problem of prison overcrowding, should criminals have the option of making restitution to their victims? How should victims of assault or rape be compensated?

NOTES

1. Robert J. Bursik, "Social Disorganization and Theories of Crime and Delinquency," *Criminology* 26 (1988), p. 611.
2. David Brownfield, "Social Class and Violent Behavior," *Criminology* vol. 24 (1988), p. 424.
3. Ibid., p. 427.
4. Bureau of Justice Statistics (Washington, DC: U.S. Government Printing Office, 1988).
5. Ibid.
6. Ibid.
7. Senator Phil Gramm (R-Tex.), press conference interview, Washington, DC, April 30, 1989.
8. Bureau of Justice Statistics, 1988.
9. Gramm press conference, April 30, 1989.
10. Associated Press, April 30, 1989 (excerpts from Rangel's speech).
11. Bureau of Justice Statistics (Washington, DC: U.S. Government Printing Office, 2000).
12. James Q. Wilson and Richard J. Herrnstein, *Crime and Human Nature* (New York: Simon & Schuster, 1985), p. 117.

13. Andrea Dorfman, "The Criminal Mind," *Science Digest,* October 1985, p. 45.

14. Wilson and Herrnstein, *Crime and Human Nature,* p. 173.

15. John E. Conklin, *Criminology* (New York: Macmillan, 1986), p. 140.

16. "Juvenile Justice: Before and After the Onset of Delinquency," United States of America White Paper at the United Nations Conference on the Prevention of Crime and the Treatment of Offenders (1984) p. 122.

17. *The Washington Post,* March 23, 1989, p. 1.

18. Bureau of Justice Statistics, 1988.

19. Gary McCuen and R.A. Baumgart, *Reviving the Death Penalty* (Hudson, NY: McCuen Publications, 1985); David Bender and Bruno Leone, *The Death Penalty* (St. Paul, MN: Greenhaven Press, 1986).

20. Philip Roth, "The Case Against Capital Punishment," *America,* November 12, 1988, p. 363; A.R. Mark Kleiman, "Dead Wrong," *The New Republic,* September 26, 1988, pp. 14–16.

21. "Public Opinion and Gun Control," *Annals of the American Academy* (May 1988), p. 27.

22. Yankelovich Partners, August 12, 1993, pp. 1–4.

23. Federal Bureau of Investigation (1993).

24. *The New Republic,* January 23, 1989, p. 20.

25. Christopher Simser, "Biting the Bullet," *National Review,* March 1987, p. 30.

26. Federal Bureau of Investigation, *Uniform Crime Reports* (1988).

27. University of Michigan, the Institute for Social Research (1988).

28. Vincent P. Doherty, "Keeping White Collars Clean," *Security Management,* vol. 31, no. 4 (April 1987), pp. 53–55.

29. Joseph Waldron et al., *Microcomputers in Criminal Justice* (Cincinnati: Anderson Publishing, 1987), p. 4.

30. Katherine Hafner, "Is Your Computer Safe?" *Business Week,* August 1, 1988, pp. 64–72.

31. Anne Reilly, "Computer Crackdown," *Fortune,* September 17, 1984, p. 141.

32. "Equal Opportunity Looting," *U.S. News and World Report,* May 18, 1992, p. 25.

SUGGESTED READINGS

BENNETT, GEORGETTE. *Crime Warps: The Future of Crime in America.* New York: Anchor Press, 1987.

BOESKY, IVAN F. *Merger Mania.* New York: Holt, Rinehart and Winston, 1985.

CORNWALL, HUGO. *Datatheft.* London: Heinemann, 1987.

DOLAN, EDWARD. *Youth Gangs.* New York: Messner Publishing, 1984.

DRAPER, THOMAS. *Capital Punishment.* New York: Harcourt Brace Jovanovich, 1986.

FRANK, NANCY, and MICHAEL LOMBNESS. *Controlling Corporate Illegality.* Cincinnati: Anderson Publishing, 1988.

FRANTZ, DOUGLAS. *Levine and Co.: Wall Street's Insider Trading Scandal.* New York: Henry Holt, 1987.

GRAHAM, MARY G. "Controlling Drug Abuse and Crime: A Research Update." *National Institute of Justice Reports,* April 1987.

JORDAN, DAVID C. *Drug Politics: Dirty Money and Democracies.* Oklahoma University Press, 1999.

LEDDY, EDWARD F. *Magnum Force Lobby: The National Rifle Association Fights Gun Control.* Lanham, MD: University Press of America, 1987.

REUTER, PETER, et al. *Sealing the Borders: The Effects of Increased Military Participation in Drug Interdiction.* Santa Monica: Rand Corp., January 1988.

SPITZER, ROBERT J. *The Politics of Gun Control.* Chatham, NJ: Chatham House Publishers, Inc., 1995.

WILSON, JAMES Q., and RICHARD J. HERRNSTEIN. *Crime and Human Nature.* New York: Simon & Schuster, 1985.

Chapter 5

The Politics of Terrorism

It must be a cardinal principle of liberal democracies in dealing with problems of civil violence and terrorism, however serious they may be, never to be tempted into using methods of tyrants and totalitarians.

—Paul Wilkinson, *Terrorism and the Liberal State* (1986)

It is the duty of all Muslims to kill U.S. citizens, civilian or military, and their allies everywhere.

—World Islamic Front for Jihad Against the Jews and Crusaders (February 1998) established by Osama bin Laden in 1990

Rather than invading our beaches or launching bombers, these adversaries may attempt cyber-attacks against our critical military systems and our economic base . . . or they may deploy compact and relatively cheap weapons of mass destruction.

—President Clinton in an address to the U.S. Naval Academy (May 1998)

Terrorism is not a new problem confronting the U.S. government, either at home or abroad. In the United States, the use or threat of violence against symbolic targets to obtain publicity and force political concessions is an old tactic dating back to the American Revolution. In this chapter, the different sources of the terrorism confronting the United States are discussed, including both domestic and international terrorism. How the government responds to the increasingly complex challenges posed by terrorism is reviewed, and the options, policies, and organizations involved in the fight against terrorism are examined.

From the kidnapping and murder of American diplomats to the bombings of the World Trade Center, the Murrah Federal Building in Oklahoma City, the

Centennial Park and abortion clinics in Atlanta during the 1996 Olympic Games, and attacks against the U.S. airbase in Dahran, Saudi Arabia, and U.S. embassies in Kenya and Tanzania in 1998, terrorists use violence in pursuing goals they otherwise have failed to accomplish. (Would-be bombers were halted in New England and Seattle and in Amman, Jordan, on December 31, 1999, on their way to kill Americans.) Destroying property, taking lives, and sowing fear widely through the electronic media, terrorists undermine Americans' confidence in their government's ability to protect them. Because terrorism has become a visible and increasingly popular means of manipulating governments, and because terrorism employs the increasingly sophisticated technology (in international communication, travel, and weaponry) of the twenty-first century, students and government officials alike must understand this phenomenon better. Terrorism represents one of the persistent forms of violence that will continue threatening Americans' security both at home and abroad.

SOURCES: TERRORISM

At home, the roots of terrorism in American political history have been obscured and are usually forgotten. Resorting to violence to obtain political objectives is not accepted practice in the United States today, when so many courses of legitimate political action are available, including lobbying, voting, demonstrations, civil disobedience, and litigation. But colonial Americans did resort to the use of violence against symbolic targets to obtain publicity and further their political goals. Tea was dumped into Boston Harbor, Tory sympathizers were tarred and feathered, and officials such as the king or stamp distributors were hung in effigy. The terrorist's aims were similar to those of today's terrorists; those symbolic acts of violence in the 1700s triggered greater repression by the British government, eventually culminating in a revolution.

Terrorism also preceded the Civil War, most notably in the attacks led by John Brown against proslavery groups. Six men were killed with broadswords at Pottawatomie, Missouri, in 1856; in 1859, John Brown led a raid on Harpers Ferry, Virginia, seizing a federal arsenal and hoping to set up a free state in the slave-owning South. The end of the Civil War saw the creation of an organization dedicated to terrorizing blacks, Republicans, and carpetbaggers: the Ku Klux Klan (KKK). Although federal authorities stamped out the Klan in 1871, it reappeared in 1915 and remains small but active today. The modern KKK has been involved in the murder of civil rights workers in Mississippi in 1968 and in random killings to terrorize blacks, such as the 1981 murder of Michael Donald in Alabama.

The federal government has been targeted by Puerto Rican terrorists regularly since 1950, when an attempt was made to assassinate President Harry Truman. In 1954, Puerto Rican separatists opened fire with machine guns on the floor of the U.S. House of Representatives, injuring five congressmen. Between 1980 and 1986, Puerto Rican independence groups were responsible for 55 percent of domestic terrorist attacks, according to the Federal Bureau of Investigation (FBI). The Puerto Rican independence movement still receives occasional attention from the media.

The idea of a nationwide threat of domestic terrorism first began to emerge in the late 1960s. The federal government started taking domestic terrorism seriously when the anti–Vietnam War protest movement began to spin off several domestic terrorist groups. The Weathermen, a violent splinter group of Students for a Democratic Society (SDS), bombed police stations in New York City, Chicago, and Detroit; courthouses in California and Long Island; and the U.S. Army Mathematical Research Center in Madison, Wisconsin, in 1970. In addition, they bombed a U.S. Senate men's restroom in 1971, the Pentagon in 1972, ITT corporate offices in 1973, and the U.S. Department of State in 1975. The Black Panthers, who broke with the Student Non-Violent Coordinating Committee (SNCC) in 1966, invaded the California state legislature the following year and took part in gun battles with police on the streets of Oakland. The Black Liberation Army (BLA) became active in 1971 and targeted police officers for assassination, claiming responsibility for eight murders before it was eliminated in 1973. That same year, the Symbionese Liberation Army (SLA) was organized, earning public attention in 1974 with the kidnapping of heiress Patty Hearst and the million-dollar food give-away that they demanded in exchange for her release. Instead, Patty Hearst joined the SLA, adopted the name of Tania, and participated in a bank robbery before she was captured.

The antiwar protests of 1966 had triggered concern in Washington that foreign subversion had inspired or directed many groups' activities. Several members of the Black Panthers, for example, had traveled to Algeria, Cuba, North Korea, and the Soviet Union soliciting aid and support. In 1967, President Johnson instructed the Central Intelligence Agency (CIA) to collect, coordinate, and analyze intelligence regarding communist influence on domestic dissident groups. "Operation Chaos" lasted over six years, and the CIA created 13,000 files with the names of over 300,000 people.[1] Meanwhile, the FBI, legally responsible for internal security and domestic counterintelligence activities, conducted its own investigation of subversive activities and terrorist groups. (The FBI had originally received presidential instructions in 1936 to collect data on communist subversion.) The FBI investigated the Weathermen, Black Panthers, BLA, and SLA, as well as nonviolent antiwar protest groups, the civil rights movement, and women's liberation groups. Some individuals, including Dr. Martin Luther King, Jr., were kept under surveillance as well. Congressional investigations of the FBI program known as COIN-TELPRO (Counterintelligence Program) found that the FBI kept more than 500,000 domestic intelligence files on American citizens and groups, with evidence of illegal covert action ("black bag jobs") and surveillance.[2] No evidence of a communist conspiracy to organize or direct American terrorist groups was found. Today, the FBI focuses on abortion clinic bombers, right-wing racist terrorism (KKK, Aryan Nations), cyberterrorism and drug-related narcoterrorism, in addition to its ongoing fight against organized crime. The 1995 truck-bombing of the Murrah Federal Building in Oklahoma City, however, permanently altered the previous view that violent militia activity in the United States was no threat to citizens or the federal government—especially after FBI investigative work led to the arrest and prosecution of two antigovernment activists, Timothy McVeigh and Terry Nichols.

TABLE 5.1   Hijackings, United States to Cuba

1966	0
1967	1
1968	14
1969	20
1970	13
1971	5
1972	6
1973	1

Source: Alona Evans and John Murphy, *Legal Aspects of International Terrorism* (Lexington, MA: D.C. Heath, 1978), p. 68.

During the late 1960s and early 1970s, international terrorism became an urgent concern on the American political agenda. The hijacking, or skyjacking, of commercial aircraft from the United States to Cuba received intense publicity until an extradition agreement with Fidel Castro was reached in 1973. Table 5.1 shows the hijacking activity between these two countries. Improved airline security technology (luggage x-ray and walk-through metal detectors) also helped reduce the hijacking of American jets to Cuba.

In 1972, Americans were stunned by the terrorist attack on Israeli athletes at the Olympic Games then underway in Munich, West Germany. No Americans died, but the world watched as eleven Israeli athletes were killed during a hostage-taking incident and aborted rescue attempt. During the decade that followed, American military personnel stationed in NATO countries were killed by car bombs, American diplomats and businesspeople were kidnapped and assassinated, and the American embassy in Tehran, Iran, was occupied, with fifty-five U.S. citizens held hostage from November 1979 to January 1981. International terrorism (see Table 5.2) displaced the problem of domestic terrorism both in incidence and in the sense of urgency attending the problem. The continued rise of international terrorist attacks gripped the American public and media over the course of the next two decades.

TABLE 5.2   Incidents of International Terrorism, 1968–1999

1968	120	1979	434	1990	437
1969	192	1980	499	1991	565
1970	315	1981	489	1992	363
1971	286	1982	487	1993	431
1972	540	1983	497	1994	322
1973	360	1984	565	1995	440
1974	433	1985	635	1996	361
1975	400	1986	612	1997	304
1976	457	1987	665	1998	274
1977	419	1988	605	1999	392
1978	530	1989	375		

Source: United States Department of State, GPO, *Patterns in Global Terrorism,* Washington, DC: April 2000, Appendix.

The car bomb attack on U.S. Marines in Beirut in October 1983 and the kidnapping of nine Americans held hostage from 1985 to 1991 in that city focused American attention on international terrorism. The 1980s also saw the murder of Americans during terrorist attacks (Seaman Robert Stethem died during the hijacking of TWA Flight 847, and Leon Klinghoffer died during an attack on the cruise ship *Achille Lauro* in 1985), which resulted in numerous policy responses by the United States, including the 1986 bombing raid on Libya, the arms-for-hostages deal of the Iran-Contra affair, the creation of antiterrorism assistance programs, and the creation of counterterrorism response and rescue teams. The December 1988 bombing of Pan Am Flight 103 over Lockerbie, Scotland, led to an embargo in 1991 against Libya, which was lifted in 2000 when Libya extradited two men accused of the bombing to stand trial before a Scottish court sitting in The Hague, Netherlands. In the next section, we examine the many policy options and responses Washington has considered and implemented in its fight against terrorism, both domestic and international.

STATUS: AMERICA'S RESPONSES TO TERRORISM—OPTIONS AND POLICIES

Twenty years of terrorism at home and abroad have created new problems for a U.S. government committed to protecting the security of American citizens and their property. In 1980, Deputy Secretary of State John C. Whitehead spelled out how broad the problem has become:

> What once may have seemed the random, senseless acts of a few crazed individuals has come into clearer focus as a new pattern of low-technology and inexpensive warfare. . . . While it is an alarming pattern, it is a threat that we can identify, combat, and, ultimately, defeat. Terrorism is a sophisticated form of political violence. It is neither random nor without purpose.

Today, humanity is confronted by a wide assortment of terrorist groups whose stated objectives may range from separatist causes to ethnic grievances to social and political revolutions. Their methods include hijackings, bombings, kidnappings, and political assassinations. But the overarching goal of virtually all terrorists is the same: to impose their will by using force against civilians.

The horrors they inflict on the defenseless are calculated to achieve very specific political purposes. They want people to feel vulnerable and afraid; they want citizens to lose faith in their government's ability to protect them; and they want to undermine the legitimacy not only of specific government policies but of the governments themselves.[3]

As the incidence of terrorism has increased, studies have shown that there are three basic categories or types of terrorist threats confronting the United States today. These include:

1. *Separatist causes:* Nationality or ethnic groups seeking national autonomy or independence may resort to violence to achieve their goal. Examples include the American Indian Movement (AIM), EPB Macheteros (Puerto Rico), Irish Republican Army (IRA),

Popular Front for the Liberation of Palestine (PFLP), Basque Homeland and Freedom (ETA), and Armenian Secret Army for the Liberation of Armenia (ASALA).

2. *Political revolutionary movements:* These organizations are committed to radical and rapid change in the political system through the use of violence. Examples include Sendero Luminoso (Shining Path) of Peru; the Red Army Faction of West Germany, which sought an end to capitalism, imperialism, and NATO in Europe; and Hezbollah, the Party of God, which seeks an end to Western influence in Lebanon, the establishment of an Islamic state, and an Islamic world revolution.

   American groups such as the Weathermen, the Black Panthers, and the SLA fit this category in the 1960s and 1970s. Currently, organizations like the Aryan Nations, committed to the establishment of a whites-only traditional society, now qualify as violent revolutionary American terrorist movements. These include forty groups, with approximately 10,000 members across the United States. Their "bible," *The Turner Diaries,* describes the arming of white militants to resist federal government authority, which they view as the servant of Jewish and black interests. This fictional work, depicting the ultimate "race war," gives a chilling, conspiracy-laced view of the underground and violent militia movements.

3. *State-sponsored terrorism:* Governments secretly use terrorism against their enemies (dissidents or other states) when more overt forms of conflict are too risky or too costly. Pakistan's President Zia ul-Haq was killed in August 1988, reportedly by agents of Afghanistan's Soviet-backed government. U.S. Ambassador to Pakistan Arnold Raphel also died in the attack. Libyan leader Colonel Muammar Gaddafi was accused of sponsoring the terrorist bombing of a West Berlin discotheque frequented by U.S. military personnel in April 1986. The United States also has employed state terrorism in its foreign policy (see Terrorism As an Instrument of American Foreign Policy later in this chapter). State terrorism can be conducted using state employees or foreign proxies, but like other forms of terrorism, it uses violence or the threat of violence to obtain political goals.

An attempt on the life of former president George H. Bush while he was visiting Kuwait in April 1993 was labeled by the United States as an act of state terror and attributed to the regime of Saddam Hussein of Iraq. (A retaliatory bombing raid against Iraqi radar facilities was ordered by President Bill Clinton.)

The number of groups using terrorism has ballooned in the past twenty-five years, and given the significant American presence abroad, the opportunity for American paths to cross those of terrorists has also grown. American tourists, overseas businesses operations, business staff, U.S. military personnel stationed abroad, our foreign bases, American diplomats, and diplomatic facilities have all been targeted by various terrorist organizations. U.S. policy to counter the threat of terrorism rests on four pillars. The United States

1. offers no concessions to terrorists and will not ask or pressure other governments to do so;
2. brings pressure on states that support terrorism;
3. pursues international cooperation in counterterrorism;
4. develops practical measures designed to identify, track, apprehend, prosecute, and punish terrorists.[4]

This four-pillar policy embodies the lessons of many years of study and experimentation, failure and success in dealing with terrorism. The dangers of trading TOW missiles (antitank weapons) to the Iranians to expedite the release of American hostages in Beirut became clear during the investigations of the Iran-Contra scandal of 1987; President Ronald Reagan often stated publicly that the United States would never negotiate with terrorists, but in secret talks his administration paid for the release of three Americans held hostage in Beirut. Unfortunately, three more Americans were promptly taken hostage in their place, and the deal was revealed in the Beirut press. International cooperation has proven more and more successful in capturing terrorists, often before they can carry out an attack, as seen in the case of a Japanese Red Army terrorist caught carrying explosives into New Jersey in April 1988. Such measures, however, failed to prevent the midair explosion of Pam Am Flight 103 over Lockerbie, Scotland, in December 1988. Practical counterterrorism measures run the gamut from airport metal detectors to "watch lists" and computerized databases of terrorists. The following sections review four categories of responses to terrorism: diplomatic/legal, economic, technical, and military/intelligence options.

Diplomatic and Legal Responses to Terrorism

In April 1988, fifteen members of the Covenant, the Sword and Arm of the Lord, and the Aryan Nations were tried in the United States on charges ranging from attempted murder of a federal judge and an FBI agent to conspiracy to commit civil rights violations in the Denver murder of radio talk show host Alan Berg. In 1997, the federal trial of Timothy McVeigh and Terry Nichols for bombing the federal building in Oklahoma City was a culmination of the criminal prosecution process used by the FBI to fight domestic terrorism, though the approach left many Americans wondering why terrorist conspiracies cannot be detected and prevented prior to such a great loss of life. The FBI has also helped bring to trial abortion clinic firebombers in Pensacola, Florida, and KKK lynch mob members in Alabama. Domestic terrorism in the United States is consistently treated as criminal activity and is dealt with as such by the law enforcement community.

The FBI has very limited power to surveil or wiretap suspected terrorists and often relies on civilian watch-groups like the Southern Poverty Law Center and B'nai B'rith to report suspicious activity. As they targeted the Weathermen and Black Panthers twenty years ago, federal agents have infiltrated the KKK, informants are used to gather evidence, and wiretaps and other forms of surveillance are employed to build criminal cases and produce indictments.

In 1988, the leading Colombian drug dealer and narcoterrorist Carlos Lehder Rivas was successfully prosecuted and sentenced to life in prison without parole. In 1996, Sheikh Omar Abdel Rahman was convicted for his role in the conspiracy to bomb the World Trade Center in New York. Law enforcement officials now must worry about hostage-taking ploys that try to obtain the release of convicted terrorists.

Curiously, abortion clinic attacks—which have included murder, vandalism, arson, bombing, assault and battery, burglary, death threats, and stalking—have not been treated as terrorism or criminal conspiracy by the FBI, at least not until 1993, which saw the murder of Dr. David Gunn outside a Pensacola, Florida, abortion clinic, and the attempted murder of Dr. George Tiller outside his Wichita, Kansas, clinic. Domestic terrorism, occurring with less publicity and far fewer casualties than gang wars or crack operations, has so far been contained with traditional law enforcement techniques. In May 1994, President Clinton signed the FACE bill (Federal Access to Clinic Entrances). The new law mandates prison terms and heavy fines for those who block abortion clinic entrances or threaten or attack patients or clinic employees. By 1997, the FACE legislation had reduced, but not eliminated, violence against abortion clinics. In January 1997, clinics were bombed in Tulsa and Atlanta, and in 1998 anthrax hoaxes closed clinics in seven cities across the country, reminding us that clinic terror continues despite greater vigilance and tougher laws.

Unfortunately, a law enforcement or legal approach to international terrorism also has proven less than effective. The inability of law enforcement to prevent terrorism was demonstrated by the February 1993 bombing of the World Trade Center in New York City. Despite prior knowledge of a conspiracy from a well-placed informant, the FBI could not prevent the spectacular terrorist attack, which resulted in more than $500 million in damage, cost six Americans their lives, and wounded more than 1,000 people.

International terrorists who threaten or harm Americans abroad know that the complexities of international law often work in their favor. Many countries refuse to extradite individuals who have committed political crimes and subsequently requested asylum, that is, protection from extradition. In 1987, for example, the Federal Republic of Germany refused U.S. requests to extradite the Hamadei brothers, accused of air piracy and murder in the 1985 hijacking of TWA Flight 845 to Beirut. Likewise, since 1917, IRA members have fled to the United States after attacks in Britain or Northern Ireland and have successfully avoided extradition back to the United Kingdom to stand trial. The Reagan administration concluded a treaty with the United Kingdom to close this loophole, often called the political exception, and the United States is no longer a sanctuary for the Irish Republican Army. The difficulty surrounding extradition, even when treaties exist between countries to expedite the process, continues to impede the prosecution of terrorists. Given this problem, some states have begun to kidnap terrorists and avoid the legal wranglings altogether. Fawaz Younis claims that U.S. agents kidnapped him in 1987 and brought him to Washington, D.C., to stand trial for hijacking Jordanian Airlines Flight 401 in 1985. After the *Achille Lauro* hijacking in 1985, U.S. F-14 jet fighters forced an Egyptian airliner carrying the suspected terrorists to land in Sicily. Italian authorities in Sicily insisted on taking the suspects into custody since the *Achille Lauro* was an Italian ship. The United States was very disappointed to lose the opportunity to prosecute the individuals involved in the murder of American Leon Klinghoffer, particularly when the Italians allowed the hijackers' leader, Abu Abbas, to leave the country without facing charges.

Legally, U.S. options in dealing with international terrorism are constrained by difficulties in extraditing suspects back to the United States. In May, 2000, the State Department reported that from 1993 to 1999, only thirteen extraditions of accused terrorists had been carried out. To combat the problem of extradition and to generate greater international cooperation in the struggle against terrorism, the United States has been very active at the United Nations. In 1972, the United States introduced a Draft Convention for the Punishment of Certain Acts of International Terrorism, but the measure was rejected by the General Assembly. Support in many countries for people's struggles for national liberation made it impossible to agree on who was a terrorist and who was a hero in the struggle for national independence. The U.N. General Assembly approved resolutions calling for the punishment of acts of terrorism against diplomats and the taking of hostages, but this legislation has no enforcement mechanisms. The United States also led efforts to punish or extradite hijackers in the Tokyo Convention (1963), the Hague Convention (1970), and the Montreal Convention (1971). Like legislation in the United Nations, these conventions produced agreements that lack automatic enforcement mechanisms.

The U.S. House of Representatives and the Senate have left a legal track record in the fight against terrorism, including passage of laws that

1. allow the offering of large rewards (up to $2 million) for information leading to the arrest and capture of terrorists, to the arrest of the mastermind of the World Trade Center bombing, and to the arrest of the designer of a much more massive bombing conspiracy against targets in New York, including the FBI and U.N. headquarters, as well as the Holland and Lincoln Tunnels;
2. authorize federal prosecution of terrorists who attack U.S. citizens abroad;
3. identify and label terrorist states like Libya for diplomatic punishment per the Lautenberg Amendment of 1987, which called for automatic sanctions against sponsors of terrorism.

Economic Responses to Terrorism

Economic sanctions against states that employ or support international terrorism have been part of the U.S. counterterrorism policy since 1979 when the American Embassy in Tehran was seized. The U.S. Department of State identifies six nations that repeatedly support international terrorism: Iran, Libya, Syria, Cuba, Sudan, and North Korea. It is the position of the United States that these states help terrorists by providing weapons, money, training, safe houses, false identification, and diplomatic pouch privileges. U.S. policy calls for concerted pressure, in conjunction with other friendly nations, to isolate terrorist nations "from the community of civilized nations by imposing economic, political, diplomatic, and—if all else fails—military pressures."[5] Economic pressure or sanctions may take several forms:

1. Trade embargoes, like the cutoff of pipeline equipment and technology to Libya in 1986 and Iraq in 1991.

2. Termination of aid, arms sales, or credit. The president is empowered to prohibit financial transactions if a national emergency is declared. Most Favored Nation (MFN) status may be revoked.

3. Cooperation with other nations collectively to pressure or punish terrorist states, as in November 1986, when the European Community (EC) imposed trade sanctions against Syria for its support of terrorism.

4. Freezing assets—for example, Iranian property in the United States remains frozen until relations are normalized.

5. Issuing travel alerts, which may discourage U.S. tourists from patronizing areas with poor security like the Athens International Airport or Lebanon.

The difficulty involved with economic sanctions hinges on (a) knowing which states to punish and (b) ensuring that economic sanctions by the United States will not be circumvented by other nations willing to fill the economic void. Coordination must involve other targeted nations to be effective. Sanctions tend to work slowly and may prove costly to American companies and workers, but allies who cooperate with the U.S. economic sanctions do represent an important form of non-violent leverage in U.S. counterterrorism policy. In 2000, the United States began easing its sanctions against Libya, Iran, and Cuba.

Economic responses to terrorism also include some positive incentives. The United States offers Anti-Terrorism Assistance Program (ATAP) aid to friendly governments trying to fight terrorism. More than 4,000 individuals from forty different countries have received antiterrorism training in ATAP since 1984,[6] and rewards up to $2 million for information are paid out of a $10 million fund created in 1985.

Technical Responses to Terrorism

Scientific technology has provided some of the most effective methods for preventing or minimizing terrorist attacks. Commercial aviation now routinely subjects passengers to metal detectors, and passenger luggage is x-rayed to detect weapons or bombs. Some airlines, like Israel's El Al, require passengers to personally load their luggage onto luggage carts immediately prior to boarding a plane. If a bomb goes undetected, the bomber will be aboard to share the fate of the victims. El Al also has armored baggage compartments to permit an airliner to survive a midair explosion. X-ray and metal detectors will soon be supplemented by devices that can detect plastic weapons and can "sniff" explosive materials (called thermal neutron analysis devices, or TNA). The politics of applying technology to the fight against terrorism is not always simple. The Clinton administration found in 1996 that Congress would not agree to a requirement to place "taggants" or trace elements in explosives, to enable the FBI to trace bombers' suppliers. The chemical industry argued that such additives might make their materials unstable, although the British government's experience with taggants indicated just the opposite.

Identifying terrorists, however, can be more difficult than locating their bombs. U.S. counterterrorist efforts include technical means to identify, track, and apprehend terrorists, but the FBI still lacks a state-of-the-art computerized system to assist its investigation. In Wiesbaden, Germany, the Komissar system stores and analyzes data on terrorists, groups, methods of operation (modi operandi), and contacts. Members of the European Community (EC) have developed mechanisms to pool and exchange data on terrorists; but the FBI's only tie into this system is an agreement with INTERPOL (International Criminal Police Organization) to notify European governments when the United States issues arrest warrants for terrorists. Clearly, many technical opportunities in the realm of computer databasing remain undeveloped in the United States, possibly because the threat of terrorism at home remains fairly low compared to the European experience.

One of the cheapest and most effective low-tech devices to prevent terrorist attacks is the traffic barrier used to prevent truck bombs. Now placed in front of U.S. embassies, the State Department, and the White House, these barriers have become a security fixture that we take for granted, like x-ray machines at airline terminals. Long metal poles with mirrors on the end are now used routinely to check automobile traffic entering U.S. diplomatic facilities for bombs attached to the underside of vehicles. Some of the technical fixes used in counterterrorism seem almost too simple.

Technical means also have proven extremely useful in minimizing the damage of terrorist attacks when they do occur. Congress has appropriated funds to improve overseas physical security of U.S. diplomatic and military facilities, including

1. armoring vehicles and "hardening" facilities with bulletproof windows;
2. installing improved internal and perimeter security systems, such as computer-assisted Marine security guard control;
3. operating DESIST, an interagency computer library that contains worldwide terrorism information used to prevent or respond to terrorist attacks;
4. organizing the Office of Counter-Terrorism and Emergency Planning (M/CTP) Terrorism Incident Management in the State Department to prevent or respond to attacks on Americans abroad.

In addition to the technical fixes that have proven to be among the most effective means of preventing or minimizing terrorist attacks, there now exist a number of techniques that official or civilian Americans can use for personal protection against terrorism. The personal protection techniques include the following:

1. When flying overseas:
   a. remember that American carriers usually have excellent security.
   b. avoid sitting on the aisle, where most hijacking casualties occur.
   c. travel with a tourist passport.
   d. wear quiet, civilian clothing.
   e. avoid traveling with religious pilgrims.
   f. don't carry official documents.
   g. watch your luggage at all times.
   h. avoid waiting lounges, ticket counters, and security stations.
2. When working abroad:
   a. take a defensive driving seminar, since over 90 percent of individually targeted attacks (bombs, kidnappings) involve vehicles.

b. alter your driving routes and departure times.
c. stay alert to State Department or local law enforcement security warnings.
d. be sure that a reliable person knows your itinerary and whereabouts at all times.
e. consider wearing a bulletproof vest and using an armored vehicle.
f. always use office and home security systems.

The technical and practical responses to terrorism also include the management or censorship of media coverage of terrorist attacks. In April 1988, a hijacked Kuwaiti airliner was moved out of range of television video cameras and the publicity given to the hijackers dropped off quickly, as did pressure on the Kuwaiti government. The murder of hostages stopped, and the crisis was soon resolved. Among U.S. journalists, however, an adversarial relationship with the government leads to uncensored and occasionally sensationalistic coverage of terrorism. No technical fix appears likely to resolve the tension between the public's right to know and terrorists' sophisticated manipulation of print and electronic news media, which puts pressure on governments and makes them look incompetent.

In May 1998, President Clinton appointed Richard Clarke to coordinate efforts to counter unconventional threats, including preparing a plan to protect the computer networks operating the nation's power grid, utilities, and communications systems. The new terrorism "czar" has been charged with improving the Centers for Disease Control's ability to detect and deal with a biological weapon assault, such as the introduction of anthrax or botulism into the environment. All active-duty servicemen and women in the U.S. armed forces are being inoculated against anthrax, and in May 2000, the largest field test ever run in the United States examined how well-prepared local, state, and federal authorities have become in the new age of counterterrorism. The exercise was called TOPOFF, and included a simulated biological weapon attack in Portsmouth, New Hampshire, and a simulated chemical weapon attack in Denver, Colorado. Legislation now permits Army Reserve and National Guard units trained in biological and chemical weapons detection and response to train with local law enforcement, as well as the Federal Emergency Management Administration and the Department of Health and Human Services.

Military and Intelligence Responses to Terrorism

Pooling intelligence reports on terrorism groups and activities, in addition to preventive security measures, holds the most promise for deterring terrorist attacks. The intelligence community in the United States and its European counterparts go beyond the collection and sharing of information: Terrorist organizations can be infiltrated and surveilled, their membership and plans revealed. While U.S. intelligence had some success in penetrating domestic terrorist groups in the late 1960s and early 1970s, terrorist organizations in the 1980s became smaller, more compartmentalized, and much more security conscious. British efforts to infiltrate Irish groups, and American and Israeli efforts to penetrate groups in Beirut, were successfully frustrated. Such groups as the Provisional IRA in Northern Ireland and Hezbollah in Beirut are often built on units composed of family members who are not likely to compromise others in the group or to accept bribes to reveal group plans.

Technical intelligence, which does not immediately involve agents or human intelligence, employs electronic and satellite surveillance to locate and identify terrorists and their training camps. More than a dozen terrorist training camps in Afghanistan and Libya alone are under surveillance, and camps in Syria, Iran, Lebanon, and Iraq are also monitored by satellite. Police and intelligence agencies in the United States are also urging Congress to require chemical tagging of explosives so those materials can be traced after bomb attacks.

Infiltration and technical intelligence, representing the slow and painstaking methods in the intelligence community's repertoire, are joined by covert operations to punish, weaken, or destroy terrorist operations. Israel's counterterrorism covert operations conducted by MOSSAD (Institution for Intelligence and Special Services) have included the assassination of PLO deputy Khalel Al-Wazir (Abu Jihad) in 1988, as well as tracking down and killing twelve Arabs who planned and carried out terrorist attacks against Israelis, including the 1972 Munich Olympics massacre. U.S. counterterrorism operations, when publicized, have usually been carried out by the military, unfortunately with less success than Israeli operations.

Military options among the counterterrorism responses available to the United States include

1. declaring war
2. military reprisals
3. military rescue operations

Most states do not publicly acknowledge their support for or participation in terrorism—a legal convenience called "plausible deniability." Evidence of their responsibility for terrorist attacks is difficult to produce; and consequently, terrorism rarely leads directly to declarations of war. The assassination of Archduke Franz Ferdinand in 1914 by the Serbian Black Hand is a significant exception to this rule.

Military reprisals for terrorist attacks have been employed frequently by Israel against Palestinian camps in Lebanon and by the United States against Libya in 1986, against Iraq in 1993, and against Sudan and Afghanistan in 1998 following the bombings of U.S. embassies in Africa. Muammar Gaddafi was implicated by his praise of the Christmas 1985 bombings of the Rome and Vienna airports and by Libyan aid to the bombers of a Berlin bar patronized by U.S. military personnel in April 1986. The United States raid on Libya was described by the president as an act of self-defense, although others have characterized it as an attempt to assassinate Colonel Gaddafi. The Libyan leader survived, but his support for terrorism has become far less vocal since the raid.

The United States developed an antiterrorist military force in 1977, the First Special Forces Operational Detachment Delta, popularly known as Delta Force. Led originally by Colonel Charles Beckwith, Delta Force's first major assignment, known as Operation Eagle Claw, was to rescue Americans held hostage in the embassy in Tehran. The April 1980 rescue attempt was aborted in the Iranian desert, but U.S. forces performed successfully in 1985, forcing the jet carrying the hijackers of the *Achille Lauro* to land in Sicily. Delta Force, based at Fort Bragg, North Carolina, is trained to resolve hostage situations involving planes, ships, trains, or buildings anywhere in the world. Delta Force is on instant alert, but the opportunity to rescue American hostages in Beirut was stymied by a lack of solid intelligence as to the hostages' location. Rescue of hostages within the United States is the responsibility of local police or the FBI Hostage Rescue Team.

Ironically, the last U.S. hostages held in Beirut were released in December 1991. Their release took place because the prisoners in Kuwait (for whom the hostage-takers hoped to swap the Americans) had been set free when Saddam Hussein's forces invaded Kuwait in 1990.

U.S. Government Organization for Combating Terrorism

The many options available to the United States to combat terrorism have resulted in a very complex counterterrorism organization, with many bureaucratic participants. Table 5.3 shows the organizational structure of federal agencies in the fight against terrorism.

TABLE 5.3   U.S. Government Bureaucracies Participating
in Counterterrorism Efforts

Office of the President
National Security Council
Senior Interdepartmental Group
Interdepartmental Group on Terrorism

CIA	Department of Transportation
Department of Defense	Department of the Treasury
Department of Energy	National Security Council
Department of Justice	Office of the Vice President
Department of State	

Advisory Group on Terrorism

Agency for International Development	Federal Emergency Management Agency
Arms Control and Disarmament Agency	Federal Protection Service
Bureau of Alcohol, Tobacco, and Firearms	Immigration and Naturalization Agency
Centers for Disease Control	International Communications Agency
Defense Intelligence Agency	Joint Chiefs of Staff
Department of the Army	Metropolitan Police Department
Department of Energy	National Security Agency
Department of the Interior	Nuclear Regulatory Agency
Department of Justice	Office of Management and Budget
Department of State	U.S. Coast Guard
Department of Transportation	U.S. Customs Service
Department of the Treasury	U.S. Postal Service
FAA	U.S. Secret Service
FBI	

More than thirty offices, agencies, or departments participate in this complex counterterrorism organizational structure. The process by which policies are made and implemented is cumbersome, although terrorist crises are handled by the much smaller Special Situation Group established by President Reagan and chaired by the vice-president. Because so many groups participate in the war against terrorism, as the Reagan administration called it, the Department of State created the Office for Combating Terrorism (1979), which has become a key voice in shaping and articulating U.S. policy on terrorism. This office attempts to weave together the work of the thirty-plus bureaucracies into a coherent policy, and the Four Pillar Policy is a product of its efforts. For its domestic and international audience, the State Department reiterates that U.S. policy to combat terrorism includes

1. granting no concessions to terrorists;
2. placing pressure on sponsors of terrorists;
3. gaining international cooperation to combat terrorism;
4. developing practical measures to prevent, punish, or minimize terrorist attacks.

While the Four Pillars appear to be simple and coherent, coordinating the many agencies' efforts against terrorism has proven difficult. The checks and balances built into this system may have contributed, in part, to the arms for hostages scheme carried out by Oliver North. Out of frustration with working within the regular—but unsuccessful—channels, North implemented a 1986 scheme to purchase the freedom of American hostages in Beirut. In 1987, the Department of Justice led an effort to close the New York and Washington, D.C., offices of the Palestine Liberation Organization (PLO) as punishment for its use of terrorism against Israel. The Department of State opposed the closings, arguing the need for direct contact—but not diplomatic recognition—between the United States and the PLO. In 1994, the State Department opposed President Clinton's order to issue a visa to former IRA member and then-president of Sinn Fein, Gerry Adams. Formulating and implementing consistent counterterrorism policy have been difficult tasks for the U.S. bureaucracy, problems that will continue to challenge governmental participants in the war against terrorism.

Terrorism as an Instrument of American Foreign Policy

No activity of the Central Intelligence Agency has engendered more controversy than "covert action," the secret use of power and persuasion. The contemporary definition of covert action as used by the CIA—"any clandestine operation or activity designed to influence foreign governments, organizations, persons, or events in support of United States foreign policy"—suggests an all-purpose policy tool. By definition, covert action should be one of the CIA's least visible activities, yet it has attracted more attention in recent years than any other U.S. foreign intelligence activity.[7]

This observation, made in the course of the 1976 Church Committee Report on the CIA's use of covert action, was part of a larger study on the government's use of propaganda, political action, and paramilitary tactics to promote American interests abroad. The Church Committee (U.S. Congress, Senate Select Committee to Study Government Operations with Respect to Intelligence Activities, 1974–1976, chaired by Senator Frank Church of Idaho) found evidence that the CIA had participated in assassination plots and conspiracies to topple unfriendly governments. Although the term *terrorism* is not used in the report, the tactics described employed the use or threat of violence against symbolic targets to obtain political goals. Fidel Castro of Cuba, for example, was the target of numerous CIA assassination plans, including the use of poison cigars, exploding seashells, and a contaminated diving suit. The CIA at various times tried to dose Castro with drugs to make his beard fall out or to administer LSD to him before a public address. The CIA also explored plans to use Sam Giancana and other underworld figures in later murder schemes against Castro, all of which aborted or failed.

The Church Committee found that Rafael Trujillo of the Dominican Republic, Patrice Lumumba of the Congo, and Colonel Rene Schneider of Chile were also targets of CIA or CIA-approved assassination schemes. CIA conspiracies to topple governments (Iran, 1953; Guatemala, 1954; Cuba, 1961; Chile, 1973) continued into the 1980s, focusing on the Marxist regimes in Nicaragua and Afghanistan. Weapons and money were supplied to the Contras and *mujahedin,* known as freedom fighters to some, terrorists to others. These are the proxies of state terrorism. The CIA also mined Nicaraguan harbors in 1981, a more traditional act of war, and published a manual for the Contras, *Psychological Operations in Guerrilla Warfare,* which recommended the assassination of court judges, police, and state security officials. The United States' F-111s bombed the residence of Muammar Gaddafi in April 1986 (over a dozen terrorist training camps in Libya went untouched), which was denounced by many states as an act of state terrorism. CIA plans to topple Panamanian strongman Manuel Noriega were aborted in a failed coup in 1988 that followed revelations of his connections to drug traffickers Fidel Castro of Cuba and Daniel Ortega of Nicaragua. Another coup attempt failed in October 1989. Then the United States intervened militarily in December 1989 to remove Noriega from power and bring him to Miami to stand trial on drug charges.

The United States has been the target of state terrorism and also has used state terror as part of its foreign policy repertoire. Since the Church Committee Report, assassination has been forbidden as an instrument of American foreign policy, a prohibition confirmed most recently by President Clinton.

PROSPECTS: DOMESTIC AND INTERNATIONAL TERRORISM

Terrorism at home and abroad, experts agree, will continue to threaten American lives and property as we enter the twenty-first century. The U.S. government must remain committed to promoting the security of its citizens and will continue to search for new methods to prevent, punish, or minimize the damage terrorists cause. Media coverage of sensational acts of terrorism, such as the October 2000 suicide bomb attack on the *USS Cole* in Yemen, will rivet public attention on this problem, even though relatively few American lives will be lost to terrorism. The underlying causes of terrorism—frustrated struggles for national liberation or radical causes and state sponsorship—will continue to produce groups willing to resort to violence to achieve their political goals. Those underlying causes, such as the Kurds' desire for a homeland or conservatives' opposition to legal abortion, have many deeply committed followers who will not readily give up their struggles.

The violence will continue, but the final question remains: Will terrorism inside the United States worsen? The answer is unclear, for although law enforcement and intelligence agencies are alert to the threat and the number of domestic "patriot" terrorist groups declined significantly in 1999 (down from 435 in 1998 to 217, according to the Southern Poverty Law Center's Intelligence Project), a commission created by Congress in 1998 reported in 2000 that the United States must get tougher on terrorism. Although social tolerance of political violence in the United States is low because of the many avenues of expression available to domestic groups pursuing political causes, the country is vulnerable to terrorism due to the unregulated media coverage of terrorist actions, the ease of travel and communication, and public access to weapons. Terrorism, the commission warned, is likely to find an easy target in the United States, and it is also unlikely to diminish or disappear as a threat overseas. Americans abroad must continue to be alert to terrorist attack where their government cannot protect them, and the troubling vulnerability to domestic terrorist attacks may indicate that the U.S. government cannot completely protect its own citizens at home, either. This, of course, is no surprise to the African American community, which in the late 1990s saw an upsurge in the number of black or racially mixed churches torched by arsonists. Federal, state, and local authorities in the United States identified 318 church burnings between January 1995 and December 1996, at least seventy of which the FBI considers to have involved race as a motive. In his 1997 budget request, Bill Clinton supported a $10 million federal loan guarantee program to help rebuild those churches.

Internationally, the terrorist threat against American targets remains a constant risk. Media coverage of American targets of terrorism remains intense. In December 1988, the in-flight explosion of Pan Am Flight 103 over Lockerbie, Scotland, which killed 259 people on the plane, including 189 Americans, and 11 people on the ground, was in all likelihood a retaliation for the U.S. Navy's accidental downing of an Iranian airliner over the Persian Gulf the previous summer. In 1989, another democratic state, Israel, resorted to kidnapping Lebanese Sheikh Obeid in order to obtain the release of three Israeli hostages held in Lebanon. From 1987's Iran-Contra revelations to 1988's Lockerbie tragedy to 1989's videotape of Lieutenant Colonel Higgins's hanging, the threats of international terrorism remain difficult and numerous. The U.S. government's deep frustration in its many efforts to deal with international terrorism may provoke more creative solutions and perhaps a resort to the use of force.

While no Americans were killed when Sarin, a deadly nerve gas, was released in 1995 in the Tokyo subway, the vulnerability of American cities was driven home by the Oklahoma City bombing a month later. Perhaps the leading anti-American figure to emerge in the late 1990s was Saudi Arabian exile Osama bin Laden. The son of a Saudi billionaire, bin Laden fought the Soviets in Afghanistan, then turned his fundamentalist energies and resources against the infidel Jews and "Crusaders" who "offended Islam," supported the Saudi monarchy, and safeguarded the state of Israel at the expense of Arabs. Osama bin Laden has been linked to the 1993 World Trade Center bombing, the 1996 Dahran dormitory bombing, the 1998 U.S. embassy bombings in Africa, and the 2000 bombing of the *USS Cole* in Yemen. The U.S. government placed a $2 million bounty on his head in 1998 when he fled Sudan for sanctuary in Afghanistan.

Developments in international affairs had an impact on terrorist activity and created a mixed picture as the 1990s opened. The Iron Curtain fell in 1989, and the 1991 collapse of communism and the Soviet Union removed a major sponsor of international terrorist groups. The West German RAF, which lost its sponsor and operating base in the former East Germany, for example, entered a dormant stage as many members sought amnesty. Loss of Soviet support and the defeat of its Arab ally, Iraq, during Desert Storm brought the Palestine Liberation Organization into serious negotiations with Israel. In September 1993, the PLO agreed to peace accords with Israel, signaling the end of PLO-sanctioned terrorism against Israel and its American supporters. (Internecine terrorism continues, however, as PLO members and supporters and Israelis are targeted by Palestinians who reject the accords with Israel. Fundamentalist groups like HAMAS continued terrorist attacks after the second "intifada," or uprising, that began in September 2000.) In Peru, the government of Alberto Fujimori declared all-out war on Sendero Luminoso, having captured and convicted the group's leader, Abimael Guzman, in 1992 after suspending the constitution and declaring a state of emergency. A major potential source of international terrorism is feared to be coalescing in Colombia, where the government and the largest U.S. military mission in Latin American history are battling another drug-revenue-rich terrorist group, the Revolutionary Armed Forces of Colombia, or, in local jargon, the FARC-NARC, which the CIA estimated in 2000 enjoyed annual profits of $600 million from the drug trade. With access to nearly unlimited cash, the FARC has bought a massive arms cache and controls nearly half the countryside.

In addition to attacks on Americans at home or abroad, a serious technical issue has been added to the list of threats posed by terrorists. With the proliferation of nuclear, chemical, and biological weapons, terrorists can now gain access to materials that will greatly increase their destructive capabilities, and his interest in purchasing such technology has placed Osama bin Laden at the top of American terrorist threats. With the increasing use of nuclear-powered electric generating facilities and with continued development of small, battlefield nuclear weapons, terrorists now have many more targets of opportunity to steal fissionable material with which to construct a bomb or acquire an operational nuclear device. Binary chemical weapons, which contain materials that are inert until mixed, are much simpler for terrorists to handle. And consider the public hysteria that would result if a terrorist group announced that it had obtained a live sample of the AIDS virus, or perhaps anthrax, and threatened to contaminate a city's food or water supply. Terrorists occupying a nuclear power plant could threaten a city with a core meltdown unless their demands were met. In short, technology now offers far more lethal and sensational weapons to terrorists—a threshold waiting to be crossed. Although most groups obtain publicity and occasionally concessions using only simple technology (plastic explosives, kidnapping), the risks of high-technology terrorism cannot be discounted. As we enter the twenty-first century, the threats posed by terrorism will continue to grow more complex. Will democracies have the strength and creativity to respond effectively?

STUDY QUESTIONS

1. Define terrorism. Give examples of the different types of terrorism.
2. Describe the policies and measures that the U.S. government has employed against international terrorism. Which are effective, which are not, and why?
3. Should the United States have a terrorism czar to coordinate the governmental fight against terrorism similar to the drug czar who coordinates the war on drugs? Why or why not?
4. What are the root causes of terrorism? What might the United States do to attack the roots of the problem?
5. Why are democracies more prone to terrorism problems than authoritarian states? How can democracies fight terrorism and remain democratic?

NOTES

1. Rockefeller Commission Report on CIA Activities Within the United States, Special Operations Group, "Operation Chaos," *Findings*, 1975, p. 16.
2. Church Committee Report, "The Scope of Domestic Intelligence," 45B, p. 6.
3. Secretary of Defense, "Annual Report to the Congress, Fiscal Year 1986," February 4, 1985, p. 12; U.S. Department of State, "Patterns of Global Terrorism" (1988).
4. *Fundamentals of U.S. Foreign Policy* (Washington, DC: U.S. Department of State, Bureau of Public Affairs, Office of Public Communication, March 1988).
5. *International Terrorism* (Washington, DC: U.S. Department of State, Bureau of Public Affairs, April 1992).
6. Ibid.
7. Church Committee Report, "History of U.S. Covert Action," 45A, p. 14.

SUGGESTED READINGS

BJORGO, TORE, ed. *Terror from the Extreme Right*. Portland, OR: Cass Series, 1995.

CHALMERS, DAVID. *Hooded Americanism: The History of the KKK*. New York: Franklin Watts, 1981.

CRENSHAW, MARTHA, ed. *Terrorism in Context*. University Park: Pennsylvania State University Press, 1995.

DEES, MORRIS. *Gathering Storm: America's Militia Threat.* New York: Harper Perennial, 1996.

DYER, JOEL. *Harvest of Rage: Why Oklahoma City Is Only the Beginning.* Boulder, CO: Westview, 1997.

HOFFER, ERIC. *The True Believer.* New York: Harper Perennial, 1951.

LAQUEUR, WALTER. *The Age of Terrorism.* Boston: Little, Brown, 1987.

LAQUEUR, WALTER. *The New Terrorism.* New York: Oxford University Press, 1999.

LIVINGSTONE, NEIL C., and TERRELL E. ARNOLD. *Fighting Back: Winning the War Against Terrorism.* Lexington, MA: Lexington Books, 1984.

MACDONALD, ANDREW (pseudonym). *The Turner Diaries.* Arlington, VA: National Vanguard Books, 1980.

MERKL, PETER H., and LEONARD WEINBERG, eds. *The Revival of Right-Wing Extremism in the Nineties.* Portland, OR: Frank Cass, 1997.

NACOS, BRIGITTE L. *Terrorism and the Media.* New York: Columbia University Press, 1994.

POWELL, WILLIAM. *The Anarchist Cookbook.* Secaucus, NJ: Barricade Books, 1971.

Public Report of the Vice President's Task Force on Combatting Terrorism. Washington, DC: U.S. Government Printing Office, 1986.

REICH, WALTER, ed. *Origins of Terrorism.* New York: Cambridge University Press, 1990.

RISEN, JAMES, and JUDY L. THOMAS. *Wrath of Angels: The American Abortion War.* New York: Basic Books, 1998.

WILKINSON, PAUL. *Terrorism and the Liberal State.* 2nd ed. New York: New York University Press, 1986.

Chapter 6

The Politics of Arms Racing and Weapons of Mass Destruction

I am become death, destroyer of worlds.

—J. Robert Oppenheimer, quoting from the Bhagavad-Gita, after witnessing the
first atomic blast at Alamogordo, New Mexico (1945)

*Eighteen months after U.S. and British warplanes badly damaged its missile
factories, Iraq has restarted its missile program and flight-tested a short-
range ballistic missile that could carry conventional explosives or the
chemical and biological weapons that Iraq is still suspected of hiding.*

—U.S. Department of State spokesman (July 1, 2000)

From the end of World War II through the Cold War, Americans generally accepted
the conventional and nuclear arms race "simply as an effort to keep up with or stay
ahead of the Russians."[1] As the United States adjusted to its new postwar role as superpower, it needed to maintain the capability to project force globally because it had
entered a global competition with the Soviet Union. To secure its citizens and the
American way of life, the United States committed itself to the containment of the
Soviet Union's expansionist tendencies. This was accomplished through a variety
of means, including the reconstruction of Western Europe and Japan, the establishment of a series of security treaties and military bases in nations on or near the Soviet
Union's borders, and the creation of a national security policy geared to conducting
and winning an arms race with the Soviets. As the U.S.–U.S.S.R. relationship ma-
tured and as the need to manage their nuclear relationship grew increasingly obvious, the superpowers cautiously tempered their arms race with arms control
measures.

The Cold War ended with the collapse of communism and the splintering of
the U.S.S.R. in December 1991, seeming to confirm the strategy of containment.

But the Cold War adversaries were left with large weapons arsenals still pointed primarily at each other. The international system collectively spent more than $700 billion on weapons in 1996, and the transition from a bipolar world to a multipolar system proceeded with uncomfortable uncertainty. Wider proliferation of nuclear and chemical weapons technology accompanied an increase in bitter civil wars—for example, in the former Yugoslavia, Afghanistan, Chechnya, and across Africa; and the "peace dividend" many had hoped for did not immediately materialize at the end of the Cold War.

In this chapter, arms racing, weapons proliferation, and the implicit specter of global annihilation by weapons of mass destruction (WMD)—perhaps the greatest threat to personal and national security—are examined. The general concept of an arms race and the course and sources of the prolonged U.S.-Soviet rivalry are reviewed, with emphasis on the technological stimulus that exacerbated the proliferation of weapons of mass destruction beyond the American-Russian rivalry. The aftermath of the Cold War and arms control efforts to slow the development and spread of the technology of WMD are also examined, with emphasis on the prospects for control of the increasingly sophisticated technologies of destruction. These issues, like the national problems of health care, poverty, and crime, have become more complex and more urgent. They are too important to be left to the politicians and technical experts, as are the problems of managing the new biomedical and biotechnological knowledge now becoming available (see Chapters 7 and 8). Albert Einstein observed that the "unleashed power of the atom has changed everything save our modes of thinking, and thus we drift toward unparalleled catastrophe."[2] Success in arms control over the last thirty years and the end of the Cold War have dampened fears of catastrophe, but new concerns threaten international peace and U.S. security. Progress in the new millennium on nuclear, chemical, and biological weapons proliferation must be as successful as U.S.-Soviet efforts were in managing their rivalry. Otherwise, both of the former adversaries will face continuing threats to national and global security, not from one another, perhaps, but from other nations that have bought or built such weapons or from terrorists who may have stolen them.

SOURCES: THE U.S.-SOVIET ARMS RACE

If war is part of policy, policy will determine its character. As policy becomes more ambitious and vigorous, so will war, and this may reach the point where war attains its absolute form.

—Carl von Clausewitz, *On War*[3]

Here is war that requires no national effort, no draft, no training, no discipline, but only money and engineering know-how of which we have plenty.

—Walter Lippmann, on nuclear weapons

Following World War II, the United States and the Soviet Union confronted a situation unlike any faced before in international relations. The context in which world politics is played out had been changed forever by four developments:

1. The practice of total war (such as the firebombings of Dresden and Tokyo, air raids on London, and the nuclear bombing of Hiroshima and Nagasaki) converted civilian populations and industrial bases into participants and targets of war strategies.
2. Nuclear weapons had been developed and had proven useful and relatively inexpensive over the course of the war.
3. Ideology (fascism, Marxism-Leninism, liberal democracy) delineated the major lines of political conflict during and after the war.
4. The Cold War quickly took shape, embodying the ideological chasm between the remaining two power centers (the United States and the Soviet Union) and reflecting their intention to compete politically and militarily through a conventional and nuclear arms race in lieu of the potential holocaust of another hot war. That arms race would be global in scope and would involve a level of technological competition in the realm of WMD never before seen.

Defining the Arms Race

What exactly is an arms race? When two or more nation-states consciously participate in a relationship marked by hostility and competition, with high levels of military spending, an **arms race** can be said to exist between them. Their relationship will be interactive; that is, the countries involved will act and react to each other, to their perceptions of their rivals, and to forces within the nation-state that participate in the arms race. An arms race does not have to spiral steadily upward. Bruce Russett captured the essence of an arms race in an analogy:

> If two long-distance runners maintain a steady pace, we consider them to be in a race just as much as if their speed were continually increasing; it is the element of competition, or interaction, that makes the race.[4]

Three elements trigger and maintain arms races: perception of a hostile opponent, bureaucratic and domestic interests, and reciprocity.

Perception of a Hostile Opponent. The international environment is one in which all nation-states face scarcity of resources and wealth, which leads to competition and insecurity. To protect their people and territory, which are the two requisite components of any nation-state, governments conduct internal and external security operations using police and military forces. The state must anticipate, identify, and respond to threats in the environment, making *perception* a key function in national defense. The intentions and capabilities of a nation's friends and enemies comprise central concerns of a government's perception of the international environment. Unfortunately, states often misperceive the actions and intentions of their enemies due to a phenomenon called the *mirror-image effect.*

In a mirror-image situation involving two states such as the United States and the Soviet Union, each side sees itself as moral, correct, and acting defensively, while the other side is seen as evil, hostile, and behaving offensively. After the onset of the Cold War in the late 1940s, when the United States and the Soviet Union were already alienated by ideology and disagreements over war spoils (especially the status of Germany and Poland), mutual misperception contributed to the start of the arms race. The Soviets saw Lend-Lease (U.S. materiel for the war against Germany) aid and assistance cut off unexpectedly early, and Marshall Plan resources for reconstruction were offered on terms unacceptable to them. Having suffered 20 million deaths in World War II, they were denied reparations from Germany (except from the eastern, Soviet-occupied zone), Japan, and Italy, and they were confronted by a nuclear-armed United States committed to containing the Marxist-Leninist state to the death. The United States saw an expansionist Soviet Union, committed to global communism and continuing to occupy Eastern Europe despite an agreement to allow democratic elections in the area. (U.S. businesses also had looked forward eagerly to participating in the reconstruction of the Eastern European states, from which the Soviets had barred them.) Each superpower began to make the most hostile interpretation of the other's actions and the intentions behind them. This set the stage for the next two elements of an arms race: Bureaucratic and domestic interests began to buy into the mirror image (and arms racing), setting into motion the cycle of reciprocity that would propel the arms race onward.

Bureaucratic and Domestic Interests.   Once the foundation of a hostile relationship had been laid, bureaucratic and domestic interest groups moved into place to shape the manner in which the rivalry would be expressed. In the postwar United States, President Dwight Eisenhower labeled this process the "acquisition of unwarranted influence, whether sought or unsought, by the military-industrial complex." This complex, often called the *iron triangle,* is illustrated in Figure 6.1.

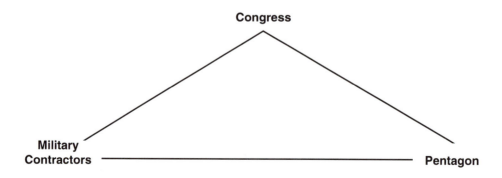

FIGURE 6.1   The Iron Triangle

This arrangement was by no means unusual in American politics, but in the realm of defense policy its influence was of tremendous importance in maintaining high levels of defense spending targeted at the Soviet Union. This was especially true when nurtured by presidential support and budgetary requests. Three fourths of congressional districts enjoyed often-substantial Pentagon spending, accounting for local employment by military contractors and stimulation of the economy. Contractors also contributed to the campaigns of key congressional committee members, such as members of the Senate Armed Services Committee and Defense Appropriations Subcommittee and the House Armed Services Committee and Defense Appropriations Subcommittee.[5] Major military contractors became dependent on defense-related contracts for a large share of their business and acquired a vested interest in a continuing arms race. Relationships developed among bureaucrats in the Pentagon, congressional committee members, and military contractors, none of whom would benefit from a reduction in the perceived Soviet threat or lower defense expenditures.

A similar phenomenon developed in the Soviet Union (now Russia), where a military-industrial establishment (but without a private business sector) still plays a powerful role in the economy and in defining what threatens and what enhances national security. Both superpowers had military-industrial complexes that were justified by the need for national security, a need sharpened by a hostile image that each held of the other. Each complex could appeal to patriotic sentiment or self-interest (less than 20 percent of U.S. defense procurement is met through competitive, formally advertised contract bids),[6] and the complexes have proven remarkably adaptable to changes in the environment. The Soviet Red Army, for example, supported Mikhail Gorbachev's restructuring of the economy and arms control overtures to the United States, hoping that a modernized and more efficient system, built during a breathing spell from the arms race, would better provide for the military in the next high-technology phase of national security competition. In the United States, weapons like the B-52 strategic bomber, about to become obsolete, enjoyed "built-in interest groups pressing either to modernize it . . . or replace it with something else that [would] do a similar job and keep the same people and resources employed."[7] Those interest groups put forward and lobbied for programs that included the B1-B and B-2, or Stealth, bombers. Both of the enormous military-industrial complexes in the United States and the former Soviet Union now face the enormous challenge of conversion to civilian research, development, and production. In one of the ironies of the post–Cold War era, the United States had spent nearly $150 million by 2000 to help the Russian government convert or destroy factories building WMD.

Reciprocity. **Reciprocity** describes the relationship of two or more states locked into an arms race when an action on one side will produce a reaction on the other. An increase in Soviet defense spending or the initiation of a new weapons system research project would produce a response on the part of America's military-industrial complex, and vice versa. The history of this reciprocal process in the U.S.–U.S.S.R. arms race can be traced in Table 6.1, showing the chronology of conventional and nuclear weapons developments.

TABLE 6.1   Select Chronology of Reciprocal U.S.–U.S.S.R. Weapons
Systems Development

Weapons Advance	U.S.	U.S.S.R.
Atomic bomb	1945	1949
Intercontinental bomber	1948	1955
Thermonuclear bomb	1952	1953
Nuclear-powered submarine	1955	1958
ICBM (intercontinental ballistic missile)	1958	1957
Supersonic bomber	1960	1975
Computer-guided missile	1960	1968
SLBM (submarine-launched ballistic missile)	1960	1968
Nuclear-powered aircraft carrier	1961	1992
Surface-to-air missile	1963	1961
Multiple warhead	1966	1968
ABM (anti-ballistic missile)	1972	1968
MIRV (Multiple Independently Targetable Re-entry Vehicle)	1970	1975
Sea-launched cruise missile	1982	1971
Neutron bomb	1983	?
Single warhead mobile ICBM	1987	1992
Binary chemical weapons	1987	?
Stealth bomber	1989	?
Strategic Defense Initiative	?	?

Sources: Lester R. Kurtz, *The Nuclear Cage* (Englewood Cliffs, NJ: Prentice Hall, 1988), p. 60; and Ruth Leger Sivard, *World Military and Social Expenditures 1987–88* (Washington, DC: World Priorities, 1987), p. 14.

The phenomenon of reciprocity, or the action-reaction cycle, is driven by technology and the military-industrial complex, where the process of technological momentum has been institutionalized. Weapons system research and development "employs a half million of the best-qualified scientists and engineers worldwide and absorbs one-third to one-half of the world's human and material resources devoted generally to research and development (R&D)."[8] These scientists and engineers on campuses and in corporate and military research laboratories around the world compete among themselves to produce breakthroughs in weapons technology. Because the lead time on their projects will span years, if not decades, the researchers and the bureaucrats who fund them rarely let projects die. Research programs acquire technological momentum and sometimes are applied in ways their designers never anticipated. For example, the decoys designed to confuse Soviet **ABM** defenses later became **MIRVs** (multiple independently targetable reentry vehicles). Unanticipated spin-offs and bureaucrats' reluctance to kill research programs with years of research and millions of dollars invested in them result in tremendous pressure to keep R&D projects running until an application can be found, further fueling pressure on the adversary to do likewise. This momentum and competition drove the arms race by providing increasingly sophisticated technologies that had to be matched and countered by a better defensive or offensive weapon. Thus, the cycle of reciprocity continued.

Any arms race, including the U.S.–U.S.S.R. arms race, has these three elements:

1. perception or misperception of a hostile adversary;
2. bureaucratic and domestic interests that benefit from participating in the arms race (although not necessarily war), and, hence, strive to perpetuate it;
3. the element of reciprocity or interaction among the participants, especially driven by technological momentum to match every offensive innovation with a defensive counter, and vice versa.

All three of these elements come under scrutiny when arms control efforts are undertaken, for it was clearly understood by the superpowers that control of arms racing could only succeed when the United States and the Soviet Union changed the way they perceived each other. Only then could bureaucracies redirect their efforts, including research and development and acquisition of new weapons.

With this working definition of an arms race (high levels of defense spending, perception of a hostile rival, iron triangle, and reciprocity), three questions arise regarding the U.S.–U.S.S.R. competition. First, how and why did the two states adopt arms control agreements? Second, what course did U.S.-Soviet arms control take? And third, where are U.S.-Russia arms control efforts headed?

Origins of Superpower Arms Control Agreements

The superpower arms race moved through several phases. As described by Bruce Russett in *The Prisoners of Insecurity*, there were four distinct periods in the U.S.–U.S.S.R. arms race:

> Phase I   1945–1952 American monopoly
> Phase II   1953–1957 American dominance
> Phase III 1958–1966 Soviet buildup
> Phase IV   1967–1991 Essential equivalence, or "parity"[9]

The United States enjoyed a brief nuclear monopoly (1945–1952) and then a period in which it alone had a sizable stockpile of warheads and a bomber force to deliver them (1953–1957). The shift away from uncontrolled arms racing to a more managed competition that included arms control came in Phase III, with the 1962 Cuban Missile Crisis. The crisis in October 1962 made the risk of nuclear war a tangible possibility, as President John Kennedy threatened a strike against Cuba and perhaps the U.S.S.R. if Soviet medium-range ballistic missiles were not removed from Cuba. The superpowers went to the brink of nuclear war and peered into the abyss. The risks of their hostile competition and the growth in both superpower arsenals resulted in movement toward both arms control and arms proliferation.

First, the initial hot line agreement was signed in 1963, establishing direct telegraph and radio contacts between the United States and the Soviet Union in case of emergency. This agreement (upgraded in 1971, 1978, and 1984) reflected the superpowers' recognition that a nuclear crisis required cooperative management

TABLE 6.2   U.S. and U.S.S.R./Russian Military Expenditures (in current U.S. billions of dollars)

Year	U.S.	U.S.S.R./Russia (estimates*)
1970	75.6	67
1975	90.9	132.9
1980	144.0	213.2
1985	282.0	266.0
1990	292.4	250.6
1995	268	100
2000	290	20

*Estimates of Soviet and (after 1991) Russian defense spending vary, due to Soviet secrecy and economic practices that did not employ reliable methods of costing out defense expenditures. The Stockholm International Peace Research Institute (SIPRI), for example, cited figures usually one-third to one-half lower than ACDA estimates of Soviet defense spending. Since 1991, instability and the lack of convertibility of the Russian ruble continue to make accurate estimates of Russian defense spending difficult.

Source: U.S. Arms Control and Disarmament Agency, 2000.

and communication if nuclear war were to be avoided. In 1963, the first Partial Nuclear Test Ban Treaty was signed, a multilateral agreement among nations prohibiting nuclear explosions in the oceans, in the atmosphere, and in space.

Second, following the Cuban Missile Crisis and the improvement of superpower emergency lines of communications, the Soviets greatly speeded up their military spending. As seen in Table 6.2, this would soon demonstrate the costly nature of the arms race, in addition to the risks of nuclear holocaust.

The risk of nuclear war and the costs of continued arms racing became unacceptable to the United States after the burden of conducting the war in Vietnam (1965–1974) began to take its toll. During this same period, the Soviet Union achieved essential equivalence, or rough parity, with the United States. Both sides had acquired second-strike capability—that is, nuclear arsenals sufficiently large and diversified to enable either side to withstand a first strike from the other and to deliver enough surviving warheads to retaliate with a devastating second strike. This established a nuclear doctrine of **mutual assured destruction (MAD),** deterring both superpowers from initiating nuclear war. With the acceptance of parity and MAD in the late 1960s, the competitiveness of the arms race was tempered with increasing concern that the nuclear relationship should be managed in order to limit its costs and risks. With stable deterrence achieved and an economic pinch being felt in both systems, the time for arms control had arrived. By 1996, the U.S. defense budget still exceeded $250 billion, and its Russian counterpart was roughly one third that amount. By 2000, the American defense budget neared $300 billion, and Russia was spending an estimated $20–30 billion on its crumbling defense establishment.

The Course of Superpower Arms Control Agreements

President Lyndon Johnson had initiated arms control talks with the Soviets in 1965, but the first successful limits on nuclear offensive and defensive systems were reached during the Nixon administration with the 1972 SALT I agreements.

Defensive systems known as antiballistic missiles (ABMs) were limited to two sites per nation (reduced to one site in 1974) to ensure both sides' vulnerability to nuclear retaliation, thus securing mutual assured destruction and deterrence. In addition, the number of offensive submarine-launched ballistic missiles (**SLBMs**) and fixed land-based intercontinental ballistic missiles (**ICBMs**) was frozen until 1977 (the freeze was later extended to 1980). During talks to produce these defensive and offensive arms control agreements, the United States and the Soviet Union were also at work on a new Nuclear Accidents Agreement that obliged both nations to improve safeguards to prevent an accidental launch of nuclear weapons. Signed in 1971, the accidents measures also included notification arrangements in case of an accidental launch. In 1973, the Nuclear War Prevention Agreement established further measures to help the superpowers avoid a nuclear exchange during international crises. The 1974 Threshold Nuclear Test Ban Treaty prohibited underground tests of weapons with yields above 150 kilotons but was not ratified, nor was the 1976 Peaceful Nuclear Explosions Treaty, intended to prohibit the peaceful use of nuclear explosions, such as in mining operations.

Superpower efforts to put caps on the type and quantity of offensive weapons continued with SALT II in 1979, which the U.S. Senate never ratified. Both superpowers abided by its limits (2,400 delivery vehicles; 1,320 MIRVed systems, with a sublimit of 1,200 MIRVed ICBMs; and a maximum of ten warheads on any ICBM) until 1986. By that time, new Strategic Arms Reduction Talks (START) were underway, this time involving the actual reduction of weapons, not simply setting caps on weapons increases. In 1987, the Nuclear Risk Reduction Centers (NRRCs) Agreement further enhanced communications facilities linking Moscow and Washington, and the Intermediate-Range Nuclear Forces (**INF**) Treaty was signed in Washington by Mikhail Gorbachev and Ronald Reagan. The INF Treaty provided for the elimination of all American and Soviet nuclear missiles with a range of 300 to 3,400 miles. The Soviets were obliged to destroy 1,752 missiles and the United States 859 missiles. Landmark on-site **verification** protocols accompanied the treaty, allowing twenty short-notice visits per side in the first five years, ten visits per side in the second five years, and five visits per side during the last three years of the treaty.

President George Bush (1989–1993) continued the arms control initiatives of his predecessor and successfully concluded an agreement with the Soviets on conventional forces in Europe and long-range nuclear weapons, but the collapse of the U.S.S.R. left open many questions about compliance and verification of the CFE and START agreements (see the next section, Status: U.S.-Russia Arms Control). As the 1990s unfolded, the Russians and Americans continued their dialogue on arms control in eight functional areas (see Table 6.3 for details). Arms control has become a cumulative process, with the major bilateral (or two-sided) arms agreements between the two nations reflecting their growing commitment to managing the arms race (see Table 6.4). President Bill Clinton has continued this trend, successfully urging the Russian parliament to ratify START II in February 2000, shortly after the election of President Putin. President Clinton also led the international community in renewing the Non-Proliferation Treaty indefinitely in 1995, and was the first signatory of the Comprehensive Test Ban Treaty at U.N. headquarters in New York in 1996.

TABLE 6.3 Categories of U.S.-Russia Arms Talks

1. Strategic arms reductions
2. Intermediate-range forces
3. Conventional forces in Europe
4. Space-based weapons
5. Nuclear testing
6. Nuclear nonproliferation
7. Confidence-building measures
8. Chemical and biological weapons

Improved lines of communication and production limits figured prominently in these accords, confirming the original purposes of arms control: avoidance of accidental war and some cost control. Where the superpowers failed to reach agreement, controls on research (such as Star Wars or other new technologies) typically were the stumbling blocks. MIRV technology, for example, was discussed and considered a target for possible limitation during SALT I negotiations, but the United States was reluctant to limit a technology in which it enjoyed a lead, and the Soviet Union feared being frozen into an inferior position. Thus, MIRV technology enabled the superpowers to nearly triple their arsenals until SALT II imposed temporary limits on multiple warheads. On-site inspection to verify compliance with arms agreements, resisted by the Soviets since SALT I, represented a breakthrough achievement for the INF talks. Ronald Reagan's commitment to arms reduction and his insistence that the United States "trust but verify" Soviet behavior represented the beginning of a new phase in arms control.

Confidence-building measures and levels of cooperation surpassing anything previously known in the superpower relationship were ushered in by Gorbachev's new thinking and U.S. acceptance of Soviet parity. Both sides' commitment to the

TABLE 6.4 Major U.S.-Soviet Arms Control Agreements

Signed	Treaty
1963	Hot Line Agreement
1971	Hot Line Modernization Agreement
1971	Nuclear Accidents Agreement
1972	SALT I, ABM, and Offensive Arms Agreements
1973	Nuclear War Prevention Agreement
1974	Threshold Nuclear Test Ban Treaty (unratified)
1976	Peaceful Nuclear Explosions Treaty (unratified)
1979	SALT II Offensive Arms Agreement (unratified)
1987	Nuclear Risk Reduction Centers Agreement
1987	Intermediate-Range Nuclear Force (INF) Agreement
1990	Conventional Forces in Europe (CFE) Treaty
1991	Strategic Arms Reduction Treaty (START I)
1992	Strategic Arms Reduction Treaty (START II)
1994	Pact with Ukraine on denuclearization

containment of risks and costs associated with the arms race led to the establishment of arms control talks as a permanent fixture in the superpower relationship. The American public came to expect arms agreements and summit meetings with cordial displays of mutual respect between the American and Soviet heads of state. In the next section, ongoing efforts at arms control are examined, as well as the eight areas in which the United States and the Russian Federation continue efforts to eliminate or restrain the proliferation of WMD.

STATUS: U.S.-RUSSIA ARMS CONTROL

The United States and the Soviet Union discovered four useful functions or benefits that stem from arms control:

1. Based on regular arms talks, the United States and the Soviet Union could more confidently predict the size and composition of each other's nuclear forces.
2. They could reduce the number of nuclear weapons, the costs of maintaining them, and their reliance on those weapons (and the risk of MAD).
3. They could control costs inherent in technical modernization competition.
4. They could improve accident and crisis management and communications, hence enhancing their chances of avoiding nuclear war.[10]

These benefits, which became obvious to both sides over the course of time, have led arms control to evolve into eight functional categories of arms talks which Russia and the United States currently pursue, as illustrated in Table 6.3.

Strategic Arms Reduction Talks (START I and II)

Strategic nuclear weapons have been the subject of U.S.–U.S.S.R. arms talks at Geneva since 1982. Strategic weapons, those located on U.S. soil, submarines, or bombers that can strike the Soviet Union, now Russia, and vice versa, have been the object of negotiations that may reduce their numbers by two thirds.

President George Bush, who watched the disintegration of the Soviet empire begin with the collapse of the Berlin Wall in November 1989, worked with the last general secretary and president of the U.S.S.R., Mikhail Gorbachev, to sharply reduce the strategic arsenals of both superpowers via the Strategic Arms Reduction Treaty I (see Table 6.5), as the Cold War clearly was drawing to a close. President Bush continued negotiations with Russian president Boris Yeltsin after the U.S.S.R. collapsed in December 1991 and further reduced the strategic arsenals with START II in June 1992 (see Table 6.5), which the U.S. Senate ratified by a 93–6 vote in October of that year. The earlier agreement would have reduced the number of warheads in the American arsenal to 8,500 and in the Russian arsenal to 6,200, but the latter treaty, START II, cut even deeper and included guarantees that the Soviet stockpile would not be scattered among the former republics of the U.S.S.R. but was to be consolidated under Russian control. (The U.S.S.R. had land-based strategic nuclear weapons in Belarus, Ukraine, and Kazakhstan.) Newly independent Ukraine delayed

TABLE 6.5   Strategic Arms and START

	Land Based	Sea-Launched	Air-Launched
1990			
U.S.A.	2,450	5,760	4,436
U.S.S.R.	6,612	2,804	1,596
START I			
July 1991			
U.S.A.	1,400	3,456	3,700
U.S.S.R.	3,153	1,744	1,266
START II			
June 1992			
U.S.A.	500	1,728	1,272
Russia	504	1,744	752

Source: Arms Control Association.

approving START II for several reasons: It feared Russian imperialism and views its 1,240 nuclear weapons as a security guarantee; it viewed the possession of nuclear weapons as a means to obtaining recognition as an important new state; and it tried, unsuccessfully, to leverage more aid from the United States by retaining the strategic weapons until a general aid package arrives. START II also required that Ukraine, Belarus, and Kazakhstan join the Nuclear Non-Proliferation Treaty as nonnuclear states, a provision with which Ukraine still had not complied by the end of 1993. In January 1994, Ukraine agreed to return its nuclear arsenal to Russia in exchange for economic assistance, and in 1996, the last nuclear weapon left Ukrainian soil.

START II negotiations also involved arrangements to verify compliance that are even more extensive than the landmark provisions for verification in the INF Treaty. START II requires twelve types of on-site inspections, exchange of data, open displays of weapons for satellite monitoring, twenty-four-hour monitoring of missile production plants, and a ban on the encryption (secret coding) of radio signals on test flights of new or experimental weapons. Unfortunately, none of the provisions of START II will go into effect until all five parties (the United States, Russia, Ukraine, Belarus, and Kazakhstan) exchange formal diplomatic "instruments of ratification" of the treaty. START II, which should be completed by the year 2007, will lead to a remarkable reduction in nuclear arsenals, made possible because of a successful arms control process, the demise of the U.S.S.R., and the end of the Cold War. If fully complied with, START II will reduce the total U.S. strategic arsenal from 12,646 warheads in 1990 to 4,250 in 2003 and the Russian arsenal from 11,012 to 4,250 warheads; by 2007, each side should have further reduced its stockpiles to 3,500 warheads apiece.

Intermediate-Range Forces

The INF (Intermediate-Range Nuclear Forces) Treaty, signed in December 1987 by Ronald Reagan and Mikhail Gorbachev, eliminated the entire class of U.S. and Soviet missiles with a range of 300 to 3,400 miles (500 to 5,000 kilometers). The treaty entered into force within three years of the signing, or 1990. The INF agreement fulfilled Reagan's 1981 zero-option proposal to eliminate intermediate-range weapons, and Reagan simultaneously succeeded in keeping other North Atlantic Treaty Organization (NATO) allies' INF missiles separate from the agreement. The INF Treaty of 1987 was the first arms reduction agreement between the superpowers and included historic on-site verification provisions never before agreed to by either the United States or the Soviet Union. (Resident inspectors oversee operations at key final missile assembly facilities.) The INF Treaty also included an unprecedented exchange of information on the launchers and missiles covered by the treaty, including numbers, locations, and technical data on operational characteristics. By eliminating the land-based nuclear missiles that the United States would use to defend NATO in case of a Soviet attack, the INF Treaty also raised the issue of the gross imbalance over the conventional forces of NATO enjoyed by the Warsaw Pact (U.S.S.R., East Germany, Czechoslovakia, Poland, Hungary, Bulgaria). The United States and its NATO allies (Belgium, Canada, Denmark, France, Great Britain, Greece, Iceland, Italy, Luxembourg, the Netherlands, Norway, Portugal, Spain, Turkey, West Germany) relied on a strategy that used nuclear weapons to deter a Warsaw Pact invasion, avoiding the more expensive burden of large standing armies. This strategy was also intended to present a purely defensive posture to the Soviets, who remembered Napoleon's and Hitler's invasions from the West. Successful conclusion of the INF Treaty meant that the conventional imbalance could no longer be ignored, even though the United States could still defend Europe with nuclear missiles located elsewhere. (The British and French control smaller nuclear arsenals of their own as well.)

Conventional Forces in Europe

The Soviet Union and the United States had discussed the problem of asymmetrical forces in Europe since 1973. Originally called the Mutual Balanced Force Reductions (MBFR) talks, negotiations included the United States, Canada, the Soviet Union, and seven countries whose territory hosts the front-line deployments of troops and armaments: Belgium, Luxembourg, the Netherlands, West Germany, East Germany, Poland, and Czechoslovakia. In 1986, the Soviets proposed including all NATO and Warsaw Pact countries in the negotiations, which would aim to reduce troops and armaments "from the Atlantic to the Urals." Although suspicious that this proposal was intended to sow discord among the NATO allies, the United States and all members of the Atlantic Alliance agreed to the Soviet proposal. In March 1988, these goals of the Western allies in the renamed Negotiations on Conventional Armed Forces in Europe were announced:

1. To establish "a secure and stable balance of conventional forces at lower levels."
2. To eliminate the disparities "most prejudicial to stability and security," that is, the Warsaw Pact's gross advantage in tanks, artillery pieces, and armored personnel carriers—armaments considered vital to capturing and holding territory in an invasion. NATO wanted to lock in tanks at 20,000 per side, APCs at 28,000 per side, and artillery at up to 24,000 per side.

3. To eliminate the "capability for launching surprise attacks." On this point, President Bush agreed in July 1989 to include helicopters and planes in the negotiations as well. A limit of 5,700 combat aircraft per side was proposed.

President Bush had made redressing the imbalance of conventional forces in Europe a top agenda item following the conclusion of the INF Treaty by the Reagan administration. As the Cold War ended and the U.S.S.R. and the eastern European defensive pact known as the Warsaw Pact broke apart in 1991, troop reduction agreements would also help speed Soviet and now Russian troop departures from countries across Eastern Europe.

Concluded in November 1990, the Conventional Forces in Europe (CFE) Treaty was designed to be implemented over a forty-month period after it was ratified. The CFE Treaty was signed by the U.S.S.R. and its five Warsaw Treaty Organization (WTO), or "Warsaw Pact," allies and by the United States and its fifteen NATO allies. The CFE Treaty called for the scrapping of 51,000 pieces of nonnuclear military equipment by November 1995 (35,000 by WTO and 16,000 by NATO). The CFE Treaty was overtaken by the remarkable course of events in Europe after the fall of the Berlin Wall in 1989, which led to the breakup of the Warsaw Pact and the U.S.S.R. in 1991. Poland, Hungary, the Czech Republic, and Slovakia have accomplished the removal of Soviet troops and most Soviet equipment from their territories, and the last former Soviet troops left eastern Germany at the end of 1994.

Despite appearing obsolete in the face of a Soviet collapse, the CFE Treaty still holds at least symbolic value, epitomizing the waning of the Cold War, which many believed had begun in and must end in Europe. Signatories are abiding by the treaty and destroying weapons as called for by CFE. Conclusion of the CFE Treaty also gave impetus to continued U.S. troop withdrawals from and base closures in NATO countries. U.S. troop strength in Europe fell to 100,000 in 2000, down from a Cold War peak of 351,000 in 1988. President Clinton and Manfred Woerner, secretary general of NATO, agreed in 1993 that a minimum of 100,000 U.S. troops should remain in Europe. (The U.S. Air Force will reduce its tactical wing strength in Europe from seven to two and a half.) Base closures overseas continued as the U.S. Department of Defense announced in August 1992 that it would end or reduce operations at seventy more bases abroad by fall 1995, all of them in Europe. From January 1990 to January 1994, a total of 628 facilities were closed, representing a 38 percent reduction in the total number of U.S. military installations.

The CFE Treaty and the end of the Cold War have placed more pressure on the members of NATO to revise the basic mission of the organization (to deter and defend against a Soviet assault) and to justify NATO's continued existence and expense. Many Europeans now call for reduced military spending, with greater resources devoted to integrating Europe's economy and rehabilitating the former Soviet republics and satellite states.

Their counterparts in the United States similarly argue for "conversion" from military spending and defense-related research and development to civilian investment in worker training and upgrading the U.S. infrastructure. NATO has shifted its attention to other regional threats, like civil war in the former Yugoslavia (Bosnia, Kosovo), and the threat of regional weapon proliferation. NATO moved ahead in 1994 with its own restructuring by announcing the Partnership for Peace (PFP) program, whereby prospective new members could open formal relations (joint training, offices in the alliance headquarters for liaison, etc.) with NATO, and most former members of the Warsaw Pact joined promptly. By July 1997, NATO was prepared to admit several new members such as Poland, Hungary, and the Czech Republic. This caused great anxiety in the Russian Federation, prompting newly appointed Secretary of State Madeleine Albright to suggest possible new talks between Russia and NATO on another conventional arms reduction treaty for central Europe. And despite continued Russian objections, NATO admitted Poland, Hungary and the Czech Republic to the alliance during its fiftieth anniversary celebration in 1999.

Space-Based Weapons

In Reykjavik, Iceland, in 1986, Ronald Reagan and Mikhail Gorbachev disagreed over controls on space-based weapons, delaying completion of the INF for nearly a year. By the end of 1987, Gorbachev signed the INF Treaty in Washington with no provisions for limiting the Strategic Defense Initiative (SDI). The Soviets and the United States continued, however, to discuss the issues of space-based weapons and how to conduct research, development, and testing of such weapons while continuing to observe the 1972 ABM Treaty. The issue of space-based defense and offense was raised by Ronald Reagan in March 1983 when he announced the Strategic Defense Initiative. A research program supposedly geared to the construction of a comprehensive national defense, or peace shield, today referred to as national "ballistic missile defense" or BMD, SDI highlighted the technological—and expensive—character of the arms race, how it has moved into space, and how deeply the Soviets feared a new, high-tech competition with the United States. The Soviet Union deployed the only functional antiballistic missile system (surrounding Moscow) and had its own version of SDI under research and development. Neither the United States nor the Soviet Union, however, signaled a desire to withdraw from the ABM Treaty, which either may do with one year's prior notice. The Soviets argued, along with many Western critics of SDI, that it could undermine deterrence by raising hopes of achieving invulnerability from nuclear attack or retaliation. It is the fear of retaliation that has made MAD a successful deterrent to nuclear war for more than twenty years. SDI critics argue, "It [deterrence] isn't broke, so don't fix it." SDI supporters argue that ballistic missile defense represents a reasonable safeguard against an accidental launch, a prudent program in the face of Soviet efforts along similar lines, and a "safer and more stable means of deterring aggression than the current exclusive dependence on the threat of retaliation."[11]

   A national ballistic missile defense system resurfaced as a political issue when the National Intelligence Council released a report in September 1999 concluding that "during the next 15 years the United States will most likely face ICBM threats from Russia, China, and North Korea, probably from Iran, and possibly from Iraq." Congress responded by enacting the National Missile Defense Act of 1999, which President Clinton signed in July, committing the United States to deploy such a system "as soon as technologically possible." BMD is not the only technology that has been added to the arms control agenda. Antisatellite systems (ASAT)—the offensive answer, possibly, to SDI—further complicate discussions about managing the arms race in outer space, and in the case of ASAT systems, the Soviets had the world's only system. Despite the 1967 Outer Space Treaty signed by the United States and the Soviet Union, which prohibits military activity on the moon or other planets and in outer space, the militarization of space has been underway since the Soviets orbited Sputnik in 1957. Space-based weapons, defensive and offensive, promise to pose great difficulties for arms control because of their cutting-edge technological promise. The Soviet Union was committed to limiting or slowing the development of such technologies, with the United States headed squarely in the opposite direction.

By 1993, Russia and the United States had agreed to collaborate on a joint space station to be built by the United States. Many opponents of SDI feared that the two former rivals would begin in earnest a joint project to build a space platform on which an antiballistic missile system could be tested and operated. By joining the project, Japan and the European Union allayed fears that the space station would be solely a military platform. Exploration of space and research projects involving the earth's atmosphere and oceans have been added to the work expected to be conducted on the space station.

Nuclear Testing

Defense programs utilizing nuclear weapons require the testing of those devices. Underground testing is permitted by existing treaties, and the superpowers' talks on the subject were based on their agreement that the first step must be to reach agreement on measures that would provide effective verification of the existing, but unratified, 1974 Threshold Test Ban Treaty and the 1976 Peaceful Nuclear Explosions Treaty. In their present form, these treaties cannot be effectively verified.[12] The United States and the Soviet Union agreed in principle that testing should be eliminated along with nuclear weapons in a parallel process. The first round of negotiations on nuclear testing began in November 1987, and the superpowers agreed to exchange teams that would inspect each other's test sites. In September 1996, fifty-one years after the first nuclear test explosion at Alamogordo, New Mexico, the U.N. General Assembly voted almost unanimously to open for signature the Comprehensive Test Ban Treaty to ban all further explosive nuclear testing. All the known nuclear powers (the United States, Russia, France, Britain, and China) support the treaty, and the "threshold states" (Israel, Pakistan) believed to have some warheads support the treaty as well, with the important exception of India. After India, followed by Pakistan, detonated nuclear devices in 1998, Pakistan promised to sign the CTBT and India promised to do so if Pakistan lived up to its promise. This treaty cannot take effect until all forty-four nations with nuclear installations on their soil have ratified it, although a clause in the treaty will allow signers to apply it provisionally if full signature is not met within three years.

Nuclear Nonproliferation

The issue of reducing and eventually eliminating nuclear test explosions is closely related to the problem of nuclear proliferation. States like India or Iran that seek to develop nuclear weapons refuse to renounce nuclear testing, and the United States is committed to preventing the further spread of nuclear weapons. The United States has sought to strengthen the United Nations' International Atomic Energy Agency (IAEA) and its powers to regulate nuclear exports and is also approaching the problem of proliferation from a political angle—that is, the local or regional security problems that drive states to seek nuclear weapons. In 1989, Pakistan renounced any plans to stockpile nuclear weapons, a real success for U.S. policy-makers seeking to prevent the spread of nuclear weapons, at least until Pakistan's successful nuclear tests in June 1998. In the same region, the Bush administration also decided to ban the sale to India of a missile-testing device and has pressured the French government not to sell advanced rocket technology to Brazil. In March 1990, U.S. and British agents intercepted the shipment of nuclear triggers to Iraq, which has been working to develop its own nuclear weapons for more than ten years.

After Iraq's invasion of Kuwait in August 1990, concern over Iraq's nuclear weapon development program grew. After the U.S.-led coalition ejected Iraqi forces from Kuwait in Operation Desert Storm in 1991, U.N. and IAEA inspectors began supervision of the dismantling of Iraq's nuclear weapon production facilities. The inspection teams were expelled from Iraq in 1998, and the U.N. has continued to impose sanctions on Iraq until the inspectors are allowed to resume their work to ensure that Iraq has dismantled its WMDs. In 1993, North Korea refused to comply with IAEA inspection protocols of its nuclear facilities, further raising international tension and concerns over nuclear weapons proliferation (see the discussion of new nuclear states in a later section, Prospects: Arms Control). In 1996, North Korea agreed to resume inspections and also to open discussions on modernizing its nuclear facilities with reactors that do not produce surplus plutonium. In 1998, North Korea tested a ballistic missile capable of reaching Alaska, firing it across Japan and triggering talk of a US-Japan regional or "theater" BMD system to counter the threat.

The United States and Russia have signed and ratified, along with 134 other states, the Treaty on the Non-Proliferation of Nuclear Weapons. In 1985, at an international conference to review the treaty's implementation since it entered into force in 1970, the United States and the Soviet Union confirmed their support of the treaty. Control of technology, however, has proven difficult to achieve, and the Western states that possess nuclear weapons have been much more likely than Moscow to share or sell nuclear technology to other states. Unfortunately, once nuclear technology has been sold, control of the nuclear weapons it produces disappears.

A ban, or moratorium, on nuclear testing represents another approach to controlling the proliferation of nuclear weapons. Although the spread of technology has proven extremely difficult to halt, the test explosion of nuclear devices can be detected by monitors. Russian President Boris Yeltsin and President Bill Clinton agreed in July 1993 to work for a Comprehensive Test Ban Treaty. The former superpower rivals agreed that a permanent ban on nuclear testing by the world's five major nuclear powers (Britain, China, France, Russia, and the United States) was an appropriate strategy to convince all nations to sign a Comprehensive Test Ban Treaty. Such a treaty would slow and perhaps halt the development and stockpiling of nuclear weapons because such weapons would not be considered reliable if they were not tested. In May 1995, the United States led a global conference that renewed the Non-Proliferation Treaty indefinitely. In the agreement extending the treaty were nonbinding disarmament goals that included

- completion of negotiations in 1996 on a universal and internationally effectively verifiable test ban treaty
- development of regional nuclear free zones, starting in the Middle East
- steps to assure nonnuclear weapon states that they will not be subject to nuclear attack
- increased capability of the IAEA to detect undeclared nuclear activity

Confidence-Building Measures

Perhaps more than any other euphemism in the language of arms control, confidence-building measures address the key component in any arms race: shared perceptions of a hostile adversary with aggressive intentions. Confidence-building measures were understood by Europeans to lie at the heart of any hopes for political and military normalization of their continent. The then thirty-five-nation Conference on Confidence- and Security-Building Measures and Disarmament in Europe reached agreement in 1986 on a series of measures to monitor military activity in Europe. Prior notification of any activity involving more than 13,000 troops or 300 tanks was required. Observers must be present at troop exercises or war games involving more than 17,000 personnel.[13] In August 1987, the United States sent observers to a Soviet military exercise for the first time in Europe since World War II, and that inspection was considered an important step in the "process of improving openness and enhancing confidence- and security-building in Europe."[14] Two months later, the Soviet Union was invited to observe NATO maneuvers in West Germany and Turkey involving U.S. personnel.

Bilaterally, the United States and the Soviet Union created Nuclear Risk Reduction Centers (NRRC) in Moscow and Washington, D.C. These centers provided direct communication links between the superpowers, intended to assist in the data exchanges required by arms control negotiations. The NRRCs will also be used for the notifications required by the INF Treaty; ideally, the centers represent another small step toward reducing the dangers of nuclear war posed by accident or miscommunication.

Chemical and Biological Weapons

In 1984, at the Geneva conference on disarmament, the United States presented a comprehensive treaty proposal to ban the development, production, use, transfer, and stockpiling of chemical weapons. In 1985, Congress voted to end the eighteen-year ban on American production of chemical weapons. In 1986, U.S. experts began bilateral talks with Soviet experts on the problem of chemical weapons proliferation. In 1988, Iraq used chemical weapons to kill 5,000 Kurdish civilians in Halabja, as it had done earlier in its war with Iran, from 1980 to 1988. By 1997, 160 countries had signed the Chemical Weapons Convention (CWC). Exactly what are chemical weapons, and why are they on the U.S. arms control agenda?

Chemical weapons (CW) were used in warfare as early as 429 B.C., when the army of Sparta combined burning pitch with sulfur to produce a poisonous gas beneath the city walls of their enemy. There are six types of chemical weapons, defined by the damage they inflict:

1. tear gas
2. vomit gas
3. blistering agents
4. blood agents
5. choking agents
6. nerve agents

First, tear gas is the most common poison gas. Some forms are mild enough for use in riot control, but stronger battlefield varieties of tear gas completely incapacitate victims. Second, the Soviet Union has employed a super tear gas that causes vomiting. The Red Army has used it to force enemy troops out of buildings and caves. Third, blistering agents (sulfur mustard and nitrogen mustard gas) also cause nausea and vomiting but do further damage to eyes and skin, causing blistering, temporary blindness, and potentially lethal respiratory damage. Mustard gas was used in trench warfare in World War I, which led to the signing of the Geneva Protocol of 1925, prohibiting its use in war. But the Geneva Protocol, signed by 131 nations, does not ban production or stockpiling and has no enforcement mechanism. Fourth, blood agents (hydrogen cyanide and cyanogen chloride) disrupt the blood's transport of oxygen and cause tearing, choking, and sometimes death. Mustard and cyanide gases were used by Iraq in 1988 against the Kurds in Halabja, killing an estimated 5,000 men, women, and children. Fifth, choking agents (chlorine, phosgene, and chloropicrin) attack the lining of the victims' lungs and lead to drowning, as the lungs fill with fluid. Phosgene caused 80 percent of the gas fatalities suffered during World War I. Finally, nerve agents (VX, Sarin, Tabun) are the most deadly chemical weapons and are both odorless and colorless. They may be absorbed through the skin or inhaled and kill within minutes of exposure. They are the most commonly stockpiled of the chemical weapons. Nations reported to possess one or more of these chemical weapons include the United States, the former Soviet Union, Iraq, Iran, Libya, Syria, Afghanistan, France, China, North Korea, and Vietnam. Nations suspected to possess chemical weapons include Burma, India, Pakistan, Egypt, Ethiopia, Israel, Somalia, and Taiwan.

Chemical weapons, sometimes called the poor man's nuke, began to receive more attention in U.S. arms control efforts after two events in 1988. West German chemical manufacturer Imhausen Chemie was discovered constructing a pesticide factory in Rabta, Libya, a facility also capable of producing chemical weapons. In March 1990, a mysterious fire severely damaged the Rabta plant. In March 1988, Iraq used chemical weapons against its Kurdish citizens, bringing the issues of chemical weapons production and the export of the necessary technology under scrutiny. U.S. efforts in this area operate on several levels. Through the Department of State's Office of Munitions Control, the International Traffic in Arms Regulations governs the export of chemical weapons. Efforts to coordinate U.S. efforts to control exports and constrain proliferation are coordinated through the Australia group. This group of nineteen industrialized nations (twelve members of the European Community, the United States, Australia, Canada, New Zealand, Japan, Norway, and Switzerland), formed in 1984, works to discourage or block chemical weapons proliferation by harmonizing national export controls on precursor chemicals and by networking on the proliferation problem.

On January 13, 1993, in Paris, more than 120 states, including Russia and the United States, met at the headquarters of the United Nations Educational, Scientific and Cultural Organization (UNESCO) to sign an agreement banning the manufacture, stockpiling, and use of chemical weapons. Like the INF and START Treaties, the Chemical Weapons Convention includes an extensive set of verification measures. The pact also provides sanctions, or punishment, for nations that refuse to sign. The newly established Organization for the Prohibition of Chemical Weapons will carry out verification checks, emphasizing the ban on twenty-nine toxic chemicals and fourteen "families" of chemical subject to international supervision. (The United States began to destroy its chemical weapons in 1992.) The convention went into effect January 15, 1995, and set a new standard for arms control regimes, especially in the realm of biological weapons, which are banned by a 1972 convention that has no provisions to enforce or verify compliance. And the treaty only applies to states, as the international community was reminded when a Japanese cult, Aum Shinrykyo, released deadly sarin gas in the Tokyo subway in March 1995, killing twelve and sickening thousands.

Biological weapons (BW) may represent the next technological generation of weapons. The twentieth-century bioengineering revolution and the potential of recombinant DNA (rDNA) may provide living organisms that can be used as weapons. Common diseases in plants, animals, and humans may be altered to become more lethal. For example, an attack on an enemy's grain crop with a potent new fungus strain might be difficult to manage and attribute. Bacteria, viruses, and toxins might be altered to spread forms of remedy-resistant anthrax or cholera. Dengue fever (a debilitating tropical virus), Q-fever (similar to typhus), and bubonic or pneumonic forms of plague could be enhanced by genetic engineering. The prospects of the use of such weapons in war or in the hands of terrorists have concerned Washington. The United States has accused the Soviets of producing biological weapons and actually using them in Afghanistan and Southeast Asia.

Like chemical weapons, biological weapons are not new to the arsenals of nations. The modern development of biological weapons began in World War II, with experiments conducted in Japan, Germany, France, the United States, and the Soviet Union. The Japanese conducted the most extensive experimentation, focusing on plague and anthrax, as well as delivery systems (bombs, artillery shells, and spray tanks). The Japanese tested these weapons on living prisoners of war in their notorious Unit 731, where at least 3,000 human subjects died in BW experiments. The Japanese and Nazi biological weapons programs both involved breeding insects to carry disease and attack crops. In the United States, wartime efforts culminated in U.S. Army testing of germ warfare by spraying unknowing Americans,[15] which came to light in the 1970s. The United States unconditionally renounced all forms of biological weapons in 1969 and led efforts for an international ban culminating in the 1972 Biological and Toxin Weapons Convention, signed by 110 countries. The convention lacks verification and enforcement provisions, like the 1925 Geneva Protocols, and is equally limited in its effectiveness. In 1989, the United States estimated that several countries have the ability to produce biological weapons and that Syria, North Korea, and Cuba actually possess the weapons. According to CIA Director William Webster, "at least ten countries are working to produce biological weapons." The State Department, in testimony before the U.S. Senate, expressed its concern about the "spread of biological weapons in unstable areas and about the prospects of biological and toxin weapons falling into the hands of terrorists or into the arsenals of those states which actively support terrorist organizations."[16]

Prospects for control of both chemical and biological weapons hinge on cooperative efforts among the United States' friends and allies to prevent the proliferation and use of these weapons. Efforts also continue in other international forums, especially with the former Soviet Union, to limit the spread of these latest instruments of war. While these efforts will not completely eradicate biological and chemical weapons, arms control efforts should slow their spread. Meanwhile, the United States maintains a defensive program at Fort Detrick, Maryland, where research on vaccines, antidotes, and decontamination in case of biological warfare continues.

PROSPECTS: ARMS CONTROL

The Reagan administration simultaneously undertook the modernization of U.S. strategic forces (essential to the ongoing superpower arms race) and the pursuit of verifiable arms control and arms reduction agreements for U.S. and Soviet arsenals. The technological momentum of the arms race was most clearly expressed in the programs encompassed by the Strategic Defense Initiative, which became a major impediment to continuing progress in arms control. The Bush administration accepted and promoted all three elements: modernization (MX, Stealth bomber, Trident D4), verifiable arms control, and SDI. In September 1996, President Clinton led nearly every member state of the United Nations in signing the Comprehensive

Test Ban Treaty, while his administration continued to work with Russia, Europe, and Japan on building a space station for purposes much broader than providing a military platform in space. The Clinton administration also affirmed the end of the Cold War and worked with the successor states to the Soviet Union to ratify START I and II and to assist in the dismantling of the old Soviet strategic arsenal of nuclear, chemical, and biological weapons.

Arms racing and the proliferation of weapons of mass destruction to rogue states and terrorists are taking on new dimensions in the post–Cold War world. Priorities have shifted with the end of a bipolar ideological conflict, and multiple new problems and choices confront the United States. These are discussed in the following paragraphs.

New nuclear states are challenging efforts to limit proliferation tendencies and thereby the risk of nuclear wars. Plutonium produced by breeder reactors may provide an affordable source of fuel for nuclear power generation—fuel that might be diverted to weapon programs. Potential new nuclear states that may produce warheads by the end of this decade include Algeria, Egypt, Iran, Libya, North Korea, and Syria. Israel and India already possess stockpiles of more than a hundred weapons, and Pakistan has at least ten. Arms control measures, diplomacy, and sanctions have kept the lid on Pandora's box. One instance of a preemptive military strike (Israel's 1981 raid on the Osirak facility in Iraq) and U.N. mandatory inspections and dismantling of nuclear facilities in the same country in 1992 and 1993 did, however, set precedents for alternative means of halting nuclear proliferation.

Budgetary pressures provide ongoing incentives to both the United States and Russia to fulfill arms control agreements that will enable them to focus their defense spending on modernization or to redirect those resources elsewhere. Given the admittedly horrendous state of the Russian economy, the present may hold the greatest opportunity yet for the United States to conduct further arms talks, enhance mutual perceptions of confidence and reliability, and pursue conversion of the military-industrial complex.

A strategic build-down may result from the budgetary pressures and simultaneous urge to modernize felt by both Russia and the United States. A strategic build-down would allow modernization of nuclear weapons while reducing their number. Two senators, Sam Nunn (D-Ga.) and William Cohen (R-Me.) proposed the idea of destroying two nuclear warheads for each new one deployed. This idea was incorporated into the Reagan administration's START package but was criticized by some analysts as harmful to the weapons redundancy that guarantees stable deterrence.

Proliferation and terrorism will persist and may eventually dominate the arms control process as the Cold War winds down. Binary chemical weapons (which have 2 components that remain safe until mixed) are now safely storable, transportable, and much easier for governments or terrorist groups to handle. Biological weapons would be extremely difficult to trace if used. (The Iranian government, for example, tried to buy poison-producing fungus strains from Canada and the Netherlands in 1989. The fungus, found on grass and wheat, produces mycotoxins that can injure humans and animals by damaging cells' ability to synthesize proteins.) Until it invaded Kuwait in 1990, the Iraqi government's research agencies had been able to purchase live anthrax cultures for "agricultural" research projects from the U.S. government's Centers for Disease Control. And the proliferation of nuclear generating facilities has resulted in a large increase in the amount of plutonium and uranium available for diversion. A terrorist group no longer needs to build a bomb; occupation of a nuclear reactor facility or theft of plutonium followed by a threat of dispersion into the air or water supply would hold a government hostage for some time. The Energy Policy Project Report commissioned by the Ford Foundation indicated that nuclear power plant security safeguards are so lax that it is only a matter of time before terrorists can steal fissionable material to use for their own purposes.[17]

An unexpected problem has recently arisen: the tremendous cost of dismantling America's chemical weapons arsenal. The Chemical Weapons Convention obliges the United States to dispose of its stockpile within ten years. The U.S. arsenal consists of nearly 400,000 M-55 rockets filled with liquid nerve gas, and since 1983, the Army has detected over 1,300 rockets leaking sarin and VX gas. The Army wants to incinerate nerve and mustard gas in a 2,000-degree furnace in the desert in Utah, but environmentalists have sued to block the burning. In 1997, the United States stored 31,496 tons of chemical weapons in 33 different states, and at least 215 sites of buried weapons were on a list for cleanup (estimated cost: $17 billion). Russian officials have estimated their cost of compliance at nearly $10 billion, which the financially strapped Russian Federation cannot afford. In 2000, the United States acknowledged it may miss the 2007 deadline for destroying its CW stockpiles. The U.S. Army was blamed for poor management of the $15 billion program devoted to the destruction of the chemical weapons.

The arms racing/arms control relationship between the United States and Russia has entered a more mature post–Cold War phase, benefiting from the cumulative confidence earned in earlier successful negotiations. With the 1987 INF Treaty, a threshold was crossed regarding on-site inspections. The intrusive verification measures agreed upon reflect a higher level of trust and the greater sense of urgency now attending the nuclear arms race. Only by continuing to manage the arms race through arms control can the United States and Russia hope to guarantee the security of their people and their homelands from the horrors of a nuclear exchange, or assault by chemical or biological weapons. Improvement in the relationship, however, has been offset by the proliferation of modern weapons (biological, chemical, and nuclear) beyond the control of either the United States or the former Soviet Union. All that is certain as the new millennium begins is that arms racing and the proliferation of WMD will persist, as will the urgent need to constrain these threats with arms control.

STUDY QUESTIONS

1. Define an arms race. Describe the events and conditions surrounding the U.S.–U.S.S.R. arms race.
2. What is the military-industrial complex? What role does it play in the arms race?

3. Examine the list of major arms control agreements between the superpowers. What trends do you detect? What is missing? In what area will the next arms agreement be reached?

4. What benefits do states enjoy through arms control? Can success in nuclear arms control agreements lead to biological and chemical weapons agreements?

5. Of the eight categories of current U.S.-Russia arms negotiations, which one is most threatening to American national security? If you were the president's national security adviser, in what order would you list U.S. arms control priorities?

NOTES

1. *Arms Control and the Arms Race: Readings from Scientific American,* with Introductions by Bruce M. Russett and Bruce G. Blair (New York: W.H. Freeman, 1985), p. 4.

2. Otto Nathan and Heinz Norden, eds., *Einstein on Peace* (New York: Schocken, 1968), p. 376.

3. Carl von Clausewitz, *On War,* Michael Howard and Peter Paret, trans. and eds. (Princeton, NJ: Princeton University Press, 1976), p. 606.

4. Bruce Russett, *Prisoners of Insecurity* (New York: W.H. Freeman, 1983), p. 70.

5. Gordon Adams, *The Politics of Defense Contracting: The Iron Triangle* (New York: Council on Economic Priorities, 1981).

6. Lester R. Kurtz, *The Nuclear Cage* (Upper Saddle River, NJ: Prentice Hall, 1988), p. 95.

7. Russett, *Prisoners of Insecurity.,* pp. 77–78.

8. Ibid., p. 79.

9. Ibid., pp. 6–13.

10. Harold Brown and Lynne E. Davis, "Nuclear Arms Control: Where Do We Stand?" *Foreign Affairs,* Summer 1984, pp. 1145–1146.

11. *Fundamentals of US Foreign Policy* (Washington, DC: United States Department of State, Bureau of Public Affairs, March 1988), p. 17.

12. Ibid., p. 19.

13. Ibid., p. 20.

14. Ibid.

15. Leonard Cole, *Clouds of Secrecy: The Army's Germ Warfare Tests over Populated Areas* (Totowa, NJ: Rowman & Littlefield, 1988).

16. Statement by Reginald Bartholomew, Under-Secretary for Security Assistance, Science and Technology before the Subcommittee on International Finance and Monetary Policy of the United States Senate (Washington, DC: Committee on Banking, Housing and Urban Affairs, June 22, 1989).

17. Mason Willric and Theodore Taylor, *Nuclear Theft: Risks and Safeguards* (Cambridge, MA: Ballinger, 1974).

SUGGESTED READINGS

ACKLAND, LEN, and STEVEN McGUIRE, eds. *Assessing the Nuclear Age.* Articles from the 40th Anniversary Issue of the Bulletin of Atomic Scientists. Chicago: University of Chicago Press, 1986.

BLACKWILL, ROBERT D., and ALBERT CARNESALE, eds. *New Nuclear Nations.* New York: Council on Foreign Relations, 1993.

BROWN, HAROLD. *Thinking About National Security: Defense and Foreign Policy in a Dangerous World.* Boulder, CO: Westview Press, 1983.

GOLDBLAT, JOZEF. *Arms Control.* Thousand Oaks, CA: Sage Publications, 1996.

HARRIS, JOHN B., and ERIC MARKUSEN, eds. *Nuclear Weapons and the Threat of Nuclear War.* New York: Harcourt Brace Jovanovich, 1986.

RUSSETT, BRUCE. *Prisoners of Insecurity: Nuclear Deterrence, the Arms Race, and Arms Control.* New York: W.H. Freeman, 1983.

SMOKE, RICHARD. *National Security and the Nuclear Dilemma.* 2nd ed. New York: Random House, 1987.

WALLENSTEEN, PETER, JOHAN GALTUNG, and CARLOS PORTALES, eds. *Global Militarization.* Boulder, CO: Westview Press, 1985.

PART II

Glossary

ABM Antiballistic missile, a defensive means of countering strategic ballistic missiles.

arms control Agreements between two or more states to control arms racing.

arms race A relationship between two or more states marked by competition in the acquisition of weapons, interaction, and reciprocity.

biological weapon (BW) A living organism or toxic biological product used to produce injury or death—for example, anthrax.

chemical weapon (CW) An inorganic gas or poison used to inflict injury or death—for example, nerve gas.

confidence-building measure A practice designed to enhance mutual understanding of military activities in order to reduce the risk of war through miscommunication or accident.

deterrence Preventing war by threatening terrible retaliation.

ICBM Intercontinental ballistic missile, a rocket, fixed or mobile on land, capable of delivering a warhead in excess of 5,500 km; operates outside the atmosphere for much of its trajectory and is unpowered during most of its flight.

INF Intermediate-range nuclear forces, land-based missiles, and aircraft capable of striking targets beyond the battlefield but short of ICBM range.

MIRV Multiple independently targetable re-entry vehicle—multiple warheads with multiple targets on one launch vehicle.

Mutual Assured Destruction (MAD) The last phase of the United States–Soviet Union arms race (1967 to 1991), characterized by essential equivalence between the two superpowers' arsenals. Each side was able to withstand a nuclear "first strike" by the other and retain enough offensive capability to deliver a devastating retaliation, or "second strike." Since neither side could win a nuclear war, neither side would start one, which produced a "stable deterrence" and created enough security that both sides became interested in arms control.

Reciprocity A characteristic of the relationship between two or more states engaged in an arms race, wherein the action of one state will trigger a reaction by the other(s). For example, if the United States builds a national ballistic missile defense system, the Russians may expand their offensive missile capability to overwhelm that defense.

SLBM Submarine-launched ballistic missile.

verification Process and means of establishing compliance with treaty provisions.

PART III

Biology and Politics

INTRODUCTION

The science of the next fifty years is biology; the technology of the next fifty years is biological manipulation.

—Jacob Bronowski, mathematician and scientist

The intimate relationship among money, violence, and politics is clear and needs little justification. However, the importance of including biological perspectives in an examination of public policy and political behavior is not as well known and warrants comment. Biopolitics is *not* an effort to reduce all behavior to biological phenomena; it is simply a call to recognize the human individual as a rational, social, and biological creature and to include biological data in the study of human behavior.[1]

WHY STUDY BIOPOLITICS: SIX ARGUMENTS

There are a number of compelling theoretical and practical reasons why the intimate relationship between biology and politics ought to be explored. But three arguments in each area should be sufficient to make the case for this intellectual endeavor.

Theoretical Reasons

1. To date, the fundamental questions of politics have been based on an incomplete and flawed model of human nature. This results in a misleading model of how human beings function. Nothing could be more serious, because all political theory is ultimately based on one's model of human nature.

Consider the following: Explaining behavior is absolutely central to political science as a discipline, but the explanation can only be as good as the base on which it is constructed. So far, virtually all political scientists have explained behavior in terms of two variables—social and psychological behavior determinants. The problem is that a third component, a biological dimension, today demands our consideration. This biopolitical perspective suggests that there are *three,* not two, bases that must be analyzed if one is to adequately explain political behavior.[2]

For centuries political theory has addressed the issue of human nature. Every one of the great philosophers, from Plato and Aristotle to St. Thomas Aquinas and Machiavelli and on to Rousseau, Mill, and Marx, addressed this monumental question. Each contributed important insights. For example, Marx pointed out the important role that economic relationships play in human lives; St. Thomas demonstrated the nature and role of reason in all human beings; and Machiavelli noted the egoistic and materialistic nature of human beings in their political life. If political scientists are to continue to contribute knowledge about human nature and behavior, then the recent developments in biology may be very helpful. Granted, inquiry into the biological aspects of behavior is a relatively new development in the discipline. Yet, if political behavior is influenced, even in part, by biological forces and factors, then these elements can be employed in our efforts to realize political, economic, and social goals. In sum, the study of political life in isolation from biology is an oversimplification.

2. A biopolitical perspective can help us explain and predict political behavior.

Three concepts are stressed by biopoliticians when discussing behavior—evolution, ethology, and sociobiology.

Evolution refers to a process of continual change and development. Charles Darwin's theory of natural selection in 1859 suggests that our present-day plants and animals have their origin in preexisting types and that variation and differences are due to modifications in successive generations. It further suggests that limited resources generate the struggle for existence and the survival of the fittest, which combine with inheritance and mutation (random changes in the genetic code inherited by the next generation) to produce significant modifications in a species over time. Changes in climate and the earth's surface, as well as destruction by other organisms, drive some species to extinction. Evolution proceeds in several directions at different rates and is a continuing process. Today, some scientists contend that natural selection occurs even at the molecular level, in the DNA itself, prior to the development of the organism.

Ethology is the systematic inquiry into the nature and evolution of behavior patterns in animals. Ethologists claim that behavioral traits, like physical ones, can and should be examined from the evolutionary viewpoint, and that natural selection shapes behavioral patterns that identify a species and contribute to its fitness (defined as the ability to leave behind offspring).

Sociobiology focuses on the social behavior of animals and emphasizes the significance of the biological bases of behavior. "One area of prediction and hypothesis has been of considerable controversy, the application of sociobiology to

Homo sapiens. Sociobiologists argue that some principles used to investigate the social behavior of animals can be applied to investigate the social behavior of humans."[3]

Few social scientists argue with the first two concepts, evolution and ethology. However, there is serious controversy concerning the third—sociobiology. Here *Homo sapiens* is involved, and here emotions are aroused. The question is, does *Homo sapiens* begin life genetically predisposed toward particular behavior patterns? Is *all* behavior learned or is there, in some instances, an inherited tendency to behave in a particular fashion, given certain stimuli? This is the area of disagreement. Though many concepts are involved, a brief comment on three of them—aggression, territoriality, and dominance-deference patterns—should serve to illustrate the problem.

Aggression is "intentional injury to person or damage to property."[4] There are three competing theories that seek to explain human aggression: the sociological theory of *learned behavior*, the psychological hypothesis of *frustration-aggression*, and the biological thesis of a *genetic (ethological) base*. The learned behavior theory of sociology sees aggression as a consequence of naturally benign individuals being driven to violence by environmental circumstances. The psychologist views aggression as being caused by frustration in goal attainment. The ethologist sees aggression as an innate characteristic, genetically encoded in humankind through natural selection. The problem is that commitment to any of the three theories involves a leap of faith. There are simply three seemingly irreconcilable ways of viewing aggression, none of which can boast of being more rational than the other two—although each faction has erected monuments of empirical evidence to support its position.[5]

Territoriality suggests that all human beings have a sense of territory. This may be reflected in a passive love of country (patriotism) or in the active nationalism of Iranians since their 1979 revolution, Palestinians in their struggle with Israel, and Jews in their vow to see Jerusalem forever united under Israeli rule. Human beings who emigrate often find themselves strangers forever in their adopted land. All of us have experienced a longing for our hometown, and most people talk nostalgically about their roots. Our very identity is tied into territory. In many ways, people know who they are in terms of geography. If this is true, even in part, then hopes for the peaceful accommodation of tensions in international politics will be forever unrealizable in a world of continual mobility and movement.[6]

Dominance-deference theory suggests that "man's biological nature incorporates strong propensities to establish and sustain . . . hierarchies within his social groupings; that is the stratification of political authority, power and influence may be by nature intrinsic to human social existence."[7] Dominance here suggests rule while deference implies obedience. Again, there are only two ways to view the dilemma: Either political relations are, as Marx believed, transitory arrangements, doomed to wither away in the new world; or humans are, as Aristotle said, political animals destined to live life in political relationships forever. In the former case, a temporarily hostile but ultimately benign theory of human nature prevails. In the latter instance, one accepts humankind as it is—good and evil, selfish and selfless, egoistic and altruistic—and constructs social, economic, and political relations reflective of that reality. In the former case, authoritarian rule is required as there is a task to fulfill. In the latter case, people can work for a more humane politics as it will be with us always.

3. Intellectually, the significance of biopolitics for conceptualization at all levels of political science is profound.   Every area of theoretical development and research is affected—political philosophy, political behavior, methodology, and the systemic models. Knowledge of biopolitics will not, for example, solve the theoretical problems associated with concepts such as power, authority, influence, religion, and history. But the new information of biopolitics can help expand, illuminate, and develop scholarship in these areas. The dialogues and debates generated by the pioneers of this new field in the study of politics can help social scientists test existing theories. To paraphrase John Stuart Mill in his book *On Liberty*, if some of the ideas of biopolitics are correct, we can benefit by exchanging error for truth. If some of the ideas are incorrect we can gain almost as great a benefit—an opportunity to gain a clearer perception of the truth produced by its collision with error.

Practical Reasons

1. Every one of the great issues of biopolitics raises major questions of public policy.   From the obvious issues of the environment and the earth's climate, such as holes in the ozone layer of the earth's atmosphere, waste disposal, deforestation, and population overload, to the complex issues involving human reproduction (frozen embryos, artificial twinning), the harvesting of human organs, the formidable puzzles of chemical and biological weapons, mapping and sequencing of the human genetic code, and gene transfer and genetic screening, the explosion of biological knowledge generates momentous philosophical, religious, legal, and political problems. Each one touches on the dignity of the human individual and on the vitality of our free democratic society.

Biology has given human beings solutions, but those very solutions have created staggering problems for government at every level. Today, political leaders must develop new policies, assume new roles, and revise the allocation of scarce resources. The nation desperately needs policies for every issue just mentioned—and scores more not cited—plus regulation of biotechnological research and development and new guidelines for government, business, and academia. All are involved. How citizens think about the environment must be changed if they are to survive. How people think about human beings must be altered if they are to continue life, with dignity, in an authentic political community.

2. Public understanding of the great issues of biopolitics stands at a dismal level.   In the presidential campaign of 2000, science and technology were virtually left out in the cold. Very little of the dialogue among the candidates involved the complex relationship between science, technology, and the nation's future. Yet these issues are as important to the nation's future as economics, social policy, and foreign affairs. Science and technology, in large part, were ignored by the candidates and the media as they talked of the future. "Science *is* the future and any candidate with a vision of the next decade" should be talking about these issues.[8] Without discussion and debate, we can expect little from government. Illumination of the issues is therefore urgent, for it is public opinion that generates governmental acts. Consider just one example: In 1950, world population was 2.5 billion. By the fall of 1987 it had doubled to 5 billion—all in thirty-seven years. And where did this increase occur? As expected, in the Third World countries. The migratory pressure and the necessity to escape, to "go north," is already accelerating, leading to serious social problems and the rise of racist doctrines in a number of countries in Europe (Germany, France, Great Britain, Belgium, the Netherlands) and the United States.

3. The formerly veiled, now open, threat to the order and stability of our social system is at hand. It is here now—not fifty years from now. If biological manipulation of behavior is possible (and it is), then our democratic system is potentially at some peril. Democracy presupposes human beings as free moral agents, not manipulated agents of bureaucratic conditioners. To maintain and nourish our democratic institutions, we need to take into account the revolution in biology and its explosive technology.

We live in a world of approximately 186 sovereign states that are, for the most part, accountable only to themselves. Yet the world ecological issues transcend the nation-state. Global issues and the sovereign state system do not auger well for thoughtful policy on biopolitical issues. Every ideology will view these problems in a different fashion. Think how differently the issues of eugenics, medical ethics, reproductive technology, and the ecological crisis might be viewed from the perspectives of liberalism, conservatism, fascism, and communism. The facts of biology and the values and beliefs of the various ideologies stand in obvious tension with one another. Nationally and internationally, the struggle to set priorities, to determine the nature of the key issues, and to know how to handle them will be animated, to say the least.

What Are the Great Issues of Biopolitics?

Public policy directs its central attention to the biomedical issues, issues associated with biotechnology, and the ecological crisis.[9] Since the focus of this text is on political issues, these topics form the subject matter of the three major chapters that constitute this section on biology and politics.

Biomedical Issues (Chapter 7): In order to understand the origin, nature, and politics of the major biomedical issues to be discussed, the reader is first introduced to three topics: ethics and law, the legal and ethical concepts employed in biomedical issues, and the principal codes of conduct that limit the behavior of medical professionals. The heart of this chapter (the "Status" section) employs two major concepts to organize the data—"Reproductive Technologies" and "Life-Maintenance Technologies." Each of these two great issues of biopolitics presents humanity with new challenges requiring imaginative decisions. Each requires that human beings face the unbridgeable gulf between what is and what ought to be and reconcile the two in public policy. The chapter concludes with some commentary on future trends in the area and the political and legal complexities entailed.

Biotechnology (Chapter 8): After a brief explanation of the history and development of biotechnology in the "Sources" section of the chapter, the focus of the chapter ("Status") is organized under two major subtopics—biotechnology and genetic engineering. The section on biotechnology addresses four major concerns: the five industries most affected, major areas of risk, regulation, and relationships. The next major subtopic—genetic engineering—discusses three problems: the genome project, the repair of deficiencies, and the improvement of organisms. The chapter closes with a résumé of the important legal, commercial, and ethical questions associated with the burgeoning new phenomenon of biotechnology.

The Ecological Crisis (Chapter 9): The basic analysis in this chapter on the worldwide ecological crisis is divided into two sections—biotic and abiotic—in the section labeled "Status." The discussion of the biotic crisis deals with the problems attendant to our living systems—population, plants, and animals. The world's population explosion is discussed in some detail, and then the dangers implicit in the diminution or extinction of plant and animal species is examined. The abiotic analysis is organized under the categories of air, water, and land. The analysis here inquires into a host of related issues such as the ozone layer, the greenhouse effect, toxic chemicals, expansion of deserts, problems with drinking water, deforestation, and the like. This chapter concludes with an analysis of recent public policies and national and international proposals that purport to deal with these questions.

NOTES

1. Thomas C. Wiegele, *Biopolitics: Search for a More Human Political Science* (Boulder, CO: Westview Press, 1979), pp. 7–8.
2. Ibid., pp. 26–28.
3. Sebastian Haskel and David Sygoda, *Fundamental Concepts of Modern Biology* (New York: Amsco School Publications, 1972), pp. 18 and 22.
4. James C. Davies, "Aggression: Some Definition and Some Physiology," *Politics and the Life Sciences*, August 1987, vol. 6, no. 1, p. 27.
5. Ibid., p. 37.
6. Albert Somit, "Review Article: Biopolitics," *British Journal of Political Science* 2, April 2, 1972, p. 218.
7. Fred H. Willhoite, Jr., "Primates and Political Authority: A Biobehavioral Perspective," *The American Political Science Review* 70, 1976, p. 1110.
8. Frank Press, editorial in the *Dayton Daily News*, April 10, 1988, sec. B, p. 7.
9. Bryan Hunter (ed.), *The Statesman's Yearbook: 1995–96* (New York: St. Martin's Press, 1996), p. 7.

Chapter 7

Biomedical Issues

Beginning in the year 2001, and for the first decade of the new millennium, there are a number of weighty biomedical issues confronting the citizens and government of our modern democratic state. How we resolve, or fail to resolve, these issues will determine, in part, the kind of human individuals we shall become; the nature and vitality of our most basic social institution, the family; the class structure of our free society; and the very vitality of our democratic political economy.

To understand the origin and nature of the major biomedical issues to be discussed, three topics must be introduced: the nature of ethics and law, the major legal and ethical concepts employed in biomedical issues, and the principal codes of conduct that limit behavior of medical professionals. The goal here is, of course, to illuminate the historical and philosophical antecedents contributing to the development of these issues.

Next, two major conceptual phrases are employed to organize the mass of data associated with these great issues of biomedicine—reproductive technologies and life-maintenance technologies. Each of these issues presents us with new, unforeseen, and sometimes startling legal and moral problems demanding that policymakers face reality objectively and create priorities and hierarchies in our national value system, since each issue implies different ethical outcomes. Each requires that we face the unbridgeable gulf between what is and what ought to be and reconcile the two in public policy. For what is right, ethical, and *ought* to be must ultimately be united with what *is* in the cauldron of power politics.

Reproductive technologies constitutes the heart of this chapter, and it is here that science has given us the most staggering inventions. Today, we virtually manufacture babies, families, and society.

Originally, the family had its origin in the union of a man and a woman. It was they, and they alone, who had a role to play in any expansion of the family. Today, in many instances, the expansion of the family may involve many more actors playing technical and biological roles. To cite just one widely publicized example: In the fall of 1987, a forty-eight-year-old South African woman gave birth to her daughter's test-tube triplets. She thus became "the world's first surrogate mother of her own grandchildren."[1] Eggs from her daughter, whose uterus had been removed, were fertilized with sperm from her daughter's husband and implanted in the prospective grandmother, who subsequently produced the triplets. Since South Africa has no laws to deal with such a phenomenon, the daughter had to adopt her own genetic issue.[2] This illustrates just one of a host of issues. Today, one woman may be the donor of ova, a second woman may carry the fertilized eggs, and a third woman may adopt the child. Thus, when the child cries for its mother, three women might legitimately step forward. Civil law, religion, and ethicists have hardly begun to deal with such a problem, and this is truly a problem of simple proportions compared with others facing today's families.

In the past, the class structure of modern democratic society was a function of one's parents' economic position or the special talents of the individual. Ted Kennedy had the good fortune to be born into a wealthy and politically active family. Ted Turner had the organizational talent and personality skills requisite to organize and run CNN, the Cable News Network. Bill Gates, the mastermind of Microsoft software used in personal computers, is today the richest man in the world, and from this position of wealth and knowledge he exercises tremendous influence in virtually all aspects of human relationships. All exercise an inordinate amount of control over public opinion and public policy in America. Today, society can be rationally planned—and it will be as technology advances. We can and have produced superkids. And when one produces such children, one has, by definition, produced normal kids and subnormal kids. Perhaps we will forgo the labels of Gammas or Deltas as employed by Aldous Huxley in *Brave New World,* but the labels *superkid* or *Gamma* are only convenient euphemisms employed to satisfy our psychic needs.

The section on *life-maintenance technologies* deals with the dark side of the development of machinery to maintain life artificially. It also covers the transplanting of human organs such as the heart, liver, kidney, and cornea; hormone treatment; and cybernetics, in which a human function is replaced by a machine, or a body part is replaced with a mechanical device. As each problem is examined, an effort is made to clearly describe the nature of the technological development along with the ethical and legal controversy associated with its use. In addition, the intense competition for certification by the government among private agencies that retrieve kidneys and other organs for transplanting is analyzed. Who are the agencies involved, and why is the struggle so fierce?

This section of the chapter also explores and critically analyzes a number of issues confronting society in the area of medicine and health from a religious, ethical, political, and legal perspective. Here we inquire into some of the basic ethical principles and operative ideals of our society by applying them to specific biomedical issues such as death and dying, abortion, the newborn, experimentation on human subjects, informed consent, and the allocation of scarce resources.

The chapter concludes with some speculation on future trends in the area of biomedical issues as seen "through a glass darkly."

SOURCES: BIOMEDICAL ETHICS

On the Nature of Ethics and Law

Ethics is the discipline concerned "with what is good and bad and with moral duty and obligation . . . [it involves] a set of moral principles and values. . . . [and in medical practice] accepted professional standards of conduct."[3] Ethics also involves the relation of ends to means, because frequently situations arise in medical research and practice that demand resolution of such moral dilemmas. Medical ethics thus involves a pattern of values accepted as valid in a particular professional or institutional setting. It is binding on those who belong to the group, such as members of the AMA, and is backed up by sanctions that might include loss of license for those who fail to obey the code.

Civil law is related to politics and differs dramatically from ethical codes such as the Hippocratic Oath in both scope and sanction. David Easton's concept of "the authoritative allocation of values for a society"[4] is perhaps the most useful phrase available to clarify the difference. Law is binding on all individuals and groups in society, not some, and is backed up by coercive force—the police and armed forces of the state, if necessary. Sanctions imposed on those who disobey the law may even involve the execution of the transgressor. The distinctions should thus be clear: Codes of ethics apply to *some* individuals and groups in society, and physical punishment, if permitted at all, is strictly limited. Civil law applies to *all* individuals and groups in a social system, and sanctions may, in some cases, even involve the death of those who violate the law. For example, the state can and does set limits on the physical punishment parents may inflict on their own children. Yet, paradoxically, the state may at some later date hang, shoot, or inject with a lethal dose of poison that same child for failure to obey the law.

Medical professionals are constantly making moral decisions with major legal implications. Traditionally, they have employed four ethical theories to justify their decisions: *consequences* of the procedure (greatest good for greatest number); *duty* as defined by some ethical code (Ten Commandments); the *rights* and claims of the human individual; and personal *intuition* of the attending professional.[5]

Major Ethical Concepts of Biomedicine

To participate intellectually in the discussion that follows, it is very important to understand some key concepts. Lawyers, politicians, physicians, technicians, theologians, and ethicists are all involved. And for good or ill, they commonly use some terms that must be understood. Five crucial concepts are briefly discussed here; other lesser but important ones are defined in the glossary at the end of Part III.

1. *Human Beings:* Professionals involved in decision making constantly refer to human beings, to their nature and rights. A problem of biology and politics is specifying what constitutes the essence of human life. The concept of consciousness may be helpful here. Animals possess consciousness. Human beings have self-consciousness, that is, they are aware of their awareness. This is the turning back of the mind upon itself and

the quality that distinguishes human beings from beasts, the quality that reflects their uniqueness and dignity.

2. *Autonomy:* The autonomy of the human individual refers to a quality of self-direction and self-control. Autonomy implies self-directing freedom and moral independence. Human beings are free moral agents. They choose and make decisions. For example, democratic politics is choosing a destiny rather than simply making adjustments to environmental conditions. Autonomy means that one has control over one's life, is responsible for the decisions made, and has an area of discretion (judgment) within which control over the self is operative. In politics, autonomy refers to self-government. In biomedicine, it refers to self-direction and personal responsibility.

3. *Informed Consent:* In medicine, nothing should be done until the patient has been determined to be mentally competent to make a decision in the case, has had the procedure carefully explained, and has then given his or her free consent to the procedure.[6] Informed consent may well be the fundamental problem of bioethics. Does the patient understand the problem, and has his or her agreement to allow the procedure been freely given? For example, can a child agree to complex procedures, or an elderly person in a coma? Obviously not. Here other human beings are involved in the decision-making process and a kind of paternalism exists. This paternalism is prevalent in medicine today and has been for 2,500 years. In these cases, actors other than the patient are involved in decision making and, in such cases, informed consent is a consequence of their analysis of the situation.

4. *Rights:* Moral rights are based on one's value-belief system and the product of information privately revealed to particular individuals. Civil rights are legal claims spelled out in common, statutory, and constitutional law. The sanctions of the former may involve damnation. The sanctions of the latter include financial penalty, imprisonment, or both. Patients have moral rights that vary depending on their value system, but all have legal rights in a free society, guaranteed by the state and civil law. The rights of patients, doctors, institutions, and the public will be a part of every substantive issue examined in the next part of this chapter.

5. *Malfeasance:* In biomedical issues, malfeasance refers to wrongdoing or misconduct by a researcher or practitioner. The medical professional is duty bound to help others and, if this is impossible, to do no harm. The duty to help others and avoid harm is explicit in every code of ethics for medical researchers and practitioners from the Hippocratic Oath to the Geneva Convention Code. This is a high-priority concept for doctors.

Principle Codes of Conduct Regarding Medical Ethics

The **Hippocratic Oath,** written in 500 B.C., seeks to protect the rights of patients and to define the proper relationship between physician and patient, particularly the notion of confidentiality. The oath also warns the physician to be alert to and avoid any malfeasance in practice.

The Principles of Medical Ethics of the American Medical Association, first established in 1847 and updated ever since, states guidelines for physicians in their relationships with patients, colleagues, and other health professionals. These guidelines refer particularly to honesty, competence, and the rights of all. In addition, the code demands that physicians expose colleagues who are incompetent or who engage in fraud or deception. Finally, physicians are called to perform community service and to seek to improve public policy as needed.

The Nuremburg Code was created after World War II in response to the Nazi medical abuses practiced by some physicians in Hitler's Germany. The object of concern of this code is medical experiments and research. The code demands voluntary, informed consent of the subjects of experiment, requires prior animal experimentation, demands that all unnecessary physical and mental suffering be eliminated, and prohibits any experiments where there is good reason to believe death or disability will follow.

The Declaration of Helsinki provides detailed guidelines for biomedical research involving human beings and acts as an update of the Nuremburg Code. It was established during the decade from 1964 to 1974. This code includes a detailed set of principles to guide those involved in experimentation. It deals with ethical behavior in clinical research (research combined with professional care) and nonclinical biomedical research.[7]

STATUS: BIOMEDICAL ISSUES

Reproductive Technologies (Birth)

Consider the following:

- A husband and wife killed in a plane crash left some embryos in a freezer in Australia; their children are now involved in a legal battle with relatives who say they are acting on behalf of the frozen embryos.
- A lesbian couple requested artificial insemination and, when the clinic refused, the state of Michigan intervened on behalf of the couple.
- Doctors can now impregnate women who have passed menopause.
- Five Nobel laureates have donated sperm to an exclusive sperm bank.
- Twins can now be artificially created.
- Doctors nourished a baby inside the brain-dead corpse of a woman and in August 1993 delivered a healthy child.
- A grandmother's legs, which were covered with venous ulcers, are now covered with skin that can be traced back to her grandson: A doctor did a circumcision and sent the removed foreskin to a laboratory, where the cells in the foreskin were grown in a culture; after three weeks, sheets of the new skin were sent to doctors, who applied them to the grandmother's legs.[8]
- A single woman in Vermont "drops a seventy-five-dollar check in the mail to a health center in northern California, gets back sperm packed in dry ice and impregnates herself."[9]
- In 1999, a woman in California "had a baby using sperm that was extracted from her dead husband as he lay in the morgue."[10]

Developments in the biological sciences have produced moral, social, and legal questions of great complexity. For example, the new reproductive technologies necessarily imply that vital decisions must be made on eugenics, the science deal-ing with improvement of a race by control of procreation. Some genetic material will be viewed favorably and some unfavorably. In addition, our capitalist economic system, a marvel of productivity, will surely be a part of the problem as business-men seek commercial advantage from the new discoveries. Few, if any, guidelines exist, so our entrepreneurial system may well exacerbate an already difficult and complex situation. Further, some in the feminist movement are concerned that the new technology is little more than an unmitigated attack on women. They argue that the new reproductive technologies demand that we redefine what it means to be a woman.[11] Just think of the malpractice charges to which physicians will be subject in the future. The lack of clear legal guidelines plus the reality of physicians shar-ing decision-making responsibilities suggests more and more litigation.

That the new reproductive technologies generate complex problems is patent-ly true. It is equally true that they offer great benefits; namely, they can assist infertile couples in having children (a source of great happiness and reduction of stress and anxiety); create conditions where, through surrogacy, a childless couple can have a child that is partially their own genetic product; and gain new knowledge by manipulating the basic material of life via genetic engineering.

We live at the dawn of the third millennium, a period in which our technolo-gy has run far ahead of our religious, moral, and legal codes. The new technology stands in opposition to the old morality: We have sexless reproduction but still de-fine parenthood in the same way. The contradiction must be resolved. Three concepts are employed here to organize and explain the multitude of reproductive tech-nologies available today: designer babies, ersatz families, and programmed society.

Designer Babies

The All-New Conjugal Act.   Until recently, the vast majority of babies were obtained by the sexual union of a man and a woman in the privacy of the bedroom. Today, quite a variety of alternatives are available to those who want to have a baby. Consider the following:

1. *Artificial insemination (AI):* In this procedure, sperm from the husband, or from a donor when the husband is infertile (AID), is injected into the wife's genital tract to induce conception.
2. *In vitro fertilization (IVF):* Here an egg is removed from a woman's ovary and fertil-ized with sperm from a man. Forty-eight hours after this external procedure, the fer-tilized egg is put into the woman's uterus so that gestation can begin. This procedure might, of course, involve only a husband and wife or it might involve either an egg or sperm donor.
3. *In vivo fertilization (IViF):* This technique is used when a woman cannot produce viable eggs, but can gestate a baby. Sperm from the husband of woman A is used to fertilize woman B. Five to seven days after conception, B's womb is flushed and the embryo transferred to A's uterus, where gestation occurs.[12]
4. *Gamete intrafallopian transfer (GIFT):* Technicians induce and monitor development of eggs in the ovaries. They then collect the eggs from the woman, the sperm from the

man, and put the eggs and sperm into the fallopian tubes together to secure fertilization. In IVF, fertilization is external. In GIFT, it is internal. Again, this may or may not involve egg or sperm donation.[13]

5. *Fertility drugs (FD):* Drugs are employed to artificially stimulate a woman's ovaries (superovulation) to ensure that several eggs are produced in a cycle. This procedure is frequently employed prior to IVF.

6. *Egg, embryo, and sperm donation (EESD):* As noted above, EESD may be involved in AI, IVF, IViF, and GIFT. Nevertheless, it is vital to note these aspects of reproductive technology separately, as they imply peculiarly pressing social, ethical, and legal questions.

7. *Single sperm direct injection (SSDI):* This technique, invented by Belgian scientists, may allow almost any man, no matter how few, misshapen, or immobile his sperm cells, to father a child. The method involves "the direct injection of a single human sperm into a human egg in a petri dish."[14] So far the scientists have produced more than three hundred pregnancies through SSDI and one hundred babies have been born.

What are some of the questions raised by the new reproductive technologies? What are the major ideological postures around which the debate centers? Three perspectives stand out today—the feminist movement, the Warnock Committee, and the Roman Catholic Church.

On the issues associated with designer babies, the easiest position to explain is that of the Roman Catholic Church as expressed in its "Instruction on Respect for Human Life in its Origin and on the Dignity of Procreation" (Rome, 1987, hereinafter called "Instruction"). This well-written and logically impeccable document contends that none of the reproductive technologies noted here are morally licit; all violate the conjugal union of a man and wife and, in so doing, deprive the procreation of its "unitive meaning." The use of third-party egg, embryo, and sperm donors; technicians; masturbation; and external fertilization, as well as the disposal of fertilized eggs, all are seen by the "Instruction" as morally illicit.[15]

Many in the feminist movement are also concerned about the application and effects of the new reproductive technologies. For instance, they are particularly concerned that valid informed consent was obtained from those women involved in the experiments leading to the development of these technologies. In addition, they are concerned that the new technologies may demean motherhood, turn women's bodies into mere commodities that men can simply rent for a short period in order to carry a child created by AI, and give politicians and doctors control over their lives during pregnancy.[16] Finally, some contend that these technologies are limited and should be available to those with all forms of sexual preference, including not only those in heterosexual but also in homosexual relationships.

"The Warnock Report on Human Fertilization and Embryology" (England, 1985) explains the technology, presents pros and cons on each, and then makes its recommendations. For example, the Warnock Report recommends that there be time limits on keeping an embryo alive in vitro; that children born where a donor is involved should receive information on ethnicity and genetic health at age eighteen; that all involved in IVF be licensed; that any unauthorized use of embryos derived via IVF be a criminal offense; and that no research on embryos may occur after the fourteenth day of gestation. These and a host of other thoughtful recommendations are addressed to the new technology.

Improving Babies.   Science has provided technology that enables us to control the transmission of some hereditary diseases and to achieve gender identification. Diagnostic screening can detect abnormalities and genetic defects, and the Warnock Report suggests that donor eggs, sperm, and in some cases embryos, should be offered to those who may transmit hereditary disorders. We may soon produce infants free of many genetic defects. Regarding sex selection, this can be important in cases involving certain sex-linked genetic disorders such as **hemophilia,** a defect almost always associated with males and characterized by an inability to clot blood, with subsequent hemorrhaging. Where either partner is determined to be a carrier, this defect can be avoided by amniocentesis and, if the disease is present, abortion.[17] The new technology also may help couples in other ways; for example, in the United States, recent surveys show that "when a couple already has a boy, there is a very strong preference that the next child be a girl."[18] The technology is simple but effective (sex chromosomes in girls are XX; in boys, the combinations are XY) and is patented by Gametrics Limited of Montana. "Sperm swim through a test tube filled with a specially prepared gel. The sperm that make it to the bottom are more likely to have a Y [male] chromosome."[19] If a couple wants a girl, the woman is inseminated with sperm from the top of the tube, while those who wish a boy are inseminated with the sperm from the bottom. The 50–50 odds that characterize traditional sex selection are significantly changed to a 72 percent success rate.[20] A recent technique developed at Genetics & IVF Institute claims the clinic can offer couples an 85 percent chance of producing a girl. Sperm are given a dose of a DNA staining chemical since the X chromosome in a sperm designed to produce a girl has a bit more DNA than the Y chromosome. A laser then is targeted on one sperm at a time, making it glow. Since the female-producing sperm shines more brightly, a machine automatically separates the brighter from the dimmer sperm. Voilà—a girl is conceived in 85 percent of cases.[21]

The tragic side of changing the odds so dramatically is to be found in countries such as India and China, where there are strong cultural biases against females. This bias is exacerbated in China by that nation's policy of only one child for a couple. Some experts claim that thousands of female babies are aborted or killed each year.

Still other techniques that are in the immediate future include **artificial twinning** and gene insertion. Cattle breeders in the livestock industry presently have the technology to divide the embryo of a valuable animal and create twins. "There is no technical reason why this could not be attempted with humans";[22] and in October of 1993, Dr. Jerry L. Hall of George Washington University in Washington, D.C., "successfully cloned human embryos, splitting single embryos into identical twins or triplets."[23] This is the first report of such an accomplishment. Scientists have already inserted "genes into the eggs of mice during the IVF process. The genes are . . . then passed on to their offspring."[24] This procedure creates conditions in which cures for genetic diseases become a probability, not a mere possibility.

Finally, some argue for **sterilization** of mentally retarded people without their consent. The argument here is that mentally retarded parents cannot fully care for and provide for their children; that taxpayers are therefore forced to pay to raise the child with funds that might have been used in a more utilitarian manner (immunization); and that in cases where the cause is genetic rather than environmental (not a result of malnutrition, for example), the offspring of mentally retarded parents often create a continuing social problem. However, some also demand that we answer important legal and ethical questions. What are the ethical limits on research? Who should decide what these limits are, if any? How shall we reconcile the conflicting values of our search for knowledge versus respect for the human individual? To test the level of volatility implicit in some of these procedures associated with reproductive technologies, consider the following hypotheses:

1. Unauthorized use of an embryo conceived in vitro would (would not) constitute a criminal offense.[25] An embryo derived in vitro, "whether frozen or unfrozen," may (may not) be kept alive, "if not transferred to a woman,"[26] after fourteen days.
2. When a couple who have stored a frozen embryo dies, the right to dispose of or use the embryo passes to the storage authority (the relatives).[27]
3. Do-it-yourself sex selection kits should (should not) be controlled by the state.[28]
4. A child born to "a woman following donation of another's egg"[29] shall (shall not) be considered the child of the birthing mother, the donor to have no legal rights whatsoever.
5. A donor of sperm should (should not) be limited to ten children[30] fathered by this process of donation.

There are literally hundreds of unanswered ethical and legal problems involved. Just consider the issue of inheritance and cryopreservation (frozen embryos) technology to get some idea of the complexity of the problem.

"Ersatz" Families

Surrogacy. Virtually every American is familiar with the much publicized Baby M case. It provoked debate in homes, churches, and legislative assemblies. For about three months Mary Beth Whitehead fought for the custody of a child she had given birth to under a $10,000 contract with William Stern. She called the child Sara. He called the child Melissa. Stern's sperm had been used to fertilize Whitehead's egg through AI. Stern wanted a child to whom he was genetically linked. The New Jersey Superior Court said the contract was a valid one and Stern was awarded custody in March 1987. However, in February of 1988, the New Jersey Supreme Court overruled the March ruling by Judge Harvey Sorkow and held that commercial surrogate contracts are illegal.[31] Whitehead's parental rights cannot be denied—she is the mother. Though legally binding only in New Jersey, this decision seriously clouds the whole practice of commercial surrogacy contracts.

What is **surrogacy?** "Surrogacy is the practice whereby one woman carries a child for another with the intention that the child should be handed over after birth."[32] AI or IVF is employed in this procedure. The egg may be the product of the commissioning mother or it may be that of the surrogate; the sperm may be that of the commissioning father or that of an agreed-upon donor; the surrogate mother carries the embryo through the gestation period and then turns the baby over to the commissioning couple[33]—many combinations are possible. Surrogacy frequently involves payment, but may be done for humanitarian reasons. The Baby M case does not make all surrogacy invalid, only that involving a commercial agreement where payment is involved. This could run from $10,000 to $25,000 for the surrogate mother, $10,000 for the lawyer who drafted the contract, and $5,000 for medical expenses.

The basic argument for surrogacy is that it offers a couple who have no children a chance to have a child that is genetically related to one of them. The danger of surrogacy is that a woman's uterus is used for profit. In essence, her body is transformed into a commodity to be bought and sold, like corn or cattle. For this reason the Warnock Report recommends that surrogacy contracts and agreements should be declared illegal and unenforceable in the courts.[34] The "Instructions" of the Roman Catholic Church clearly state that surrogacy is morally illicit because it violates the sanctity of the traditional conjugal act. Finally, feminists express grave concerns about surrogacy contracts because, they say, they reinforce our class-stratified society, expose women to economic exploitation, will ultimately lead to cross-racial surrogacy when embryo transfer has been perfected, and permit men to hire women at a rate of $10,000 for nine months,[35] or for about $1.50 per hour, simply to expand their own gene pool.

Surrogacy poses fascinating problems related to the family and parenthood. For example, consider the case where a child cries out for its mother and three women rush forward—the one who donated the egg, the one who carried the egg through the nine months of gestation, and the adoptive mother. Who *is* the mother? What stress and anxiety will the child suffer in later life? To this could be added, of course, two fathers—the one who donated the sperm and the adoptive father. Legally and ethically we are not in tune with our technological achievements. Will this enfeebling of the mother-infant bond ultimately corrode us as a species? Will marriage and the family be further enfeebled? The "Instructions" of the Roman Catholic Church certainly think such is the case. They contend that the institution of the family, society's fundamental building block, is seriously weakened by such arrangements.[36]

Consider the following examples that demonstrate the complexity of surrogacy. Women who are past menopause are now giving birth to children. In Italy, a sixty-two-year-old widow became pregnant after "implantation of an ovum fertilized by the sperm of her late husband (the donor of the egg was not identified)."[37] In California, a fifty-three-year-old grandmother became pregnant with twins from donated eggs fertilized with sperm from her thirty-two-year-old husband.[38] In Houston, in November of 1993, a woman rented a billboard on the highway that said, "Womb For Rent! Educated, Loving, Surrogate Mother Available." The woman said the price was negotiable.

In Ohio the law says that the woman who delivers a baby is its mother. Problem: Shelly Belsito, of Kent, had her cancerous uterus removed in 1992. However, she continues to produce healthy eggs, which were fertilized with her husband's sperm and then implanted in her sister's womb. According to law, the Belsitos must adopt their own genetic issue because the hospital is required to list Mrs. Clark, the birth mother and sister of Shelly Belsito, as the real mother. A county judge decides the case.[39]

One more example should make the case for the complexity of surrogacy. A woman in Michigan agreed to be a surrogate mother for $10,000. She gave birth to twins, a boy and a girl. The commissioning parents did not want two children because they felt it would be added stress. They took the girl but refused the boy, who is now being raised by the surrogate mother and her husband. This could well be an economic and marital nightmare for the families in the future.

In an effort to deal with all the complexities of surrogacy, New York State recently banned surrogate parenting for profit. The state legislature was pressured to pass the bill by an unusual coalition that included the National Organization for Women (NOW) and the New York State Catholic Conference. Though surrogacy for profit is now illegal, people in New York can still act as surrogates for relatives or friends.

Scientific Parenting. In 1983, doctors in Australia "announced that the first woman to become pregnant with a frozen embryo will give birth [to the baby] 13 months after the baby was conceived."[40] The embryo had been stored at a temperature of minus 200 degrees for four months, thawed, and placed in the woman for gestation.[41] **Cryopreservation** (freezing of sperm, eggs, or embryos) prevents fertilized eggs from being destroyed. It also allows technicians to save fertilized eggs in the event the initial IVF fails. The greatest conflicts arise over the status of the embryo. The Vatican's "Instructions" insist that it must have the full rights of personhood, since life begins at conception. Australia, a leader in the area of reproductive technology, has established guidelines that limit cryopreservation to a maximum of ten years.[42] This technique of delayed pregnancy is common in animal husbandry; it is relatively new in its relation to human beings, however, and raises grave questions. But the technique is a fact of life: It works, and the procedure must be thoughtfully analyzed. The first baby from a frozen embryo was born in March 1984 in Australia, a five-and-a-half-pound girl born by caesarean section, conceived by IVF from the egg and sperm of a husband and wife. The embryo was frozen for only two months, but it could have been ten or twenty years. This raises staggering legal questions.[43]

To further clarify the tension between law and technological change, consider these two facts: (a) Federal law relies on state law in determining who gets Social Security; and (b) Under Louisiana law a child conceived after the father's death is not recognized as his heir. In 1995, Ed Hart developed cancer and had his sperm stored, fearing that chemotherapy would make him sterile. Hart later died, his wife was impregnated with his sperm three months after his death, and subsequently she gave birth to a little girl. When she applied for Social Security survivor benefits ($700 per month), her petition was denied and the little girl was declared illegitimate. Nancy Hart sued the Social Security Administration, and in March 1996, the bureaucracy of Social Security reversed its position and agreed to pay. Law and technology were again in correspondence—at least for the moment.[44]

The most celebrated case in the United States relating to cryopreservation was resolved after a four-year struggle in the courts. In Maryville, Tennessee, a man (Junior L. Davis) divorcing his wife (Mary Sue Davis) went to court to prevent her from becoming pregnant with fertilized eggs they had placed in frozen storage. The argument centered on who should control the couple's seven frozen embryos. "The embryos in the Davis case were less than two days old when they were frozen, and consist of four to eight undifferentiated cells each."[45] In September 1989, the court ruled that the fertilized eggs should go to Mary Sue Davis. Junior Davis appealed the decision and after a four-year custody fight with his ex-wife, the embryos were finally awarded to him. Davis's major argument was that he did not want to become a father against his will. Subsequent to the award by the appeals court, the seven frozen human embryos were destroyed. There was simply no precedent for this dispute.[46] Nothing in our law, religion, or philosophy prepares us for such decisions. Yet technological advancement in biology demands that we resolve such challenges. More are certainly on the way.

Embryo transfer is the movement of a human embryo from one uterus to another for the period of gestation. This can be done for either medical or social reasons. Medically, a woman may be able to produce, conceive, and carry an embryo for a short time. But if she cannot carry the embryo or fetus for the full period, it can simply be transferred to a surrogate for the period of gestation. Embryo transfer might also occur when a wealthy or active woman simply does not care to go through the inconvenience of a nine-month pregnancy. In this case, transfer of the embryo to a surrogate produces the genetic offspring of the commissioning couple.

"Programmed Society." Challenges to a free society abound in the new reproductive technologies. These challenges exist in the very nature of the human beings who are born into the social system. We know that social classes exist as a product of both fortune and initiative, but what happens now that we can select the qualities we want our children to possess? Consider the following: "Five Nobel laureates have given sperm to an exclusive sperm bank to be matched with the 'right' women in hopes of producing exceptional children."[47] Many people see this as a way to preserve genius. Why not preserve the sperm of an Einstein, a Beethoven, or a Picasso? Why should we not have exceptional children rather than just plain kids? The sperm can be frozen for years and then be thawed, used to fertilize an egg, and successfully gestated. Why not sterilize those who have genetic defects or are mentally retarded? Better yet, a new technology makes it possible that gestation of human embryos in other species will be available soon. Recently a quarter-horse mare gave birth to a normal, well-developed zebra in Louisville, Kentucky. The fertilized egg of two zebras was implanted in the womb of the mare and she produced the small zebra almost one year later.[48] In Cincinnati the embryo of a rare female eland, after being frozen one and a half years in a plastic straw at

383 degrees below zero, was thawed and placed in the womb of a surrogate mother, a Bongo antelope, who subsequently gave birth to the young antelope. The zoo has also used Eland mothers as surrogates to produce Bongo antelopes. This is a new technique used by scientists to preserve an endangered species; here, a common species was employed to gestate a rare species.[49]

There are really few limits to the possibilities. Shopping at sperm banks is a reality. Embryo banks and egg banks may well follow. In February of 2000, a couple advertised that they would pay $100,000 "for the eggs of a bright, young, white athlete."[50] Ellen Goodman recently argued in an article that rules ought to transcend the law of supply and demand. She was commenting on an ad run in newspapers near some of America's most prestigious schools (Harvard, Stanford, MIT, Yale) saying that a couple would pay $50,000 for the eggs of a woman over 5'10" with combined SATs of over 1400.[51] Finally, the Internet site www.ronsangels.com is allegedly set up to sell the eggs of beautiful women to the highest bidder. This is a "beauty egg auction," and is only one example of what may happen. Now if parents don't have the "right" traits, they can buy them on the Internet.[52] Now one can truly have high-tech adoption and select one's children with care. The commissioning couple, probably well off financially, simply goes to a fertility clinic, has eggs and sperm drawn, fertilized in vitro, and transferred to a healthy woman for gestation. They then stop back in nine months and pick up their child.

Cloning of human beings is also a possibility in the future, according to some scientists. The cloning procedure works like this: A mature human egg is obtained from a woman; the nucleus of the egg cell is removed; the nucleus of a body cell of a donor is removed and placed in the egg cell (it could be that of the woman who donated the egg); the renucleated egg will then develop just as other eggs develop; birth occurs.[53] The clone will have the same genotype as his or her parent.[54]

So, as the twenty-first century begins, we are faced with the possibility of new carriers; embryo, sperm, and egg shopping; superkids; cloning; and high-tech adoption. To close this section, consider the following startling procedure. In May 1987, the dean of anthropology at Florence University in Italy said that new technologies make it possible to create "a new breed of slave, an anthropoid with a chimpanzee mother and a human father. . . . The cross-breeding of a female chimpanzee, fertilized with human male sperm, had resulted in the formation of an anthropoid embryo."[55]

Even issues of war and peace can be overwhelmed by technological innovations such as the ones just discussed. It is, perhaps, past time to make these issues a part of the political agenda in America.

Life-Maintenance Technologies

This section addresses some, but not all, of the key technological issues associated with life maintenance. Three concepts organize the mass of technological material to be discussed here—informed consent, life, death. Consent is addressed first, as it is involved in every other case, is quite complex, and is frequently the cause of ethical and legal dilemmas.

Informed Consent

To consent is to give approval to what is done or proposed by another. The Senate must give its consent to treaties signed by the president before they become part of the law of the land. Government in the United States bases its legitimacy on the consent of the people. Consent transforms power into authority—ruling into right-ruling.

In medical research and practice, the concept of consent implies that an individual, or the parents or guardian in the case of a minor, has given permission to the physician or medical researcher to perform some procedure that involves touching, examination, and possibly treatment. Informed consent includes this but goes beyond it in its requirement that the patient be competent to understand the nature of the illness. Four doctrines combine to define the concept of informed consent:

1. what the procedure is and how it is to be performed;
2. possible risks involved as well as expected results;
3. any alternative procedures or treatments and their risks;
4. results if no treatment is given.[56]

Ethically, informed consent is implied in the concepts of individual autonomy and self-determination, as well as the patient's dignity as a human being. The central question here is, What does it mean to be an authentic human being? If the answer is that human beings are free moral agents, then informed consent is mandatory. Paternalism and the decision on just how much information is necessary is, has, and will forever be a problem. Complicated procedures are frequently involved. Nevertheless the effort must be made.

Legally, informed consent and adequate disclosure have been held by the courts to be the duty of the research scientist or physician, who must inform the patient about the possible and probable consequences of the treatment.[57] Failure to do so may involve severe sanctions. The Nuremburg Code is particularly important in consent associated with medical research. The voluntary consent of the individual is "absolutely essential" and stated as such in the first principle of this code. Nuremburg also demands "capacity to consent," elimination of all "force, fraud, deceit, [and] duress," and full disclosure of the "nature, duration, and purpose" of the procedure. Finally, it charges all who initiate, direct, or engage in the research as responsible agents.

Life

Allocation of Scarce Resources.   Allocation of scarce medical resources occurs at two levels, macroallocation and microallocation. Macroallocation decisions relating to scarce resources refers to decisions made by Congress (Medicare), state legislatures (health-systems agencies), health insurance companies (Ohio's insurer for retired teachers is Aetna, for example), and health organizations (heart and cancer funds, for example). Microallocation decisions are made by individuals or small groups at hospitals or offices. The impact of the human individual on the decision-making process is inversely related to the level of decision making; that is, at the micro level, the particular individual (a doctor, patient, or technician) plays a major role, while the same individual at the macro level, in the vast majority of cases, plays a minor role. Simply, as one moves from the level of an office or hospital to the state, nation, or world community, the impact one has on decision making becomes less important. This is as true in medicine as it is in political decision making.

Consider the ethical and legal implications of some of the following cases reported in the press.

1. In Japan, only one heart transplant has been performed in the last thirty years and only 800 kidney transplants are done each year (10,000 a year are done in the United States). Why? Because of Japan's definition of death. Japanese law says that death is declared when the heart stops beating, while in the United States death is defined as death of the brain. Japanese watchdog groups seek murder charges against doctors who perform transplants. Thus, thousands of Japanese die each year waiting for transplants that are routine in the United States.[58]

2. Bombay, India, is the world center for buying and selling kidneys, where this practice is legal. There are about 100 recognized "kidney brokers" in Bombay who arrange to get kidneys for the ailing wealthy from Bombay's poor. These brokers have no problem lining up donors among the poor, who receive from $2,000 to $3,500 for one of their kidneys. This kidneys-for-cash practice has divided the medical profession in India.[59]

3. In London, the government moved recently to stop the sale of kidneys. Turkish peasants who donated a kidney for transplant surgery at Humana Wellington Hospital were paid $3,200 to $5,600. The argument is simple—"we are discussing a shortage of organs for transplant, particularly of kidneys. The waiting list stands at 3,500 people, but the list is growing."[60] The number of donors remains stable while the list of those waiting for a kidney grows. In the United States, the median waiting time in days for a kidney is 965 in 1997. As of February 2000, there are 43,300 people in the United States waiting for a kidney transplant according to a United Network for Organs Sharing Report issued February 29, 2000.

4. Another case involving liver transplants raises other questions. There are many more human individuals with faulty livers needing replacement than there are livers available. The question here is Who gets the liver? What criteria shall be employed? Should society allocate the available liver to the one who will pay the most, the one who has contributed the most to our society (a president or great scientist), the one who has the greatest potential (a youth with a 180 IQ), the one where the chances of success are greatest—or should the candidates simply draw straws, as in a lottery? Which people are involved in making the decision? Which one of the criteria listed above best meets the values of a free society? Now that the technology exists to perform the surgery, the decision cannot be avoided. Liver transplants for three celebrities—David Crosby (rock star), Mickey Mantle (baseball great), and Robert Casey (governor of Pennsylvania)— recently raised questions of fairness in the decision-making process. Is the waiting list for a liver transplant strictly adhered to or do wealth and fame play a part in obtaining donor organs? More than 2,000 Americans die each year awaiting a liver transplant. The expenses involved are very high: $20,000 for evaluation, $300,000 for the

operation, and $1,000 a month for antirejection medication. Many argue that the scales are weighted to favor those with a great deal of money.[61]

5. On September 3, 1999, bidding for a human kidney on the Internet hit $5.7 million. But this is illegal in the United States and the ad was cut from eBay. The very next day's newspaper wrote of an altruistic woman who gave a kidney to a stranger. The Internet advertiser was condemned; the altruistic woman was praised. One was a heel while the other was lauded as a hero. But one could argue that this is the age of the market, so why not a human spare-parts market? The black market for organs is already a thriving business in China, where kidneys, lungs, and livers go to the highest bidder. If somebody wants to sell and someone else wants to buy, what is ethically wrong? In fact, the Missouri legislature recently debated whether death row inmates could donate kidneys or bone marrow in exchange for a life sentence. There is simply a huge demand for organs and not nearly enough of them to go around.[62]

6. What groups should be licensed to retrieve kidneys and other organs for transplanting? Intense competition among private groups has emerged because there are large profits to be made, and operating expenses are frequently reimbursed by the federal government. Agencies now struggle over territory. For example, the federal government pays about $7,700 for a kidney. These agencies identify donors, arrange for the surgery, and take responsibility for preservation of the organ. To receive an approved application is the same as a federal franchise to do exclusive business in an area. This is a monopoly that may or may not be in our best interest as citizens. If federal funding is involved, then we face the real possibility of a bureaucratic morass. What should we do? Should we seek monopoly or competition? Will donors be solicited with huge payments?

7. What should be done in cases where high technology is associated with medical care? Should every hospital have a CAT scanner? Should every hospital do bypass surgery? Should kidney dialysis be available in all, some, or one central community? What about rural versus urban facilities—is this equality in ethics and law?

8. Anencephalic babies are babies born with brain stems but with the rest of their brains missing. About 200 anencephalic babies are born each year in the United States. These babies cannot survive more than a few weeks, and doctors want to salvage their hearts, livers, and other organs for other babies. The problem is that these organs are damaged by lack of oxygen, so some doctors argue that such doomed babies be considered dead so their organs can be removed for transplant. Others argue that making an exception for anencephalic babies puts us on the "slippery slope," whereby we will go on to take organs from people with other serious medical conditions. Thus the question arises, Under what conditions, if any, can doctors remove organs from patient A in order to transplant them into patient B? The ethical and practical issues demand resolution.[63]

9. The Communitarian Network, a social ethics organization, claims that thousands of people die every year awaiting organ transplants. This group contends that "everyone's organs should be made available at death, by law, unless the person or relative objects in advance."[64] The group decries "the wastage" of precious human resources and contends that in the United States we are, in this instance, giving too much attention to individual rights rather than individual duties. Opponents argue this is nothing less than "field-stripping" the dead—something that violates the philosophy of many individuals and groups.[65]

Every question raised in these examples is difficult to answer. What is the right thing to do? It is an instructive exercise to think through and argue out the implications of example 4 (What criteria shall we employ in allocating a kidney?) with friends, classmates, and relatives. The decisions people make will be startling. Each one of us is forced to think through his or her own values and belief system and establish priorities. It is a difficult task.

Prolonging Life via Artificial Means.   There are two ways to prolong one's life: natural and artificial. Natural techniques include eating a diet low in fat to minimize its damaging effects on the arteries; maintaining a body weight that is appropriate for one's height and frame; and exercising aerobically at least three or four times a week to nourish and strengthen one's cardiovascular system. In addition, life is prolonged by minimizing undue stress, eliminating the use of tobacco products, and using alcohol in moderation.

Artificial means of prolonging life involve implantation of cardiac pacemakers to assist those with weak hearts, renal dialysis for those with malfunctioning kidneys, mammographies to reveal small breast tumors invisible to the eye or touch, coronary bypass surgery for those with badly clogged arteries, and heart transplants or artificial hearts for those individuals whose hearts have been destroyed by disease. Technology also permits us to reconstruct cross-sections of the body with a CAT scanner and to transplant lungs, livers, tissue (skin or bone), and blood vessels or cartilage from one place to another in the same person. Plastic heart valves now act as replacements for human tissue, implantation of synthetic arteries has begun,[66] and spare part surgery and technological innovation are a reality. In tissue engineering, laboratories can now grow skin and cartilage for subsequent transfer to humans. In Boston, scientists have created a human ear growing on the back of a mouse. In other new departures to improve or prolong life, scientists, in December of 1995, transferred baboon bone marrow into a man with AIDS. The effort to bridge the species barrier has caused a good deal of public concern because mixing species demands that we face anew the question of what it means to be human. But perhaps the most exciting new development is the successful revival of the heart of a rat, which had been frozen to the core in liquid nitrogen at 320 degrees below zero. To date the only things frozen and then revived had been sperm and embryos, but with the new technology, scientists could use the procedure in storing human organs indefinitely, giving physicians almost limitless time to test and match tissue perfectly. Cryonicists contend that such research will enable us to preserve and revive whole bodies at some future time.[67] The benefits are great, but the potential dangers are also frightening. Society faces an era when body organs are becoming a mere commodity. Since a commodity has both a use and an exchange value, legal and illegal methods will be employed to transfer organs as supply and demand dictates. Legally they may be obtained, as in the kidney transfer, by a simple purchase agreement. Organs may also be obtained illegally by establishing human chop-shops, in which criminals kidnap and subsequently harvest the organs of A in order to sell these precious spare parts to B, who pays whatever is asked since life itself is at stake.

Experimentation.   Consider the following experiments:

- A United States Navy ship secretly sprayed a cloud of germs over San Francisco to test the residents' resistance to germ warfare.
- A government agency watched with cool detachment as syphilis destroyed 200 men selected at random for treatment with placebos (an inert substance used in controlled experiments to test the effect of another substance) when penicillin was available.[68]
- Lethal hepatitis virus was deliberately injected into mentally retarded children in an effort to gain new knowledge.[69]
- Aware of the association of high oxygen administration and blindness, investigators conducted a controlled experiment on premature babies. Six of the group tested were blinded.[70]
- To better understand the effects of radioactive fallout, the Atomic Energy Commission gave approval in the 1940s and 1950s for tests on human beings. About 9,000 Americans, children and unborn included, were used in 154 radiation tests. These figures, released in February 1995 by the Energy Department, demonstrate the scope and seriousness of the experimentation. The Energy Department also said an additional "150 or so" radiation experiments were performed on human beings. This information, released in 1995, sounds almost insane. It can and has happened here.[71]

Every year thousands of Americans become research subjects voluntarily. Without such research, medical science would collapse. The problem is the lack of clearly defined guidelines as to what constitutes ethical experimentation, with the Nuremburg Code and the Helsinki Declaration being two of the most important. How can scientists experiment on people—and human beings are the ultimate test site—in a humane manner while not depriving them of their rights? If society cannot solve this problem, research will either be stopped or go out of control. The dilemma is that human experiments must be conducted if we are to continue to make scientific advances that contribute to the welfare of all human beings. But scientific knowledge and patient welfare often stand in conflict with one another.

Researchers tend to justify medical experimentation on one of three bases: that important benefits to society will accrue, that great harm to society can be prevented, and that we owe it to those yet unborn. Many contend that these are valid arguments. Before discussing who the subjects of human experimentation are, however, one important distinction should be made between research and therapy and between the researcher–subject relationship and the physician–patient relationship. The former is concerned with testing a hypothesis and contributing to knowledge; the latter is concerned with enhancing the physical well-being of the patient as a human individual.[72]

The majority of human experimentation subjects fall into the following categories: prisoners, dying patients, students, children, retarded people, the poor, and fetuses. Prisoners are probably the largest single group selected as particularly good subjects. Society views this group as expendable and sees experimentation as a way for prisoners to establish social status—as a method whereby prisoners can pay society back for their crimes. Besides, said one scientist, they are "cheaper than chimpanzees." The payoff for the prisoner is frequently a parole. Students, particularly science students, are frequently used as subjects of experimentation. They are, claims the investigating researcher, intelligent and informed, and they freely consent to the procedures. But is this the case? Can a student freely consent to an experiment conducted by an academic superior? Some contend that those who do not volunteer in a classroom risk a damaged relationship with the instructor and perhaps a reduced academic grade. Some institutions give extra credit to those who volunteer. Is this ethical—or legal? Children are often subjects of experiments, as in the case of the 1953 Polio Pioneers. Ruling all children out of all experiments would have precluded the studies that solved the horrendous problem of polio. Finally, how do children, the mentally retarded, the psychiatrically ill, and the fetus give informed consent? How can any in this group give consent, as a patient or a subject, to procedures not directly related to his or her own physical well-being? Can they legally and ethically be used in experimentation to gain knowledge alone? These are the legal and ethical questions to be resolved. Let us close this section with a very brief résumé of one calamity in experimentation—the thalidomide tragedy.

Two European corporations, Biochemicals Ltd. and Chemie Grünenthal, sought to seize a part of the $3.5 billion sedative market in the early 1960s. They began to market a wonder sedative called thalidomide, with inadequate experimentation. The problem that arose from this negligence was the birth of 8,000 deformed babies (the babies were born with phocomelia—malformed upper limb abnormalities, arms similar to flippers on seals). In subsequent tests on rabbits it was learned that the drug, if taken between the fifth and eighth weeks of pregnancy, could cause phocomelia. The hope of great profits, careless and negligent experimentation, and lack of openness and honesty all contributed to the disaster. The example clearly shows the importance of economic motivation, political carelessness (the drug had been approved by the British Medical System), the weakness of some university researchers, and the cobweb of relations among academia, business, and medicine.[73]

Death

Euthanasia, the intentional termination of life, is not a new concept. In the past it was practiced by some Eskimo groups on young and old alike if they could not participate in hunting and the production of food. In the Netherlands active euthanasia is legal, and on August 21, 1988, the CBS program *60 Minutes* interviewed patients, physicians, and family members involved in the procedure. One physician had euthanized more than 100 patients. Debate continues on this touchy subject in the Netherlands, but the practice is becoming more widespread. The problem today in the modern democratic state is exacerbated by a number of new conditions: medical technology that enables us to maintain a person's life almost indefinitely; staggering costs for the new technology, which threaten to bankrupt the system; memories of the Nazi holocaust in World War II that frighten people about the possibility of a new genocide; and finally, the initiation of the living will (a patient's order to a physician or family to terminate life support), which poses complex legal questions.[74]

Two types of euthanasia are practiced; active and passive. Active euthanasia is the direct act of killing an individual who is hopelessly ill. Passive euthanasia means withholding treatment so the patient will die as quickly as possible. In active euthanasia the patient might be provided a lethal dose of sedative or receive an injection by the physician of a lethal dosage of a narcotic or sedative. In passive euthanasia the physician may withhold antibiotics, turn off equipment, or simply not start heart massage.[75] It is this distinction that is critical.

Arguments on the pros and cons of mercy killing appear almost every week in our daily newspapers. For example, in 1998, the AMA's president, Dr. E. Wilke, strongly reaffirmed its anti-euthanasia position. The group's House of Delegates, representing almost 300,000 members, voted its opposition "to a physician intentionally causing the death of a patient."[76] In Tampa, Florida, a hospital filed suit to remove life-support systems and let a semicomatose baby die. The judge in the case, after visiting the baby in the hospital, signed an order "allowing the hospital to disconnect the life-support system."[77] California's National Hemlock Society, with thirty chapters and more than 20,000 members nationwide, argues that terminally ill patients should have the right to request a lethal injection from their physician to minimize suffering for them and their families.[78] The ethical and legal implications are profound. Is active euthanasia simply murder, as some contend, and the first step on the path to genocide? They remind us that the Holocaust did occur, and it occurred in a modern industrial state with deep religious roots. Those against euthanasia argue that God alone has the right to decide when a person dies and that the intentional killing of another person can never be permitted. Those who believe that euthanasia is morally justified argue cogently that withholding or withdrawing extraordinary life-support systems is morally right and legally sound. This group contends that it is only humane to let such suffering be ended quickly, that it is cruel and inhumane to refuse the plea of a dying patient, and that a human individual is a free moral agent and thus always has the right to choose when and if life should continue. Finally, they hold that the patient's freedom and dignity as a human being are encroached upon when he or she no longer controls his or her own life. Idaho law, for example, states that "euthanasia could be actively administered to one who signed the [appropriate] document."[79]

In the United States the best-known case associated with euthanasia is that of a Michigan pathologist, Dr. Jack Kevorkian, who invented a device that allows terminally ill patients to kill themselves. Dr. Kevorkian has assisted over fifty individuals in committing suicide with the device, which, he says, kills painlessly in three to four minutes. Physicians and government officials are thus presented with a legal and ethical dilemma. The 70-year-old Kevorkian has been involved in this activity for a number of years, most lately in 1999, and recently was sent to jail for 10 to 25 years as punishment. Recently the courts in America have opened the way to physician-assisted suicide. The Second Circuit Court of Appeals struck down a state law in New York that prohibited physicians from helping patients die. In May 1996, the Ninth Circuit Court of Appeals in San Francisco made a similar ruling. The laws against doctor-assisted suicide in a majority of the states may be a thing of the past unless the United States Supreme Court reverses both decisions—and it may not even choose to hear the cases. The Hippocratic Oath that states "I will give no deadly medicine to anyone if asked" may soon be a thing of the past. This "absolute ethical norm," established thousands of years ago, is now blurred by U.S. courts, and some contend that this opens medical practice to abuse.[80]

What is to be done? What is the situation in America today? Polls suggest that there is overwhelming support not to maintain life-support procedures in terminal cases. In June 1986, a poll of the AMA membership voted 73 percent in favor of withholding life support from the hopelessly ill patient. The Pacific Presbyterian Medical Center in San Francisco conducted a poll that showed 90 percent favoring permitting the competent patient to refuse treatment, even over family objections. The Los Angeles County Bar Association approved guidelines concerning the forgoing of life-sustaining support for adult patients who so request.[81] A British expert, Dr. John Harris, a professor of bioethics, argues that better treatment of disease could lead to "generational cleansing." In other words, the elderly could in the future be condemned to death by suicide or euthanasia after an allotted lifespan as science creates conditions to advance the maximum age to 120 years old. Some call this "creeping longevity," a reality with profound implications for the sanctity of human life. Soon we may be forced to decide when individuals have had a long enough life and must die by suicide or euthanasia.[82] However, some ethicists and religious groups argue that human life is sacred and that no poll should be considered—that God alone has the right to decide on life and death.

Abortion. "Abortion is the termination of pregnancy before the fetus is viable."[83] An **abortion** is a deliberate act that intentionally seeks to end a pregnancy. A miscarriage is a spontaneous or natural termination of a pregnancy. The former involves human will; the latter does not. For example, an abortion-inducing drug sold in Europe and Asia, RU-486, when taken with prostaglandins (which also induce abortion), could mean that the procedure would merely involve obtaining a prescription, not undergoing surgery. It would be private action, personally administered.

In France, the cost of a drug-induced abortion in a clinic is funded by the government. There, RU-486 has been available since 1988. The entire procedure, in its 1996 practice, involves simply taking two sets of pills where formerly a clinic-administered injection was involved. This procedure means we may transform one of America's "most divisive political debates by making abortion . . . simpler, safer and more accessible"[84] around the world. Sometime soon, American women may be able to use RU-486. In the summer of 2000, the Food and Drug Administration approved the drug based on its "97 percent success rate" in Europe. Since 1.3 million of the nation's abortions are surgical, RU-486 will significantly change treatment in the United States.[85]

Change is the rule regarding laws on abortion in the United States. In 1800, no laws existed and abortion was performed on demand. As the century progressed, states established laws prohibiting abortion, and by 1900 nearly every state had made it a criminal offense to perform abortions.[86] In 1973, *Roe v. Wade* established the prevailing law of the land on abortions. In this case the Supreme

Court held that a woman's decision to terminate a pregnancy is protected by her right to privacy as guaranteed in the due process clause of the Fourteenth Amendment. The court held that in the first trimester, when 88 percent of all abortions occur, a woman may choose to have an "abortion free of interference by the state," while in the second trimester, "a state may regulate the abortion procedure," and in the third trimester the state may "proscribe abortion during that period."[87] Then, on July 3, 1989, the Supreme Court announced its decision in a case originating in Missouri—*Webster v. Reproductive Health Services.* This decision significantly enlarged the scope of state regulation of abortion. It has already prompted some state legislatures to pass rulings designed to test the fundamental doctrine implicit in *Roe v. Wade*—abortion as one dimension of the right to privacy. The Supreme Court in *Roe v. Wade* based the right of women to have an abortion on the Fourteenth Amendment's concept of individual liberty and restrictions on state action, and it suggested that the Ninth Amendment's reservation of rights may yet prove to be the firmest constitutional basis for a right to privacy that includes abortion.

Before proceeding, it is very important to define a few concepts associated with fetal development. Fertilization occurs when the male sperm cell unites with the female ovum or egg. The fertilized egg, called a **zygote,** contains the hereditary characteristics of the mother and father (twenty-three sets of **chromosomes**). These characteristics have their origin in the genetic base of life called **DNA.** The fertilized cell begins division. At the end of the second week, after implantation in the uterus, the zygote is renamed an **embryo.** It is called an embryo until brain activity begins, about the eighth week, when it is renamed a *fetus.* At about twenty-eight weeks the fetus is said to be *viable,* that is, capable of living outside the uterus. At the end of approximately forty weeks, birth occurs.[88]

Now the real problem associated with the abortion issue can be addressed. When does human life begin? Is a zygote or an embryo a human being? Until we answer that question—What does it mean to be a human being?—we cannot address or evaluate the morality or the legality of abortion. What constitutes the quintessential element that defines a human being or a person? Three important criteria that have been employed to date include life, soul, and reason. Those who argue for life say that, from the moment of fertilization and the first cell division until death, being alive equals full personhood. This is the position of Pope John Paul II, who in his 50,000-word encyclical *The Gospel of Life (Evangelium Vitae)* states his scathing opposition to abortion. The pope seeks to safeguard life from conception to death. For the Catholic Church, absolute right and wrong exist on basic moral issues—there is no accommodation with moral relativism. Further, the pope warns that democratic societies are sliding toward totalitarianism by legalizing morally wrong actions such as abortions.[89] Others say it is the existence of a soul that defines a person. The problem here is, When does the soul enter the living tissue? Some say with fertilization, while others, like Aristotle, St. Augustine, and St. Thomas Aquinas, held that the soul entered the living tissue sometime during the first trimester. Finally, some contend that reason is humankind's essential quality. For example, we frequently hear and read about people who possess no mental capacity. This third group argues that without some level of intelligence the living tissue cannot be characterized as an authentic human being.[90] Surely there are other criteria, but these three appear to be the most prominent ones.

Certainly we cannot resolve the underlying philosophical problem in this text. However, it is possible to address the problem with reason by beginning with the antithesis of life, that is, death. *Taber's Cyctopedic Medical Dictionary* defines brain death as "permanent cessation of all vital functions; the loss of brain stem and spinal reflexes and flat EEGs over at least 24 hours . . . total irreversible cessation of cerebral function." Given this definition, we can say that if one accepts the termination of all brain activity as *the end* of a person's life, then it is logically rational to accept the position that *the beginning* of a person's life occurs when the brain stem begins to function at six or seven weeks after conception, or when upper brain activity begins at eleven or twelve weeks after conception.

Until we are willing to define what it means to be human we cannot go forward. Once this is done, all can be logically resolved. There are a number of positions that one might assume—ban *all* abortions, permit *some* abortions, permit *all* abortions. Those who contend that all abortions should be banned would necessarily have to argue the position of life as the essential quality of a human being, or that the soul is congealed in the living tissue at the moment of fertilization. The advocates of abortion under certain conditions might argue the late ensoulment theory, or they might contend, as most do, that in particular cases, such as incest, rape, physical well-being of the mother, or defective genetic structure of the embryo, abortion could take place if done during the first trimester. Finally, individuals who argue for the pro-choice position usually assume one of two postures: some pro-choice advocates would permit abortion up to viability; others would permit abortion up to birth. There is certainly an unlimited number of positions on the spectrum from absolute pro-life to absolute pro-choice. And for good or ill, this is the position in which many citizens in America find themselves. Nevertheless, the only way we can begin to resolve the issue is to answer the philosophical question, What is essential to being a human? Then, and only then, can citizens in a free democratic state establish public policy that reflects the community's position on this great issue of American politics. It is as simple, and complex, as that.

PROSPECTS: BIOMEDICINE

Nobody today can foresee all the possible future developments associated with the great issues of biomedicine. Nevertheless, in the area of reproductive technologies some issues require constant review and may necessitate state licensing. First, the problem of cross-species fertilization will surely continue, but should it be made a crime if human cells capable of forming a new individual through fusion with other cells are used? Many contend that human dignity, whether from a religious, ethical, or philosophical viewpoint, is surely denied in such a procedure. Second, cloning of human beings seems a remote possibility, but cloning of replacement parts such as kidneys will go forward with renewed vigor given recent advances in the technology. Third, as IVF technology becomes more reliable, there will be a tendency to mass-produce human embryos because they may then be used to test new drugs. This commercial advantage could mean billions of dollars to the corporation that can develop such drugs. The power behind this technology lies in the drive for profits and economic advantage. Should this warrant careful control? Finally, in the struggle to overcome genetic defects there will surely be a powerful move toward more gene therapy research. Here, in order to remedy a particular genetic defect, a replacement gene is inserted and normal development can then occur. Should genetic screening be mandatory?

In the area of life maintenance there are also a few issues that, because of their nature and power, will dominate the agenda in the new millennium. First, it will be necessary to define empirically what it means to be an authentic human being. Unfortunately, we can no longer escape the issue because of the momentous economic implications involved in whatever we do. *We live in a world of scarcity.* What we spend to keep A alive (a comotose seventy-year-old degenerate), we cannot spend on B (a ten-year-old genius). Today, society cannot do both. Second, the abortion issue, perhaps the most volatile question on the agenda, will surely be the subject of more litigation. At this writing, neither extreme of the pro-life or pro-choice position seems likely to prevail. Rather, litigation and legislation that builds ever more restrictions into the *Roe v. Wade* decision seems likely to be America's operative ideal. Few individuals and groups will be completely satisfied; but we shall have to learn to live with compromise and a certain amount of uncertainty and inconsistency. Third, the issue of euthanasia will become ever more a subject for debate as we start the year 2001. As our society ages and the population increases, as resources become ever more scarce and hospital fees go beyond $1,000 per day, and as we begin to understand the full dimensions of humanhood, euthanasia, as an agenda item, will become ever more significant. Finally, the issue of human beings seen as spare parts for other human beings will become prominent. Life is seen as a supreme value by many people, and those who have the money or the will can arrange to buy or acquire the necessary body parts of other human beings. There is a great commercial potential here and a greater potential for ugly crime.

This forecast of the future "through a glass darkly" is just that—conjecture. But it is conjecture founded on trends and power realities. Biomedical issues along with biotechnology and the ecological crisis are on the agenda in the year 2001. They must be addressed thoughtfully *now*.

STUDY QUESTIONS

1. What will be the effect of the new reproductive technologies on our primary social structure—the family?
2. Under what conditions, if any, should public policy in the United States support surrogacy?

3. What are some of the legal, ethical, and political implications of cryopreservation? What limits, if any, should be built into public policy addressing this issue?

4. What are the arguments for and against the cloning of human beings and the cross-breeding of species?

5. What criterion should be used to allocate scarce resources such as a kidney or heart?

6. What does it mean to be an authentic human being? Is a comatose person human? What criterion should be employed in making the decision?

7. Should the United States adopt a policy of active euthanasia similar to that in operation in the Netherlands?

8. What is an ethical, well-designed medical experiment on human beings?

9. Should a living will be attached to driver's license renewal forms to expedite organ donation?

NOTES

1. *Dayton Daily News and Journal Herald,* October 2, 1987, p. 20.

2. Ibid.

3. *Webster's New Collegiate Dictionary* (Springfield, MA: Merriam-Webster, 1977), p. 392.

4. David Easton, *The Political System: An Inquiry into the State of Political Science* (New York: Alfred A. Knopf, 1933), p. 134.

5. For a very useful review of these positions see Thomas A. Shannon, ed., *Bioethics,* 3rd ed. (Mahwah, NJ: Paulist Press, 1987), pp. 3–5. Shannon employs different, but closely related, concepts. Also look into the text by John E. Monagle and David C. Thomasma, *Medical Ethics* (Rockville, MD: Aspen Publishers, 1988), pp. 494–495.

6. Ibid., Monagle and Thomasma, p. 496.

7. Marcia A. Lewis and Carol D. Warden, *Law and Ethics in the Medical Office* (Philadelphia: F.A. Davis Company, 1983), pp. 112–129.

8. Ronald Rosenberg, "Scientists Use Foreskin in Skin-Graft Technology," *Dayton Daily News,* November 1, 1992, p. 4F.

9. Ethan Bronner, "Biological Gains Raise Troubling Ethical Questions," in *Dayton Daily News,* September 9, 1987, pp. 24–27.

10. *Dayton Daily News,* March 27, 1999, p. 4A, "Birth Hailed As a First" (no byline).

11. Michelle Stanworth, ed., *Reproductive Technologies* (Minneapolis: University of Minnesota Press, 1987), p. 3.

12. Mary Thom, "Dilemmas of the New Birth Technologies," *Ms.,* May 1988, pp. 71–72. Thom presents a clear, succinct résumé of the three technologies in great detail in this issue.

13. Gregory Enns, "Making Babies Can Make Worries, Too," *The Sarasota Herald Tribune,* March 20, 1988, p. 1.

14. Gina Kolata, "Sperm Injection Method May Aid Male Infertility," *Dayton Daily News,* August 11, 1993, p. 4A; Ibid., August 15, 1993, p. 13.

15. Thomas A. Shannon and Lisa Sowle Cahill, *Religion and Artificial Reproduction* (New York: The Crossroad Publishing Co., 1988), pp. 155–169.

16. Lori B. Andrews, J.D., "Feminist Perspectives on Reproductive Technologies," in *Reproductive Laws for the 1990s,* Sherrill Cohen and Nadine Taub, eds. (Clifton, NJ: The Humana Press, Inc., 1988), pp. 1–3.

17. Mary Warnock, *A Question of Life* (Oxford University: Basil Blackwell, 1984), pp. 48–50.

18. Arthur Caplan, "A Bundle of Trouble," *Dayton Daily News,* June 14, 1993, p. 7A.

19. Ibid.

20. Ibid.

21. Frederic Golden, "Boy? Girl? Up to You," *Time*, September 21, 1998, pp. 82–83.

22. Robert Bapell, "In Vitro Veritas," *The New Republic*, February 15, 1988, p. 12.

23. Gina Kolata, "Human Embryos Cloned," *Dayton Daily News*, October 24, 1993, p. 1.

24. Ibid.

25. Warnock, *A Question of Life*, p. 64.

26. Ibid., p. 66.

27. Ibid., p. 56.

28. Ibid., p. 52.

29. Ibid., p. 38.

30. Ibid., p. 27.

31. Robert Hanley, "Surrogate Contracts Illegal, Court Says," *Sarasota Herald-Tribune*, February 4, 1988, p. 1.

32. Warnock, *A Question of Life*, p. 42.

33. Ibid.

34. Ibid., p. 47.

35. Wendy Chavkin, Barbara Katz-Rothman, and Rayna Rapp, "Third Party Reproduction: Dissenting Voices and Questions," in *Reproductive Laws for the 1990s*, Cohen and Taub, p. 1.

36. Shannon and Cahill, *Religion and Artificial Reproduction*, p. 172.

37. "Propriety of Pregnant Granny Raised," *Dayton Daily News*, January 30, 1992, p. 2A.

38. "Pregnant Granny: Devoted or Dumb?" *Dayton Daily News*, October 7, 1992, p. 7A.

39. "Judge Must Deliver Before Woman Does," *Dayton Daily News*, September 28, 1994, p. 4B; "Who's the Mother?" *Dayton Daily News*, September 16, 1994, p. 3B; "Son Born to Parent's Surrogate in Alcron Case," *Dayton Daily News*, October 13, 1994, p. 5B.

40. "Woman Pregnant with Frozen Embryo," *Dayton Journal-Herald*, May 3, 1988, p. 8.

41. Ibid.

42. Shannon and Cahill, *Religion and Artificial Reproduction*, p. 88.

43. "First—Baby from Frozen Embryo," *The New York Times*, April 15, 1984, p. 8.

44. Janet McConnaughey, "Feds Don't Recognize Child," *Dayton Daily News*, December 1, 1995, p. 16A; Ellen Goodman, "Law Must Reflect Present Reality," *West Hawaii Today*, January 27, 1995, p. 10A; Alan Sayre, "Social Security Catches Up," *Dayton Daily News*, March 12, 1996, p. 2A.

45. "Duel Begins for Custody of 'Pre-borns,'" *Dayton Daily News*, August 9, 1989, pp. 1 and 6.

46. *Dayton Daily News*, March 4, 1989, p. 2A; August 8, 1989, p. 4A; August 9, 1989, pp. 1 and 6; September 22, 1989, p. 1; and June 16, 1993, p. 2A. (This note is for those who wish to follow the evolution and development of this precedent-setting case.)

47. *Dayton Daily News*, February 29, 1980, p. 11.

48. *Dayton Journal-Herald*, May 18, 1984, p. 20.

49. Joe Kay, "Frozen Zoo Curb Against Extinction," *Dayton Journal-Herald*, December 26, 1984, p. 24.

50. "Couple Offers $100,000 for Eggs," *West Hawaii Today*, February 9, 2000, p. 15A.

51. Ellen Goodman, "Some Rules Should Surpass the Laws of Supply and Demand," *West Hawaii Today*, March 12, 1999, p. 10A.

52. Ellen Goodman, "Technology Eggs Us Onward and Upward," *Dayton Daily News*, November 10, 1999, p. 15A.

53. Thomas A. Mappes and Jane S. Zembaty, *Biomedical Ethics* (New York: McGraw-Hill, 1986), p. 494.

54. Ibid., p. 495.

55. Uli Schmetzer, "Scientist: Ape-men Possible," *Dayton Daily News*, May 14, 1987, p. 1.

56. Lewis and Warden, *Law and Ethics in the Medical Office*, p. 75.

57. *Canterbury v. Spence*, U.S. Court of Appeals, District of Columbia, in *Law and Bioethics*, 3rd ed., Thomas A. Shannon and JoAnn Manfra, eds. (Mahwah, NJ: Paulist Press, 1987), pp. 255–269.

58. Yuri Kageyama, "Japanese Looking for American Organ Donors," *West Hawaii Today*, January 11, 1997, p. 15A.

59. "Mugging of Kidney Donor," *Dayton Daily News*, July 16, 1989, p. 1G.

60. Robert Barr, "British Scandal Spurs Review of Body Part Trade," *Dayton Daily News*, July 16, 1989, p. 1G.

61. Bill Laitner, "David Crosby's Liver Transplant Is Raising Questions of Fairness," *Dayton Daily News*, November 29, 1994, p. 4C; Carl Senna, "How to Avoid a Vile Market in Recycled Human Body Parts," *Dayton Daily News*, June 15, 1995, p. 15A.

62. Gwynne Dyer, "Surgeons: Why Not Revive the Human Organ Market?," *Dayton Daily News*, July 3, 1998, p. 15A. See also Ellen Goodman, "In Organ-Transplant World," *Dayton Daily News*, April 8, 2000, p. 10A. See also *Dayton Daily News*, September 3, 1999, p. 1A, and September 4, 1999, p. 9A.

63. Jean Heller, "Syphilis Victims in U.S. Study Went Untreated for 40 Years," *The New York Times*, July 26, 1972, p. 1.

64. Mike Feinsilber, "Organ Donation Called 'Social Duty,' " *Dayton Daily News*, December 22, 1992, p. 8C.

65. Ibid.

66. Joseph F. Fletcher, *Humanhood* (Buffalo, NY: Prometheus Books, 1979), pp. 65–68.

67. "Ear Apparent," *Dayton Daily News*, October 25, 1995, p. 3A; Jeff Stryker, "Surgery Gives Man New Best Friends," *The New York Times*, December 17, 1995, p. 3E; Michelle Boorstein, "Defrosted Heart of Rat Revitalized," *Dayton Daily News*, September 23, 1996, p. 5A.

68. Jean Heller, "Syphilis Victims in U.S. Study Went Untreated for 40 Years," *The New York Times*, July 26, 1972, p. 1.

69. Richard Restak, "Experimentation on People Without Dehumanization," *The New York Times*, July 20, 1975, p. 15.

70. Michael Alderman, "Medical Experiments on Humans," *The New Republic*, December 2, 1966, p. 10.

71. Robert Burns, "About 9,000 Involved in Human Radiation Tests," *West Hawaii Today*, February 10, 1995, p. 9A.

72. George J. Agich, "Human Experimentation and Clinical Consent," in *Medical Ethics*, J.F. Monagle and D.C. Thomasma, eds. (Rockville, MD: Aspen Publishers, 1988), pp. 127–130.

73. Bruce Page, et al., "Behind the Thalidomide Tragedy," *Atlas* 23, no. 9 (September 1976), pp. 15–20.

74. David B. Clarke Jr., "Euthanasia and the Law," in *Medical Ethics*, pp. 219–220.

75. Lewis and Warden, p. 184.

76. "AMA Reaffirms Stance on Mercy Killing," *Dayton Daily News*, June 29, 1988, p. 8C.

77. "Judge Orders Life-Support System Discontinued," *Sarasota Herald Tribune*, January 22, 1988, p. 13, and February 10, 1988, p. 7B.

78. Ibid., January 20, 1988, p. 1.

79. Lewis and Warden, p. 185.

80. Michael D. Lemonik, "Defining the Right to Die," *Time*, April 15, 1996, p. 82; Charles Krauthammer, "First and Last, Do No Harm," *Time*, April 15, 1996, p. 83.

81. Clarke, *Medical Ethics*, p. 218.

82. Roger Hatfield, "Creeping Longevity," *The Ottawa Citizen*, April 7, 2000, p. A-9.

83. Lewis and Warden, p. 164. See also George Will, "Muddy Thinking Mars McCain," *Dayton Daily News*, August 26, 1999, p. 15A.

84. Jill Marlowe, "New, Improved and Ready for Battle," *Time*, June 14, 1993, p. 48.

85. "Group Wants to Sell RU-486," *Dayton Daily News*, April 2, 1996, p. 4A.

86. Lewis and Warden, p. 164.

87. *Roe v. Wade*, Supreme Court of the United States, 1973, in *Law and Bioethics*, Shannon and Manfra, eds., p. 26.

88. André Hellegers, "Fetal Development," *Biomedical Ethics*, pp. 456–459.

89. William D. Montalbanu, "Pope Leaves Little Room to Disagree," *Dayton Daily News*, April 2, 1995, p. 13A.

90. Fletcher, pp. 133–35. (Fletcher presents a first-rate and extended argument for all three of the positions reviewed here.)

SUGGESTED READINGS

COHEN, SHERRILL, and NADINE TAUB. *Reproductive Laws for the 1990s.* Clifton, NJ: The Humana Press, 1988.

FLETCHER, JOSEPH F. *Humanhood.* Buffalo, NY: Promethus Books, 1979.

LEWIS, MARCIA A., and CAROL D. WARDEN. *Law and Ethics in the Medical Office.* Philadelphia: F.A. Davis Company, 1983.

MAPPES, THOMAS A., and JANE S. ZEMBATY. *Biomedical Ethics.* New York: McGraw-Hill, 1986.

MONAGLE, J.F., and D.C. THOMASMA, eds. *Medical Ethics.* Rockville, MD: Aspen Publishers, 1988.

SHANNON, THOMAS A., and LISA SOWLE CAHILL. *Religion and Artificial Reproduction.* New York: The Crossroad Publishing Company, 1988.

STANWORTH, MICHELLE. *Reproductive Technologies.* Minneapolis: University of Minnesota Press, 1987.

WARNOCK, MARY. *A Question of Life.* Oxford University: Basil Blackwell, 1984.

Chapter 8

Biotechnology

The scientific concerns of today will be the political concerns of tomorrow.

—George Will, political commentator and Pulitzer prize winner

There is a lesson in today's constellation of news stories. . . . Pay as much attention to science news as to political news. Political choices are made in contexts that politicians cannot choose, and the contexts are increasingly shaped by science.

—George Will[1]

Biology is "the science of life or living matter in all its forms . . . [with special] reference to origin, growth, reproduction, structure and behavior."[2] *Technology* is that "branch of knowledge that deals with the creation and the use of technical means"[3] designed to achieve a practical purpose. In its broadest sense, the level of technological development of a society refers to the totality of technical means available to provide the necessities of life—food, clothing, shelter, fuel, medical care—for the survival and comfort of human beings. **Biotechnology** is "the technology involving the use of living organisms—cells, microbes, fungi, plants and animals—to produce useful products."[4]

Basically, there are only three ways of producing a useful product: "mechanical technology (cutting wood . . .) where the underlying physical material maintains its distinct identity; chemical technology (. . . producing baked goods) where the starting materials recombine to form a different final product; and biotechnology (brewing beer . . . producing hybrid seeds or breeding horses . . .) where living organisms are utilized to produce useful products."[5] Biotechnology is, today, the most exotic of the three. Nevertheless, it is still simply one of three technologies—the one that employs living organisms to produce a product that is useful.

Biotechnology is involved as scientists labor to produce agricultural crops that are resistant to particular diseases and are able to live longer without water, and to reduce farmers' dependence on pesticides. Biotechnology promises to help human beings in their struggle to save the environment and to control diseases such as Parkinson's disease, AIDS, and cancer. It is important to remember that biotechnology is internally related to the production of useful products; it is not merely "understanding how living organisms function"[6] (biosciences). This distinction is crucial.

This chapter on biotechnology is a general survey of the topic written for the layperson, not the scientist. It is a summary of what constitutes this emerging new technology. As such, it is divided into three parts. The first part—"Sources"—discusses the history and development of biotechnology during the last five decades. The next part, the heart of the chapter, is entitled "Status." Two major subtopics are discussed—biotechnology and genetic engineering. Biotechnology encompasses genetic engineering but goes beyond it. Nevertheless, genetic engineering is such a significant dimension of biotechnology that it has been elevated to subtopic status.

The section on biotechnology initially seeks to identify and explain the five major areas affected by biotechnology (health, agriculture, the environment, national security, and energy); the major risks involved in research and development associated with biotechnology; law, regulation, and safety related to biotechnology; international aspects of biotechnology; and the complex relationships between government, business, academe, and other professional organizations involved in biotechnology.

The section on genetic engineering directs its attention to three major areas of analysis—the human genome project, the genetic repair of deficiencies, and the production of new genetic combinations. Here new developments such as **gene splicing,** gene therapy, genetic mapping, genetic screening, cloning, sequencing, eugenics, neo-eugenics, **gene transfer,** and genetically altered plants and animals will be discussed. There is no doubt that molecular genetics is an exceptionally exciting field; but there are major social and ethical issues involved in the human genome project (the "code of codes") and in genetic repair and improvement.

"Prospects," the last part of the chapter, purports to sketch out an agenda for the future. What is to be done about regulation of biotechnology on a national and international level? What are some of the potentials and limits of biotechnology? What are the emerging new primary concerns being raised by religious groups and ethicists about biotechnology and genetic engineering? How shall we begin to resolve these complex relationships nationally and internationally? What are the real goals of the revitalized interest by the military and the police in biotechnology? How will commercialization of biotechnology affect the health of human beings and animals? Not so long ago, for example, a firm named Genentech so skillfully premarketed a heart attack drug that a newspaper reported "cardiologists across the country are salivating."[7] All these questions must be addressed as we begin the year 2001. But now is the time to clarify a few concepts and to review the history and development of biotechnology.

SOURCES: HISTORY AND DEVELOPMENT
OF BIOTECHNOLOGY

In the beginning, farmers practiced biotechnology by patiently cross-breeding living plants (wheat, corn, soybeans) in order to develop new crops that provided higher yields and were more resistant to pests and harsh environmental conditions. An example in more recent times is the work of entrepreneurs in commercial fermentation. Here a large number of microorganisms are grown under controlled conditions and then mixed with nutrients. The microorganisms eat up the nutrients, and their waste products are what we use as yogurt, cheese, wine, and beer.[8] Baking, brewing, and wine-making processes have been used for several millennia. The breeding of cows to give more milk and the breeding of horses for strength or speed also are examples of biotechnology that have existed for centuries. In every case, living organisms are employed to produce useful products. Biotechnology is involved in the selection of feed for a horse that must pull heavy loads. It includes the breeding of dogs for particular purposes—guard duty (German shepherds), speed (greyhounds), or hunting (beagle hounds).

Still other historical examples of very old applications of biotechnology include the use of human and animal fertilizer in order to produce better crops. Liquid manure wagons still turn the white snow of the Bavarian foothills of Germany a distinct brownish color. The grafting of fruit trees is still practiced throughout the world. Finally, the expanding use of biotechnology in its relation to human and animal health is perhaps best seen in diagnostics and in vaccines. All these applications of biotechnology in agriculture, animal husbandry, medicine, and industrial products involve the use of living organisms to produce useful products. But note one important factor—none of the traditional biotechnology methods interferes with the processes of nature that operate at the level of the genes. In every case it is nature that has the task of putting limitations and safeguards on these encounters.

The 1950s—Breakthrough

The breakthrough in biotechnology, perhaps the greatest scientific discovery in biology since Darwin, occurred in England at Cambridge University's Cavendish Laboratory in 1953. An American, James Watson, and his English partner, Francis Crick, discovered the structure of DNA, the molecule that stores all the information on heredity. "Given the fact that DNA was known to occur in the chromosomes of all cells . . . none of them [the scientists] seemed to take seriously the evidence that genes were made of DNA."[9] However, Watson and Crick, in their race with Linus Pauling and other scientists to discover the structure of DNA, operated on this principle and in early 1953 announced their findings to the world in a 900-word article beginning, "We wish to suggest a structure for the salt of deoxyribonucleic acid (DNA). This structure has novel features which are of considerable biological interest."[10] Watson and Crick then explained in their paper the existence of "two intertwined chains with identical base sequences [suggesting] that one chain in each molecule had at some earlier stage served as the template for the synthesis of the other chain."[11] Separation of the two chains initiates replication; two new "daughter strands" are formed; and thus two DNA molecules are created identical to the original molecule.[12] This was a scientific discovery of the first magnitude.

The 1960s—Transition

The discovery of the structure of DNA in the 1950s startled the scientific world and prompted a fundamental change that occurred during the 1960s—that is, the change from basic science to applied science, from fundamental research to applied research. The 1960s was the transition period. Traditionally, basic research is done at universities and research institutes and is not the subject of formal regulatory agencies. Prior to biotechnology's new tool, genetic engineering, this was the case. The movement to applied research and development of products frequently involved decades. For example, in the case of the first heart pacemaker, it took over three decades from the time of the basic research to the first operational unit.[13] With the discovery of the structure of DNA, the movement to the application stage occurred very rapidly. Soon research was conducted in commercial research and development laboratories as well as in university schools of agriculture, veterinary medicine, and applied microbiology.[14]

The 1970s—Rapid Development

With the transition of research from academe to private industry, development of biotechnology directed its attention to "manufacturing, packaging, and marketing the products derived from phases one and two."[15] Federal approval from the Food and Drug Administration required that trials and data collection and patent procurement be performed to get approval. In the 1970s much of the energy of private industry was directed toward achieving these goals. Consider the following examples of private industry activities related to product trial, data collection, patents, and government approval:

- Eli Lilly and Company's work to produce human insulin for diabetics through genetic engineering
- Amgen Incorporated of California's development of erythropoletin (EPO), a protein produced by the kidney that increases production of red blood cells—a possible remedy for anemia
- General Electric's securing a right to patent an oil-eating organism after a favorable ruling by the U.S. Supreme Court
- Genentech's marketing of a drug, tissue plasminogen activator (TPA), that dissolves blood clots—a boon to heart attack victims.[16]

The 1970s accelerated development and propelled early commercialization into the new decade.

The 1980s—Worldwide Commercialization

Former Senator Lawton Chiles of Florida, in a speech at the University of Florida, stated that biotechnology will help humans live longer, healthier lives, wipe out toxic waste that endangers the nation's groundwater, and eliminate dangerous chemicals employed in food processing. In these areas, the United States faces serious competition from Japan and Europe. These rivals in the global economy recognize the multibillion-dollar biotechnology market and have, unlike the United States, already established national policies regarding the next generation of biotechnological products.[17] Drugs and vaccines produced through biotechnology are already sold in the U.S. market. Many have been approved and "scores of others are in the final stages of development."[18] The reality of the worldwide economy, so dramatically demonstrated in the stock market crash on Black Monday, October 19, 1987, includes the relatively new area of biotechnology, which is changing the very nature of many industries today.

The 1990s—Competition in the World Economy

With the Cold War ended, the 1990s was a watershed in American history. General Motors, once thought unshakable, began having difficulty in world markets. The large pharmaceutical companies were having difficulty, as were the new enterprises in biotechnology. The competition was becoming ever more savage, and it had many facets. First, the gargantuan human genome project initiated in the United States came under attack by French geneticists, who were doing pioneering work and doing it faster than the Americans. The race to map the human genome was on, and it involved nations, money, and morality.[19] Second, competition emerged among biotechnology and other disciplines—physics, for example, suffered cutbacks as governments funneled more funds into biotechnology. Gene therapy to correct gene defects now garnered more and more funding.[20] Third, competition between states began to heat up. Rhode Island and Massachusetts were involved in a battle to locate EcoScience Corporation, a biotechnology firm, within their borders. Plant sites and tax breaks were offered because hundreds of new jobs were expected to be created.[21] The race to map and market the products of biotechnology and genetic engineering was on, and the 1990s was the decade of decision. New Zealand, in particular, is making exciting advances in the field of biotechnology: Biodiscovery NZ is a company producing new biological pesticides; AgResearch has patented a gene therapy that causes twins in sheep; and Malaghan Institute has focused on cellular respiration and its effect on cancer.

STATUS: BIOTECHNOLOGY AND GENETIC ENGINEERING

Two major topics are discussed in this section of the chapter—biotechnology and genetic engineering. Each of these in turn is reviewed in terms of specific subtopics. The discussion of biotechnology addresses four major areas:

1. five principal industrial areas affected by biotechnology
2. major areas of concern associated with biotechnology
3. regulation, safety, and biotechnology
4. relationships in biotechnology (national and international) between government, industry, and academe

The inquiry into genetic engineering examines three key areas:

1. the genome project
2. repairing deficiencies
3. improved combinations

Biotechnology: Five Areas Most Affected

Health Industry. "Biotechnology makes it possible to produce virtually unlimited quantities of our natural body agents . . . [and] biological pharmaceuticals that replicate body functions [while providing] greater effectiveness and fewer side effects."[22] Three biologicals marketed by Genentech Incorporated, a leading company devoted exclusively to biotechnology, demonstrate this clearly—insulin to treat diabetes (a disease that affects about 25 percent of the U.S. population); human growth hormone for treatment of dwarfism and osteoporosis; and tissue plasminogen activator (TPA) to dissolve blood clots.

Pharmaceutical products already in the research and development stage belong to several categories: blood proteins such as TPA; monoclonal antibodies (more than a hundred of these diagnostic tools) for everything from pregnancy to cancer, now employed in the growing test kit market; hormones such as insulin; and synthetic vaccines to deal with major viral diseases such as influenza, yellow fever, rabies, smallpox, and malaria. There has been a noticeable and growing shift in medicine from treatment to early diagnosis and prevention. "In a . . . survey of publicly held biotechnology companies, . . . 37 percent of the companies catered primarily to the diagnostics area, and 33 percent were devoted largely to therapeutics."[23]

Nevertheless, the race for new pharmaceuticals is still fierce. Consider the following examples:

- Interleukin 2, an anticancer drug, is undergoing clinical trials in the United States and Europe in preparation for applications to the FDA.
- **Interferons,** proteins produced by the body as a part of the immune response, are under development by the United States and also by an Italian-Swiss group. These are considered powerful weapons in the war against cancer.
- Tumor necrosis factor (TNF) is being developed by Genentech and Phillips Petroleum in the United States, and also in Japan. This white blood cell product attacks tumor tissue and is being tested as a weapon in the fight against AIDS.
- California Biotechnology is experimenting with a technique that permits human insulin to be administered by spraying the drug directly into the nose of the patient.[24]
- A patent has been awarded to Ohio University "for a mouse strain carrying a human gene that makes it resistant to viral infection . . . [the mouse strain] can be used in studies of the immune system's response to cancer . . . 15 generations continue to carry the human interferon gene."[25]
- Geneticists in the United States, Europe, and Japan are in a race for one of the "most aggressively contested trophies in science this year: BRCA-1, a gene that when defective

is thought to cause about half of all inherited breast cancer."[26] Prestige, careers, and demand by millions of women worldwide (and the profit therein) will go to the victors in this race.

- Millennium Pharmaceuticals, Inc. <www.mlmn.com> in December of 2000 announced research focus on understanding how specific changes in genes relate to disease in both therapeutic and predictive medicine. The company seeks to transform medicine at every stage of disease from gene to patient.

Genetic research plays a key role today in developing products to treat the following health problems:

1. A study sponsored by the federal government demonstrates that a genetically engineered flu vaccine can be produced faster (two months rather than nine months) than those currently in use.[27]

2. Recently scientists have zeroed in on genes associated with manic-depression on chromosomes 6, 13, and 15. This condition affects thousands of Americans every year.[28]

3. Tay-Sachs disease, a genetic disorder occurring primarily among three groups (French Canadians, Jews whose families come from Eastern Europe, and Cajuns), can now be detected early in gestation. A baby who was born free of the disease was first screened for this incurable disease when she was only *eight cells old*.[29]

4. Scientists recently discovered that a surprising number of people, perhaps one in 100 whites, have genes that protect them from AIDS. Geneticists are now trying to find a way to copy the effects of this genetic shield. The newly discovered gene is called CCR5.[30]

5. Agar-Agar <www.seatechagar.com> embarked on a new biotech application in a fall 2000 announcement. Agar is a seaweed harvested in India and employed, via biotechnology, in food processing, culture medium (plant tissue and cell culture), and pharmaceuticals associated with dental practices.

6. Finally, corporations and universities are working to develop a blood substitute employing biotechnological methods. Sources of this hemoglobin substitute include genetically altered bacteria. This oxygen-carrying substitute would be worth billions.[31]

All these and many more pharmaceuticals associated with human health are being developed.

Animal diseases are also an important dimension of biotechnology in the area of health. This is so because diseases that kill or enfeeble animals (tick-borne diseases, for example) act as an immediate constraint on the production of livestock all over the world. Ultimately, this results in a serious decrease in the production of food needed for human consumption. Since World War II, Asia, Africa, and Latin America have changed from food exporters to food importers, largely because of the population explosion in these areas. Advances in biotechnology can help to reduce crop loss in the field, improve food processing, and contribute to the health of animals, nitrogen fixation, fermentation, and waste recycling.[32] Consider the following example of genetic storage: A cattle herd left untended on a remote island in the South Pacific for about a hundred years without any husbandry or treatment for disease is being studied, and reproductive samples taken, that may help modern cattle resist disease.[33] Today we are moving from the germ theory to gene therapy.

The application "that excites doctors . . . is manipulating microbiotic genes in ways that help the immune system fight off many cancers. . . . a drug just can't get to all the cancer cells. There are too many. But the immune system can. That's what it's designed for."[34]

Agriculture.   It is impossible to predict the future impact of biotechnology on agriculture, but it certainly represents a means for pivotal change. Three areas will be affected—plants, animals, and agriculture-industrial applications.

In the area of plants, the biotechnology of cloning and genetic manipulation means "more efficient propagation, better selection of seeds, greater tolerance to environmental stress, resistance to pests and tolerance of pests."[35] Biotechnology will also aid in the animal sector by giving scientists better diagnostic tools, improved techniques for therapy and prevention of disease, and the ability to manipulate the animal genome itself in order to bring out a desired quality (more strength, more milk, bigger eggs). Finally, the new biotechnology is building a linkage between agriculture and industry—among farmers, suppliers of agricultural products, and food processors—that will create entirely new relationships. For example, the use of a growth hormone in cows may increase milk production as much as 40 percent. This reality demands that government policy and farm practice regarding milk production and subsidies must be revised. Another instance might be in the sugar market, where substitutes for sugar, in the form of high-fructose syrups, are a growing reality. Traditional producers of sugar, such as Cuba, face difficult days ahead as the new products seek to replace this commodity worldwide.[36]

In agriculture, the focus of concern has shifted from the initial interests, such as nitrogen fixation genes in cereal plants, to a more product-oriented approach. Thus, research and development today seek to improve crop strains, control insect pests, prevent plant diseases, and increase herbicide resistance. Prevention of disease is the focus today at animal health-care centers. Improved vaccine development to combat disease is a high priority in biotechnology associated with agriculture in Japan, Germany, France, Canada, and the United States.[37]

Food processing is one of the oldest examples of agricultural biotechnology, and in many ways it remains one of the most significant applications of the new technology. Three sectors in food processing combine to form the present focus of biotechnology—fermentation, enzyme technology, and downstream processing. *Fermentation* technology is the oldest use of living organisms for the production of a useful product (beer, wine, cheese, yogurt, vinegar, soy sauce). Beer is probably the oldest and is produced by the fermentation of a malted cereal, usually barley. Herbs, such as hops, are then added for flavor. **Enzymes** exist in all living organisms and are used by living cells to catalyze specific reactions. Microorganisms in yeasts have been used for thousands of years for the production of beer and wine. All commercial fermentation processes are the consequence of enzyme action. "*Downstream processing* is concerned with the separation and purification of an essential product or products from a fermentation process . . . [it] is the least glamorous aspect of biotechnology but can represent a major part of the overall costs of a process, as much as 40 percent of the total costs."[38] Improvement in downstream processing (purification) improves efficiency and reduces costs.

New agricultural applications of biotechnology designed to improve the quantity and quality of commercial products include the following examples:

- A California biotech firm, Calgene, began selling genetically engineered tomatoes in 1993 after years of field tests and regulatory reviews. The commercial launch of the biotech tomato[39] was a huge victory, and sales were predicted to be $500 million a year.
- Genetically engineered cotton "should greatly reduce the need for insecticides and increase the effectiveness of herbicides."[40] In addition, genetic engineering will also improve the properties of cotton fiber itself, hybrid seeds, byproducts, and cottonseed oil.
- Researchers at the University of Florida are using genetic engineering to make sea oats bigger and better. These grasses and shrubs help stabilize the dunes that lie on the ocean shore of the offshore islands. By using a natural beach microbe (VAM fungi) the VAM organism becomes a natural fertilizer for the sea oats and increases their size by 75 percent in height and root production.[41]
- Genetic researchers have succeeded in giving guinea pigs a tan, without sunlight, by smearing their shaved bodies with a substance like DNA. The new genetic research product is designed to give users the hue normally derived from sunbathing rather than an artificial hue. The substance is a manmade copy of a piece of DNA.[42]
- "In a laboratory in Texcoco, Mexico, [a scientist] loads a tiny corn embryo and an invisible bit of genetic matter into a 'gene gun,' a high-tech device resembling a microwave oven. Helium gas builds up and [the scientist] blasts the embryo with DNA carefully developed to make the corn insect-resistant."[43]
- By the year 2050, the world's demand for food will be about triple today's farm output. We are already farming 37 percent of the earth's land surface, and without high-yield farming the world will be forced to plow up even more of the land. Biotechnology's genetically modified "golden rice" will help eliminate vitamin A deficiencies that currently cause 8 million children in poor countries to go blind. It will also help resolve the iron deficiency that more than a billion women suffer from and that results in increased risk of birth complications. Finally, Mexican researchers have created the first acid-soil crops by inserting a gene for citric acid that defeats the aluminum toxicity in the soils. This could result in an increase in tropical food production of 40 percent.[44]

Environment. Biotechnology holds great promise for helping to resolve some of America's environmental problems and preserves its fragile ecosystem. New developments in biotechnology today will help in the future with both the biotic and abiotic issues that confront the nation, particularly in the area of monitoring and cleaning the environment. In terms of sheer volume, the treatment of sewage and wastewater—both industrial and domestic—is the greatest environmental task of biotechnology to date. Traditional applications of biological technology to sludge, waste water, and treatment of solids by biological technology will soon be complemented with projects designed to reclaim "useful substances from waste by means of genetically engineered microorganisms, and use of such organisms to effectively decompose crude oil or highly toxic substances."[45] In this new biological process, genetic engineering is involved—that is, the alteration of living organisms to improve their performance in impacting environmental problems such as solid waste, oil slicks, and toxic waste. It is here that the significance of recombinant DNA is so pronounced, because it alone provides scientists with the ability to produce new and improved biological systems to be employed in the fight to clean up our environment.

The $200 million market for biodegradation products should grow 40 percent over the next few years as biotreatment firms rush to the market. The *Exxon Valdez* oil spill of March 24, 1989, polluted Alaskan waters and created the conditions for the first major test to determine whether hydrocarbon-eating aquatic microbes can help clean up oil-soaked beaches. The results to date are encouraging, as oil degraded five times faster on treated beaches than on beaches left alone.[46] In the Dayton, Ohio, area, Environmental Biotech "sells a drain-cleaning service to restaurants, schools, nursing homes, and cafeterias. The service uses bacteria to eat grease which is not biodegradable and can be broken down into carbon dioxide and water which are biodegradable."[47] The central premise of the book and 1993 film *Jurassic Park* is that white blood cells picked up from dinosaurs by mosquito-like insects entombed in amber can be harvested, put into eggs, incubated, and in time produce dinosaurs. Genetic material of extinct dinosaurs is then used to re-create these giant new space-age dinosaurs. Researchers have been able to produce genetic material from insects that have been extinct for 20 million years; but although re-creating DNA is the first step to re-creating an animal, the rest is science fiction. Very difficult problems lie ahead in such a process—chemistry and radiation take their toll. It is one thing to get a sample of dinosaur DNA. It is quite another to resurrect *Tyrannosaurus rex*.[48] The earth's environment is certainly endangered, but the dinosaurs of *Jurassic Park* are more "reel" than real.

Biotechnology offers the possibility for effective monitoring and cleanup of our environment. The problem is that many agencies in the United States and throughout the world are more concerned with how to regulate the new technology than with how to clean up the waste. With over 6 billion people, the earth's population will soon be suffocated in its own waste and pollution unless it can move forward with the new biotechnology.

National Security.   The question of national security involves both external and internal aspects. The primary instrument of external security is the military, while internal security has as its main tool the police.

From 1946 to 1991, military security in the United States had as its immediate object of concern the Soviet Union and terrorist states such as Syria, Libya, and Iran. Other military concerns surely existed, but these were perceived as paramount during this time. The United States and the Soviet Union were both involved in research and development of defense technologies associated with chemical and biological weapons and in the technology of genetic engineering that makes these weapons possible. The history of chemical and biological warfare suggests that there is a momentous potential for new military applications of recombinant DNA (rDNA). A future hostile act could be the introduction of a small change in common diseases of plants and animals through the manipulation of an existing virus.

Such an action would be virtually impossible to detect. Gene wars are a distinct possibility.[49] Potentially, biotechnology could escalate the tension between the United States and its perceived adversaries worldwide.

The agents of biological warfare include disease-causing bacteria, viruses, and toxins—powerful weapons in the hands of terrorists. The Reagan administration increased the Department of Defense budget for biological weapons "from $63 million in 1980 to $334 million in 1987."[50] Although 111 countries signed an agreement in 1972 to ban production and use of biological and toxic weapons, the signatories are permitted to do defense research—and the distinction between defensive and offensive weapons gets very cloudy in empirical analysis. Biological agents are living cells, and the potential to manipulate bacteria and viruses for use in warfare is strong. Biotechnology allows seemingly innocuous ventures to disguise forbidden biological weapons (BW) activities. It also offers new ways to detect BW agents. This both "complicates and simplifies enforcement of the international Biological Weapons (BW) Convention,"[51] which the United States has signed. Finally, the U.S. Army has developed a process that involves engineering the gene of spider silk into bacteria that produce a fiber "stronger than a silkworm's silk—indeed, far stronger than steel."[52] The Army hopes to use this new fabric for bulletproof vests, parachute cords, helmets, and light equipment.

Biotechnology in its relation to internal security has given the police and the court system a very powerful tool: **genetic fingerprinting.** DNA is a basic material that contains within it a human being's genetic code. These patterns are like the bar codes on virtually everything purchased in a grocery store. In this case, each bar code is unique to each human individual (with the exception of identical twins) and as such, it is an invaluable aid in identification of suspects. "While traditional techniques can narrow to one in one hundred the possibility of others having that blood, DNA fingerprinting squeezes those odds to one in ten billion."[53] A geneticist in England, Dr. Alec Jeffreys, invented this relatively new form of genetic testing. It has been used in England since 1985 and is already being used in a variety of cases in the United States.

- In Preston, England, two ten-year-old boys were accused and convicted of the murder of a two-year-old child on the basis of DNA tests. Both boys had bloodstains on their shoes from the victim, and hair from the toddler was found on their clothing. The British Forensic Science Service told the court that the hair and blood samples found on the two boys matched that of the victim. The two were sentenced and imprisoned.[54]

- In Clearwater, Florida, genetic tests on a ten-year-old girl who was at the center of a "baby swap" controversy proved she was the offspring of a couple who claimed her as their biological issue, not that of the man who raised her. The test was claimed in court to show with "99.9 percent certainty" that Kimberly Mays was the biological daughter of the Twiggs, not of Robert Mays.[55]

- In Jessup, Maryland, after nine years in prison (sometimes on death row), a man convicted of rape and murder was freed by DNA tests that proved he could not have been the perpetrator of the crime.[56]

- In Orlando, Florida, a man was sentenced to seventy-eight years in prison for stabbing and raping a woman. The evidence: "the DNA in the [defendant's] blood matched the rapist's semen."[57]

- DNA proves useful in disasters by helping investigators identify victims. In the TWA Flight 800 disaster, examiners identified a victim by DNA from a toothbrush at his home.[58]

- In Bradenton, Florida, a man who denied fatherhood finally admitted paternity when faced with the "bar code." Blood tests proved the defendant was the father. This meant that the woman could collect child support.[59]

- DNA is now commonly employed in cases of adoption, rape, and paternity disputes, and by welfare departments in child-rearing cases. In June of 1998, Defense Secretary William Cohen announced the identity of a Vietnam veteran buried in the Tomb of the Unknown Soldier at Arlington, Virginia. He was 1st. Lt. Michael Blassie, shot down in Vietnam in 1972. He will be reinterred near his home; the monument to the unknown soldier may become a thing of the past.[60]

- To authenticate their paintings, some artists now incorporate part of their DNA into the ink used in signing their work.

In addition to these cases, genetic fingerprinting can also be helpful in resolving immigration disputes and in the identification of remains. Finally, representatives in Ohio have recently initiated legislation to establish a DNA data bank of genetic engineering to help in resolving crimes. More new applications of the technology are being discovered. It is likely to change the entire science of police investigations. Forty-six states accept DNA as evidence in criminal trials, according to ABC News reporting on June 14, 1996.

Energy. Today's biotechnology may well revolutionize the field of energy. A string of DNA can be separated and isolated from a cell's genome. Then it can be inserted into other organisms, which begin to function like factories for the production of gene products.

At the present time, biotechnological alternatives to fossil fuels are not seen as economically sound in most countries. Nevertheless, there are three important applications of biotechnology related to the energy supply—"conversion of biomass [for example, sugar cane into fuel alcohol] through fermentation processes to biofuels (methane and ethanol), microbiological removal of sulphur and sulphides from coal, and enhanced oil recovery."[61] In Brazil, environmental conditions are good for the production of fuel from a renewable resource, sugar cane. It is a net energy gain to Brazil because the juice of the pressed cane is fermented by heating it with the debris of the cane stalk as a boiler fuel. This heat also provides steam for local electricity production. This has been done with corn in the United States.

The enhancement of oil recovery is an additional application. "Contrary to popular belief, the oil reserves of a well are not in the form of a liquid pool."[62] Most of the oil is dispersed in the porous rock itself and must be flushed out. The traditional technique is to apply pressure with water or natural gas; but now microbial agents are used to flush the oil out. There appears to be great potential to increase oil recovery in the application of this new technology.

Major Risks and Concerns of Biotechnology

Four major areas of risk and concern are associated with biotechnology—philosophy, anthropology, sociology, and ecology. Each area's object of concern is a bit different, but there are aspects of each that overlap.

Philosophy. In contrast to the 1960s, this is neither the nuclear age nor the Age of Aquarius—it is the age of genetics. Physics has already given way to biology as the principal organizing motif as we start the year 2001. Biology is moving ever faster, and human beings are beginning to lose their capacity to control the science and the technology of biology. Consider some of the philosophical questions that confront us now. Is unfettered research ethically right? If newly created life forms might threaten the balance of nature itself, can we sit idly by? How shall we deal with medical experimentation (see Chapter 7), and is it right or just for research scientists to profit as individuals from research conducted significantly through the grant of public funds? If it is society that pays the cost, should not society receive some of the benefits? Should research ignore pressing human needs when tremendous profits are possible? Is there, or can there be, a just distribution of genetic engineering benefits between the rich and poor countries of the world?

What laws shall we pass to equate power, the political *is,* with right, the ethical *ought* in biotechnology? Can the two be synthesized? The Supreme Court has said that it is constitutional to patent new forms of animal life; but patents tend to limit the free flow of information. In addition, if patents on new forms of animal life (a mouse, in this case) are legal, will we someday patent human life? Many people are concerned that the patenting of living organisms is not in the public interest and puts humanity in jeopardy of having patents extended to higher life forms.

The Judeo-Christian religion that surrounds American society like a cocoon teaches that human life is sacred. Both Judaism and Christianity argue that God is the ultimate creator and that human life cannot be reduced to mere parts. In terms of these two powerful worldviews, are not the scientists involved in genetic engineering playing God? What does it mean to be a human being? What is the nature of human life and what responsibilities do we as human beings have for life on earth? When scientists talk about eliminating defects and improving human beings, they bring to their task a submerged ideology regarding what is better. Value judgments are involved in correcting mortal deficiency. Every eugenics program, from Plato's *Republic* with its guardian class to Hitler's breeding program of Lebensborn, implies judgments. So, too, must the new genetic engineers make crucial decisions: Judgments must be made—ethical judgments about goals and about ends and means. Some ethicists contend that genetic engineering reduces human beings to objects rather than subjects, to means rather than ends. These issues demand attention.

Animal rights are also an ethical concern of some individuals and groups. Some contend that experimentation on animals is abusive, that we are producing grotesque new life forms by transferring human genes into animals. Ethicists and religious leaders contend that this violates species integrity.

Anthropology.   DNA is the chemical alphabet of life. Scientists today can create new arrangements of genes, implant them in a bacterium, and then watch as the new "bug" divides and reproduces itself. The problem is that changing the genetic code of human beings—altering the genetic constitution of people—is a momentous step. Who decides to do this? How is it possible to know the long-term effect of such manipulation seven generations from now? The key question is, What traits should be emphasized?

Eugenics is the science dealing with improvement of hereditary qualities through breeding. The Nazi **Lebensborn** program sought to improve the quality of the German populace by breeding S.S. officers to women with such desired qualities as blond hair, blue eyes, and Teutonic nose and lips. Consider the following developments in genetics and what impact they might have on a country embracing extreme nationalism in the future. Scientists studying the biology of behavior have "identified a gene that influences how impulsive, excitable, [and] quick-tempered" an individual is.[63] In addition, geneticists have recently linked aggression in mice to a single gene. "Male mice lacking a single gene are oversexed and vicious, pressing their attacks even on rodents that have signaled defeat."[64] These mice lack the normal brake on social behavior, nitric oxide, researchers said. As some scientists work to improve animals, will not others work to produce a better human being? Genetic engineering has the potential to alter heredity through gene therapy. For human beings, however, the problem remains: What does it mean to be human? Tampering with nature and human hereditary qualities is seen by many as a risk that ought not to be assumed.

New forms of life are now possible through genetic engineering—cloning, cross-breeding, and sex choice. Scientists have already cloned frogs, mice, sheep, and cows. Scientists at Texas A&M University unveiled a disease-resistant black Angus bull that could lead to safer beef and more efficient ranching. The month-old bull had been cloned from genetic material frozen for more than fifteen years. This new animal carries the traits that make him immune to brucellosis, tuberculosis, and salmonellosis.[65] Is the cloning of human beings ever ethical? Are there circumstances when it is proper? There are arguments on both sides of the issue. Cloned body parts (heart, lungs, liver, etc.) would minimize rejection problems; an extended human life span is certainly a distinct probability. If cloning raises problems, consider the consequences of cross-breeding species. Are the predictions in Aldous Huxley's *Brave New World* about to be realized? Biotechnology and genetic engineering are creating a new tension in our approach to human problems—namely, a transition from a view that primarily values the human individual, to one that measures what is good, right, just, and proper in terms of the group—**utilitarianism.** Research and treatment in America has always been done on the basis of what is best for a specific individual. Today, however, the techniques of genetic engineering are moving us toward utilitarianism, that is, the greatest good for the greatest number. Finally, biotechnology is changing the basis of life through the new and innovative reproductive technology discussed in detail in Chapter 7. Today, we deep-freeze embryos, construct artificial wombs of steel and glass, alter behavior, assist in determining sex, and change the very basis of reproduction. All these activities are related to the question of human nature and **alienation.** Will the new technology further exacerbate, alienate, and isolate the human individual? Time will tell—and the time is now.

Sociology. Political, economic, and social institutions have concerns about the new biotechnology. Politically, the issue involves the extent and the jurisdiction of regulation, assessment of risks involved, and the role of technical experts in public policymaking. Government's role must be concerned with the environment and with the commercialization of biotechnology. The question is how to regulate the new industry while stimulating new enterprises and maintaining public safety.[66] In the late 1970s, there was a great deal of concern about health hazards caused by the new biotechnology. Most of this has died down, but concern over control of biotechnological work through federal monitoring is still very much alive in Congress. Formerly, self-regulation was the rule. Today, government regulation touches many aspects of biotechnology research and development. Biotechnology is an ever growing issue in Congress—particularly regarding who should be involved in decision making, who pays, and who benefits from biotechnology.

In the area of economics, the great issue is commercialization. The biotechnology industry is an emerging multibillion-dollar enterprise. Many concerns are being raised in this area, such as who owns the new life forms and to what extent market forces alone will, or should, determine how we shape and reshape human, animal, and plant life on earth.

Socially, there is concern about biotechnology's effect on the family, our basic social structure (see Chapter 7). In addition, to the extent that the family is enfeebled, so too are the church and school. For example, genetic screening may be very useful, but it also can be employed in an abusive manner, particularly in situations where prejudice regarding race or sex is involved.

Ecology. The major concern in the area of biotechnology and the environment is how to protect the planet and at the same time not obstruct progress in science. The ecological health of the world depends on a biodiversity that is the product of billions of years of evolutionary development. A hazard to the fragile environment can happen inadvertently—the introduction of a new species, for instance. Perhaps a new form of pollution might occur, a pollution that is itself the product of released organisms reproducing themselves millions of times. How shall the nation control this type of pollution? Can mistakes be tolerated? Is any information about nature gained without risk? These are the questions being raised by environmentalists concerned about the emerging new biotechnology.

All these areas of risk—philosophy, anthropology, sociology, and ecology—raise legitimate concerns. These concerns imply the necessity of political regulation, and it is to this question we now turn.

Regulation of Biotechnology

The problem of regulation of biotechnology is how to establish a sound system of control that ensures public safety but does not impose restrictions that might kill the infant industry in its early stages. Simply, the United States needs a regulatory system to establish standards for valid laboratory research and sound manufacturing processes.

When this problem first emerged in the mid-1970s, public opinion regarding genetic engineering was polarized from panic to panacea. Scientists themselves attempted to impose a moratorium and eventually convened the **Asilomar Conference** of 1975, a truly historic event in self-regulation organized for researchers to discuss the hazards of the new biotechnology. Little more than a decade later, after much debate and some time had passed, most individuals and groups have concluded that the biotechnology industry is someplace between the calamity of the Andromeda strain claimed by some and the minor accident noted by others. There are some serious public concerns involved, and they deserve serious public inquiry.[67]

According to former vice-president Albert Gore of Tennessee, there are three areas in biotechnology that should be addressed by public policy:

1. proper use of information derived from biotechnology
2. the use of biotechnology to produce new substances
3. the application of biotechnology to human beings

The first is concerned with how information from biotechnology is used (genetic screening and employment, for instance); the second is related to how the new substances of biotechnology alter earth's plants and animals and, thus, the very environment on which life depends; and the third is concerned with changes in the genetic constitution of human beings.[68] To understand how difficult it is to establish and administer thoughtful public policy, consider the following example: Biotech drugs are eagerly awaited by consumers as lifesavers, but the Food and Drug Administration (FDA) must approve each one, and that approval does not come easily. The process itself is long and complicated, and the FDA is overburdened with applications for drug approval. The FDA simply does not have the funds to keep pace with this burgeoning new industry, but without FDA approval, biotechnology drugs cannot be sold commercially.[69]

In addition to the FDA, three statutes combine to form the regulatory program regarding biotechnology. The Occupational Safety and Health Act (OSHA) deals with risks in the workplace; the Toxic Substances Control Act (TSCA) attempts to control environmental hazards of chemical substances; and finally, Section 361 of the Public Health Service Act (PHSA) gives the FDA authority to issue regulations related to communicable diseases.[70] These regulations address the rewards and penalties to society's health (human and animal) and environment. It is a subject of major concern as we start the year 2001.

The battle lines over genetic foods are being drawn; food manufacturers and the FDA are immersed in the struggle. Wisconsin recently moved to ban milk hormone for dairy cattle; in the fall of 1993 the first genetically engineered food reached American markets—the Flavr Savr tomato;[71] and the FDA is pondering the use of labeling genetically engineered foods. The pros and cons are not resolved at this writing.

Relationships in Biotechnology

The relationships involved in biotechnology are staggering, both nationally and internationally. Nationally, government agencies at the federal, state, and local levels may be involved in development and application of monoclonal antibodies employed in, for example, purification techniques. All levels of governmental decision making are involved, and all must establish public policies to deal with the application of biotechnology. Next in order of involvement might be business groups of many types—manufacturing, financing, distributing. Venture capital accumulation alone requires private investors, banks, and finance houses. In addition, corporations involved in transportation and manufacture must be involved. Professional and service industries associated with animal, plant, and human health, as well as environmental specialists, have a concrete interest in public policy associated with biotechnology. Academe generally, and faculty in particular, play a crucial role in biotechnology, as do institutions such as foundations, charities, and nonprofit organizations.

Internationally, the United Nations (U.N.) and many of its related agencies are participants in biological projects associated with human health (gene therapy), food and agriculture (additives for animal feed, vaccines, plant growth hormones), energy and environmental management (enhanced oil recovery), and raw material and chemicals. In addition to this, every nation in the developed world has an active interest in research and development in biotechnology.

Formerly, an entrepreneur with an idea for a useful product simply raised the venture capital, established the manufacturing plant, produced the product and, in some cases, even marketed the product. Today, all that is changed. Many other actors are involved in the decision-making process from the conception of the idea to the ultimate consumer of the product: government, professional groups, the universities, and perhaps even international organizations and groups from competing countries. The biotechnology industry bears witness to the reality of the new world economy.

Genetic Engineering: Three Major Areas

There are any number of organizing schemes that might be employed in a discussion of **genetic engineering.** Three categories of analysis—the genome project, genetic repair of a deficiency, and production of a new genetic combination—are used in this review.

Genetically engineered organisms come in one of two varieties. "They can serve as manufacturers (. . . make insulin) or as products (. . . protect crops)."[72] In the idiom of the day, the trip into the world of genetic engineering is an awesome journey, with overwhelming possibilities. Even the revolutionaries in the former Soviet Union, who for years assumed a nurturistic stance in the age-old nature-versus-nurture argument, finally embraced genetic interpretations of human behavior. "The old Marxist interpretation of human behavior had, paradoxically, become subversive to the Soviet order."[73] Consider genetic testing as just one example. About 50,000 women a year undergo an amniocentesis test. From a single ounce of amniotic fluid, scientists can determine the sex of the child, whether it will be retarded, crippled, or the victim of a fatal genetic disease. The people involved face agonizing choices, and for society and philosophy it raises questions about the very nature and meaning of human life. "Today 200 diseases are detectable within eight weeks of conception. No one of them is curable"[74] at the moment.

Genetic links have been discovered to Alzheimer's disease, manic depression, learning disabilities, mental disorders, alcoholism, and scores of other diseases. Eighteen Fortune 500 companies have reported using genetic tests to screen employees and job applicants,[75] and many other firms plan to follow their example. Insurance companies are using genetic tests to identify individuals with a family history of genetic disease. California and Utah computerize genetic records on thousands of their residents. Should a state or a corporation hire someone with a high risk of Alzheimer's disease? Should a fetus with a serious genetic disorder be terminated because of the social costs involved? The blueprint for life itself is being mapped at this moment, even as new ethical and political questions arise. Following are three areas of genetic engineering that should be examined.

The Genome Project.   The **Human Genome Project**, directed by Dr. Francis S. Collins, started officially in 1990 and was estimated to take fifteen years and cost $3 billion. The goal was to map the entire human genetic code, the "code of all codes." It has been called by some the most significant project human beings have ever mounted. The project had two principal goals: (a) to develop a detailed map of the human **genome** showing the location and function of the approximately 100,000 genes that make up the human chromosomes; and (b) to determine the order (the sequence) of the individual nucleotides in the DNA of these genomes. Progress in the development of the genome map was better than originally expected and the fifteen-year goal seemed to be a realistic one.[76] Such a map was expected to be a tremendous boon to doctors in diagnosis of such diseases as cancer, cystic fibrosis, and the more than "3,000 human diseases known to be inherited."[77] Approximately a hundred federal, educational, and corporate institutions have been involved in the development of this atlas of human geography. This project "is setting the stage for 21st century biology . . . [because] we are talking about the blueprint of life—the rawest and most fundamental type of biological information."[78] Once the location and nature of each of the 100,000 genes is known, scientists will have created the conditions conducive to treating and curing inherited diseases. Japan sees genetic engineering as the next-generation industry, and the genome project is the centerpiece of the U.S. response, that is, to "analyze all the genetic material in the human cell."[79]

In this international race to "understand all 23 [pairs of] human chromosomes and the tens of thousands of different genes they contain, . . . scientists hope to isolate the genes behind many if not all human diseases."[80] "Although the project started in American laboratories, it is now a global venture."[81] This map is being created by scientists and researchers at the Whitehead Institute for Biomedical Research in Cambridge, Massachusetts, and at Genethon in France. The map was published in December of 1995.[82] With the publication of the map, the project began a transition from basic research to applied research. New firms are being established to process the information because there are a variety of ways to make money from genomics, such as genetic testing and gene therapy.[83] There is already one striking bit of information derived from the project, i.e., that the genes for surface traits such as skin color are discounted; "the human races are remarkably alike under the skin." The variation among individuals is much greater than the differences among groups. In fact the diversity among individuals is so enormous that the whole concept of race becomes meaningless at the genetic level.[84]

But now, in the year 2000, the book of life has a new reader—a new player in the race to rapidly decode, or sequence, the genetic code. His name is J. Craig Venter and his flagship company, Celera, claims that it can decode the "human blueprint" faster than the Collins group by using hundreds of "automatic gene sequencers," supercomputers costing $300,000 each. Whether Venter and his partners can produce a text as complete as the Human Genome Project led by Collins is a matter of great debate. Venter argues that researchers all over the world will have the human genome "ahead of time" because of their work. The political question is whether anybody has the right to do what Venter proposes, that is, patent basic scientific information. His opponents contend that discoveries in nature are not inventions and that the Patent Office has violated its statute in issuing such patents.[85]

Some people have compared the Human Genome Project to the Manhattan Project and the Apollo program. It will certainly play a major role in helping the United States maintain its lead in the biotechnology industry. But there are formidable legal and ethical issues that must be resolved—information control, eugenics (improvement of the species), and the marketing of "high-grade" embryos. American policymakers are addressing none of these issues at this time.

The political problems remain, and as scientists map the genetic constitution of human beings, the makers of public policy must deal with the issues just discussed. To forecast much of the political agenda for America in the next few years, it would be wise to read *Science News* as well as *Time, Newsweek,* and *The New York Times.*

Repairing Deficiencies. Genetic engineering has conferred on human beings a power they may be ill prepared to exercise. To repair a genetic defect is surely a laudable activity, but to improve on the "book of life" is quite another thing. Unfortunately, the distinction between *repair* and *improve* in genetic engineering is not quite as clear in science as it is in language. Nevertheless, this inquiry purports to make that distinction in order to reveal some of the complexities involved in the issue. There are, after all, thousands of inheritable diseases that are likely targets for genetic research, among them sickle-cell anemia, Tay-Sachs disease, and Huntington's disease, and mental illness. In the last few years, scientists involved in genetic research have made some remarkable progress in locating the genetic root of some of these problems and in repairing the genetic deficiencies.

"Gene therapy is the supply of a functional gene to cells lacking that function, with the aim of correcting a genetic disorder or acquired disease."[86] Biologists are now in the business of putting genes into cells, and this creates an entirely new situation wherein human beings really no longer have to live with the genes they were born with. This is gene therapy, and it will help physicians cope with many kinds of genetic disorders. In principle, gene therapy permits doctors to introduce any sort of gene deemed necessary into patients lacking healthy copies of the particular gene.

Each human cell contains forty-six chromosomes constructed of DNA and protein. In genetic engineering, the DNA, which is coiled in a double helix, is chemically removed and unraveled. Then, in gene therapy, scientists snip out genes of the DNA of one organism, join it with the DNA of another organism, and insert the altered combination into a cell. The purpose is to reproduce, like a copying machine, an unlimited number of the altered composite. This technique has tremendous potential for repairing and treating particular genetic diseases. Consider how it might be employed in some of the following cases involving genetic problems in human beings:

1. A young woman had a cholesterol level so high that she suffered a heart attack at sixteen. After being treated about ten years with gene therapy, the woman's cholesterol level had dropped significantly. The new therapy will, in all probability, extend her life expectancy by years. The woman's disease, familial hypercholesterolemia, created a condition in which her liver lacked the gene necessary to remove cholesterol from the blood. Scientists used viruses to shuttle copies of the missing gene into her liver cells in the laboratory and then put the corrected cells back into the woman's liver.[87]

2. Carlene Lauffer became the first human being to get gene therapy for arthritis. Researchers "injected specially treated cells into the knuckles of her left hand. Researchers hope the cells will produce proteins that would ease the pain and halt further deterioration of the joints. . . . If gene therapy proves effective, joint replacement for arthritis may eventually become unnecessary."[88]

3. In a new procedure, Savio Woo, a scientist with the Baylor College of Medicine, "clipped what he called a 'suicide gene' from a herpes virus and injected it into tumors of mice with colon cancer. . . . The tumor cells absorbed the suicide gene, making the cells susceptible to a drug" used to treat herpes. Woo reports he saw 'dramatic' regression in the tumors. Human trials have now begun with a few patients.[89]

4. Cystic fibrosis is caused by a gene flaw. It results in a thick mucus accumulation in the lungs, intestines, and pancreas. It is the most common fatal inherited disease of Americans. "Researchers have begun transferring normal genes into cystic fibrosis patients in an experiment they hope will lead to a cure.[90]

5. Alzheimer's disease takes its victims by surprise. Researchers for years have sought the key to who is at risk for this devastating disease. Recently, "scientists have identified a gene whose presence warns of increased risk of Alzheimer's disease."[91] This single errant gene enables scientists to illuminate the disease and work toward a cure.

6. Researchers have identified a gene pattern on the "X chromosome in 40 pairs of homosexual brothers,"[92] adding evidence to the theory that the tendency to be gay can be inherited.

7. "Essential" hypertension accounts for 95 percent of all high blood pressure in the United States. Scientists recently "linked a human gene to the most common form of high blood pressure . . . a disease afflicting more than 50 million Americans."[93]

8. The potential of gene therapy as a treatment for AIDS received a boost when molecular biologists inserted a gene "into cells of [six] people affected with HIV, the virus leading to AIDS, . . . to try to reduce viral replication."[94]

9. Two French babies born with a lethal immune disease called "bubble boy disease" have been restored to apparently normal immune systems after gene therapy. The doctors involved said that they observed clinical benefits that they had never observed before.[95]

10. Spare parts for humans may be in the future. Two scientists have grown replacement organs for sheep and rabbits using the animals' own cells and lab molds to help the tissue take shape.[96]

As the genome project continues to evolve and develop, the opportunity for repair of deficiencies improves in a direct relation.

Improved Combinations. To improve something is to enhance its value, to make it better, to make it more acceptable—in short, to increase its excellence. This is the unabashed claim of science regarding genetic engineering, which has already given us bigger beef cattle, cows that give more milk, and genetically altered strawberries—berries that are bigger, better tasting, and more resistant to frost. Scientists inserted a gene that controls growth in a rainbow trout into a carp and produced a genetically altered carp that grew 20 percent faster than its natural relatives. The goal was to reproduce this experiment in catfish, thus improving the South's aquaculture.[97] The government of the People's Republic of China is also deeply involved in this research and development. The point is that genes can be demonstrably transferred from one species to another and will produce important changes. Genetically engineered fish are here to stay; they will grow to full size in a shorter period, provide more edible flesh, and pass this quality on to their offspring—but not without consequences for the environment. Scientists "are now attempting to transfer into fish [genes] from humans, chickens, cattle, and mice . . . [all designed to] substantially change"[98] the characteristics of the particular species.

Gene transfer has been used to make plants more resistant to drought and to particular herbicides and "the United States issued to Harvard University . . . the world's first patent for a higher [read *improved*] form of life: a genetically engineered mouse."[99]

Today, gene therapy is at the threshold of human trials. If animals can be improved, so can human beings. In the spring of 1989, scientists at the National Institute of Health in Bethesda, Maryland, began treating "ten terminal cancer patients by giving them back billions of their own white blood cells that have been supercharged (improved in the laboratory) to enhance their natural ability to kill tumors."[100] This was the first time the government had approved the introduction of foreign genes into human beings. The test put improved genes into the patient's body, and then the genes were removed after a month to see if they were still working. This is gene therapy, and nobody knows what will happen.

Use of the data derived from the human genome project for eugenic purposes, whether tacitly or by policy, is the most controversial policy of all.[101] The basic idea of eugenics is to improve human stock by increasing the number of allegedly desirable human beings and reducing the stock of allegedly undesirable people. The fear is that the genome project will encourage the movement to produce "superbabies" and to eliminate the unfit. "Genes for physical characteristics (sex, height, hair color, race, and eye color) as well as genes to protect against some possible future illness are being identified now." The genes for musical, artistic, and athletic ability may become known, as will the couplet of genes for the traits and abilities that comprise intelligence.[102] To adopt a eugenics policy raises fundamental social questions. Should we give up "the usual game of reproducing by 'sexual roulette' in which parents simply and blindly accept all products of conception,"[103] or do we impose controls that limit such choices so that a minimum quality standard of human health and potential may reasonably be expected? For example, the official China News Agency said on December 20, 1993, that China will use abortion, sterilization, and banned marriages "to avoid new births of inferior quality and heighten the standards of the whole population [in legislation entitled] 'Eugenics and Health Protection.'"

In 2000, the *Journal of Gene Medicine* discussed gene transfer in dealing with cancer; gene transfer to control the central nervous system; and gene therapy to help patients with severe combined immunodeficiency.[104] The great hope, according to Hadassah University Hospital and Pittsburgh Human Gene Therapy Center in December of 2000, is to understand disease at the molecular level, develop techniques to treat genetic defects, transfer genes to modify the course of disease, and to more effectively manipulate the human organism via gene therapy.

In early 1997, Dr. Ian Wilmut, an embryologist from Scotland, and his team of scientists announced that they had cloned an adult sheep—a "higher order" animal—and named her Dolly. The cloned sheep is the first mammal reproduced by inserting the DNA from a cell of a mature sheep into the unfertilized egg of a second sheep, which was then implanted into a third sheep that gave birth to the clone—Dolly. What process was employed? How was this genetic feat accomplished? First, the nucleus of a ewe's udder cell was removed and starved of nutrients so that it was dormant and nondividing (the nucleus contains the cell's DNA); second, this nucleus then replaced the nucleus of an unfertilized egg from a second sheep. Simply, the DNA of sheep number one replaced the DNA of sheep number two; third, an electric charge jump-started the hybrid egg so that it acted like a fertilized egg (in other words, like one in which a female egg is joined with the sperm from a male); fourth, the cell then grew and divided, and when it became an embryo it was implanted in a third sheep—the surrogate mother; fifth, in July of 1996 Dolly was born—proving that a cell from an adult mammal can return to an embryonic stage and bring forth new life.

The cloned sheep gives us an insight into a new era in scientific discovery that lies before humanity. Consider some of the possible benefits and hazards. Cloned animals may help us produce hard-to-make proteins, generate organs for human beings that are now in short supply (pigs are of great interest in this area), aid in research on genetic diseases such as cystic fibrosis, copy animals that yield good beef or milk, and enable scientists to edit their clones so they might have a special immune system. All this and more. However, hazards also exist—particularly in the area of ethics and morality that go far beyond the limited boundaries of science. The very idea of what it means to be a human being could be altered. What will relationship terms—parent, sibling, grandparent, ancestor—mean in the future? If humans have an identity crisis today, what will identity and human dignity mean in the future?

Some European nations have already banned cloning. The United States has not. President Clinton called the news of Dolly's birth "startling." He asked that a bioethics commission review the implications for human beings and report back to him within ninety days (by May 1997).[105] The National Bioethics Advisory Commission (NBAC) concluded that at this time (Fall 1997) it is morally unacceptable for anyone in the public or private sector, whether in research or a clinical setting, to attempt to create a child using "somatic cell nuclear transfer." They urged Clinton to maintain the moratorium and to cooperate with other nations on this issue.

At the University of Hawaii, clones of clones of clones have been born, suggesting that adult cells can be turned back into primitive cells capable of generating new tissues, organs, and even entire animals. "Designer" cattle are on the way as researchers have produced six genetically identical calves—this as reported in the *Dayton Daily News* on May 22, 1998. The implications of this new scientific capability suggest that the world we all live in will never be quite the same again. Indeed, the nature-nurture argument now takes on new dimensions. Asked if this procedure would work with human beings, a leading research scientist involved in a similar cloning experiment said he would consider it unethical.[106] The problem, of course, is what happens in a case where a scientist does not consider the cloning of humans unethical. *The Boys from Brazil* by Ira Levin is the story of a Nazi scientist with a diabolical plan to create a new Hitler by cloning ninety-four men. This novel suggests some frightening possibilities.

Scientists have long known that each of us, at conception, is female. "The embryo destined to become a boy begins as a female."[107] After thirty-five or forty days a gene labeled SRY switches on to initiate the embryo on the road to maleness. Recently, researchers have isolated this genetic switch on sex determination. SRY is the master switch.[108] The problem is what do we do with this information. If it's possible to "flip" the SRY switch, is it not probable that someday it will happen? What then?

Perhaps Robin Cook's novel *Mutation* best sums up the possibilities for the future. In this story a father arranges to have his unborn son genetically altered to be superintelligent. The results are chilling.

PROSPECTS: BIOTECHNOLOGY

The most important political need, as the nation enters the twenty-first century, is the establishment of a framework for national decision making by the federal government on the great issues of biotechnology. Federal agencies are already behind schedule as they attempt to construct regulations for the evolving biotechnology industry, and the tensions involved in public policy have been further exacerbated by the decision of the U.S. Patent Office to allow patents on bioengineered organisms.

There are still a number of important questions that must be resolved in the federal policies—for example, Who should control science? How shall we protect our environment? What does it mean to be a human being? What rights exist for human beings? What limits, if any, should exist to protect animals? What are the possible and the probable dangers implicit in biotechnology research and development? What should we do regarding biological warfare? These and a host of other questions confront policymakers at all levels of the political system. The consequences of the new technology will be momentous, and U.S. political and legal institutions must deal with the new conflicts and disagreements.

Commercial development in biotechnology is a reality now and it will soon be a multibillion-dollar international factor. New ethical and religious questions are sure to be raised, demanding that we face up to what it means to be a human being.

In the establishment of U.S. public policy, the traditional actors in the conflicts and disagreements to date have been lawyers, interest groups, and institutions. But biotechnology will, as the future reveals itself, require that other actors become involved, namely, the public and political scientists—the public because the traditional policymakers simply are not equipped to raise and cope with the social and ethical dimensions of disagreements on issues of biotechnology; political scientists because they, perhaps more than any other group, understand our institutions and processes and thus can help in minimizing conflict and in predicting policy outcomes.[109]

The prospects for biotechnology in the twenty-first century are revolutionary; we are likely to see rapid, fundamental change in our health (human and animal), agriculture, national security, energy, and environmental industries. Change is the new rule in almost every aspect of life, and this change will penetrate to the very foundations of society. Some optimism may be warranted, however, because the modern democratic state has successfully constructed the institutions and processes needed to deal with change. One need only look at the last four bulwarks left in the communist block (Cuba, China, Vietnam, North Korea) to understand that authoritarian and totalitarian systems are becoming passé because they are only theoretically, not practically, change-oriented systems. They are simply not capable of rapid, fundamental change. It is our great good fortune to live in a democratic system—a system that theoretically *and* practically is open to change. This is one of our greatest strengths.

STUDY QUESTIONS

1. Define *biotechnology* and comment on its relationship to genetic engineering.
2. What limits, if any, should be established regarding scientists' efforts to genetically "improve" on agricultural products (strawberries, potatoes, tobacco)?
3. Should the FBI establish a genetic code bank including every citizen (this could be done at birth) to aid in its fight against crime (so-called genetic fingerprinting)? If so, why? If not, why not?
4. Should the United States establish a policy of mandatory genetic screening? If so, why? If not, why not?
5. Distinguish between gene splicing and gene therapy.
6. What is the genome project and why is it a significant program for Americans today?
7. Who should participate in the debate and dialogue regarding genetic engineering, and why should these individuals and groups be involved?
8. The issue of whether someone has property rights to his or her own DNA has never been resolved by the courts. Simply, who owns genetic material once it is used in scientific research?
9. Evaluate a political system's ability to develop, regulate, and commercialize the new biotechnology.
10. Third World countries hold the "bank vault" (the wealth of genetic diversity) on new genetics. Will their natural heritage be exploited by First World wealth? Should there be any limit to state sovereignty in its relation to genetics?

NOTES

1. George Will, "The Scientific Concerns of Today Will Be the Political Concerns of Tomorrow," *Dayton Daily News*, April 26, 1989, p. 11.
2. *The Random House Dictionary of the English Language*, 2nd ed. (New York: Random House, 1987), p. 210.
3. Ibid., p. 1950.
4. Warren "Clint" Hyer, "An Overview of Biotechnology," *Biotechnology Views*, October 1988, p. 5.
5. Ibid.
6. Ibid.
7. Andrew Pollack "Genentech: New Product to Aid Heart Patients," *The New York Times*, January 5, 1988, p. 27.
8. J.E. Smith, *Biotechnology Principles* (Washington, DC: American Society for Microbiology, 1985), p. 39.
9. James D. Watson, *The Double Helix* (New York: New American Library, 1968), pp. 18 and 53.
10. Ibid., p. 140.
11. Ibid., p. 118.
12. Ibid.

13. Sandra Panem, ed., *Biotechnology: Implications for Public Policy* (Washington, DC: The Brookings Institution, 1985), p. 4.
14. Ibid.
15. Ibid.
16. Warren E. Leary, "Life Patents," *Dayton Daily News,* June 29, 1980, p. 6; Peter Coy, "Biotech Industry Comes of Age," *Dayton Daily News,* August 8, 1988, p. 6; James Flanigan, "Betting on Biotech," *Dayton Daily News,* March 29, 1989, p. 5.
17. "Biotechnology and U.S. Competitiveness," speech by Senator Lawton Chiles, sponsored by The Center for Governmental Responsibility, University of Florida, Gainesville, January 23, 1989.
18. Coy, "Biotech Industry Comes of Age," p. 6.
19. Christine Gorman, "The Race to Map Our Genes," *Time,* February 8, 1993, p. 57.
20. "More Government Funds for UK Biotech," *The Financial Times Limited,* January 17, 1992, p. 3.
21. "Contest for Biotech Companies Rages On," *The Providence Journal Bulletin,* December 16, 1992, p. 2.
22. "Biotech's New-Wave Biologicals," *Chemical Week,* December 18, 1985, p. 26.
23. "Biotechnology Growing Greener at Last," *Chemical Week,* September 30, 1987, p. 21.
24. Ibid., pp. 28–32.
25. Paul Recer, "O.U. Develops Mouse That Resists Infection," *Dayton Daily News,* December 24, 1992, p. 8C.
26. Dan Fagin, "Race Is on for Breast Cancer Gene," *Dayton Daily News,* November 18, 1993, p. 3E. See also, Dr. Harmon Eyre, "Gene Breakthrough Helps Breast Cancer Detection," *Dayton Daily News,* September 15, 1994, p. 12A.
27. Vicki Cheng, "Genetically Engineered Flu Vaccine Shows Promise, Study Finds," *The New York Times,* June 25, 1995, p. 10, sec. J.
28. Malcolm Ritter, "Scientists Zero in on Depression Gene," *Dayton Daily News,* April 2, 1996, p. 4A.
29. Joe Taylor, "First Baby Tested for Tay-Sachs Is Born in Texas," *West Hawaii Today,* January 27, 1994, p. 12A.
30. Daniel Q. Harey, "Genes Prevent AIDS," *Dayton Daily News,* August 9, 1996, p. 12A.
31. Steven Morris, "Big Problems, Big Profits in Artificial Blood," *Dayton Daily News,* December 1, 1994, p. 3A.
32. Alan T. Bull, Geoffrey Holt, and Malcolm D. Lilly, *Biotechnology: International Trends and Perspectives* (Paris: OECD, 1982), pp. 24–25.
33. "Genetic Storage," *Sarasota Herald-Tribune,* March 25, 1990, p. 6F.
34. "From the Germ Theory to Gene Theory," *Dayton Daily News,* December 21, 1999, p. 4C.
35. Organization for Economic Cooperation and Development, *Biotechnology and the Changing Role of Government* (Paris: OECD, 1988), p. 27.
36. Ibid.
37. C.M. Brown, I. Campbell, and F.G. Priest, *Introduction to Biotechnology* (London: Blackwell Scientific Publications, 1987), pp. 129–131.
38. John E. Smith, *Biotechnology Principles* (Hong Kong: Van Nostrand, 1985), p. 97.
39. David Rotman with Emma Chynoweth, "Agchem Producers Sow Plans for Rich Harvest," *Chemical Week,* August 18, 1993, p. 33.
40. "Genetically Engineered Cotton," *Genetic Technology News,* October 1991, p. 8.
41. "New Technology Makes Sea Oats Bigger, Better," *Sarasota Herald-Tribune,* February 4, 1990, p. 2B.
42. "DNA Substances Gives Sunless Tan to Guinea Pigs," *Dayton Daily News,* December 1, 1994, p. 3A.
43. Doretta Donovan and Frazier Smith, "Mexico Lab Fighting Famine," *Dayton Daily News,* November 27, 1996, p. 4A.
44. Dennis T. Avery, "Biotechnology Has Greater Potential Than Organic Farming," *Dayton Daily News,* April 15, 2000, p. 9A.
45. OECD, *Biotechnology and the Changing Role of Government,* p. 36.
46. Janet Raloff, "An Alaskan Feast for Oil-Eating Microbes," *Environment,* April 17, 1993, p. 253.
47. June Herald, "Company Profile: Environmental Biotech of the Miami Valley," *Dayton Daily News,* January 2, 1993, p. 4B.
48. Robert Cooke, "More Reel Than Real," *Newsday,* June 15, 1993, p. 64; "Nobel Prize for 'Jurassic Park' Chemists," *Press Association Newsfile,* October 13, 1993, p. 1.

49. Charles Pillar and K.R. Yamanoto, *Gene Wars: Military Control Over the New Technologies* (New York: Beech Tree Books, 1988).

50. Larry Thompson, "Scientists Say Genetic Engineering Increases the Threat of Biological Warfare," *Sarasota Herald-Tribune*, February 1, 1989, p. 12E.

51. Jeffrey L. Fox, "Impacting Biological Weapons," *Biotechnology* 2, September 1993, p. 979.

52. "Tough-as-Nails Silk Developed by Scientist," *Sarasota Herald-Tribune*, February 27, 1990, p. 10A.

53. Gayle Golden, "Crime Solving Entering New Age of Technology," *Dayton Daily News*, March 4, 1988, p. 2Z4.

54. "DNA Tests Link Boys to Killing," *Dayton Daily News*, November 11, 1993, p. 11.

55. "Tests Show Girl Is Not Child of Man Raising Her," *Dayton Daily News*, November 20, 1989, p. 1.

56. Sandra Skowran, "Convict Freed by DNA Test," *Dayton Daily News*, June 29, 1993, p. 3A.

57. "Man Gets 78-Year Term for Second Rape Conviction," *Sarasota Herald-Tribune*, February 9, 1988, p. 10-BM.

58. Malcolm Ritter, "DNA Useful in Disasters," *Dayton Daily News*, April 4, 1997, p. 2A.

59. L. Wayne Hicks, "DNA Test Fingers Man as Child's Father," *Sarasota Herald-Tribune*, March 23, 1989, p. 3.

60. Ben DiPietro, "DNA Testing Could End Honored Tradition," *Dayton Daily News*, May 29, 1990, p. 11A.

61. OECD, *Biotechnology and the Changing Role of Government*, p. 35.

62. Brown, Campbell, Priest, *Introduction to Biotechnology*, p. 112.

63. Malcolm Ritter, "Scientists Link Gene to Personality Trait," *Dayton Daily News*, January 2, 1996, p. 1A.

64. "Aggression in Mice Linked to Gene," *Dayton Daily News*, November 23, 1995, p. 5A.

65. *Dayton Daily News*, December 19, 2000, p. 1A.

66. Albert Gore Jr., "A Congressional Perspective," in *Biotechnology: Implications for Public Policy*, Sandra Panem, ed., pp. 12–18.

67. Panem, ed., *Biotechnology: Implications for Public Policy*; see the articles by Albert Gore, James J. Florio, and the conclusion by Sandra Panem.

68. Gore, "A Congressional Perspective," pp. 13–14.

69. Stephen Jones, "FDA Overburdened with Applications for New Drugs," *Dayton Daily News*, May 8, 1989, p. 2.

70. Thomas O. McGarity, "Legal and Regulatory Issues in Biotechnology," *Biotechnology and the Environment*, pp. 143–44. Edited by Albert H. Teich, Maurice A. Levin, Joe H. Pace; Washington, DC: 1995; published by the U.S. Environmental Protection Agency.

71. Maxine F. Singer, "Food Fight," *Dayton Daily News*, August 13, 1993, p. 11A.

72. "What Price Mighty Mouse," *The New Republic*, May 23, 1988, p. 7.

73. Loren Graham, "The Return of Genetics," *The Washington Post National Weekly Edition*, May 10, 1993, p. 23.

74. Robert Lee Hotz, "Genetics Testing," *Dayton Daily News*, May 27, 1987, p. Z41.

75. Ibid.

76. Belinda Rossiter and Thomas Caskey, "Medical Consequences of the Human Genome Project," *National Forum*, Spring 1993, p. 12.

77. "Scientists Urge $3 Billion Effort," *Sarasota Herald-Tribune*, February 12, 1988, p. 7A.

78. Robert Lee Hotz, "Technology Limits Plans to Chart Atlas of Genes," *Dayton Daily News*, May 27, 1987, p. Z43.

79. "Battle for the Future," *Time*, January 16, 1989, p. 43.

80. Natalie Angier, "Big Gains Reported in Project to Map Genetic Structure," *The New York Times*, October 1, 1992, p. 1.

81. "The Human Genome: The Proper Study of Mankind," *The Economist*, September 14, 1996, p. 20.

82. "Gene Map Reaches Midpoint," *Dayton Daily News*, December 22, 1995, p. 10A.

83. "The Human Genome: The Proper Study of Mankind," *The Economist*, September 14, 1996, p. 21.

84. Sribala Subramanian, "The Story in Our Genes," *Time*, January 16, 1995, p. 54.

85. Gwynne Dyer, "Hijacking the Human Genetic Code," *Dayton Daily News*, December 27, 1999, p. 7A. See also Tim Friend, "New Effort to Decode the Human Genome on the Fast Track," *USA Today*, June 9, 1998, p. 6D.

86. Rossiter and Caskey, p. 14.
87. "Gene Therapy Lowers Cholesterol," *Dayton Daily News*, April 1, 1994, p. 9A.
88. Byron Spice, "Gene Therapy Test Set," *Dayton Daily News*, July 21, 1996, p. 15A.
89. Paul Raeburn, "Suicide Genes Destroy Tumors in Lab Animals," *Dayton Daily News*, July 28, 1995, p. 11A.
90. "10 Cystic Fibrosis Patients to Get New Gene Therapy," *Dayton Daily News*, April 20, 1993, p. 4A.
91. "Higher Risk of Alzheimer's Linked to Gene," *Science News*, August 14, 1993, p. 108.
92. "Gene Pattern Linked to Sexual Orientation," *Dayton Daily News*, July 16, 1993, p. 12A.
93. "Scientists Link Gene, Hypertension," *Dayton Daily News*, October 2, 1992, p. 4C.
94. Elizabeth Pennisi, "High Tech Gene Therapy to Target HIV," *Science News*, September 18, 1993, p. 182.
95. Lauran Neergaard, "Gene Therapy Restores Immune Systems to 2 Babies," *Dayton Daily News*, April 28, 2000, p. 6A.
96. Dave Howland, "Tissue Growth Offers Hope," *Dayton Daily News*, July 23, 1997, p. 3A.
97. Keith Schneider, "A Designer Fish Raises Fears for Nature," *The New York Times*, June 12, 1988, p. 4.
98. Keith Schneider, "Carp with Genes Altered Grow Faster," *The New York Times*, June 2, 1988, p. A-20.
99. Keith Schneider, "U.S. Issues World's First Animal Patent," *Sarasota Herald-Tribune*, April 3, 1988, p. 1.
100. "Gene Therapy Reaches a Threshold: Human Trials," *Dayton Daily News*, May 22, 1989, p. 4.
101. Marc Lappe, "Justice and the Limitations of Genetic Knowledge," *Forum*, Spring 1993, p. 34.
102. Jerry E. Bishop, "Unnatural Selection," *Forum*, Spring 1993, p. 28.
103. Joseph Fletcher, "Genetic Control: A Position Paper," *National Forum*, Fall 1989, p. 43.
104. *The Journal of Gene Medicine*, May-June, 2000, Vol. 2.
105. See the following news reports and essays for more information on cloning: (a) Associated Press, "Clinton Asks Panel for Report on Cloning," *The Honolulu Adventurer*, February 25, 1997, p. A-5; (b) Matt Crenson, "It's a Brave New World—If You're A Sheep," *West Hawaii Today*, February 28, 1997, p. 6A; (c) Ellen Goodman, "We Need Not Follow Science's Lead," *West Hawaii Today*, February 28, 1997, p. 10A; (d) "Human Cloning: Unsettling and Now Perhaps Inevitable," *USA Today*, February 25, 1997, p. 14A; (e) George Will, "Dolly Raises Stakes of Philosophy," *West Hawaii Today*, February 27, 1997, p. 10A; (f) Malcolm Ritter, "Scientists Clone Adult Mammal for First Time," *West Hawaii Today*, February 24, 1997, p. 1A and 4A; (g) "Implications of Cloning Sheep Are Remarkable," *West Hawaii Today*, February 26, 1997, p. 10A; (h) Charles Krauthammer, "A Special Report on Cloning," *Newsweek*, March 10, 1997, pp. 60–61.
106. Malcolm Ritter, "Scientists Clone Sheep en Masse," *West Hawaii Today*, March 7, 1996, p. 2A.
107. " 'Master Switch' Rules in Creating Boys and Girls," *Dayton Daily News*, December 2, 1994, p. 11A.
108. Ibid.
109. Odelin Funke, "Political Scientists and Biotechnology Policy," *PS: Political Science and Politics*, Winter 1988, p. 66.

SUGGESTED READINGS

BROWN, C.M., I. CAMPBELL, and F.G. PRIEST. *Introduction to Biotechnology.* London: Blackwell Scientific Publications, 1987.

BULL, ALAN T., GEOFFREY HOLT, and MALCOLM D. LILLY. *Biotechnology: International Trends and Perspectives.* Paris: Organization for Economic Cooperation and Development (OECD), 1988.

OECD. *Biotechnology and the Changing Role of Government.* Paris: OECD, 1988.

PANEM, SANDRA, ed. *Biotechnology: Implications for Public Policy.* Washington, DC: The Brookings Institution, 1985.

PILLAR, CHARLES, and K.R. YAMANOTO. *Gene Wars: Military Control Over the New Technologies.* New York: Beech Tree Books, 1988.

WATSON, JAMES D. *The Double Helix.* New York: New American Library, 1968. This is a superb book on the scientific and human struggle to unearth one of nature's secrets: DNA.

Chapter 9

The Ecological Crisis

Ecology is a branch of science concerned with the interrelationship of organisms and their environment. Formerly, issues of war and peace dominated the national and international agenda. Today, the ecological crisis, in both its biotic and abiotic dimensions, creates security problems of a totally different kind for America and the world. Consider the following:

- A study, by Washington University scientists, of the Great Flood of 1993 found that the Missouri River near Columbia, Missouri, removed 2 million tons of soil from a 10,000-acre flood plain after it tore through levees and in return deposited 3 million tons of sand.[1]

- The ozone in the air around Chicago on August 6, 1996, was thick enough to make some throats scratchy and persuade state environmental officials to declare "ozone action day."[2]

- Massive food shortages will develop over a forty-year period as a population explosion outstrips the world's food supply.[3]

- After years of Brazilian government claims that stricter environmental laws had slowed destruction of the Amazon rain forest, newly issued figures show that deforestation has actually increased sharply since the 1992 Earth Summit was held in Rio de Janeiro.[4]

- Nearly one fourth of the world's species of mammals are threatened with extinction, and about half of those may be gone in as little as a decade, according to the most complete global analysis of endangered animal species ever compiled.[5]

These are just a few examples of the types of environmental abuse caused by human beings that today have the capacity to change the very nature of the world. The worldwide ecological crisis is a reality *now*. This is a crisis different from the Cold War, the homeless in America, terrorism, and massive budget deficits in that it cannot be negotiated away, bought off, imprisoned, or disguised and rationalized by the skillful rhetoric of politicians and public relations experts.

Environmentalists argue that this crisis is inexorably moving the world, twenty-four hours a day, toward calamity, and that tokenism such as the Clean Air Act will not work as the ecological crisis deepens. We are, they contend, destroying our own biodiversity, our own web of life, and we fail to recognize that we are a part of that fragile fabric. These issues suggest that the survival of the human species itself is at peril.

The "Sources" section of this chapter seeks to briefly describe the recent history and development of the ecological crisis and some of the worldwide conditions associated with this phenomenon. However, the real heart of this chapter is the "Status" section, which addresses the major issues. In order to deal with the host of biotic (population, plant, animal) and abiotic (air, water, land) issues as thoughtfully as possible within the limits of space provided in one chapter, some choices on what issues to include and exclude, as well as an organizing scheme for presentation of the material, is mandatory. Thus in this section of the chapter, each topic is analyzed as follows: What is the nature of the problem? What are some of the principle conditions that give rise to the problem? What are the major consequences of the problem? What proposals have been suggested to date to deal with these issues? Finally, in the section labeled "Prospects," an effort is made to identify significant new trends in our struggle to cope with the ecological crisis, along with an analysis of the possibilities and probabilities for success and failure.

SOURCES: THE ECOLOGICAL CRISIS

"Most environmental difficulties arise from a virtually universal aspiration—economic dynamism. By such dynamism mankind has made more of a mark on the environment in the last 100 years than in the preceding 3,000."[6] In the developed countries of the First World, this dynamism found its initial dramatic expression in the Industrial Revolution of the nineteenth century. The staggering technological changes in the manner in which goods were produced, and the human and ecological relationships involved changed everything. Coal for heating and steam engines for factories were the fundamental new conditions that ultimately resulted in the major ecological changes that confront us today. Think of the changes involved: small self-sufficient agricultural communities gave way to new and extremely large cities defined by industry and manufacture; merchants, bankers, and entrepreneurs became the mediators of this new age; skilled craftspeople gave up their guilds, tools, and skills to enter the burgeoning factories where division of labor fragmented the productive process and where the tools were owned by the entrepreneurs; and finally, the security once provided by the guilds was gone. Extravagant wealth and abject poverty existed in internal relationship to one another. Air, water, land, and energy pollution took a quantum leap forward as this economic dynamism spread throughout Europe and North America. Living plants, animals, and people were forced to give way to the new urban-industrial setting. Nothing—neither human beings nor nature itself—could stand in the way of the great new god, economic progress.

In America the Civil War, the era of the trusts in the 1890s, World War I, the social revolution of Franklin D. Roosevelt's New Deal in the 1930s, the world-shattering cataclysm of World War II, and the race into space fired into life by *Sputnik* in 1957 all gave rise to technological change and innovation that in turn shattered existing social, economic, political, cultural, and ecological relationships. Everything changed in a very short period, and the effect on the worldwide ecological balance was particularly disastrous. The means of transportation changed from the horse and buggy to the automobile, truck, train, and airplane with all the attendant pollution problems. In energy, the transition was from water and wood to fossilized fuel and nuclear power with its radioactive emissions. In manufacturing, the change was from the handloom to the automated factory. In agriculture today, 3 percent of the work force feeds 97 percent of the United States because of fewer and larger farms (agribusinesses) using the latest chemical fertilizers, and because of farm practices that maximize immediate profits at the expense of conservation of soil as a natural resource. The mass media, the very mode whereby we gather information and learn about problems, has changed from the newspaper and periodical to radio, television, and telecommunications.

There are two kinds of catastrophes—natural and humanmade. Natural catastrophes include plagues, hurricanes, earthquakes, tornadoes, and floods. Humanmade catastrophes involve human inventiveness and may be visible or invisible. Visible humanmade disasters include the London smog that killed 3,000 people in 1952; the 1986 Chernobyl nuclear reactor accident in the Soviet Union, in which people, plants, and animals were killed and injured through radiation; the Bhopal, India, disaster in 1984 from a toxic gas leakage that killed thousands; the 1984 disaster in Times Beach, Missouri, a small town that was virtually eradicated by **dioxin,** a chemical byproduct brought in with waste oil to hold down the dust during the summer; the massive oil spill from a sunken Argentine ship in Antarctica on January 29, 1989, threatening that pristine environment; and the hole in the ozone layer over Antarctica that has now drifted over Australia and threatens the health of thousands. The invisible humanmade actions that disastrously affect our biological diversity include such items as automobiles, deforestation, aerosol sprays, acid rain, ozone depletion, pesticides, commercial and residential development of wetlands, and the consumption of some foods (red meats, for example) in quantities that are not healthy for human beings and may be destructive to the natural environment in which the animals are raised.

It was Rachel Carson's *Silent Spring,* published in 1962, that called attention to the insecticide DDT and its insidious consequences. The book is a documented study of the consequences to our environment of chemical poisons, particularly insecticides and herbicides, developed after World War II. The book "is now credited by most environmentalists with being a consciousness-raising event that has resulted in a long-lasting environmental movement in the United States."[7] It was the spark that ignited national and international action.

Nationally, the Environmental Protection Agency, the largest regulatory agency in the country today, was created, and the Clean Air Act of 1970 was established. In addition, the Occupational Safety and Health Act of 1970, designed to ensure safety standards in the workplace, became law; President Nixon signed into law the National Environmental Policy Act, requiring environmental impact analysis on federal projects; and the first Earth Day was proclaimed in 1970. Other environmental legislative landmarks include the Water Pollution Act of 1972; the Coastal Zone Management Act of 1972 to protect the biologically productive wetlands; the Endangered Species Act of 1973; and the Toxic Substances Act of 1976, which gives the EPA more control over the manufacturing and use of pesticides. Then on January 1, 1980, President Carter, as his first official action of the new decade, announced a second Earth Day. Movement on the ecological crisis was a reality.[8]

Internationally, other important actions were also initiated: The United Nations Stockholm Conference of 1972 was convened to draw attention to worldwide ecological issues; the United Nations Environmental Program was organized in 1972 and set up in Nairobi, Kenya; President Carter's commissioned report, *Global 2000*, was ordered to inquire into the nature of the world's resources at the end of the century; the *Brundtland Report* of 1987, a U.N.-sponsored study, effectively demonstrated the intimate internal relationship between economic growth and environmental protection; and the United Nations Conference on Environment and Development, known as the Earth Summit, was held in Rio de Janeiro from June 3 to June 14, 1992. More than 100 heads of state attended this conference designed specifically to deal with the world ecological crisis. The conference addressed such issues as bans on shipping toxic waste to Third World nations, global warming, world water resources, and the destruction of rain forests. All these actions sought to awaken public opinion to the new environmental dangers and to help in the struggle to create an international consciousness regarding the worldwide ecological crisis.

Traditional environmental groups such as the Sierra Club, the National Audubon Society, the Nature Conservancy, and Friends of the Earth have now been joined by more radical environmental groups such as Earth First. Activists in Earth First "shackle themselves to trees, stage sit-ins before bulldozer blades, pour sand in the engines of earthmovers and pound spikes in tree trunks to mangle loggers' saws. They call the practice monkeywrenching"[9] and call on citizens to give up consumerism and worldly goods, highways and skyscrapers, in favor of saving the wilderness.

But our ever-accelerating technological change goes on and expands to more and more countries in the world. What is the status of the ecological crisis today? That is the subject of the next section.

STATUS: BIOTIC AND ABIOTIC ISSUES

Two major organizing concepts are employed in this section—biotic and abiotic. **Biotic** refers to that which is living, that which has a specified mode of life. **Abiotic** refers to that which is nonliving. Three biotic issues (population, plants, animals) and three abiotic issues (air, water, land) are discussed in this section of the chapter.

The worldwide dilemma is how to reconcile three seemingly irreconcilable forces—the dynamism of economic development, the environment, and the urge to procreate (to beget or bring forth offspring). "They are opposing forces, doomed to cross each other out and produce disaster unless they can be brought to a more harmonious convergence . . . the three must be considered together, an indissoluble triangle."[10]

Biotic Issues

The Population Explosion

Nature of the Problem. A time bomb is ticking away. According to some scientists, our "modern human population which started out about 43,000 years ago, has grown rapidly only in the last two centuries."[11] It was not until 1850 that the world's population reached 1 billion. Eighty years later, in 1930, world population hit 2 billion; in 1960, only thirty years after that, the third billion was realized. The population explosion continued until the world had 4 billion people in 1974, only fourteen years later. World population hit 5 billion in late 1986[12] or early 1987 (authorities disagree on this), and 6 billion in 2000. By 2010, it will hit 7.2 billion, according to the *Financial Times* of London, with 95 percent of this increase in the developing countries.[13]

To further exacerbate these staggering statistics, this dramatic increase in world population growth is occurring in the Third World, not in the developed countries. Population growth in the countries of the First World is well below 1 percent, while that of the underdeveloped nations exceeds 2 percent a year. In the last thirty-five to forty years, more than 2 billion people have been added to the population of the less developed countries. "This is equal to the entire population of the world as recently as 1932!"[14] "Uncontrolled population growth is a threat to human survival. . . . Without population control, humans are quite capable of eating and consuming themselves out of house and home."[15] It is important to note here that 4.5 billion of the world's 6.2 billion people live on an income of about $1,000 a year.[16]

China's population, which exceeds 1 billion (one out of every five human beings is Chinese), is the only one of the less developed nations that has made concerted efforts to control population. Heavy fines are employed to discourage unauthorized births, and women of childbearing age are urged to use contraceptive methods. China's birthrate in 1986 and 1987 was 1.4 percent, but even with this remarkable statistic, 22 million babies were born in 1987. This implies serious social problems ahead for both developed and underdeveloped nations.[17] Without China's efforts to control population, the Third World population explosion would be even worse. Consider the following statistics:

- The Third World has 5 billion of the world's 6.3 billion people.
- Asia has more than 3.5 billion of the world's 6.3 billion people.
- India reached a population of 1 billion people in the spring of 2000.
- Pakistan has a 3.4 percent growth in its 120 million people.

- Bangladesh has a 2.6 percent growth rate and 117 million people.
- Sub-Saharan Africa has a birthrate of 3.03 percent.
- In Latin America, birthrates run 2.3 percent.
- North Africa and the Middle East have a 3.03 percent birthrate.
- Each year more than 90 million people are added to the world.

The population explosion is a new and emerging source of political tension between the countries of the north and south. Perhaps the predictions of Thomas Robert Malthus, an Englishman, are correct. Malthus wrote an essay in 1798 entitled "An Essay on the Principle of Population, As It Affects the Future Improvement of Society," in which he argued that population will always grow faster than food supply, and that the consequence will inevitably be poverty and misery for human beings. For Malthus, the only concrete checks on population growth are war, famine, and pestilence, and efforts by government to help the poor will always be in vain.

The *Global 2000 Report* ordered by President Carter contended that new initiatives were needed to cope with poverty, population, and the implied environmental problems. However, President Reagan's administration saw little cause for concern, arguing that the free market and technological change would be able to counterbalance population increases. President Bush, following the Reagan lead, saw little if any cause for concern and, at this writing, President Clinton had not yet begun to focus on world overpopulation. The Clinton administration's instincts on family planning issues seemed to be progressive, but other issues had priority and world overpopulation had yet to be seriously addressed. Though the Clinton administration was theoretically behind the United Nations effort to control growth of world population, the president's domestic agenda left him limited resources to cope with this "ticking time bomb."

Some Conditions Associated with the Population Explosion.
Five conditions particularly contribute to the existing increases in world population—poverty, civic culture, psychology, biological forces and factors, and technology itself.

According to Barry Commoner, analysis of the relationship between poverty and overpopulation is frequently in error. Many analysts argue that it is overpopulation that determines poverty and thus that the key issue is production. To Commoner, the reverse is true—that is, it is poverty that causes overpopulation, and distribution is the key issue. To Commoner, the traditional methods of family planning, legal restriction of reproduction, and survival of the fittest simply will not work in the long run. He contends that if poverty can be eliminated, population growth will take care of itself. He documents this with convincing testimony from Germany, Japan, and the Scandinavian nations. What is needed, then, is to identify the basic problem—distribution of goods and wealth, not production—and to correctly relate cause and effect. If the problem is ever to be resolved, it is critical that the correct relationship be determined. Commoner's thesis implies the need for social change—change to more pluralistic societies—in the less developed nations, not foreign aid or legalistic measures. It is, of course, possible that humanitarian efforts will suffice; but they probably will not, and the world is built on real probabilities, not remote possibilities.

In addition to poverty as a cause of overpopulation, the social and civic culture of countries creates conditions for rapid population growth. Government alone can stimulate or depress population through indoctrination and legislation (tax policy, control of the media, and the educational system). Hitler's Germany and Stalin's Russia both established public policy designed to increase the population of certain groups (Aryans and Great Russians) and decrease the population of other groups (Jews and Ukrainians). Today, China has embarked on a vigorous program to reduce population, while Muslim fundamentalists have campaigned against the September 1994 U.N. conference in Cairo on population. The Muslim stance, along with the Vatican's offensive against artificial birth control, has population experts worried that the struggle to control population growth may be lost.[18] A U.N. Population Fund study of August 1994 argued that "the best way to avert a catastrophic global population explosion is to give women more choice . . . and greater access to education."[19] The cultural conditioning of people is a reality. It exists in all societies and it certainly affects population growth (Germany has zero population growth, while the average woman in Kenya has eight children). For cultural reasons, the strict abstinence demanded during about half of each monthly cycle couldn't be maintained in less developed countries. For the most part, natural methods of family planning do not work in the Third World.

The psychological reasons that lie behind population growth are many and varied. One may want children for personal fulfillment or simply because one wants something to love and care for. In some social systems it is only possible to gain respect or social acceptance if one has children. Thomas Hobbes, the seventeenth-century English philosopher, argued that gaining respect is one of the driving forces in human life. Finally, one may want children because of the need for economic security and because it is a way to perpetuate oneself. A child, or grandchild, is a physical extension of one's personality. It is, in a sense, a kind of immortality. One's progeny also provides social security in many countries today, such as India or Kenya.

Sociobiologists argue that life is a struggle to expand one's **gene pool.** They emphasize the biological bases of behavior and hold that people have children because they are biologically encoded to do so. They even explain some important behavior patterns between men and women in terms of genetics. For example, some sociobiologists claim that women are more selective than men in choosing a mate because they have only a few opportunities to expand their gene pool, while men can be less selective because their opportunities for gene pool expansion are much less limited. Most women produce only a few children during their lifetime, and their productive years end in their late forties; however, men can, and have, fathered children in their eighties.

Finally, technology is also a variable that contributes to overpopulation. Improvements in health care (sanitation, immunization, prenatal care, and so on) extend life expectancy and help minimize infant deaths, thus contributing to population growth. International organizations associated with institutions such as the United Nations can provide food, clothing, shelter, and fuel to sustain life by airlifting necessary supplies to a troubled area quickly. Agricultural improvements in seeds and farming methods have helped famine-ridden societies (China and India) overcome such natural disasters and have thus contributed to overpopulation.

    Major Consequences of the Population Explosion. Just as the causes of the population explosion are many and varied, so too are the major consequences. All over the world people are on the move. Migration today is a problem growing out of the population explosion, and the principle migration is from south to north; people in unprecedented numbers are leaving their homelands in the less developed nations because of economic privation and political unrest and moving north. A number of countries in the First World are confronted with a new problem—strangers living in their community. For example, Germany faces the problem of foreign workers, particularly those from Turkey; France is confronted with large numbers of Algerians, who moved to France following the war for independence in Algeria; the United States has millions of illegal aliens (Hispanics) who have emigrated from Central America and Mexico.[20] In the year 2050, the population of the United States will total about 394 million people—up 50 percent from the present numbers—according to a Census Bureau profile. In 2050, California will approach 50 million people.[21] The United States has the fastest-growing population in the developed world today as a result of immigration, and without substantial reductions, the doubling of the U.S. population in the next fifty to sixty years is a distinct possibility. A report by Population Action International shows that the greatest flow of humanity to North America comes from East and Southeast Asia, Latin America, and Eastern Europe.[22] Great Britain has, in recent years, experienced race riots due to the influx of blacks from the Caribbean area and Indians from south Asia; and the Netherlands must now cope with new inhabitants from the Dutch East Indies. The list could be extended to include virtually every developed nation. These strangers are certain to spark serious social, economic, political, and ethical issues in all the host countries. Ethnicity is a powerful force in the world today—perhaps even stronger than nationalism. One need only view the chaos, war, and anarchy in what was the communist state of Yugoslavia to see the overwhelming power of ethno-nationalism. The brutal conflict among Croats, Serbs, and Muslims bore stark witness to the dangers of a virulent ethnicity, be it founded on race, religion, language, or culture.

    A second consequence of the population explosion is the degradation of the environment. Renewable resources such as air, water, land, plants, forests, and animals are being used up at a rate that defies replacement. Conservation of natural resources may be impossible with the current population explosion because a particular resource may be so depleted that it cannot renew itself. The present biotic and abiotic conditions of planet Earth (loss of ozone, greenhouse effect, acid rain, endangered species, deforestation) suggest that it may be too late already. Energy shortages, scarce water, exhausted land, and more air pollution will combine to radically alter U.S. diets in the coming years. There will be less meat and more potatoes, beans, and pasta in the national diet as the nation's population doubles to over 500 million, says David Pimentel of Cornell University.[23]

Famine is characterized by large-scale loss of life and by social and economic chaos that destroys production potential. A recent example is the famine in Ethiopia in the mid-1980s, in which more than 1 million people perished. Here the former Marxist regime of President Mengistu initiated a resettlement program, established Soviet-style collective farms, and spent millions of dollars for arms. The combined effect was a national catastrophe—famine. Individual nation-states and the United Nations, through its Food and Agriculture Organization, tried to aid Ethiopia, but with limited success. Famine as a consequence of overpopulation occurred in 1943 in Bengal and in 1974 in Bangladesh. A more recent example of famine occurred in the East African state of Somalia. There tens of thousands starved to death as a combination of drought and environmental exploitation, exacerbated by ethnic struggle, worked out its logic of human tragedy—a tragedy the world watched on the nightly television news. Only the efforts of the United Nations and its supporting members were able to avert an even more terrible human disaster in Rwanda in 1995–1996. Where population growth outstrips water, food supplies, and adequate housing, the problems seem obvious. As the "world prospers, global famine becomes likely. . . . All we need is a few more years of declining reserves and then one really bad summer in the main grain-growing area of the northern hemisphere and we're looking at a worldwide shortfall of maybe 50 million tons of grain."[24] The pessimistic forecast of Malthus still seems relevant today.

Finally, the rush to the cities with their attendant urban chaos and the rise of ultra–right wing political parties are both directly related to rapid increases in population. Population experts point out that in the year 2000, the five largest cities (in millions of people) in the world would be as follows: Mexico City, 16.6 million; São Paulo, 16.5 million; Tokyo-Yokohama, 26.5 million; Calcutta, 12.0 million; and New York, 16.3 million.[25] In France, "Jean-Marie LePen, the leader of France's ultraright, ultranationalist party that preaches open racism"[26] has shown heavy gains in areas where Arab immigrants live. The revival of fascist doctrines may accompany such social change.

Closing Commentary. The challenge of the ecological crisis is to find some means to balance population, economic development, and the environment. This will surely be the Bermuda Triangle for *Homo sapiens* unless humanity can learn to live in harmony with nature. In addition, recent studies suggest that political upheaval at the social level and self-destructive behavior of the individual may result from crowding (for example, behaviors such as mating and parental care of infants may disappear).[27] In some parts of the world the earth's life-support system (grasslands, forests, topsoil in croplands, marine life) is beginning to break down, and the biotic consequences will be disastrous. Present estimates of the planet's capacity run from 8 to 12 billion people. We will be entering this range soon. Every year 90 million more people draw on the earth's resources, half of all renewable fresh water is being used up, and one third of the world's population lives in water-stressed areas. Africa faces the most serious food and water shortages. One fourth of the world's renewable water is in South America.[28] The rising world population must be brought under control or "Spaceship Earth" may not survive. The future of the human race depends on the actions we take now.

Plants (Forests)

The destruction of tropical forests in the world today is so extensive, so devastating, and so irrevocable that humanity may soon lose its richest, most diverse, and most valuable biotic resource. As a consequence, life will lose forever much of its capability for continued evolution. The economic, esthetic, and cultural losses to future generations will be incalculable.[29]

Nature of the Problem.   Conservation of the tropical forests is an issue of global concern. Deforestation is occurring worldwide and may be the greatest biological calamity the world has ever known. Northern forests are also affected. In Germany the phenomenon is known as *"Waldsterben"* (forest death); in the former state of Czechoslovakia, more than a million acres are severely damaged; and the damage from **acid rain,** air pollutants, and ozone concentration in sunny conditions affects many other nations in Europe and North America such as Switzerland, Sweden, Russia, and Poland.[30] In the United States, rain forests that run from California to Alaska—the last great stands of ancient trees (Douglas fir, hemlock, spruce, cedar, redwood, and sequoia)—are being cut down at a rate of 60,000 acres per year. Foreign timber companies, particularly those from Japan, are outbidding American firms, and in 1987 the timber cut from the 156 national forests reached the highest level in history—12.7 million board feet. But in November of 2000, President Clinton imposed new logging restrictions in America's national forests.[31]

Deforestation of the tropical forests in particular is one of the most threatening world problems today. The magnificent trees felled by chaining (in which two huge tractors with a chain between them sweep an area of all trees) and chemical application (Agent Orange) in Brazil, Mexico, and Panama are destroying the "lungs of the earth." These great woodlands, together with algae in the oceans, literally create the conditions for human life—absorbing carbon dioxide and giving off oxygen. The destruction of these beautiful but fragile forests implies the destruction of millions of species in Africa, Asia, and Latin America. This, in turn, means the destruction of our **biodiversity.** (Ecuador alone has 20,000 different species of plants, while all of North America has only 17,000.) Four years after Brazil hosted the Earth Summit that sought international accords on biodiversity and climate change, burning of the rain forests is reaching the worst levels ever. Subsistence farming that employs slash-and-burn crop practices may well "destroy almost half of the world's remaining 5 billion acres of tropical forest." On a daily basis, each person of the over six billion people on earth uses 3.5 pounds of wood. Over 50 percent of this is used not for building but for burning—for energy.[32]

Some Conditions of Deforestation.   Four conditions create the circumstances for deforestation; they are social, economic, political, and technological. Socially, the population explosion in the less developed nations has been so great during the last forty years that the environment cannot sustain the people. Landless peasants and rural poverty are the immediate consequence, and the long-range effect is deforestation. Governments, in their efforts to achieve social stability, ignore stewardship of natural resources and open up tropical forests for economic development. In addition, the rapid increase in population demands that more wood be available for fuel and shelter; thus population increase again means that wood will be cut faster than it can be replaced. Forests, particularly rain forests, are being burned down to serve the necessities of life (food, clothing, shelter, fuel) for more and more people.

Economic conditions play a major role in deforestation. Forest farming and cattle ranching are major sources of deforestation. Farmers simply clear and burn a section of forest to create their own farmland in Brazil's Amazon region, farm it until it is worn out, and then move on to another part of the forest. Cattle ranchers clear forest land in Latin America in order to establish grasslands for cattle production. The government supports this destructive practice because much of the beef is exported to the United States, where it is used in the fast-food industry in exchange for sorely needed dollars to support their financially unstable regimes. Some environmentalists argue that cattle are the culprits and that we must move "beyond the beef culture." These individuals and groups argue persuasively that "the aesthetic, environmental, and commercial impact of razing and burning millions of acres of ancient rain forests to make room for cattle ranching is beyond human calculation."[33] They go on to point out the destructive impact of cattle: desertification; overgrazing of the world's rangeland; the 900 pounds of vegetation consumed by an individual steer each month; the effect of their cloven hooves in compacting soil and thus reducing the land's capacity to absorb water; eroded soil; the 1 billion tons of organic waste produced each year by cattle in the United States; and finally the emission of methane gas (a potent greenhouse gas) into the atmosphere.[34]

More than a billion cows are now raised all over the world to produce meat. Seventy-eight percent of all grain harvested in America is fed to cattle. All this when the evidence suggests that vegetarianism is a healthier diet. In Asia, an area long committed to vegetarianism, lentils and rice are being replaced by meat and fatty fast foods. In Thailand, overweight young people abound while a generation ago this was almost unheard of. In India, where 80 percent of the diet is traditionally vegetarian, many are now eating fast foods. In China, where bean curd (tofu) has been produced for 2,000 years, there are now more hamburger outlets than vegetarian restaurants. In Japan, where meat went almost untouched a century ago, meat is chosen over traditional diets of vegetables, fish, and rice.[35]

Highway construction also encourages migrants to settle in the rain forest areas. Thus, the drive for economic development, population proliferation, and migration come into conflict with the environment in Brazil, Panama, Ecuador, and other Latin and Central American states. Short-term economic advantage is exchanged for long-term environmental enfeeblement. Finally, one of the last great rain forests in Papua, New Guinea, is in danger. Foreign loggers, desperate for new sources of tropical lumber, see tremendous commercial profit in these forests that have sheltered the indigenous people since the Stone Age.[36]

Government policies also create serious environmental problems. In order to increase energy capability in Altamira, Brazil, the government initiated a program to build two giant dams in the Amazon rain forest. The dams would "flood an estimated 3,000 square miles of rain forest and displace 7,000 Indians."[37] The government claims the dams are vital to economic growth. Other policies of the government in Brazil also contribute to deforestation: short-tenure logging concessions; sale of public lands to loggers at low prices; laws that forbid export of entire logs that could be processed in modern plants, and other laws that encourage local processing in outdated sawmills, which create great waste; subsidies for business to produce charcoal; and tax breaks for enterprises involved in logging and processing wood.[38]

Technological development also contributes to deforestation, particularly in the forests of the north, in the form of acid rain and ozone. Acid rain has damaged the Green Mountains in Vermont, and scientists have documented "tree disease and death from ozone and other pollutants in the family of photochemical oxidants."[39] Acid rain occurs largely through the combination of oil and coal and is one of the north's most pernicious environmental problems. These conditions are not sufficient to account for all deforestation, but they certainly represent some of the most destructive forces. Technologists at the Massachusetts Institute of Technology have developed one new and rather dramatic innovation. The idea is "to create forests by dropping saplings, packed into dart-shaped containers, from airplanes. When the trees hit the ground . . . they will impale themselves in the soil and take root. What takes all summer with hard-working tree planters might be accomplished by a C-130 in the course of a few sorties.[40]

Major Consequences. Serious biotic and abiotic effects are directly related to deforestation and encroachment on other forms of plant life. The worldwide warming trend, called the **greenhouse effect,** is directly related to deforestation. The great tropical forests act like a sponge in soaking up carbon dioxide, but as these forests are cut down, the level of carbon dioxide increases, oxygen decreases, and a warming trend in the earth's climate occurs. This has further consequences, which include the melting of the polar ice caps and a subsequent rise in the water levels of the oceans. These in turn will inundate ocean lowlands that are the habitat of many species of animals.

Deforestation has a drastic effect on soil erosion. The Panama Canal is an excellent example of how the two are related. More than 70 percent of the tropical forest surrounding the canal's route has been cut down. With the great trees gone, the slopes where they once stood are easily eroded away. This eroded soil goes into Madden Lake, built to act as a reservoir of water for the canal during periods of drought, and reduces the lake's storage capacity.[41]

Deforestation is also worsening natural disasters throughout Asia. In 1991 in the Philippines, flash floods swept down the bare hills of Leyte, sweeping entire communities in their path; in Thailand's southern province, floods and mud slides recently buried entire villages; in Indonesia, 500,000 hectares of rain forest have been lost to indiscriminate logging practices, which then create conditions for fires. China's deforestation has resulted in its worst floods in fifty years, which now inundate millions of acres of valuable farmland; and in Bangladesh, a massive flood caused by deforestation displaced one third of the population.[42]

Other consequences of deforestation include the threat to the world's supply of Monarch butterflies resulting from the destruction of the fir forests in Mexico's central highlands. This area is the breeding ground of the insects.[43]

The damage of deforestation is seemingly endless: Brazilian Indians are homeless; prescription drugs are threatened, as one in four has its origin in the tropical forests of Africa, Asia, and Latin America; and finally, forests are cut down, the earth's surface becomes "shiny," and the energy from the sun is reflected back into space. This is called the *albedo effect* and results in a disruption in rain and wind currents.[44]

Closing Commentary.   What can be done? Many measures, no one of which will suffice on its own, collectively can create conditions that will ameliorate the disastrous consequences of deforestation. Some initial moves might be efforts to curb population, as in China; efforts to improve forest growth and existing energy efficiency; and increased work on renewable sources of energy (solar, wind, thermal). If any one of the more than 186 nation-states in the world, or international organizations such as the United Nations, need a vision—a direction for policy that would benefit all human beings, all long-term economic development, and the world's environment—it might be summed up in one slogan; "Stewardship = Plant a Tree."

Animals

Nature of the Problem.   The majestic bald eagle, the mysterious wolf, the amusing and graceful dolphin, the ponderous but intelligent whale and elephant, the rare and exotic panda—these and hundreds of other animals are on the endangered species list. Biodiversity suggests that there is a crucial, intimate, internal relationship that exists between the many species living on earth. The species need each other to survive and to continue the process of evolution. The biotic resources of the world provide human beings with the material necessities of life—food, clothing, shelter, fuel, clean water, oxygen, and medicines. They also provide us with the beauty, security, imagination, and affection that are the necessary conditions for our psychological well-being. The extinction of particular species has gone on for eons. In the past, this was all part of a natural process. The extinction of species today is caused by human action. Many animals are on the endangered species list in America, among them the Aleutian Canada goose, Oregon silverspot butterfly, Colorado River squawfish, green sea turtle, key deer, Kirkland's warbler, grizzly bear, wild horse, amber snail, black lace cactus, and black-footed ferret. Around the world, many other magnificent animals are today considered endangered species (pandas, hirola antelopes, mountain gorillas, whales, dolphins, wolves, and seals).[45]

In the United States, the Endangered Species Act of 1973 is the most important piece of legislation in America's wildlife conservation program. The act establishes a comprehensive program to preserve animals determined to be endangered (seriously threatened by extinction) or threatened (likely to be threatened in the near future). The act ensures that any action by federal agencies does not jeopardize or threaten endangered species. It also provides for necessary habitat, federal-state cooperation, cooperation with other nation-states, and controls on harvest.[46] One important limit on the law is that endangered species are protected only from federally funded action. Private development is not controlled unless it results in the extinction of an endangered animal. At the present time, 1,234 species are on the endangered list, while another 1,000 have been proposed but remain unlisted.[47] In implementing the Endangered Species Act, Judge Douglas P. Woodlock, on September 24, 1996, ordered the state of Massachusetts to stop "issuing fishing permits to lobstermen and other commercial fishers who use types of nets and lines known to kill right whales."[48]

Endangered species are a worldwide problem, not just a problem of the United States. In Kenya, poachers, greedy for ivory revenues, have decimated the great elephant herds that once roamed the country. The elephant population in Africa has been cut in half the last ten years. In what is said to be a world record haul, London police seized a total of 105 rhino horns valued at almost $3 million on September 3, 1996.[49] The mountain gorillas in Rwanda are threatened by extinction. These marvelous, gentle giants have been reduced from 450 in 1960 to 280 in 1987 until today, they number only between 150 and 200. Poaching, human encroachment, habitat destruction, land for raising cattle, and trapping for zoos all contribute to the problem. Finally, many species of whales are on the endangered species list, including the sperm, bowhead, right, blue, and humpback. Uncontrolled hunting and contamination of habitat are two of the causes of depletion of these great whales.

Some Conditions of Species Extinction. Four conditions contribute to species destruction—loss of habitat, alien species introduction, economic dynamism, and contamination. Habitat destruction is perhaps the single greatest cause of endangered or threatened species. For example, ski resorts in California want to expand their recreational facilities. The problem is that this causes loss of habitat for local populations of pine marten, red foxes, and wolverines.[50] In Southern California, home building and new freeway systems encroach on the corridors of mountain lions. These magnificent animals explore the urban boundaries until they find "corridors" (narrow strips of seminatural habitat) to undeveloped areas. Without these corridors for movement, these great cats are threatened with extinction.[51] "Habitat loss occurs when river valleys are dammed, forests are bulldozed, . . . or marshes are drained for development. Pollution of our air, fresh waters, and oceans degrades ecosystems until they can no longer support wildlife."[52] Destruction of habitat (land, water, air, forest, grasslands) eliminates the very conditions that give life to all biota. Habitat loss caused by population growth and economic development is a major threat to wildlife. The northern spotted owl is threatened by the arrival of the eastern barred owl, which is driving the spotted owl from its natural home in California.[53]

Introduction of alien species is another condition that ravages indigenous biotic species. These competitors hasten the extinction of native animals. One particularly instructive example is the introduction of the canid (dogs, wolves, coyotes, foxes) into new habitats. Generally, the canids have some human help in the form of transportation or food provision. Unfortunately, dogs are very successful in adaptation. The Polynesians who colonized New Zealand brought with them a dog called the kuri. This alien animal is implicated in the extinction of many species of large birds. In Australia, the Aborigines and their dog, the dingo, pushed the wolf and Tasmanian devil into extinction on the mainland. European dogs, through interbreeding and outbreeding native wolves, have forced them into extinction.[54] In America, dogs have caused damage to deer herds but cannot be killed except when caught in the act of killing a game animal or attacking livestock.

Economic dynamism also creates conditions that endanger animals. The slaughter of baby seals less than nine days old ("white coats") off Newfoundland has been prohibited since 1982, but hunters simply shift their attention to older pups that are now hunted at sea, which makes control even more difficult.[55] Annually, the tuna industry kills 100,000 dolphins on average in the hunt to catch tuna. This occurs because the tuna fishermen "continue to catch tuna by herding dolphins that skim the surface above the tuna, netting both the fish and the mammals."[56] Overfishing for grouper, red snapper, and pompano resulted in smaller catches in Florida in 1989. Commercial fishing vessels are hauling in so much seafood from the world's oceans that more than 100 species are in danger. In October, 1996 the U.S. Court of International Trade, seeking to protect turtles from shrimp nets, ordered that Gulf shrimpers who do not employ turtle excluder devices on their trawls can no longer sell their catch in the United States.[57] These examples, when added to the problem of poaching in Africa for elephant ivory, hunting gorillas for zoos and whales for meat and oil, compound the problem. The drive, the powerful urge for personal gain within human beings, and for economic development within social systems, combine to destroy animals and blunt the effects of the endangered species program.

Finally, contamination of our water, soil, grassland, and forests by chemicals and waste destroys many animals, and the potential benefits are lost to humankind forever. The diversity of animal species available to us in the future is thus further limited. A recent example of this contamination is the timber industry on the U.S. West Coast, which has ruined fishing for Pacific salmon. This occurred because the loggers clear out the forests, which fills the salmon runs with silt and thus destroys the watersheds the salmon need for successful spawning.[58]

Major Consequences.   The very existence of human beings depends on our stewardship of the animals of the world. Dead sand crabs and shrimp that float ashore from waters polluted with raw sewage, tar, grease, refuse, and fecal matter not only ruin beaches but deprive humanity of food. The world needs a reliable ecosystem in which everything from small sea animals to giant redwoods can survive.

In addition to food, wildlife provides natural beauty. In fact, nature is the very criterion against which the artist's rendering of an eagle, bear, or fish is measured. Aesthetically, humanity is impoverished each time a species, no matter how small, is driven to extinction. We have lost reality and can only see an image of existence—not existence itself. If the magnificent mountain gorilla is gone, it's gone, and we can only see pictures or fiberglass models of what once existed.

Destruction of species also has economic consequences. Thriving industries and products will cease to exist and will become mere relics, like the buggy whip. The whaling industry is in tatters. The great buffalo herds were decimated in a few years, as were all the related industries.

Finally, many people believe that humanity has a moral obligation to protect life and the endangered species of our planet. That life has a purpose, and that a moral order exists, provides the moral foundation upon which many people build their lives. If this is the case, then the survival of humans and animals is internally related and the senseless killing of animals must cease. Radical activists are now turning to violence in some circumstances.[59]

Life on earth exists in a narrow area on our planet. All creatures living in this **biosphere** have necessary conditions under which they must live. Humans must approximate a "75-degree cocoon"—whether on earth or on the moon. Animals must also enjoy minimum conditions for life or they cease to exist. The activities of human beings have threatened these conditions. We must change our lifestyles and establish public policies to enforce new behaviors.

Abiotic Issues

Air

Three distinct problems are involved in analyzing issues associated with air— the greenhouse effect, ozone depletion, and pollution. Clarity demands that each be addressed separately because the characteristics of each problem differ. But each issue will be analyzed in the same manner as the biotic issues, that is, in terms of the *nature* of the problem, some of the *conditions* associated with its origin, and the major *consequences,* in that order.

Three pieces of environmental legislation address the problems of air pollution in the United States. The Clean Air Act of 1970 was established to assign responsibility and allocate powers to the federal and state governments. The act also provides assistance programs, technical expertise, and financial aid to areas thought to endanger public well-being. The next most important piece of legislation was the Comprehensive Environmental Response, Compensation and Liability Act of 1980, commonly known as the Superfund. This statute is intended to address problems associated with hazardous waste, which may also include work associated with air pollution. Finally, the Clean Air Act of 1987 (the Mitchell Bill) sought to reduce air pollution by mandating rigorous regulatory standards for control of sulphur dioxide (SO_2) and other emissions.[60]

Greenhouse Effect.   The greenhouse effect, or global warming, occurs when carbon dioxide (CO_2) from burning fossil fuels (coal, oil, natural gas) and other gases (methane and nitrogen) rise into the upper atmosphere. "These gases let incoming heat from the sun reach the Earth, but block the Earth's own heat from traveling into space, much as a greenhouse traps heat indoors."[61] The pollutants prevent excess heat from escaping into space and the heat is reflected toward the earth's surface. Simply, solar heat is trapped by the pollutant gases from factories and automobiles; it accumulates in the atmosphere that encircles the planet like a blanket and acts as an insulating barrier (like the panels in a greenhouse), and the planet becomes warmer each year.

Scientists claim that elevated levels of carbon dioxide, caused by the burning of coal, oil, and other energy sources of combustion, are responsible for 50 percent of the greenhouse effect. The United States is responsible for 26 percent of all worldwide emissions of carbon dioxide, Russia 21 percent, Western Europe 17 percent, China 11 percent, and the developing countries 20 percent.[62] There is one bright spot in all this: The White House has now joined in the attack on the greenhouse effect. At the International Climate Change Conference in Geneva in 1996, the United States announced a dramatic reversal of policy. As of that date "the principle of universal, mandatory cuts in greenhouse gas emissions has been accepted by the international community."[63] There is much to be done, but at least it's an agreement on principle.

A second condition that creates the greenhouse effect is the growing population of the world. A growing population implies the need to expand economies, which in turn means increased demand for energy and greater combustion of fossil fuels emitting CO_2, and this in turn warms the earth's climate. If the planet's population continues to grow until it reaches 11 billion within the next twenty-five to thirty years, the number of rice consumers will certainly go over 5 billion. The problem here is that "cultivation of rice, the only major grain used almost exclusively for food, results in the emission of some 14 percent of the methane—a major greenhouse gas—caused by human activities"[64] and by animals.

Third, the destruction of the earth's forests creates conditions for climatic change. Forests, which absorb carbon dioxide, are being destroyed all over the planet; thus the "sponge effect" of the forests regarding CO_2 is lost. Finally, other gases such as chlorofluorocarbons (CFCs) in aerosol cans, and Styrofoam and methane employed in refrigerant solvents, also pollute the atmosphere and contribute to global warming.

The major consequences of the greenhouse effect can be disastrous, according to climatologists. Industrial soot and brown clouds are disguising the greenhouse effect over American cities. This helps keep them cool, but rural areas are experiencing warmer temperatures. The problem is that these greenhouse effects last for decades in the atmosphere, and we are doing less to reduce use of fossil fuels, particularly gasoline, that fuel the greenhouse gases.[65] Continued greenhouse warming means climatic change—drought, flood, dust bowls, and rising sea levels. A dramatic rise in the level of the sea, changes in the pattern of the world weather system, and the inability of warmer Antarctic seas to absorb CO_2 are seen by scientists as three major catastrophes associated with the greenhouse effect. If carbon dioxide doubles in the earth's atmosphere sometime in the middle of the next century, as some scientists forecast, a new computer simulation suggests that major climate changes could lie ahead.[66]

Finally, even those individuals and institutions that have traditionally fought against stricter regulation have now begun to retreat. Why? Because of fear: fear that "more severe storms caused by global warming may gut the insurance industry . . . fear that melting polar ice and rising sea levels may drown some entire small countries (Kiribati, Tuvalu, Tonga) . . . and swamp . . . big chunks of Bangladesh and the Netherlands . . . and fear that it's already too late to stop global temperatures from going up a couple of degrees.[67]

Ozone Depletion in the Stratosphere.   The world's protective ozone-rich air in the stratosphere, called the **ozone layer,** absorbs and reflects almost all of the sun's ultraviolet rays. Chlorofluorocarbons (CFCs) used in refrigeration, foams, solvents, and aerosol propellants, along with halons—chemicals used in fire extinguishers—rise into the stratosphere. The CFCs break down when exposed to the sun's ultraviolet rays, releasing chlorine and bromine. These then attack ozone molecules and break them up. As the protective layer, or shield, of ozone in the stratosphere breaks down, more ultraviolet rays reach earth. The ozone layer in the stratosphere absorbs more than 99 percent of the ultraviolet rays of the sun. CFCs, or Freon, was developed by the DuPont Company in the 1930s and has many commercial applications. E. I. DuPont is the world's largest producer of CFCs, and the United States produces one third of the world's total.

In the past few years the ozone layer over the Arctic has been experiencing some significant losses because of global warming. But at the moment, ozone depletion is more severe over the Antarctic, where there is an actual hole in this protective layer. The problem is the ultraviolet radiation that can cause skin cancer and interrupt animal reproduction.[68] Scientists claim that it will take centuries to correct the damage to the earth's ozone shield. Though there has been a ban on the production and sale of CFCs since January 1, 1996, in the United States, satellite measurements in 2000 showed that the protective ozone layer had dropped to record low levels in the stratosphere above much of the planet and is worst over the Antarctic.[69] One explanation for this is the new and lucrative business of Freon smuggling. U.S. customs agents in Miami, Florida, uncovered an "elaborate smuggling scheme for a new contraband . . . 'R-12,' the ozone depleting chemical refrigerant commonly known as 'freon.'"[70] Millions of dollars are at stake in illegal profits and excise taxes because of the 1996 ban on production and import.

Some nations believe natural phenomena such as cyclones are primarily responsible for ozone depletion, but most Western scientists argue, with persuasive evidence, that CFCs are the basic cause of ozone depletion in the stratosphere. These chemicals are used extensively in air conditioners, refrigerators, and plastic foams.

The consequences of ozone depletion are many. Consider the following: climatic changes, increased skin cancer, damage to plants, growth impedance, destruction of plant immune systems, decline of forests by decreasing the tree's ability to absorb needed nutrients, damage to marine life, damage to crops, eye cataracts, reduction of crop productivity, and suppression of immune system efficiency.[71]

The March 1989 conference of 123 nations in London ended with the United States and Europe taking the lead in agreeing to reduce ozone depletion. Many nations in the Third World were less pessimistic and lagged behind. However, the conference did raise world consciousness regarding the ozone problem and the need to phase out CFCs by the year 2000. Obviously this provision has not been realized.

Air Pollution.   Air pollution is simply contamination of the air by waste products. The measuring system employed to gauge the quality of air is the **Pollutant Standard Index (PSI).** This measure was developed by the Environmental Protection Agency (EPA). PSI ratings range from 0 to 500, with readings below a mean of 100 characterized as clean and healthy, and readings over 100 labeled dirty and unhealthy. States are required to issue a PSI alert when readings over 200 are recorded. Recently, the EPA leveled record fines for polluters in America. In March of 2000, the agency said in its annual enforcement report that in all criminal and civil cases that had been initiated, $166.7 million in fines were levied against violators.[72]

Four elements are measured in the PSI: *particulates* from smoke, dust, coal, and fly ash; *sulphur dioxide*, SO_2, produced by the combustion of fossil fuels; *carbon monoxide* from automobiles; and *ozone* produced by the reaction between nitrogen oxides from the smokestacks of power and industrial facilities and hydrocarbons found in automobile exhaust fumes. (The ozone that exists near the earth's surface is commonly called bad ozone, while the "good" ozone exists in the stratosphere.) These are the four major conditions that produce air pollution in the United States. The combination of these contaminants is called smog—particularly the combination generated by surface ozone and carbon monoxide. To deal with the problem of pollution, San Diego is installing smog-control equipment on older cars (1975 through 1981 models). Another source of pollution, according to the EPA, are the millions of gas-powered lawn mowers that belch out 6.8 millions tons of waste products each year—about 10 percent of all pollution in the air.[73]

The consequences of air pollution can be deadly. More than 4,000 people in London died from air pollution in 1952. In New York City, in 1966, 168 deaths were caused by a three-day inversion. Air pollution not only harms humans, it inhibits plant growth, affects climate, and harms the respiratory systems of animals. A study called "State of the Air 2000" graded metropolitan areas in the United States based on the number of unhealthy smog days they experienced. The Los Angeles area was the worst, but smog levels in Houston, Atlanta, and St. Louis were close behind. At the moment, 132 million Americans live in an area where the air quality has failed the Environmental Protection Agency recommendations.[74]

Water

The very survival of the human species depends upon the maintenance of an ocean clean and alive, spreading all around the world. The ocean is our planet's life belt.

—Jacques-Yves Cousteau, Marine Explorer (1980)

Nature of the Problem.   Water is the most precious liquid on earth and is crucial to life on earth. Since renewable fresh water has remained the same for eons and since the human population has more than doubled since 1958—from 2.8 to

6 billion—the amount of available water has dropped by about 58 percent. The water supply of the world has been taken for granted until recently. But a new report says that "water scarcity is a spreading global problem . . . by 2025, one out of three people will be living in countries with inadequate fresh water supplies . . . and there are no substitutes—as human populations grow, there's less renewable water for each person."[75] Even in the United States, which has a good water supply nationally, regional demands often exceed supply—witness the problem of water shortage in Southern California. There, wells are a lifeline, and overpumping has enfeebled underground water supplies, which results in brine from the sea being sucked into ocean-floor vents that once spouted clear springs.

Industrial expansion, the population explosion, sprawling megacities, and wasteful use of water have resulted in catastrophic water pollution. "Two thirds of the Earth's surface is covered with water, but most of this is salty and cannot be used directly for human or agricultural nourishment. Only 2.5 percent of water on Earth is fresh, and two-thirds of that is locked into ice caps and glaciers. Less than one-hundredth of 1 percent of Earth's water is both drinkable and renewed each year by rainfall and other precipitation."[76] The problem of the oceans of the world is global—from sewage in the Mediterranean and oil spills in Antarctica, Alaska, and the English Channel, to the red tides in Japan's Inland Sea and the filth that drives bathers from beaches in New Jersey and Long Island. In simple terms, pollution threatens the biotic life of the oceans. Pollution problems associated with the world's oceans are most serious in the coastal waters, marshlands, bays, and rivermouths of the oceans. These areas constitute only a minute percentage of the surface areas of the world's oceans but are extremely sensitive to contamination.

The problem of water pollution also extends to rivers, lakes, streams, and ultimately the groundwater—favorite dumping grounds for industrial waste, municipal sewage, garbage, and toxic waste. These are the major freshwater sources of our drinking water. The problem of contaminated groundwater is particularly acute because it is difficult to clean up. The world will spend $600 billion over the next ten years to increase water supplies. Urbanization and agriculture are creating new demands. Eighty countries are already experiencing water shortages (countries in the Middle East and sub-Saharan Africa, along with southern India, northern China, and Mexico). All this occurs while the global demand for water increases at 2.3 percent a year.[77]

Some Conditions of Water Pollution.   The conditions that contribute to world ocean pollution are to be found on both land and sea. Land-based pollution is caused by a number of factors—nonbiodegradable plastics; agricultural runoff of fertilizers and pesticides into our rivers and streams and ultimately into the oceans; wastewater and toxic substances from factories and sewage treatment plants; and raw sewage and sludge simply dumped into rivers that flow to the oceans. Sea-based pollution originates directly from oil spills, acid rain, garbage from boats and ships, sludge dumping, and algae bloom (**red and brown tides**). Incinerating toxic waste products at sea is also harmful because it threatens the ocean's rich surface layer. Two of the most serious water pollutants, acid rain and oil spills, are so destructive they warrant special mention. Acid rain is the precipitation (rain, snow, hail, fog, mist) of sulphur dioxide resulting from coal-burning generating plants and nonferrous ore smelters, and nitrogen oxides from automobile and fuel-burning emissions. Acid rain is believed responsible for some major aspects of water pollution in addition to the well-known effects it has on hardwood and conifer forests. Both Canadian and American lakes have suffered from acid rain damage, and hundreds of lakes have been rendered lifeless by this humanmade plague.[78]

Wars, introduction of a new species, and international waterways also contribute to the shattering of our water ecosystem. In the Persian Gulf War, the smoke plume from hundreds of oil wells burning in Kuwait stretched for hundreds of miles across the Gulf itself, affecting regional weather and water supplies. In addition, the ecological impact of the oil spill into the Gulf ordered by Iraqi President Saddam Hussein was estimated to be four times the size of the *Exxon Valdez* spill in Alaska. Oil-covered birds, polluted beaches, damage to vegetation and animal life from the heavy tars made this war a major ecological disaster.[79] Next, the inadvertent immigration of new alien species causes problems. The zebra mussels that recently appeared in the Great Lakes were "brought over from European rivers by accidentally getting flushed out of the ballast of a large cargo ship in Michigan's Lake St. Clair in 1988 . . . [these] thumbnail-size creatures cluster in the water intake pipes of electric power plants [and] factories,"[80] crippling some of these facilities. Finally, the debate over the plastic-covered tomato farms along Maryland's Eastern Shore became an issue. Environmentalists asserted that these farms were fouling the local water with chemicals used in fertilizing the tomato plants. Joining the fight against the tomato farmers were members of the shellfish agriculture industry.[81] Competition for water is increasing, and new tensions are arising between countries because of water shortages (between Israel and Syria and between Ethiopia and Egypt, for example). Water, not oil, is becoming the major problem in the Middle East.

Since the massive *Amoco Cadiz* oil spill off the coast of France in March 1978 dumped 1.3 million barrels of crude oil into the water, there have been scores of similar accidents.

- A crippled Argentine ship dumped 250,000 gallons of diesel fuel into the unspoiled waters of Antarctica in February 1989;[82]
- A grounded tanker threatened to spill its "cargo of 3.7 million gallons of crude oil . . . [on] Oahu's beaches in March 1989;[83]
- An oil slick off the Florida Keys . . . two miles long . . . was of unknown origin;[84]
- "A tanker filled to capacity with crude oil ran aground and ruptured Friday 25 miles from the southern terminus of the Trans Alaskan Pipeline, spewing her cargo into water rich in marine life. By evening the ship, the *Exxon Valdez,* had sent more than 200,000 barrels of oil into the frigid water of Prince William Sound, making this the *largest tanker spill in U.S. history.*"[85]
- There is a powerful antipollution sentiment in Germany spearheaded by the Green Party. When Royal Dutch Shell attempted to sink an oil rig in the Atlantic Ocean, the

Green Party called for an economic boycott of the 1,728 Shell stations in Germany. It worked. The stations lost 30 percent of their business and Shell abandoned its plan. The Green Party feared another oil spill.[86]

Major Consequences of Water Pollution.   Nonbiodegradable plastic destroys marine life. Millions of birds and tens of thousands of marine mammals (pelicans, sea turtles, sea lions) die from eating or becoming entangled in monofilament line. The oceans are being used as a garbage dump by ships at sea, boat owners, fishermen, and visitors to the beach. Recently, a 50,000-gallon raw-sewage spill forced the closing of Seal Beach in California.[87]

Half the nation's drinking water comes from groundwater, which contains many contaminants. This is a serious problem throughout the United States, and much of it is caused by hazardous waste facilities, industrial landfills, septic tanks and cesspools, and underground storage tanks for oil and gas. Reports indicate that rusted-out underground storage tanks are losing 11 million gallons of oil and gas into the ground each year.[88]

Our drinking water and ocean waters are also seriously damaged by toxic waste, as is that of lesser developed countries, where the toxic waste is sometimes dumped. There is, however, a plan to carry millions of tons of fresh water to the Arabian Gulf and to California. In the Arabian Gulf, giant tankers, usually associated with transporting oil, could soon be carrying a more precious cargo—water. The plan is to move fresh water to the Arabian Gulf from Malaysia and Turkey. The project is projected to cost $600 million and is being developed by Milcon Gulf, a trading concern. In another case in the United States, an entrepreneur, Terry Spragg, planned to fill 500 foot-long fabric bags with water from the Olympic Peninsula and tow the bags to Southern California's parched cities. The water would be used for drinking and industrial use only—not agriculture. Spragg demonstrated that he could do this by filling two demonstration bags with 770,000 gallons of water. The bags float, of course, because fresh water is lighter than salt water.[89]

Hazardous waste of any kind makes water useless to human beings. Nationally, we simply must do a better job in the future or we shall have no future at all—only a past of individual irresponsible behavior and ineffective public policy. There is no way to talk ourselves out of this problem. It must be addressed and resolved.

When the environmental aftereffects of the great floods of 1993 in the Mississippi Basin were analyzed, there were found to be both punishments and rewards. The punishment was primarily for people. Lives were lost, billions of dollars in property damage was suffered, and the flooding posed serious threats to people insofar as disease and illness were concerned. In addition, the floods gave rise to swarms of mosquitoes and to pollution by toxic chemicals that homeowners and businesses had to remove from their flooded property. However, there were a number of rewards—benefits—from the 1993 flood. Plants along the "Mississippi River have been newly fertilized by sediment from the floods. Ducks and other waterfowl that feed on the plants are thriving . . . fish have been dispersed to large new bodies of water . . . the eagles and hawks that feed on the fish can look forward to a banner year . . . and flood waters deposit rich nutrients on low-lying fields."[90] The 1993 flood spread the ecosystem to land the river had not visited in years.

Land

Nature of the Problem.   Soil erosion is a quiet crisis throughout the world. It far exceeds the natural formation of topsoil, one inch of which takes nature 250 to 1,000 years to build. Land all over the world is being plowed under and stripped of trees. In addition, grasses are burned and bulldozed for shopping centers and highway construction, all to meet the demand for food to feed our growing population. Earthquakes and volcanoes attract most of the attention, but soil erosion is occurring every minute—the land is literally being washed and blown out from under our feet by water and wind. In China, the Yellow River carries off 1.6 billion tons of topsoil per year; the Ganga River in India annually removes 1.5 billion tons of topsoil; and the Mississippi River in the United States carries off 300 million tons per year.[91]

In the United States the situation of **desertification** is dangerous. Consider the following:

- One dust storm in Bakersfield, California, in 1977 carried away 50 million tons of soil because ranchers had overgrazed hills and farmers had eliminated windbreaks;
- Half the topsoil of Iowa has been eroded away;
- In Missouri, about half the topsoil is gone and the rest is eroding quickly;
- Ten percent of the Palouse region of eastern Washington has lost all its topsoil;
- California's Lake Tahoe now has soil-clouded water instead of its once pristine clear supply;
- Near Salt Lake City an entire hillside collapsed into a housing development because contractors had stripped the hillside of trees.[92]

In Brazil, a new 500-mile highway is being constructed through the Amazon forest, across the Andes, and down to the Pacific Coast. Over it will flow the enormous hardwoods of the tropics to be shipped to Japan for its burgeoning construction projects. Japan wants the lumber; environmentalists want to preserve the forest; but the Brazilian government, needing help for its rapid population growth, wants the foreign exchange and the jobs associated with this new venture in economic dynamism. Again and again, the triangle emerges—economic development, population increase, and the environment. This contradictory triangle lies at the heart of virtually every ecological issue in the world. This triangular web of reality affects and is affected by the United States every hour, every minute of the day. Our decisions, and nondecisions, affect virtually every aspect of the triangle because of the tremendous economic power of the United States (see Figure 9.1).

Some Conditions of Land Erosion.   Two natural conditions (wind and water) and four major humanmade conditions (population growth, farming techniques, deforestation, and government policy) combine to account for the vast amount of

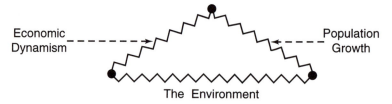

FIGURE 9.1   The Tension between Human Beings and the Environment

soil erosion in the world today. To date, there is not much any nation can do to prevent the corrosive effects of great rain- or windstorms. These will continue to strip the land of millions of tons of topsoil. However, it *is* possible to do something about the four humanmade conditions that exacerbate the erosion of our land worldwide.

World population growth from 2.5 billion in 1950 to 6.2 billion in 2000 is perhaps the most outstanding sociological feature that impacts on loss of land, particularly topsoil. Occupancy of more and more land by human beings simply implies less and less land for plants and animals. Space is limited, and the recent explosion in population, particularly in Third World countries, has had a disastrous effect on soil. More people increase demand for food and fiber, and higher demand means more intensive farming of existing cropland along with introductory farming of marginal lands. This, in turn, implies loss of topsoil and a hampering of the growth potential of croplands in the United States and throughout the world.

Farming techniques are a second salient condition of land and topsoil loss. A host of factors are at work here: failure to practice crop rotation, failure to let fields lie fallow, farming on slopes, logging, fall plowing rather than no-till farming, farming marginal land, increased use of fertilizer, failure to do proper terracing, failure to employ proper tile drainage systems, use of large equipment, and ever-larger farms. These eleven practices themselves have causes, of course, but the concrete reality cannot be explained away. Farmers and farm policy in the United States and throughout the world (whether the farms are privately owned, corporately owned, or collectively owned, as in the remaining communist countries) are all responsible, as all of them practice the above techniques. A recent example in California demonstrates the problem. In Sonoma County, California, the region's premium wine grapes are in very high demand. To meet this demand, growers are cultivating the surrounding hillsides; but environmentalists say this new practice portends ruinous soil erosion and degraded water quality.[93]

Deforestation and logging practices, with the attendant landslides and frequent misuse of hillsides, also contribute to soil loss. Consider the examples already discussed regarding Brazil, Panama, the United States, and other nations.

Finally, government policies contribute to soil loss. Governments put pressure on farmers to produce; through zoning and planning commissions at the local level, governments authorize shopping center development; they also finance interstate highway systems, permit surface mining, and allow the use of off-road recreational vehicles. All these policies lead to practices that use land, sweep away our diminishing topsoil, and further estrange human beings from their environment.

Some Consequences of Soil Erosion.   As productive land is exhausted, the cost of food must increase. To date, the laws of supply and demand still dictate economic activity. In addition, crop yields are reduced significantly because less land is left to cultivate, and what is left is lower in potential productivity. This in turn increases the expenses associated with the production of food and fiber. Loss of soil reduces navigability of rivers, causes flooding, reduces the capacity to irrigate, increases the cost of dredging rivers, and requires that more food be imported. The soil crisis is, as stated, a quiet crisis, but it is an environmental problem of great urgency. The United States and the world community, perhaps through the United Nations, had best lea.n to balance soil conservation or there will be food shortages significantly more severe than those of the past.

PROSPECTS: THE ENVIRONMENTAL CRISIS

As we begin the twenty-first century, the United States must cope with all kinds of issues—crime, drugs, abortion, poverty, corruption, terrorism, the arms race, nuclear war and proliferation, health care, racism, and many more. But only one issue actively threatens the existence of human beings as a species on Planet Earth—the environmental crisis. Some contend that environmental issues are now recognized as critical global issues. Unfortunately, research on this topic suggests that the voice in the wilderness is just that—a small, weak voice. If there were a cliché to sum up the trend for the next few years, it would be "More of the same." Pollution threatens every dimension of our biotic and abiotic biosphere, and as human beings occupy more and more space on earth, the problems are further exacerbated.

What can be done? How can we transcend our estrangement as human beings from Mother Earth? When can we begin to address causes instead of symptoms? What can we do to slow the destruction of the biosphere? Three problems seem of paramount importance in the struggle to cope with the ecological crisis—the nation-state, worldwide poverty, and our conception of property.

The organization of human beings into nation-states lies at the root of the ecological crisis. We are still living in about 186 tribes, and this tribal mentality is ecologically disastrous. Human beings are divided, under the rubric of nation and state sovereignty, into *they* and *we*—alienated, separated groups that see all others as strangers. Every state thinks of itself as the centerpiece of humankind and constructs an ideology of language, religion, and culture that reinforces this perspective. As a result, it is not human beings who confront world problems, but Americans, Japanese, Brazilians, Germans, Russians. As citizens of nations we begin our analysis of world ecological problems from an abstract position (as Americans, Egyptians, or Spaniards), not a human position, and thus our analysis of the nature, cause, and consequences of the ecological issues will forever be flawed, as shown in Figure 9.2, which attempts to describe the estranged relationship.

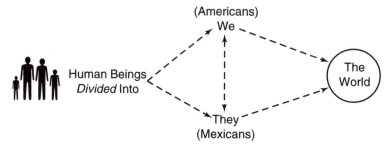

FIGURE 9.2 The Nation-state and Ecological Alienation

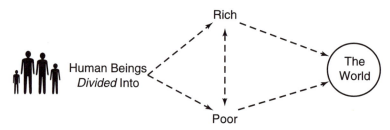

FIGURE 9.3 The Relationship between Poverty and Overpopulation

Ozone depletion, deforestation, and the slaughter of whales are not national problems; they are worldwide problems and demand worldwide answers. We live in a state of constant tension between nations, and our relation to the world is forever abstract.

Poverty exists throughout the world, and it is this condition that lies at the heart of the population explosion. As Barry Commoner points out, we have mistaken causes for effects, and vice versa, in our understanding of poverty and population. The common wisdom suggests that it is overpopulation that causes poverty (a), when in fact the reverse is true, that is, poverty causes population increases (b). If one subscribes to condition (a), then the rational program is to increase production. However, if (b) is the correct relation, then the problem to resolve is distribution. To date, U.S. and U.N. policies have generally subscribed to (a) and as a result the world has made little or no progress in slowing down the population explosion. Commoner's case is compelling in its demonstration that as states begin to resolve their poverty problems, the population problem solves itself. Again, the population problem is an issue of estrangement.

Rich and poor nations are in conflict with each other and understand their relation to Planet Earth in terms of their wealth or poverty. Within a particular nation-state, rich and poor stand in opposition to each other and to their immediate biotic and abiotic conditions. This is shown in Figure 9.3. Each is concerned with his or her own welfare, and the biosphere—the conditions of life for all—is largely ignored. Thus, some die from indulgence (obesity, high cholesterol) while others die for lack

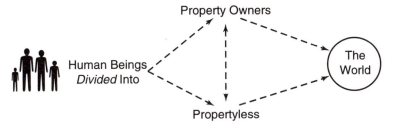

FIGURE 9.4   Private Property: The Need for a New Consciousness

of the necessities of life (food, clothing, shelter, fuel). Reduce poverty worldwide, and within nations, and the population problem can be stabilized.

Finally, we must revise our conception of private property. This is *not* a clarion call to abandon property as an institution; the failure of the communist bloc is vivid testimony that property is one of humankind's salient values. The argument here is only to modify the conception, to transcend property as sacrosanct, and to subscribe to Edmund Burke's notion of property as **stewardship.** Surely Burke, who saw the welfare and stability of society as his supreme value, would see the dangers implicit in our cavalier treatment of property and the environment, and would speak out for responsible ownership. When ownership of property is absolute, exploitation of our world's natural resources has frequently been the result. When public ownership of productive forces is the operative ideal, as in socialism and communism, there has again been exploitation, since no responsible steward can be identified. Both positions encourage irresponsible behavior.

In both cases we no longer have human beings directly dealing with the environment, but instead, the owners of property and the propertyless. What is needed, then, is to encourage the development of a new consciousness regarding property—a consciousness that pays tribute to private ownership as a valuable institution for all humankind but one that is limited by the necessary rights of others. Stewardship of property—property held as private but also in service of the public welfare—may be the best proximate solution (see Figure 9.4).

STUDY QUESTIONS

1. How is it possible to reconcile the conflict and environmental dangers implicit in the triangular web of reality made up of the following: economic dynamism, population growth, and the environment?
2. How can a world of human beings divided into more than 186 nations ever deal effectively with the worldwide ecological crisis?
3. Compare and contrast the views of the world as seen from the rich countries of the north and the poor countries of the south.
4. Is it time to develop a new consciousness regarding property? Would the concept of stewardship be a useful alternative? What can be done to encourage responsible use of private property insofar as the environment is concerned?

5. Consider the issue of the worldwide population explosion: What *is* and what *ought to be* America's position on this issue—nationally and internationally?
6. Biodiversity: What is the meaning and significance of this concept?
7. What innovative methods can be employed to deal with the following: deforestation, endangered animals, acid rain, sewage treatment, recycling waste, farming practices?

NOTES

1. William Allen, "High Tech Helps Assess Flood Damage," *St. Louis Post Dispatch,* June 5, 1995, sec. B, p. 1.
2. Peter Kendall, "As If It Wasn't Bad Enough, Ozone Pollution Takes Our Breath Away," *Chicago Tribune,* August 7, 1996, sec. 1, p. 1.
3. "Report Sees Rising Population Leading to Global Food Shortage," *Boston Globe,* August 14, 1996, p. 2.
4. Diana Jean Schemo, "Burning of Amazon Picks Up Pace, with Vast Areas Lost," *The New York Times,* September 12, 1996, sec. A, p. 3.
5. Rick Weiss, "One-fourth of Mammal Species Face Extinction," *Washington Post,* October 4, 1996, sec. A, p. 3.
6. George Will, "Take Comfort: This, Too, Shall Pass," *Dayton Daily News,* September 18, 1988, p. 7B.
7. Bayard Webster, "The Lasting, But Partial Influence of 'Silent Spring,'" *The New York Times,* January 9, 1977, p. 22.
8. Tom Ferrell, "After 10 Years, Earth Day Again: How Well Are We Doing?" *The New York Times,* April 20, 1980, p. 18E. This is an excellent summary of some biotic and abiotic issues and of legislation designed to cope with these problems.
9. Sue Cross, "Environment Activists Howl at Detractors," *Sarasota Herald-Tribune,* April 3, 1988, p. 7F.
10. Flora Lewis, "Darkness Was in Our Vision," *Sarasota Herald-Tribune,* January 19, 1989, p. 15A.
11. Bruce Bower, "Population Overload: Mice Advice," *Science News,* May 31, 1986, p. 347.
12. Leonard Silk, "Modern Views on Population," *The New York Times,* July 9, 1986, p. 26. See also Flora Lewis, "We Are Five Billion Now and Growing," *Dayton Daily News,* May 29, 1987, p. 10.
13. Arthur Caplan, "U.S. at Last Joins Rest of World in Recognizing Population Problem," *Denver Post,* February 20, 1994, p. E-4.
14. Speech by Peter H. Raven, *Wall Street Journal,* December 19, 1984, p. 12.
15. Rowland Nethaway, "Population Growth Must Be Curbed," *Dayton Daily News,* November 25, 1996, p. 9A.
16. Joel E. Cohen, "The Myths of Population," *Discover,* April 1996, p. 47.
17. *Sarasota Herald-Tribune,* February 16, 1988, p. 13A.
18. "Muslims to U.N.: Cancel Population Meeting," *Dayton Daily News,* August 22, 1994.
19. William E. Schmidt, "U.N. Population Report," *The New York Times,* August 18, 1994, sec. A, p. 8.
20. Margaret W. Sullivan, "How Do I Stop Them Coming?" *The Washington Post,* September 2, 1985, p. 10.
21. Randolph E. Schmid, "U.S. Population to Jump 50% by 2050," *Dayton Daily News,* November 19, 1998, p. 9A.
22. Lindsey Grant and Leon F. Bouvier, "Enough Is Enough," *Dayton Daily News,* August 23, 1994, p. 6A. See also "Refugees Jam World's Host Nations," *Dayton Daily News,* June 14, 1994, p. 2A.
23. Associated Press, "Big Changes for U.S. Diet," *The Honolulu Advertiser,* February 18, 1995, p. A-11.
24. Gwynne Dyer, "Hungry Times Ahead," *Dayton Daily News,* November 27, 1996, p. A-11.
25. *The 1999 World Almanac* (The World Almanac Book, 1999).
26. Flora Lewis, "We Are Five Billion Now and Growing," *Dayton Daily News,* May 29, 1987, p. 10.
27. Bower, *Science News,* p. 346.
28. National Geographic Society, October 1998, "Population and Resources" (map).

29. Hugh H. Iltis, "Tropical Forests: What Will Be Their Fate?" in *Global Ecology,* Southwick, ed., p. 224.

30. Sandra Postel, "Air Pollution, Acid Rain and the Future of Forests," in *Global Ecology,* Southwick, ed., pp. 124–130.

31. Timothy Egan, "America's National Forests Are Falling Beneath the Saw," *Sarasota Herald-Tribune,* March 20, 1989, p. 11. Kim Murphy, "Clinton Calls for Landmark Conservation," *Los Angeles Times,* November 14, 2000, part 1, p. 1.

32. Gary Lee, "Slash-and-Burn Farming Could Claim Almost Half of Tropical Forest," *Washington Post,* August 5, 1996, sec. A, p. 11. See also Diana Jean Scheme, "Amazon Is Burning Again, As Furiously As Ever," *The New York Times,* October 12, 1995, sec. A, p. 3; "Total Log Ban," *Business World,* Sept. 14, 2000, p. 1.

33. Jeremy Rifkin, "Are Cattle the Culprits?" *Environmental Action,* Fall 1992, p. 11.

34. Ibid., p. 12.

35. David Nibert, "A Step Forward for Humans," *Dayton Daily News,* July 7, 1997, p. 11A. See also Denis Gray, "Vegetarians Bemoan Growing Asian Taste," *West Hawaii Today,* January 24, 1999, p. 19A.

36. Philip Shenon, "In Isolation: Papua New Guinea Falls Prey to Foreign Bulldozers," *The New York Times,* June 5, 1994, sec. 1, p. 1.

37. "Brazilian Indians Fight Amazon Dams," *Sarasota Herald-Tribune,* February 21, 1989, p. 13.

38. Janet Raloff, "Unraveling the Economics of Deforestation," *Science News,* pp. 366–367.

39. Postel, p. 128.

40. "Incoming! Using Planes to Plant Trees," *Cleveland Plain Dealer,* August 2, 1996, p. 11B.

41. John Borrell, "Trouble Ahead for the Canal," *Time,* March 1987, p. 63.

42. Ramon Isberto, "Asia: Deforestation Worsens National Disasters," *Inter Press Service,* November 13, 1991, p. 13.

43. Homero Aridjis, "Twilight of the Monarchs," *The New York Times,* January 26, 1996, sec. A, p. 27.

44. Norman Myers, *The Primary Source* (New York: W.W. Norton, 1984), p. 10.

45. "Animal Harm," *Boston Globe,* October 11, 1996, p. 18. See also John Tueten, "Altered Habitats Threaten Flightless Birds," *Houston Chronicle,* September 27, 1996, sec. D, p. 3.

46. United States Department of the Interior, *Selected List of Federal Laws and Wildlife* (Washington, DC: U.S. Government Printing Office, 1980), p. 6.

47. Julie Anderson, *Omaha World-Herald,* "Agency's Backlog," December 17, 2000, p. 6B.

48. Scott Allen, "Gadfly's Win on Whales Could Curtail Mass. Fishing," *Boston Globe,* September 27, 1996, sec. A, p. 1.

49. Duncan Campbell, "Record Haul of Rhino Horns in Garage, *Guardian,* September 4, 1996, sec. 1, p. 7.

50. "Picture-Perfect Pine Martens," *Environment,* September 1993, p. 24.

51. Elizabeth Pennisi, "Heavy Cougar Traffic at City Edges," *Science News,* June 26, 1993, p. 410.

52. Curtis A. Moore, "Poison in the Air," *International Wildlife,* Vol. 25, #5, September 1991, p. 38. Also "Dark Skys, Changing Climate," Vol. 29, #5, September 1999, p. 27.

53. Glen Martin, "Newest Danger for Spotted Owl," *San Francisco Chronicle,* November 12, 1996, sec. A, p. 1.

54. We wish to recognize the research on canids by WSU student Elizabeth J. McLean. Also see "Wild Wolves Extinct in Western Europe," *The Guardian* (London), December 16, 2000, p. 17.

55. "Seal Slaughtering Is Protested," *Sarasota Herald-Tribune,* March 19, 1989, p. 11.

56. Myron Levin, "Tuna Industry Criticized for Dolphin Deaths," *Sarasota Herald-Tribune,* March 5, 1989, p. 18.

57. Jane Kay, "Stripping the Seas," *San Francisco Chronicle,* October 20, 1996, sec. A, p. 1. See also Gloria Tueten, "Turtles and Trade," *New Orleans Times-Picayune,* October 18, 1996, sec. B, p. 6.

58. Glen Martin, "Logging Has Decimated Salmon," *San Francisco Chronicle,* April 5, 1993, sec. E, p. 9.

59. Matr Bai, "Breaking the Cages," *Newsweek,* September 29, 1997, p. 66.

60. "Major Legislations in the 100th Congress," *Public Utilities Fortnightly,* August 20, 1987, p. 32.

61. "Greenhouse May Be Irreversible," *Dayton Daily News,* August 31, 1988, p. 2.

62. Matthew L. Wald, "Fighting the Greenhouse Effect," *The New York Times,* August 28, 1988, p. 1 and sec. C, p. 8.

63. Gwynne Dyer, "Policy Makers Finally See Global Warming as Threat," *Dayton Daily News,* August 6, 1996, p. 7A.

64. Kathy A. Sackelmann, "Limiting Rice's Role in Global Warming," *Science News,* July 10, 1993, p. 30.

65. Bill Scanlon, "Soot Masks Greenhouse Gas Effects," *Denver Rocky Mountain News,* March 14, 2000, p. 19A.

66. "Looking Far Ahead into the Greenhouse," *Science News,* August 14, 1993, p. 111.

67. Dyer, August 6, 1996, p. 2A.

68. Usha Lee McFarling, "Scientists Warn of Losses in Ozone Layer," *Los Angeles Times,* May 27, 2000, p. 20.

69. "Ozone Layer Shows Record Thinning," *Science News,* April 24, 1993, p. 260. "Profound Ozone Loss over the Antarctic," *The Independent,* London, December 7, 2000, p. 2; David Montgomery, "Largest Ozone Hole Ever," *The Scotsman,* November 9, 2000, p. 3.

70. Warren Richey, "Freon Smuggling Lucrative Business," *Dayton Daily News,* April 28, 1996, p. 19A.

71. Tom Wicker, *Sarasota Herald-Tribune,* March 8, 1989, p. 12; Philip Shabecoff, *Sarasota Herald-Tribune,* February 18, 1989, p. 11; Sam H. Verhovek, *Dayton Daily News,* October 23, 1988, p. 15.

72. James L. Nash, "EPA Sets Record for Enforcement," *Occupational Hazards,* Vol. 18, No. 3, p. 18.

73. Rae Tyson, "Air-Fouling San Diego Cars Get Free Fix-Up," *USA Today,* August 8, 1996. See also Sam Walker, "Beware: Your Lawnmower Is an Environmental Enemy," *Christian Science Monitor,* August 12, 1996, sec. 3, p. 1.

74. Rita Rubin, "Smog Clouds Nation's Health," *USA Today,* May 23, 2000, p. 8D.

75. David Briscoe, "World's Residents Expected to Get Thirsty," *Dayton Daily News,* November 8, 1993, p. 1.

76. Dr. William Reville, "Water, Water Everywhere—But Not For Everyone," *The Irish Times,* May 15, 2000, p. 9.

77. Slobodan Lekic, "Report Fears Water Crisis," *Dayton Daily News,* August 7, 1995, p. 3A.

78. Nancy Paige Smith, "Paradiplomacy Between the U.S. and Canadian Provinces: The Case of Acid Rain Memoranda of Understanding," *Journal of Borderlands Studies* 3, no. 1, pp. 13–38; and Nancy Paige Smith, "Transboundary Relations and Acid Rain," *Journal of Borderlands Studies,* Spring 1990. These articles are an absolutely first-rate analysis of the nature of the problems associated with acid rain.

79. Michael A. Hiltzik, "Environment," *Los Angeles Times,* March 5, 1991, p. 3.

80. "Zebra Mussels Spread Inland," *Dayton Daily News,* August 20, 1993, p. 2B.

81. Todd Shields, "Tomato Farms Plastic Has VA Watermen Seeing Red," *Washington Post,* July 7, 1996, sec. B, p. 5.

82. "To Battle a Massive Oil Spill," *Sarasota Herald-Tribune,* February 2, 1989, p. 18.

83. "The News in Brief," *The Christian Science Monitor,* June 11, 1996, p. 2. U.S. Supreme Court rules against Exxon shipping regarding tanker that ran aground.

84. "Oil Slick off Keys No Immediate Threat," *Sarasota Herald-Tribune,* March 4, 1989, p. 9.

85. "Crews Work to Refloat Tanker," *Sarasota Herald-Tribune,* March 4, 1989, p. 9; "Valdez Spill Leaves Lasting Impact," *Science News,* February 13, 1993, p. 102, 110.

86. Arthur Allen, "Greenpeace Halts Shell with Boycott in Germany," *Dayton Daily News,* June 23, 1995, p. 6B.

87. Seema Mehta, "Raw Sewage Closes Seal Beach," *The Los Angeles Times,* June 10, 2000, p. 7.

88. Laura Tangley, "Groundwater Contamination," in *Global Ecology,* C.H. Southwick, ed. (Boston: Sinauer Associates, 1985), pp. 141–145.

89. Danny Westneat, "One Man's Dream: Dragging Water Bags," *Dayton Daily News,* April 28, 1996, p. 17A. See also Alan George, "Huge Tankers Carry New Resource," *Dayton Daily News,* June 2, 1996, p. 15A.

90. Keith Schneider, "The Midwest Flooding," *The New York Times,* July 30, 1993, p. 14.

91. Lester R. Brown and Edmund C. Wolf, "Soil Erosion: Quiet Crisis in the World Economy," in *Global Ecology,* C.H. Southwick, ed., pp. 165–175.

92. Peter Steinhart, "America's Topsoil . . . Slip, Sliding Away," Ohio Department of Natural Resources, *GroWildlife,* March 1985, pp. 2–3.

93. Glen Martin, "High Price for Hillside Grape Harvest," *San Francisco Chronicle,"* November 16, 1995, sec. A, p. 17.

SUGGESTED READINGS

FERRELL, TOM. "After 10 Years, Earth Day Again: How Well Are We Doing?" *The New York Times,* April 20, 1980, p. 18E.

KING, CAROLYN. *Immigrant Killers.* Auckland: Oxford University Press, 1984.

MURRAY, ANNE FIRTH. "A Global Accounting." In Robert Jackson, ed., *Global Issues.* Guilford, CT: Duskin Publishing Group, 1987.

MYERS, NORMAN. *The Primary Source.* New York: W.W. Norton, 1984.

Nature Conservancy Magazine, the journal of a unique international membership organization committed to the global preservation of natural diversity.

SMITH, NANCY PAIGE. (2 articles). "Paradiplomacy Between the U.S. and Canadian Provinces: The Case of Acid Rain Memoranda of Understanding," *Journal of Borderlands Studies,* vol. 3, no. 1, Spring 1988, pp. 13–38; and "Transboundary Relations and Acid Rain," *Journal of Borderlands Studies,* Fall 1989. These two articles constitute a first-rate analysis of some of the major international political problems associated with acid rain.

SOUTHWICK, CHARLES H. *Global Ecology.* Boston: Sinauer Associates, 1985.

Glossary

abiotic Refers to that which is nonliving (air, water, land).

abortion Termination of pregnancy before the fetus is viable.

acid rain Caused largely from the combustion of oil and coal. Acid rain has damaged the Green Mountains in Vermont, the forests of Canada, and the Black Forest in Germany.

alienation Refers to the separation, isolation, and estrangement of human beings from each other, society, and their environment.

artificial insemination A procedure in which male sperm is injected into the female genital tract to induce conception.

artificial twinning The technology employed by cattle breeders in the livestock industry that divides the embryo of a valuable animal and creates twins.

Asilomar Conference A conference called by scientists in 1975 to discuss the hazards of biotechnology and genetic engineering. Asilomar is a signal event in the effort at self-regulation by scientists.

biodiversity Suggests that there is a crucial, intimate, and internal relationship that exists between the many species of life on earth, and that each species needs the others to survive and continue the process of evolution.

biology The study of all life on earth.

biosphere The area on and around the earth that acts as a support system for all life on earth.

biotechnology The technology involving the use of living organisms to produce useful products.

biotic Refers to that which is living—that which has a specified mode of life (people, plants, animals).

cell The basic structural unit of life. The smallest living unit.

chromosome Chromosomes are contained within the cell nucleus (forty-six in the cell of a human being) and are the basic structural unit of genetic material of the cell.

clone (cloning) A genetically identical organism produced by asexual reproduction. This is an important element in genetic engineering.

cryopreservation   A technique of delayed pregnancy—common in animal husbandry. Now used in humans, it involves the freezing of sperm, eggs, or embryo. Used to prevent fertilized eggs from being destroyed.

desertification   The condition in which fertile land is transformed into desert because of agricultural practices.

dioxin   A chemical byproduct that was used in conjunction with waste oil to hold down dust in Times Beach, Missouri.

DNA   An elongated molecular ladder on which an organism's genetic code is inscribed.

embryo   At the end of the second week of gestation, after the fertilized egg is implanted in the uterus, the zygote is renamed an embryo.

embryo transfer   Movement of a human embryo from one uterus to another for the period of gestation.

enzyme   A special type of protein produced by living cells that causes a reaction but does not become a part of the reaction. Metaphorically, enzymes play a "broker role" in chemical reactions.

ethics   The discipline concerned with moral duty, principles, and values. Ethics also involves the relation of ends to means.

eugenics   The science dealing with the improvement of hereditary qualities through breeding.

euthanasia   The intentional termination of life.

fertility drugs   Drugs employed to artificially stimulate a woman's ovaries (superovulation) to ensure that several eggs are produced in a given cycle. Frequently used prior to IVF.

gene   Genes are locations in linear form on specific portions of chromosomes. Genes function to express a particular characteristic of heredity (color of eyes, etc.) and to control production of an enzyme or protein.

gene pool   All the genes of all the individuals that are included in the same species.

gene splicing   A procedure in which scientists snip out genes of the DNA of one organism, join it with the DNA of another organism, and insert the altered combination into a cell to realize a specific function.

gene transfer   A procedure that may be employed by scientists to make plants more resistant to drought and to particular herbicides. Many other applications are possible.

genetic engineering   An effort by scientists to repair and/or improve living organisms via techniques such as gene splicing or gene therapy. The purpose is to produce a useful product or to help human beings lead healthier, happier lives (since human beings are not usually thought of as "useful products").

genetic fingerprinting   A form of genetic testing that can be employed to help authorities identify particular individuals in rape, murder, immigration, and paternity cases.

genome   The total genetic constitution of a particular organism—a collection of all genes in the human cell.

Global 2000   A report, commissioned by President Carter, to inquire into the nature of the world's resources at the end of the century. The report contended that new initiatives were needed to cope with environmental problems.

greenhouse effect   The greenhouse effect, or global warming, occurs when carbon dioxide (CO_2) from burning fossil fuels (coal, oil, natural gas) and other gases rise into the upper atmosphere. These gases permit the heat from the sun to reach the earth but block the earth's heat from traveling into space. It works like a greenhouse—it *traps* heat in the atmosphere.

hemophilia   A disease, almost always associated with the male, characterized by an inability to clot blood and subsequent hemorrhaging.

Hippocratic Oath   Written in 500 B.C., this oath seeks to protect the rights of patients and define the relationship between physician and patient.

Human Genome Project   A $3 billion effort by the National Research Council to map the entire human genetic code involving 100,000 genes.

informed consent   In medical practice this concept means that the individual (or the parent or guardian of the individual) *understands* the nature of the illness and has given *permission* to the medical professional to perform some procedure.

interferons   Proteins produced by the body as a part of the body's immune response. These are considered important weapons in the fight against cancer.

in vitro fertilization (IVF)   A procedure in which an egg is removed from a woman's ovary and fertilized with sperm from a man. Later the fertilized egg is put back in the woman's uterus so that gestation can begin.

in vivo fertilization (IViF)   A procedure used when a woman cannot produce viable eggs but can gestate a baby. Example: Sperm from the husband of woman A is used to fertilize woman B. Five to seven days after conception, B's womb is flushed and the embryo transferred to A's uterus, where gestation occurs.

Lebensborn   The Nazi eugenics program that was designed to produce a superior human being by mating S.S. officers with women possessing desired characteristics of hair, eyes, stature, and so on. About 250,000 children were produced in Germany between 1935 and 1945 in the Lebensborn program.

malfeasance   Refers to wrongdoing or misconduct. In biomedical issues this refers to the behavior of researchers or practitioners.

nucleus   The part of the cell that directs and controls all cell functions.

ozone layer   A protective layer of ozone-rich air that surrounds the earth in the stratosphere and absorbs and reflects almost all of the sun's ultraviolet rays.

Pollutant Standard Index (PSI)   Four elements combine to measure the PSI—particulates, SO_2, carbon monoxide, and ozone.

red and brown tides   Poisonous algae bloom that occurs in the oceans, caused by both natural phenomena and human action (agricultural runoff). It results in massive fish kills.

RNA   A messenger or delivery vehicle that leaves the nucleus and disseminates the protein dictated by the original gene's DNA. RNA functions in the decoding of hereditary data.

sterilization   A procedure designed to destroy the capacity of a human being or other animal to reproduce.

stewardship   The theory that property held as private should also be used in the service of the public welfare.

surrogacy   The practice whereby one woman carries a child for another with the intention that the child will be handed over after birth.

tissue   A group of similar cells that work together to perform a function (such as blood or nerve cells).

utilitarianism   The philosophical argument that what is good, right, just, and proper should be determined by the greatest good for the greatest number.

zygote   Fertilization occurs when the male sperm unites with the female ovum. This fertilized egg is called a zygote.

Index

Ethology, 156
Eugenics, 202
Euthanasia, 179, 184
Evolution, 156
Experimentation, 178
Exxon Valdez, 198, 237

F

Federal Election Campaign Act
  (FECA), 56–60
Feminist movement, 167
Fenwick, Millicent, 60
Fermentation, 196
Fertility drugs, 167
First World, 218, 221
Fisk, Robert, 68
Food and Drug Administration, 192,
  204
Food stamps, 14, 29
Foster, Vincent, 67
France, 159, 181, 196, 224, 225

G

Gallagher, Cornelius, 61
Gamete intrafallopian transfer, 166
Gates, Bill, 162
Gaylin, Willard, 39
Genentech, 190, 192
Gene pool, 223
Gene therapy, 193, 208
Genetic engineering, 193, 197, 205,
  207, 209
Genetic fingerprinting, 199
Genetic screening, 158
Gene transfer, 158, 190, 209
Germany, 159, 191, 196, 222–24,
  237
Gilder, George, 28
Gingrich, Newt, 50, 63
Goldwater, Barry, 54
Goodman, Ellen, 173
Gore, Albert, 204

Great Britain, 159, 191, 224
Greenhouse effect, 232
Gun control, 84, 87, 93–95

H

Habitat destruction, 230
Hakim, Albert, 64
Hall, Jerry L., 168
Harding, Warren G., 51
  Teapot Dome, 51
Harris, Dr. John, 181
Hart, Ed, 171
Hart, Nancy, 172
Harvard University, 209
Hate crime, 81
Hays, Wayne, 61
Health Maintenance Organizations
  (HMOs), 44, 45
Health Security Act, 44
Helsinki Declaration, 178
Hemophilia, 168
Hippocratic Oath, 163, 164, 181
Hitler, Adolf, 165, 201, 223
Hobbes, Thomas, 223
Hollings, Ernest, 59
Holocaust, 180
Human genome project, 190, 193,
  206, 207
Humphrey, Hubert H., 56
Hunt, E. Howard, 56
Huntington's disease, 207
Hussein, Saddam, 237
Huxley, Aldous, 162, 202

I

India, 168, 175, 219, 221, 223, 227
Informed consent, 164, 174
Intel Corporation, 4
Interferons, 194
Intermediate-range nuclear force
  reduction, 80, 137, 140–41, 143,
  146, 148